HUMAN RESOURCE DEVELOPMENT
IN A KNOWLEDGE ECONOMY

Human Resource Development in a Knowledge Economy

AN ORGANISATIONAL VIEW

ROSEMARY HARRISON

and

JOSEPH KESSELS

First published 2004 by
PALGRAVE MACMILLAN
Houndmills, Basingstoke, Hampshire RG21 6XS and
175 Fifth Avenue, New York, N.Y. 10010
Companies and representatives throughout the world

PALGRAVE MACMILLAN is the global academic imprint of the Palgrave Macmillan division of St. Martin's Press, LLC and of Palgrave Macmillan Ltd. Macmillan® is a registered trademark in the United States, United Kingdom and other countries. Palgrave is a registered trademark in the European Union and other countries.

ISBN 0–333–99015–3

This book is printed on paper suitable for recycling and made from fully managed and sustained forest sources.

A catalogue record for this book is available from the British Library.

Library of Congress Cataloging-in-Publication Data

Harrison, Rosemary.
   Human resource development in a knowledge economy : an organisational view / Rosemary Harrison and Joseph Kessels.
      p. cm.
Includes bibliographical references and index.
   ISBN 0–333–99015–3 (pbk.)
   1. Knowledge management. 2. Human capital—Management. 1. Kessels, J. W. M. (Joseph W. M.), 1952– II. Title.
   HD30.2 .H374 2003
      658.3'01—dc21

                                    2003050970

Editing and origination by Aardvark Editorial, Mendham, Suffolk

10   9   8   7   6   5   4   3   2   1
13 12 11 10 09 08 07 06 05 04
Printed in China

To our partners and families

Contents

List of Figures and Tables   x

List of Case Examples   xi

List of Research Examples   xii

Notes on the Authors   xiii

Preface   xiv

Acknowledgements   xvii

part one
THE EMERGING KNOWLEDGE ECONOMY   1

1   **Setting the Scene**   3
     Introduction   3
     The book: rationale, scope and structure   3
     The book: themes   6
     An economic base for knowledge, learning and development   11
     Developing knowledge workers in a knowledge economy   15
     The HRD function in a knowledge economy   17
     Conclusion   18

2   **Organisational Perspectives: Strategising ...**   20
     Introduction   20
     Linking HR strategy to competitive capability   20
     Pressures on the employment relationship   26
     Calculating the HR investment   28
     Testing assumptions   31
     Do we need a new HR paradigm?   35
     Conclusion   38

3   **... and Organising**   39
     Introduction   39
     Perspectives on structure   40
     Organising for knowledge creation   43
     Organising for innovation   50
     Organising for economies of expertise   53

Conclusions from research   54
Conclusion   59

4   **HRD: Country Frameworks**   **61**
Introduction   61
The drive for competitive advantage   62
NVET systems: some key features   63
The Netherlands   66
Germany   67
France   69
The United Kingdom   71
The USA   73
Japan   75
The way forward   77
Conclusion   79

5   **HRD: Emerging Challenges**   **83**
Introduction   83
Clarifying the HRD field   84
Achieving strategic thrust through integration   89
Building a learning culture   91
Promoting workplace learning   95
Developing managerial and leadership capability   97
Conclusion   103

6   **HRD: The State of Play**   **104**
Introduction   104
Achieving strategic thrust through integration   104
Building a learning culture   109
Promoting workplace learning   112
Developing managerial and leadership capability   114
The state of play: key themes   116
Conclusion   118

part two
BUILDING KNOWLEDGE-PRODUCTIVE ORGANISATIONS   119

7   **Notions of Knowledge**   **121**
Introduction   121
Knowledge as control   122
Knowledge as intelligence   124
Knowledge as relationships   129
Knowledge as commodity   134
Issues for HRD practitioners   140
Conclusion   141

8   **The Knowledge-Productive Organisation**   **145**
Introduction   145
Knowledge-productive organisations   146
The corporate curriculum framework   155
Issues for HRD practitioners   158
An organisational case study   161
Conclusion   162

9   **Researching Knowledge Productivity**   **163**
     Introduction   163
     Designing research projects on knowledge productivity   164
     Researching knowledge-productive organisations   166
     Towards a research framework and strategies   175
     Wider research issues   177
     Conclusion   180

10   **New Technology, the Knowledge Process and HRD**   **182**
     Introduction   182
     New technology, education and learning   183
     New technology and the knowledge process   186
     Collaborative technology and virtual teams   190
     New technology: tasks for HRD professionals   194
     Conclusion   196

part three
HRD: CHALLENGES IN A KNOWLEDGE ECONOMY   **199**

11   **The Ethical Dimension**   **201**
     Introduction   201
     Ethics and the business   202
     Learning and development in a knowledge economy   205
     Ethics and the HRD professional   213
     An ethics framework to aid the HRD professional   216
     Conclusion   220

12   **Conclusions: Where To Now for HRD?**   **222**
     Introduction   222
     Main themes   222
     Work and learning in a knowledge economy   228
     Knowledge workers and their supporting personnel   229
     Where to locate HRD?   231
     Performance versus learning   232
     HRD roles and tasks in a knowledge economy   233
     Conclusion   235

APPENDICES   **237**

1   **Assignments**   **239**
     Chapter 2   Strategising   241
     Chapter 3   Organising   245
     Chapter 4   HRD: Country frameworks   249
     Chapter 5   HRD: Emerging challenges   250
     Chapter 6   HRD: the state of play   252
     Chapter 7   Notions of knowledge   255
     Chapter 8   The knowledge-productive organisation   258
     Chapter 9   Researching knowledge productivity   261
     Chapter 10 New technology   263

2   **Case Companies (Scarbrough and Swan, 1999)**   **266**

     References   267
     Index   286

List of Figures
and Tables

Figures

2.1	Three dimensions to the global HR professional role	23
6.1	The factors influencing change in training and development	105
9.1	A provisional conceptual framework for researching knowledge productivity	166
9.2	The corporate curriculum in the health and welfare sector, the Netherlands	167
9.3	An initial conceptual framework for self-regulated learning and development	169
9.4	A fuller conceptual research framework for knowledge productivity	176
11.1	The downward spiral of difference	211

Tables

1.1	OECD policy recommendations for lifelong learning	13
1.2	Average percentage change in key worker groups, 1992–99	15
3.1	N-form vs. M-form	47
4.1	A comparison of country NVET systems	80
5.1	Typology of learning to support the development of learning organisations	96
7.1	The cognitivist view of knowledge	125
7.2	The self-productive view of knowledge	130
7.3	Conflicting views of organizational knowledge	136
7.4	Views of the world, and their impact on notions of knowledge	142
7.5	Issues for the strategising, organising and knowledge processes in organisations operating in a knowledge economy	144
8.1	Features of practical judgement	152
8.2	Emotional intelligence, spiritual intelligence and practical judgement	154
8.3	The eight learning pillars of the corporate curriculum	156

List of Case Examples

1.1	The changing face of car manufacturing and purchase	7
1.2	The Dutch national action programme for lifelong learning	14
2.1	Aligning SHRM with business needs	25
2.2	Hutton Borough Council, UK	32
3.1	Product development in Ford of Europe in the 1980s and 90s	45
3.2	The Learning Company	48
3.3	Asea Brown Boveri (ABB)	56
4.1	Employer/union partnership in training, USA	74
4.2	Lifelong learning: the Singaporean approach	78
5.1	Reorganising at Procter & Gamble	100
6.1	Improving workplace training and education in the UK	112
7.1	The knowledge-sharing initiative at Multicorp	133
7.2	Transforming the knowledge process at Buckman Laboratories, 1992–98	138
8.1	Agro-food complex, the Netherlands	147
8.2	The Corporate Curriculum of Rabobank	158
8.3	The Shell Learning Initiative	161
10.1	Harnessing new technology to training and learning processes	184
10.2	ICT systems to support personalised learning	188
11.1	The World Bank's approach to ethics	203
11.2	British Airways, 1980s–90s	204
11.3	Birmingham City Council and race relations training	209
11.4	Training in a UK educational institution	212
11.5	Xerox's adoption of meta standards	215

List of Research Examples

4.1   'Learning islands' in German companies   69
5.1   Seven organisations seeking 'leanness'   94
6.1   Competence managers in HRD functions   106
6.2   Knowledge-productive teams in the workplace, the Netherlands   111
6.3   Workplace learning: progress in Europe   114
7.1   The photocopier technicians   129
7.2   The knowledge-development process in different organisational settings   137
9.1   Researching learning functions of the corporate curriculum   167
9.2   Developing self-regulated learning in a pensions firm   170
9.3   Designing work-related learning projects: a constructivist approach   172
9.4   HRD professionals' transformational tasks in knowledge-creating
      organisations   173
9.5   Some findings on effective and ineffective knowledge transfer   178
10.1 Trainers and new technology   185
10.2 Collaborating in virtual teams   191
10.3 The role of collaborative technology in facilitating learning in
      virtual teams of professionals   192
10.4 Interactions between geographically dispersed teams   193
10.5 HRD professionals and the harnessing of ICT to corporate learning processes   195
11.1 Behind the rhetoric of the new economy   208
11.2 Achieving cross-boundary knowledge creation   218

Notes on the Authors

Rosemary Harrison is Chief Examiner, Learning and Development with the UK's Chartered Institute of Personnel and Development. She was formerly Lecturer in Human Resource Management and Director of the HRD Research Centre, University of Durham. She is author of many articles, texts and chapters on human resource management and development, and has a long record of consultancy and research in the strategic HRM and HRD fields.

Joseph Kessels is Professor of Human Resource Development, University of Twente, the Netherlands, and held a similar chair at Leiden University. He is a partner in Kessels & Smit, a consulting firm that does most of its work in the field of corporate learning and development. He is author of many articles and books on human resource development, and is adviser to the Dutch Minister of Education, Culture and Science, in matters that concern co-operative education and work-based learning.

Preface

SCOPE OF THE BOOK

In this book we seek to link the domain of organisationally based human resource development (HRD) powerfully to that of learning and knowledge in an emergent knowledge economy. Our aim is a critical text that reviews HRD's development and current status as an organisational process, and that identifies new HRD roles and tasks in an emergent knowledge economy. By that we mean an economy in which the application of knowledge to continuous improvement and radical innovation in goods, services and processes is the most important source of advantage for organisations. In such organisations the ideal is that:

> People at all levels have accumulated knowledge about what customers want, about how best to design products and processes, about what has worked in the past and what hasn't. A company that can collect all that knowledge and share it between employees will have a huge advantage over an organisation that never discovers what its people know. (Skapinker, 2002:1)

We explain in our opening chapter that the emergence of a knowledge economy requires a fundamental shift in ways of understanding organisations and of facilitating learning and development of those working for, or in partnership with, them. This shift creates an urgent need to evaluate the contribution that HRD processes can make to organisations operating in such an economy. That is our task in this book. It has led us to survey a broad-based literature of HRD and learning within a wider context of business strategy and human resource management, and against analysis of HRD practice at international, national and organisational levels.

Our task has given the book a special character. It means that our concern throughout is with critical strategic issues concerning the function that HRD can fulfil in organisations operating in a new type of economy, and with the changing roles and challenges for HRD practitioners that are involved here. Our primary emphasis is on processes of strategy, organising, knowledge development and new information and communication technology. We have paid proportionately less attention to operational tasks and techniques to do with the design, development, facilitation and review of learning activities, the production of instructional material and the assessment of learning outcomes.

THE BOOK'S READERSHIP

The book's scope covers research and key texts from many countries and from a variety of academic disciplines, and so is relevant for readers who work for, or are studying, organisations with a wide geographical spread across the global economy.

- Human resource (HR) professionals will find that the book provides an integrated approach to strategising, organising, working and learning. This should be helpful in stimulating a process of critical reflection on current HR practice and on likely future developments.
- Those whose responsibilities lie mainly in the HRD field will find encouragement and a clear rationale to move away from activity that is currently mainly to do with training, to a sphere of operations that is strategically focused and incorporates processes of learning, of knowledge creation and of knowledge management.
- General managers will find wide-ranging analysis of how the workplace environment is affected by the operation of a knowledge economy, and of ways in which they can help to transform it into an environment that is conducive to what we call 'knowledge productivity'. In such a workplace people work together in knowledge creation and knowledge sharing in order to continuously improve and radically innovate in goods, services and processes that enable the organisation to make sustained progress in a rapidly changing business environment.
- Academics and students in the domains of strategic management and of human resource management and development will find overviews and evaluations of up-to-date theories and research findings, a special focus on practice in the field, and learning aids to enable their active engagement with the text.

LEARNING AIDS

It seems to us that, in a book devoted to an exploration of an emergent knowledge economy and its implications for human and social capital in an organisation, it is vital to engage readers actively in a reflection on, and critical examination of, major issues likely to affect them in their current organisational roles, in those to which they aspire, and in those that they may have to assume in future. The concept of knowledge as a process that is continuously formed, developed and changed by human interactions goes to the heart of the book, and is therefore mirrored in its design. We have conceived the text as a type of ongoing dialogue with readers whose involvement we seek through a variety of interactive learning activities:

- *Reflection*. Each chapter includes moments for reflection whose purpose is to help readers absorb and fully evaluate a previous section of text.
- *Case examples*. Most chapters contain case examples that enable readers to relate complex areas of theory to real-life practice and challenges. Such examples should help to develop that critical faculty that is vital in a field (HRD) too often dismissed as lacking in rigour and business significance.
- *Research examples*. These are provided especially for readers who wish to explore relevant research in the field. Each example relates to a previous section of text, and is explained and annotated to facilitate access to primary sources. Students preparing theses or dissertations should find these sources of information particularly helpful.

Reflections, case and research examples are all boxed in the text so that they are easily identifiable yet can also be passed over when the reader prefers to maintain an uninterrupted train of thought.

■ *Assignments*. There are assignments for each chapter except Chapters 1, 11 and 12. We hope that these will add value by stimulating the development of consultancy and research-based skills, notably of those involved in advanced professional and academic programmes. We have designed the material in ways intended to help the transfer of theory to practice. In order not to break continuity within and between chapters, we have placed all assignments in an Appendix (1).

TERMINOLOGY

Throughout the book we refer to the *HRD function* loosely to indicate the body of activity that comprises HRD as an organisational process. *Function* therefore does not imply a specialist HRD department unless that is specifically indicated in the text. In the same way we use the term *HRD practitioners* to encompass all who hold key HRD responsibilities in an organisation, whether or not they are HRD professionals. The term *professional* is used in the generalised sense unless otherwise indicated. Unless the text states to the contrary, terms such as *firm*, *company*, *enterprise*, *organisation* and *business* are used interchangeably and refer to organisations of whatever size, type, purpose and sector.

We hope that the scope of the book and the learning aids that it incorporates will help readers to experience the unique mix of excitement, frustration and continuing drive to 'know' that we ourselves have felt as we have grappled with many barriers in our customary ways of thinking in order to enter and explore the ambiguous, formidable but extraordinarily enticing 'new world' of HRD in an emergent knowledge economy.

ROSEMARY HARRISON AND JOSEPH KESSELS

Acknowledgements

All real-life material reported in the book relates only to situations current at the time. Unless otherwise indicated, comments on such material are the authors' own, and do not represent any official views held by the organisations concerned. We acknowledge with thanks the organisations that have allowed us to publish accounts of their business and human resource policies and practice.

We thank Rob Veersma and Scott Beaty at Shell for their co-operation related to the Shell case example in Chapter 8 and for Shell's permission to use it there. We also thank Linda Emmett at the UK Chartered Institute of Personnel and Development for her willingness to allow us to quote and include extracts at different points in the book from the following CIPD Research Reports: *Case Studies in Knowledge Management* (CIPD, 1999), *Workplace Learning in Europe* (CIPD, 2001), *Globalising HR: Executive Briefing* (CIPD, 2002), *Organising for Success in the Twenty First Century: A Starting Point for Change* (CIPD, 2002). We are grateful to Rolanda Black, a CIPD qualifying student in 2002 in Northern Ireland, who worked with us to produce one of the assignments in Appendix 1.

Finally, we acknowledge with thanks permissions to reproduce/summarise findings based on the following copyright materials:

Brewster, C., Harris, H. and Sparrow, P. (2002) *Globalising HR: Executive Briefing*. London, Chartered Institute of Personnel and Development. Figure 5, p. 14.

Guile, D. and Young, M. (1999) 'The question of learning and learning organisations'. Working Paper. London: Lifelong Learning Group, Institute of Education, University of London, 55 Gordon Square, London WCIH ONT. Figure on pp. 15–16.

Harrison, R. (2002) *Learning and Development* 3rd edn. London: Chartered Institute of Personnel and Development. Figure 6, p. 149.

Hedlund, G. (1994) 'A model of knowledge management and the N-Form corporation'. *Strategic Management Journal*, Special Summer Issue. Vol. 15, p. 83. By permission of John Wiley & Sons Ltd.

Organization for Economic Co-operation and Development. (2001a) *The New Economy: Beyond the Hype. The OECD Growth Project*. Paris: OECD, Tables on pp. 56, 70.

Reumkens, R. and Snijders, I. (2002) 'Het Rabobank Corporate Curriculum' [The Rabobank Corporate Curriculum]. *Opleiding en Ontwikkeling*. Vol. 15, 4, pp. 30–3. By permission of Reid Business Information BV.

Scarbrough, H. (1998) 'Path(ological) dependency? Core competencies from an organizational perspective'. *British Journal of Management*. Vol. 9, p. 229. By permission of Blackwell Publishing.

Sparrow, P. and Hiltrop, J.-M. (1994) *European Human Resource Management in Transition*. Hemel Hempstead: Prentice Hall. Figure 10.1, p. 362. By permission of Pearson Education Limited.

Van Lakerveld, J., Van den Berg, J., De Brabander, C. and Kessels, J. (2000) 'The corporate curriculum: a working–learning environment'. In Proc. Annual Academy of Human Resource Development Conference: Expanding the Horizons of Human Resource Development (CD-ROM). Raleigh-Durham NC.

The Emerging Knowledge Economy

chapter one

Setting the Scene

INTRODUCTION

Two core propositions underpin this book: that in a knowledge economy the competitive advantage of organisations relies on capability to adapt to the changing environment by the continuous generation and application of new knowledge; and that the human resource development (HRD) process is key to ensuring that capability.

Our principle purpose in writing this book is to explore HRD and 'knowledge productivity' as an interactive process that can enhance the ability of organisations to make progress in a knowledge economy. Through an evaluative but essentially future-oriented text we hope to stimulate reflection on HRD's past and current organisational role and its future potential. We also seek to involve readers in the analysis of HRD's place in an increasingly knowledge-based environment, encouraging creative responses to the challenging organisational scenarios presented in the book.

In this chapter we explain our rationale for focusing the book on HRD in a knowledge economy, and identify key issues that underpin the book's structure and themes. We set the scene for subsequent chapters by reflecting on the nature and causes of the emerging knowledge economy and on macro-level issues that provide the framework for HRD as an organisational process. We conclude by examining some of the needs and challenges facing that process.

THE BOOK: RATIONALE, SCOPE AND STRUCTURE

Rationale

The framework for this book is the rapidly emerging knowledge economy. So the first question we must answer is: what is meant by a knowledge economy?

In traditional economies, added value is achieved by maximising the interactive potential of capital, labour and material. However, in a knowledge economy the critical added value is gained from the continuous application of knowledge to the enhancement and innovation of work processes, products and services. As performance differentials and competitive advantage become determined more by intellectual than by physical resources, traditional tangible physical assets become less important than intangible knowledge-based assets. In other words, a knowledge economy is emerging.

The next question we need to respond to is: why should the book focus on HRD? The emergence of a knowledge economy is one of the most dramatic shifts to have taken place in society since the industrial revolution of the late 19th century. With the impact of the World Wide Web and the increasing globalisation of business and communications that the Web has made possible, that economy is fast becoming a dominating force in relation to national economic and social policies and to work organisations. Some of the fundamental changes are taking place at organisational level. These, coupled with changing patterns of employment, are having a dramatic impact on HR policies within organisations. It is therefore an important task of academics to focus on the HR arena. Within it, however, we believe that it is the HRD domain that currently calls for special attention.

Much has been written on the relationship between HR strategy and business policy in changing organisations (see for example Schuler and Jackson, 1999; Brewster et al., 2002; Pettigrew et al., 2002). When we first began to plan this book nearly three years ago the strategy literature already contained a distinctive strand on organisational learning and knowledge management. Subsequently that strand has become a field in its own right yet there is surprisingly little on HRD as a key process for organisations operating in a knowledge economy. One major United Kingdom (UK) report (Stewart and Tansley, 2002) has reviewed new roles and tasks for trainers in such an economy, and a European research project has examined HRD strategies and practice in nearly 200 'learning oriented' organisations across Europe (Tjepkema et al., 2002). However, much of the United States' (US) and European literature on HRD is in reality primarily about training, and HRD comprises far more than that.

In a rapidly evolving environment where knowledge is the main organisational currency, firms must be able to learn fast, adapt regularly to new challenges, ensure that their workers can construct and share strategically valuable knowledge as well as acquire technical and interactive skills, and continuously improve and innovate. In other words, such organisations must be 'knowledge-productive'. The reason why we have chosen to focus on HRD in this book is because we believe that the HRD process has extraordinary potential here, albeit a potential that is often ignored, underplayed or misunderstood. A knowledge economy needs HRD professionals whose attitudes and competencies are very different from those they are expected to exercise in more traditional contexts. Many of those professionals will want and need to be educated and developed in new ways.

Our rationale for the book explains the three features that we hope give it both uniqueness and currency:

1. First, the book reflects our belief that there is now an urgent need to assess from both theoretical and practical viewpoints the contribution that organisationally based HRD can make to a knowledge economy, and to explore its underlying research base in that connection. What do we mean by 'HRD' in this sense? We explain in Chapter 5 that the term has many interpretations. However in our view:

   HRD as an organisational process comprises the skilful planning and facilitation of a variety of formal and informal learning and knowledge processes and experiences, primarily but not exclusively in the workplace, in order that organisational progress and individual potential can be enhanced through the competence, adaptability, collaboration and knowledge-creating activity of all who work for the organisation.

Our definition infers that if the HRD process is to add value in a knowledge economy, then there is a need for a fundamental shift from a preoccupation with immediate performance improvement to a greater focus on lifelong learning and work-based learning strategies.

2. Second, the book is concerned primarily with HRD's contribution to the production, dissemination and application of knowledge that has a strategic value for the organisation. It therefore explores ways in which the HRD process might be able to enhance knowledge productivity. That concept was first developed by Kessels and refers to an organisation's ability to generate, disseminate and apply knowledge to products, processes and services (Kessels, 1995, 1996; Garvey and Williamson, 2002).

3. Third, through the original conceptual framework of the 'Corporate Curriculum' (Kessels, 1996, 2001) the book explores ways in which to ensure the collaborative stimulation and facilitation of learning and developmental processes, initiatives and relationships, and to do so while respecting and building on human diversity in the workplace. In a knowledge economy organisations rely especially on tacit knowledge – that is to say, on knowledge that is embedded deep in the individual or collective subconscious, expressing itself in habitual or intuitive ways of doing things that are exercised without conscious thought or effort (Nonaka, 1991). Tacit knowledge is the property of individuals and cannot be wrested from them. They must agree to put it at the service of the collective whole. The learning that either produces or springs from tacit knowledge must therefore rest upon a recognition of mutuality of interest and of responsibility between organisation and individuals.

Scope

In writing this book we have drawn mainly on literature from the UK, the US and Continental Europe. There are several reasons for this:

- The knowledge economy is emerging with its fullest force primarily in the West, which at present is where it is having the greatest impact on business strategies, processes and practice and where, as a phenomenon, it is under the most lively debate (see, for example, Swanson and Holton, 2001; Garvey and Williamson, 2002; McGoldrick et al., 2002; Tjepkema et al., 2002a;).
- In organisations operating at international and global levels – that is, in organisations most affected by the emerging knowledge economy – the main template currently in use for human resource strategies and practice is generally Western, albeit with a considerable interest still in Japanese practice.
- The book's primary focus is on organisationally based HRD and some of the most significant research current at the time of writing (Tjepkema et al., 2002) has indicated that there are more similarities than differences between HRD practice in Europe, Japan and the US. The only major exception to this appears to be in relation to HRD professional roles, where practice in Japan has always differed significantly from that in other countries (we discuss Japanese practice in Chapter 4).

Structure

The book is divided into three parts. In Part I we explore the business and human resource agenda facing organisations that operate in the emerging knowledge economy. In Part II we move into those organisations to examine theoretical and practical approaches to the construction, sharing and utilisation of knowledge that can drive and sustain progress. In this part of the book we suggest how rich knowledge-productive work environments can be developed, paying special attention here to the role of new information and communication technology and drawing on some of the most recent empirical research into knowledge productivity. In Part III we discuss ethical issues related to strategies for learning and development in organisations operating in a knowledge economy. In our final chapter we summarise the main themes that have emerged through the book in order to identify the challenges and opportunities facing the HRD function and its practitioners in that economy.

THE BOOK: THEMES

Part I: The emerging knowledge economy

The backdrop to the six chapters that comprise Part I is the changing business and employment environment and competitive landscape of the firm. Before looking specifically at themes covered in this part, we need to review briefly the nature of that backcloth.

Interest in the internal forces that can bestow competitive advantage is a natural response to the changes that have transformed the competitive landscape since the 1970s. Throughout the 1980s there were significant movements in market share among various manufacturers, and an increase in financially driven business strategies. During the 1990s there was rapid and discontinuous economic and political change in the international environment as the Cold War ended. New commercial opportunities emerged as Eastern Europe opened up, the European Union grew in stature and the hitherto seemingly impregnable Japanese economy moved into recession. This was an era of corporate networks, multinational alliances, corporate ventures and continuing restructuring (Bowman et al., 2002: 33–4).

Throughout the same period technological convergence, changing stakeholder demands and shorter product life cycles were altering the shape of the competitive landscape (Ghoshal and Bartlett, 1994: 109). To respond to these, more sophisticated management tools and concepts were being developed in the form of information systems, quality deployment processes, team-based organisations and multi-skilled workforces. By 1993 Peter Drucker was noting the advent of a 'transformational' knowledge economy. In the rapidly growing service sector, for example, the declining role of physical labour, rapidly developing processes of collaborative engineering and new information and communications technology were already attesting to the superior value of applied knowledge over traditional economic factors. Collectively, these changes made 'a profound impact on the organizational structures and processes of companies and, more specifically, on the roles of individuals and in their relationships with their organizations' (Ghoshal and Bartlett, 1994: 110). However, it was the 'dizzying pace' of technological change that held some of the greatest strategic implications (Bettis and Hitt, 1995). This pace has continued, with consequences including an 'information-rich, computation-rich, and communications-rich organizational environment' (ibid), a heightened level of knowledge intensity, and globalisation.

The word 'globalisation' has become a kind of mantra. But what does it mean? It can refer to the geographical spread of an organisation, to the degree of transnationality of its assets, sales and employment, to the production of 'global' products, and to the global integration of processes (Brewster et al., 2002: 7). Crucially, however, it is a process directly linked with the Internet and the pricing and information revolution that it has made possible. Through the World Wide Web anyone can gain access to prices across the world and carry out his or her own comparative analysis. Buyers and sellers can come together naturally, speedily and continuously, with the consumer being the ultimate victor, as the case of auto companies demonstrates (see Case example 1.1).

Prahalad and Ramaswamy clarify the ways in which the 'consumer-centric culture of the Internet, with its emphasis on interactivity, speed, individuality and openness' has given the consumer a hitherto unimaginable influence on value creation:

> Today's companies know just how dramatically 40 million consumers networking with each other and challenging the status quo online, in categories as different as music and mortgages, are shaking up the business world. (Prahalad and Ramaswamy, 2002: 52)

They argue that companies that do not quickly learn to co-create value with their customers and capture the intelligence that illuminates what those customers value will soon lose competitive advantage. They identify (ibid: 56–7) five powers that the Web has given to 'connected customers'. These are to do with:

■ *Information access* – enabling consumers to develop the knowledge to make informed decisions

Case example 1.1

The changing face of car manufacturing and purchase

With the advent of the Internet, consumers can now rapidly identify dealers across the world who have the best offers on their preferred models. The manufacturers have taught consumers that patience will bring big rewards, so increasingly they are biding their time either until the bargains they want come through, or until the car companies capitulate. The car companies lose, as their profit margin diminishes: it is now the consumer who has become king (Stelzer, 2002). The same story holds true across two other key industries: airlines and retail clothing: there too the basic structure is changing in response to consumer attitude to price: an insistence on low cost plus high value for money (ibid). Low cost is in its turn facili-

tated by the manufacturing of goods to the most complex specification now increasingly being able to be carried out wherever is cheapest because of the ability to transmit through the Internet vast amounts of information virtually free (Collins, 2002).

This combination of easily accessible pricing data for buyers and increasing use by manufacturers of lowest-cost producers means that unprecedented economies of scale are now possible for companies with the biggest buying power. Manufacturers who cannot expand face closure. Producers get less than formerly, but they gain through much reduced advertising costs and an assured demand for their output. 'This, in a nutshell, is globalisation' (Collins, 2002).

- *Global view* – as described in the car trade case (Case example 1.1)
- *Networking* – enabling customers to form 'communities of interest … without geographic constraints and with few social barriers'
- *Experimentation* – the Web allows consumers to compare experiences, and to experiment with and develop products, especially digital ones
- *Activism* – all of the above give consumers increased confidence to 'speak out' and make clear the kind of value they expect.

This 'quiet revolution' has been 'fomented by a shift in how value is perceived and created' and by the way in which innovation and flexibility rather than efficiency have become the main drives of value (ibid: 61). It signals a need for major changes to traditional concepts of strategy and structure. We explore such changes in Chapters 2 and 3.

Organisations operating in a knowledge economy must develop strategy processes that ensure old ways of thinking and doing do not dominate, locking in customary ways of thinking, inhibiting innovation and preventing progress (Bettis and Hitt, 1995). This has direct implications for HR strategising. When tacit knowledge and human interactions are central to the construction and effective application of new knowledge, and traditional patterns of employment combine with other forces to place unique pressures on organisations' human resources, there is a need for new HR approaches in organisations. In Chapter 2 we look at the issues here.

A related theme that emerges in Chapter 2 concerns the future of the management role. Managers are still crucial to the success of implementing and maintaining strategic and structural change in organisations, but in a knowledge economy they are seeing radical changes in their roles at every organisational level. Their rate of job loss continues to be high as their roles are pressured from above and squeezed out or into new shapes from below, where many work teams are being reorganised to operate on a self-managing basis under tight performance control (Sparrow, 1999). They are intimately affected by the need to co-create value with customers and the changes in organisational strategies and design that this need is producing (Prahalad and Ramaswamy, 2002).

In Chapter 3 ('Organising') we discuss the impact of both the new competitive landscape and the knowledge economy on organisational design. Firms now need to be flexible in two major ways: in producing new strategic responses as old recipes become obsolete, and in rapidly, often almost continuously, redeploying and co-ordinating the resources needed to implement those responses (Sanchez, 1995). In a traditional economy organisations have focused on strategy and structure as products of formal planning. In a knowledge economy the rapid pace of change and its increasingly discontinuous nature create a need for a new focus: on strategising and structuring as dynamic processes. We discuss in Chapter 3 the need to find new organisational forms and to continuously adapt those forms to new contingencies.

Researchers such as Eisenhardt and Santos (2002) argue that in an emerging knowledge economy firms need to generate dynamic capabilities that rely on combining internal competencies with the know-how of external entities. In Chapter 3 we also discuss some of the ways in which the organisation can achieve what Venkatraman and Subramaniam (2002) refer to as 'economies of expertise' through leveraging intellectual capital and knowledge flows in a complex network of internal and external relationships.

Reflection

- What is the predominant view on 'knowledge' in your own organisation (or one with which you are familiar)?
- What are some of the ways in which this view is typically expressed in practical roles, tasks or activities in your own workplace?

Across Western countries and others more widely, notably Singapore and Japan, the focus and shape of HRD in organisations is being influenced by national policies on vocational education and training (VET), and by national initiatives related to lifelong learning. We explore a number of country VET systems in Chapter 4 ('HRD: Country Frameworks') in order to gain a better understanding of the economic, cultural and societal pressures that help to explain the focus and coverage of HRD at micro levels. A major issue discussed in that chapter is the increasing convergence in external challenges facing organisationally based HRD, yet the great disparity in national policies and systems aimed at ensuring firms respond effectively to those challenges.

In Chapters 5 and 6 HRD as an organisational process comes centre stage. In Chapter 5 ('HRD: Emerging Challenges') we explore findings from research since the early 1990s into HRD across Europe and more widely in order to identify the key challenges that it now faces. In Chapter 6 ('HRD: The State of Play') we examine how the HRD function and its practitioners seem to be coping with those challenges. Although some of the messages emerging from recent research are ambiguous, there is a generalised consistency in findings. We are forced to conclude that HRD has a considerable way to go before it becomes a credible business function in organisations currently, let alone in any new and even more challenging scenarios.

Part II: Building knowledge-productive organisations

Having focused in Part I of the book primarily on the changing world of work, learning and development in an increasingly turbulent business environment, we move into the workplace in Part II in order to explore issues related to the development of organisational capability to continuously improve and to innovate – in other words, to become knowledge-productive.

In organisations operating in traditional economies, knowledge has tended to be regarded as an objective entity, codifiable and often protected by patents. In Chapter 7 ('Notions of knowledge') we trace some of the ways in which, from the start of the 20th century and throughout most of its duration, this notion of knowledge as a resource to which the organisation has proprietary rights influenced corporate policy-making, the managerial role and HRD activity.

By the turn of the 20th century, the changes discussed in Part I of the book were drawing increasing attention to the tacit dimension of knowledge, and to the importance of 'knowing' as a social process. However, in their literature review, Eisenhardt and Santos (2002) found that in most organisational research 'knowledge' was still at that time being treated relatively simplistically as a resource. Drawing on arguments proposed in this book's earlier chapters, we contend in Chapter 7 that the source of competitive advantage in dynamic knowledge-based environments cannot be knowledge as organisational commodity alone, since the value of all commodities is eroded by obsolescence, imitation and poaching. We argue for a paradigm where the organisation is viewed as a system of learning and knowing processes and activity, situated in workplace communities of practice. The concepts underpinning the paradigm are not new (Vygotsky, 1978; Lave and Wenger, 1991; Sternberg, 1994). However, where once they were mainly debated in the educational and social theory domains, now they are gaining prominence in the literature and practice of business strategy and HRD (Wenger and Snyder, 2000).

We explain in Chapter 8 ('The Knowledge-Productive Organisation') that this paradigm has profound implications for organisational leaders and managers, for human resource professionals, and indeed for all who work in and for the organisation. Learning processes in the workplace constitute a major vehicle for knowledge creation. In practice, however, it can be extremely difficult to organise a work environment in such a way that learning plays a prominent role in day to day activities. The reason is less a lack of inspiring examples, more that it can be hard to recognise those examples for what they are. Too often our perceptions are conditioned by a traditional educational paradigm where working and learning are treated as two separate states. Too often, also, the focus of educational systems is the control of chosen individuals' performance and development rather than the development in all potential learners of talent, inspiration, co-operation and trust.

These and other problematic issues are the focus of discussion in Chapter 8 and also in Chapter 9 ('Researching Knowledge Productivity'). Like other commentators in this evolving field, we have no prescriptions to offer. Instead we see value in suggesting some new constructs for building and maintaining a knowledge-productive organisation, and in critically appraising the research base of those constructs. In doing so we draw on emerging as well as on historical research studies, in order not only to identify 'evidence' but also to explore the experimental. In a field that has emerged so rapidly and that is subject to discontinuous change, no historical precedents are reliable. One message of these chapters is that all researchers and practitioners in the knowledge productivity field have to learn how to speculate and innovate as well as to replicate and validate.

In a knowledge economy managers and HR practitioners need to know how to apply new information processes and systems to their own areas of work, and how to contribute to the development of an effective interaction between structure, technology and knowledge productivity when new strategies are to be introduced. In Chapter 10 ('New technology, the knowledge process and HRD') we argue that at present such knowledge is often lacking. Drawing on research studies from across Europe, we describe developments in information and communication technology that have direct implications for learning and knowledge construction in the organisation. We explore aids and barriers to the harnessing of such technology to learning and development in the workplace, and identify areas where HRD practitioners appear to need new strategies and expertise.

Reflection

■ As adaptation, improvement and innovation become critical characteristics of organisations in a knowledge economy, how do you think this might be reflected in the day to day workplace?

■ Why do you think many organisations are slow to take up the opportunities offered by new information and communication technology to enhance training and learning in the workplace?

Part III: HRD: Challenges in a knowledge economy

In Part III we integrate and discuss the main issues that have emerged from earlier chapters and explore their major implications for the HRD process and its practitioners. However, we first examine one major area often ignored or underplayed in HRD texts: ethics.

In earlier parts of the book we refer from time to time to ethical issues associated with the operation of the HRD process in a knowledge economy. These form the focus of our discussion in Chapter 11 ('The ethical dimension'). Some writers argue that the treatment of organisational learning and knowledge in the literature tends to be normative, ignoring critical issues of power and ethics. They claim that even in the so-called post-Fordist workplace discussed in Chapters 7 and 8 ('Notions of knowledge' and 'The knowledge-productive organisation') workplace learning has a 'potentially repressive power' where 'the management of training means differences are rendered invisible as learners' experiences are constructed/structured to fit a centrally controlled norm' (Solomon, 1999: 124). Such a claim raises important questions. In a globalising business environment, approaches to workplace learning need to respect and build on diversity in order both to respect ethical principles and to aid knowledge productivity at individual, team and collective levels of the organisation.

In Chapter 12 ('Where to now for HRD?') we identify key issues that have surfaced throughout the book and explore implications for HRD strategies and practice in organisations. We also gaze into HRD's crystal ball and speculate on likely future challenges, opportunities and directions for the process and its practitioners. Our conclusions point to a concept of HRD and the tasks it involves in knowledge-based organisations that differs significantly from that prevailing in more traditional contexts. This view has a particular resonance for the education and career development of HRD professionals. It presents those professionals as no mere training technicians or learning providers, but as strategic players who need a repertoire of broad-based and high-level expertise. That expertise ranges from the ability to deal with social and cultural factors of learning in communities to being an effective partner in the development and implementation of strategies at business unit and corporate levels, where integrated thinking on adaptation to the environment, building networks, innovation and learning is essential.

AN ECONOMIC BASE FOR KNOWLEDGE, LEARNING AND DEVELOPMENT

The macro-level context

At the start of this chapter we referred to Drucker's (1993) notion of a transformational knowledge economy. Many writers have subsequently commented on such an economy, using a variety of synonymous terms including:

The Information Society (Giddens, 1994)
The Learning Society (European Commission, 1996)
The Network Society (Castells, 1998)
The Learning Economy (Field, 2000; Lundvall, 2000)

Concepts of learning and collaboration are key to such definitions. Sustained competitive advantage depends on the rapid generation and application of 'dynamic capabilities', defined as the firm's ability to integrate, build and reconfigure uniquely valuable competencies. Organisations must learn quickly, drawing on information from many sources, in order to be able to repeatedly alter their resource configuration in response to market change (Eisenhardt and Santos, 2002).

At macro level, the relationship between education and economic prosperity has always been of great importance for governments and industry. One of the main tasks of publicly funded education is to invest in the development of a high-level workforce. Such expenditure is considered as a necessary investment in human capital (Becker, 1993). In studies carried out by Bassanini and Scarpetta (2001), the coefficients on human capital suggested relatively high returns to education. They calculated that one extra year of average education (corresponding to a rise in human capital by about 10%) would lead to an average increase in steady-state output per capita of around 4–7%.

A European Community (EC) advisory committee for vocational training and an education committee meet regularly with union and employer bodies to discuss training as part of the 'social dialogue' – a process involving the social partners in training policy in order to encourage employers to contribute to long-term profitability and economic performance rather than training only for immediate needs. This dialogue enables stakeholder interests, in the shape of organisations representing employers and unions, to agree on policy that is informed by practical knowledge and expertise, and increases the likelihood of successful implementation. Together, the Community's social partners have produced a series of joint opinions endorsing the importance of education and training within the Single European Market. As we explain in Chapter 4, most member states (apart from the UK) mirror this Community-level approach by having some form of regulation of the vocational educational system, and by incorporating employer and trade union interests into the policy-making process.

Across the Community the need to invest heavily in human capital has for over a decade expressed itself in a drive for lifelong learning. Adopted by UNESCO as its mission in the 1970s, the vision of lifelong learning was espoused by the EC in the early 1990s. The global initiatives that followed included the *World Initiative on Lifelong Learning* and the *European Lifelong Learning Initiative* (Homan and Shaw, 2000: 1). In 1995 the European Commission presented the White Paper *Teaching and Learning. Towards the Learning Society* (EU, 1996). It highlighted five objectives:

1. Encouraging general knowledge development
2. Strengthening the ties between regular education and companies and institutions
3. Preventing social exclusion
4. Promoting and managing several languages
5. Promoting continuing education.

Reflecting these objectives, 1996 was designated the European Year of Lifelong Learning. The Organization for Economic Co-operation and Development (OECD) supported a similar policy in its reports *Lifelong Learning for All* (1996), *Literacy Skills for the Knowledge Society* (1997) and *Knowledge Management in the Learning Society* (2000). In 2001 two OECD publications, *The Well-being of Nations: The Role of Human and Social Capital* (2001) and *The New Economy: Beyond the Hype: The OECD Growth Project* (2001a), contained a strong plea for major investment in education, training and lifelong learning to enhance economic growth. Key policy recommendations in the latter publication include those shown in Table 1.1.

Table 1.1   *OECD policy recommendations for lifelong learning*

- *Invest in high-quality early education and childcare:* These investments are more cost-effective than later interventions to remedy school failure and they help boost participation in the labour market.

- *Raise completion of basic and vocational education and improve the quality of the system:* Dropout rates from secondary education have to be lowered. ICT literacy has become part of basic competencies and has to be improved, notably by recruiting qualified teachers and making pay more competitive.

- *Improve school-to-work transition:* Create or strengthen pathways that combine education with workplace experience; to ensure cost-effectiveness of the system, establish mechanisms of co-financing between employers, trainees and government.

- *Strengthen the links between higher education and the labour market:* This can be achieved through developing shorter course cycles with a healthy orientation to job market requirements. Involving firms in the definition of curricula and funding can be valuable, as can strengthening performance-based financial incentives.

- *Provide wider training opportunities:* Increase possibilities for adults and workers to participate in higher education. Innovative instruments, such as individual learning accounts and systems of recognition of competencies, can enhance incentives to engage in training while helping to control costs. Ensure that firm training is not penalised by tax systems.

- *Reduce obstacles to workplace changes and give workers greater voice:* Employee involvement and effective labour–management relationships and practices are key to fostering change and raising productivity – governments must allow this to develop. Ensure that working time legislation and employment regulations do not hamper efficient organisational change; adapt collective bargaining institutions to the new economic environment.

Source: Adapted from *The New Economy: Beyond the Hype: The OECD Growth Project*, p. 70. OECD copyright, 2001a

In an attempt to provide the vision of lifelong learning with a sound educational base, the EC is working to improve the level of basic education in certain states, to spread scarce skills more efficiently across the Community and to increase the stock of those skills. It is widely accepted in EC countries that the mobility of labour that is crucial to an efficient labour market relies heavily on common vocational standards and transferability of qualifications. To that end, in June 1999, 29 countries signed the Bologna Declaration, whereby all qualification standards and structures are to be linked by 2009 into an overarching European qualifications structure.

OECD statements focus not only on familiar types of activities whose aim is to increase participation levels in formal education and reduce dropout, but also on pre-school education in the family and the world of work as powerful learning environments. The OECD studies (2001) stress the direct influence of better education and also of good healthcare, welfare, and social and political commitment in creating the kind of climate for living and learning in which knowledge development can occur. In such a climate, co-operation and trust play a crucial role. They help to provide the basis for the formation of networks in which the exchange of relevant information and collaborative approaches to generate new knowledge should enable the knowledge economy to thrive (OECD, 2001).

National policy frameworks

We show in Chapter 4 that in EC countries there are variations in the extent to which, at institutional and company levels, lifelong learning is facilitated by substantial investment in continuing education and training. In Germany and France, local chambers of commerce make available training for employed workers, and in most countries there are now arrangements to train the unemployed – often, too, to help those likely to become unemployed. Ideas from the 1960s and 70s about continuing education and educational leave have resurfaced in both the UK and the Netherlands in national action plans for lifelong learning, in clauses on training facilities in collective labour agreement negotiations, and in measures to make people more employable.

We detail national VET frameworks and their impact on workplace learning in Chapter 4. Case example 1.2, however, illustrates one country's approach to lifelong learning.

This example, short though it is, demonstrates that in a knowledge economy the encouragement of education, training and development is no longer the exclusive role of government, executed through the formal academic system. Firms, institutions and voluntary organisations have an equally important part to play in ensuring learning opportunities for their members. In a knowledge economy, education policy should therefore be a responsibility shared between government, citizens and market partners.

Reflection

■ At macro level there is a clear relationship between expenditure in education and the development of economically valuable knowledge. What policies covered in the chapter thus far aim to promote knowledge development at national *and/or* international levels?

■ Traditionally, governments see the need for high quality educational provision to be their prime responsibility. Who do you see to be key educational players in a knowledge economy – and why?

Case example 1.2

The Dutch national action programme for lifelong learning

The Dutch national action programme Een Leven Lang Leren [Life Long Learning] (OC&W, 1998) provides tax incentives for training and grants for employability consultants. Small and medium-sized enterprises, the elderly, and unskilled individuals receive special consideration. Companies that invest in ongoing staff training receive a certificate.

Unorthodox types of learning are under development, as many staff have trouble with conventional programmes and drop out. Appreciation is growing for competencies acquired outside the educational system. Assessment centres enable professionals to demonstrate their skills and obtain certificates. Combining working

and learning is becoming more popular, and the skill to learn independently – learning to learn – is deeply valued. Information and communications technology is used to support learning to learn.

The state is trying to help young children, especially from non-Dutch speaking families, keep up with their peers. Starting compulsory schooling at the age of four rather than five is one example. Reducing class sizes and coaching less-gifted students are other efforts in this direction. The Ministry of Education, Culture and Science has commissioned exploratory research on how the knowledge society has affected the educational system.

DEVELOPING KNOWLEDGE WORKERS IN A KNOWLEDGE ECONOMY

Knowledge workers

When looking at the workplace as a site for learning, it is important to investigate how employees are regarded by other stakeholders. Are they regarded as suppliers of labour, identified for use in some carefully designed plan? Or as problem solvers, sensitive receptors for information, potential improvers and innovators? Identifying and understanding the range of perspectives held by powerful organisational stakeholders will help to decide how to develop an organisation oriented towards 'learning', where learning, work and innovation are intricately intertwined (Brown and Duguid, 1991).

Perceptions of 'knowledge workers' constitute a case in point. Definitions here vary greatly. The OECD growth project (2001a) defines the knowledge worker as belonging to the group of scientists, engineers, ICT specialists and technicians that generate knowledge. On the other hand the CPB (the Dutch National Planning Office) gives three different definitions of knowledge workers (CPB, 2002):

- **Researchers and scientists**. These knowledge workers form 0.6% of the total labour force, of which 50% is active in the private sector and 50% is active in universities and knowledge institutions. (This is the most narrow definition of the three.)
- **Alumni of higher education**. These knowledge workers form 28.2% of the total labour force. (This definition is based on the level of general education, with knowledge workers categorised as those achieving at the highest level.)
- **HRST (Human Resources in Science and Technology)**, **including alumni of higher education + managers, teachers and engineers with secondary vocational education level**. These knowledge workers form 36.3% of the total labour force in the Netherlands. (This definition includes personnel who have achieved at the secondary level of vocational education.)

According to OECD data applying to the US and to EC countries, knowledge workers defined in any of the above ways form the fastest growing group in employment. The growing importance of knowledge-intensive employment is shown in Table 1.2.

So 'knowledge workers' form a vital part of the knowledge economy, and it is logical to predict that they will pay increasing attention to their own employability and economic attractiveness as they become more aware of their market value. They are likely to put organisations under increasing pressure to ensure a learning environment that caters for their needs.

Training, self-direction, personal development and coaching are important ingredients in the careers of knowledge workers (Alheit, 1999; Field, 2000), but as they gain

Table 1.2   *Average percentage change in key worker groups, 1992–99*

Group of occupations	Average annual percentage change, 1992–99
Knowledge workers	+ 3.3
Service workers	+ 2.2
Management workers	+ 1.6
Data workers	+ 0.9
Goods-producing workers	− 0.2

Source: Adapted from *The New Economy: Beyond the Hype. The OECD Growth Project.* Figure IV.1., p. 56. OECD copyright, 2001a

more autonomy in determining their own learning goals and in organising their own learning activities, so the control that central management and the HRD function can exercise over their learning processes will decrease. There is always likely to be a need for central co-ordination and steering of the development of competencies involving subject matter expertise and problem solving. To that extent the traditional training function will always be valued. However (as we show in Chapter 8) it will be difficult to centrally organise activities for developing those less easily defined and highly indi-vidualised skills that are crucial in a truly knowledge-productive organisation. Such skills are to do with reflection, co-operation, the building of mutual trust, the finding of personal development paths, and the exercise of independent judgement and prac-tical wisdom. Even where the organisation can offer opportunities for such skills to develop, it cannot compel individuals to use them. Knowledge workers may see training useful where it enables them to update or acquire skills that they see to be immediately relevant, but they cannot be forced to acquire those that they may not regard as relevant, nor can they be made to develop in particular ways for the longer term. The question therefore arises: what role, if any, can HRD play in fostering the more broad-based and long-term work-related learning capacity of knowledge workers?

The question is vital for HRD professionals. When the firm is understood as an evolving system of knowledge production and application, with self-organising prop-erties that result from the activities of workers who are relatively autonomous in their networks (Spender, 1996), this presents puzzling challenges to HRD professionals schooled in a very different organisational context.

Non-knowledge workers

Equally important questions arise in relation to those employees who do not partic-ipate in what is commonly regarded as the core of 'knowledge work' but who supply the vital infrastructure for specialist knowledge workers' activity. Consider at this point the following description of human and social capital by the OECD (2001):

■ *Human capital:* 'the knowledge, skills, competencies and attributes embodied in individuals that facilitate the creation of personal, social and economic well-being'. It is developed in the contexts of family, early childcare setting, formal education and adult education, daily living and civic participation, as well as in formal training and informal learning at work and through specific activities such as research and innovation or participation in various professional networks (p. 18).
■ *Social capital:* 'networks together with shared norms, values and understandings that facilitate co-operation within or among groups'. Trust may be viewed as both a source and an outcome of social capital as well as being a very close proxy for many of the norms, understandings and values which underpin social co-operation (p. 41).

As we discuss in the next section and again in Chapter 2, in many of today's organ-isations there is pressure to invest only or primarily in the short-term training of human capital and in retaining 'key' personnel. In such organisations the coverage of training and career development planning tends to be selective, with 'key' personnel such as managers and 'knowledge workers' having priority, and far fewer opportuni-ties being available for other occupational groups. Yet if we broaden the definition of knowledge workers to incorporate any who contribute to the core of economic activity in an organisation whose profitability and progress depend primarily on effective knowledge work, this should change the parameters of the HRD investment.

We argue in this book that for organisations operating in an emerging knowledge economy, where the tacit dimension of knowledge and its social construction is a vital source of competitive advantage, the focus of the HRD investment should be on building social as well as human capital. Social capital is to do with the interactions of *all* workers in an organisation. Personnel such as service workers, data workers, and goods-producing workers all belong to the networks of a knowledge activity system that enables continuous adaptation to a dynamic environment through improvement and innovation in work processes, products and services. Their learning and development are crucial to the organisation's continued success. Surely, then, the HRD process must encompass the entire workforce, non-knowledge workers as well as knowledge workers? All form part of the organisation's vital social capital. In a knowledge economy all, in a real sense, are knowledge workers.

THE HRD FUNCTION IN A KNOWLEDGE ECONOMY

New roles and tasks for HRD professionals

The questions we have just posed make it clear that those who have special expertise to contribute to the design and maintenance of learning environments, to tackling barriers to learning, and to facilitating the development of learning skills in individuals and in teams, possess a capability critical to the progress of organisations in a knowledge economy. In Chapters 5 and 6 we review the roles and tasks that HRD practitioners currently hold and the organisational activities in which they are mainly involved. We examine evidence from research that relates to their performance and to the status and focus of the HRD function. In subsequent chapters we propose new HRD roles and tasks in organisations seeking to be knowledge-productive. In Chapter 12 we look across the whole spectrum of current and likely future activity for HRD practitioners and identify what we believe to be core tasks for the profession in a knowledge economy.

The performance–learning debate

One of the questions that arises from our discussion of HRD as an organisational process concerns the extent to which its focus should be on performance or on learning. A lively debate has been taking place over this issue among HRD researchers in Europe and the US (Swanson and Holton, 2001; Holton, 2002). It is relevant to introduce it here before expanding on it in Chapter 5 and drawing our final conclusions in Chapter 12.

The productivity revolution of the 20th century was mainly due to the effective management of standardised production, and to the application of smart routines and procedures (Drucker, 2001). This type of management was extremely successful in the domain of mass production, and the skill of analysing work processes and performance improvement is still applied in business process redesign projects. It found its way into human performance technology where it was combined with behavioural learning theory (Rosenberg et al., 1992; Stolovitch and Keeps, 1992). In those knowledge management systems that rely heavily on the concept of storing 'knowledge' in databases and making efficient use of this knowledge by means of well-organised search engines, the same skill of performance analysis remains relevant.

At the heart of the performance–learning debate, however, lie the questions of whether the HRD process should be focused on performance improvement or on more open-ended continuous learning, and whether HRD activity should support individuals in their learning and development or in tasks primarily related to the achievement of their current work targets. We argue throughout this book that once the focus in an organisation shifts from rules, procedures and systems to the enrichment of work, the exploration of opportunities, and the involvement and reciprocal learning of all organisational members, then there should be a radical reconsideration of HRD's focus. Sustained investment in a work environment where knowledge productivity is the main aim is not only likely to be attractive to employees; it also seems essential for the organisation if it is to achieve and sustain progress in a knowledge economy.

Reflection

- The knowledge worker has just been introduced as a protagonist on the scene of a knowledge economy. In what sense can all employees in knowledge-productive organisations be termed 'knowledge workers'?
- When learning, development and work are intricately intertwined, how do you think it will affect the role of HRD professionals (that is, those who have undergone specialist HRD training and education)?

CONCLUSION

In this scene-setting chapter, our twofold purpose has been to explain our rationale for focusing the book on the organisational process of HRD in an emerging knowledge economy, and to identify key themes that underpin the book's structure and content.

Two of the book's major themes introduced in this chapter are that:

- in an emerging knowledge economy the capability to add value by means of knowledge creation and knowledge application is becoming more important for organisations than the availability of the traditional factors of capital, material and labour, and that
- learning and developmental processes have a crucial role to play in building that capability.

Running through both these themes is another, which has to do with changing notions of knowledge. We observed in the early part of the chapter that if knowledge is regarded as a type of commodity, organisations will tend to be preoccupied with knowledge transfer (moving items of knowledge from one location, person or group to another). If, however, it is regarded as a process, a type of activity system, the greater concern will be to create and sustain a learning culture where that process can flourish through human interactions shaped by social context and harnessed to a shared organisational purpose. Once knowledge-productive relationships in the workplace are understood as key to competitive advantage, this signals major changes for business and human resource strategies and practices. In this chapter we have opened the door to issues of strategising and organising that we pursue in Chapters 2 and 3.

As long as knowledge is regarded as an objective resource, it is also natural to rely on organisational models based on the centralisation of planning and control, and managed from the top through delegated authority and specialist expertise. Once attention is focused on workplace learning as a primary source of tacit knowledge that has a unique value in ensuring continuous improvement and innovation, then traditional organisational forms and management paradigms become problematic, as do the wider societal, political and economic logics that have hitherto sustained them. Another theme in this introductory chapter has therefore been the linkages between international and national policies to do with lifelong learning and the organisational policies that focus on those same processes.

It is at this point that the role of the traditional HRD function – the final major theme announced in this chapter – comes under review. In the chapter we have highlighted but two of the many critical questions facing the HRD function and its practitioners as organisations increasingly compete and collaborate in a knowledge economy:

- When the organisation starts to be viewed as an evolving, quasi-autonomous system of knowledge production and application, with emergent and self-organising properties that result from the activities of relatively free agents in their internal and external networks, what – if any – role has the HRD professional?
- If, increasingly, there is a tension between the needs and wants of knowledge and non-knowledge workers, between the push for performance improvement and the pull for continuous learning, and between the development of human and of social capital in the organisation, what skills, organisational base and professional qualities do HRD practitioners need if they are to play a decisive part in tackling those tensions?

The themes and questions raised in this introductory chapter mark the starting point of our enquiry into HRD's identity and role in the new world of a knowledge economy. In subsequent chapters our purpose is to achieve an integrated perspective on strategising, organising, working and learning, in order that we can propose major roles and tasks for HRD professionals in organisations operating in that world.

chapter two

Organisational Perspectives: Strategising ...

INTRODUCTION

> (In a knowledge economy) organizations need strategies for growing and maintaining a deep understanding of their own current and long-term strategic interests in the midst of a core workforce that grows and evolves with the company ... Changes in approaches to training and development are important, but they are only one piece of the puzzle. (Mohrman and Lawler III, 1999: 437)

This is the rationale for this chapter: that without an understanding of an organisation's strategic management process and of its overall human resource (HR) policies and practices, it is impossible to determine appropriate HRD strategies for the organisation. In the chapter we identify reasons for the heightened importance of HR strategies in organisations confronting radically changing business environments. We explore new pressures on the employment relationship and typical effects on management's investment in its workforce. We then test some assumptions commonly made about strategy and human resource management (HRM), and conclude by assessing the value of two different HR paradigms, one based on a unitary view of organisations, the other on a pluralist perspective, given the issues that face HRM in organisations operating in an emerging knowledge economy.

LINKING HR STRATEGY TO COMPETITIVE CAPABILITY

Adding value through HR strategies

The field of HRM has traditionally been defined as incorporating the specific practices, formal policies and overarching HR philosophies whereby an organisation's workforce is secured, deployed, retained, rewarded and nurtured (Jackson and Schuler, 1995). In this view, HRM is an umbrella term relating to a function that includes HR planning, recruitment and selection, training, appraisal and development, incentive and compensation systems, and employee relations. The traditional HR function is often perceived to be about controlling labour costs and securing a steady supply of competent employees for the organisation (Mohrman and Lawler III, 1999).

A cost-cutting function does have value in organisations where labour constitutes the single largest operating cost. However, cost-cutting does not of itself *create* value. Over the past two decades, as organisations have come under acute pressures from their competitive environment, HRM has been widely criticised for a failure to add value for the business. The resource-based view of the firm (RBV), one of the most influential bodies of contemporary strategy theory, has a special preoccupation with identifying ways in which the firm's people can contribute to its competitive advantage (Lengnick-Hall and Lengnick-Hall, 1988; Jackson and Schuler, 1995).

RBV theory views an organisation's competitive performance as determined not only by its relative position in the industry but also by the ability of its strategic management to understand and mobilise the potential offered by the organisation's internal resources and capabilities. It therefore explores how internal capabilities can be generated, combined, utilised and sustained in order to bestow competitive advantage. RBV theory highlights the firm's HR base as an asset, not a cost, to the business, because it has the potential to produce valuable organisational capabilities (Selznick, 1957; Penrose, 1959; Wernerfelt, 1984; Barney, 1991).

To explain some key terms here: first, 'capabilities'. One well-known definition is:

> the capacity for a team of resources to perform some task or activity. (Grant, 1991)

Organisational capabilities are 'valuable' when they enable the firm to exploit opportunities and reduce threats (Barney, 1991). They do this by:

- meeting or creating a market need
- having uniqueness (scarcity value) and sustainability
- being hard to copy (because their basic components interact in complex and non-linear ways to generate value for the organisation)
- being path dependent (that is to say, so deeply embedded in the fabric of the organisation through their development over time that they cannot be poached by competitors).

'Organisational resources' are those:

> stocks of available factors that are owned or controlled by the firm. Resources are converted into final products or services by using a wide range of other firm assets and bonding mechanisms ... These resources consist, inter alia, of knowhow that can be traded (e.g. patents and licenses), financial or physical assets (e.g. property, plant and equipment), human capital, etc. (Amit and Schoemaker, 1993: 35)

Finally, the term 'human resource base' refers to:

> the accumulated stock of knowledge, skills and abilities that the individuals possess, which the firm has built up over time into an identifiable expertise. (Kamoche, 1996: 216)

It is interesting that in RBV theory such definitions refer to 'individuals' and to 'human capital', but not to social capital. We will come back to this towards the end of the chapter.

Reflection

- What is meant by an organisation's 'human resource base'?
- What are some of the ways in which that base can enhance an organisation's ability to compete in its environment?

If HR policies and practices are to contribute to competitive capability in today's fast-moving environments, then HRM as it currently exists in many organisations needs to change fundamentally. Research shows that often the function is no more than an incoherent set of practices, produced and implemented in isolation from one another (Wright and McMahan,1992: 298). What is needed is a truly strategic approach. 'Strategic HRM' (SHRM) differs from 'traditional HRM' by comprising:

> the pattern of planned human resource deployments and activities intended to enable an organization to achieve its goals. (Wright and McMahan, ibid)

To achieve a strategic approach means that HR practitioners must work as business partners who operate at multiple levels in order to integrate their operations with business activity throughout the organisation (Mohrman and Lawler III, 1999).

The impact of globalisation

Research sponsored by the UK Chartered Institute of Personnel and Development shows that SHRM is playing a crucial role in organisations exposed to an increasingly globalised business environment. The CIPD's flagship project on 'Globalising HR' is one of the most ambitious research projects of its kind, incorporating an on-line survey of HR professionals, a postal survey of major international organisations and interviews with some of their leading personnel. Its findings have revealed that while social and strategic reactions to competitive pressures and labour market changes vary from country to country, all organisations in Europe now operate under broadly the same capitalist system. Because of increasing internationalisation and globalisation of businesses, all face similar challenges and in many, HR professionals are occupying a strategic role (Brewster et al., 2002).

Brewster et al. (2002) identify four strategic drivers for companies entering a globalising environment:

- maximising shareholder value
- forging strategic partnerships
- creating core business processes
- building global presence.

In order to respond to these drivers, HR functions in such companies are using four main delivery mechanisms (Brewster et al., 2002):

- *Rationalisation of costs* – the drive for cost efficiency.
- *Knowledge management* – a term used loosely to describe a drive to create and share knowledge that can be applied to continuous improvement and radical innovation in goods, services and processes. Here, however, the research finds that technical specialists are taking the leading role at present.

- ■ *E-enablement of HRM* – the drive related to harnessing new information and communication technology as part of the pursuit of better ways to do things. The impact on global HRM 'could be immense' but none of the companies surveyed 'felt they were anywhere other than at the beginning of it' (ibid: 3).
- ■ *Centres of excellence on a global scale.* HR itself is evolving in some companies into a series of global centres of excellence, for example with Shell Oil. Centres of HR excellence are often born when groups of specialists – or even individuals with a strong interest in a certain area – gather like-minded people around them, many using virtual networks. Such centres enable big business ideas to come to life. They also help talented HR people to get a global perspective and to work on major international projects.

Figure 2.1 shows that in more globalised businesses the routine work that HR specialists tend to carry out in domestically based or traditional multinationals is giving way to activity to develop organisational capability. This involves HR professionals working more closely with business leaders, with many having a seat on the board (ibid).

The HRD process features heavily in the task of developing organisational capability, as Figure 2.1 shows, and the core competencies highlighted here apply equally to HRD professionals as to other HR specialists (Brewster et al., 2002: 18). They are:

- ■ Strong personal networking skills
- ■ The ability to think strategically, work virtually and tolerate ambiguities and uncertainties of new business situations
- ■ High-level political skills
- ■ Skills in dealing with cultural diversity
- ■ A grasp of the link between HR activity and effective business performance across the world.

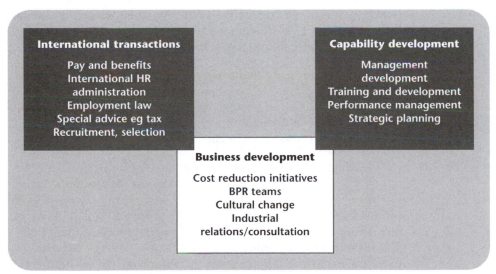

Figure 2.1   *Three dimensions to the global HR professional role*

Source: Brewster, Harris and Sparrow, 2002, p. 14. Reproduced with permission of the Chartered Institute of Personnel and Development

The researchers have identified a broad set of HR competencies that are needed to respond effectively to the challenges facing SHRM across countries in the capitalist society of the West. Despite the growing convergence in those challenges, and a corresponding convergence in generalised goals for SHRM, the ways of achieving those goals vary widely. That, however, is appropriate, since it indicates a responsiveness to context, and especially to 'local cultures, national legal and institutional frameworks, business practice and ownerships structure' (Sparrow and Hiltrop, 1994: 48). It shows recognition for the need for 'fit', as described in the following section.

Achieving fit

There are two kinds of fit to consider here. There is the fit of HR practices and processes with each other, so that what is done in recruitment, for example, is carried through in HR policies of training, development and rewards. We call this horizontal fit. There is also the fit of HR strategy and practices to the needs of the business and to external challenges and changes, so that SHRM contributes to company performance. We call this vertical fit. SHRM's task is thus to:

> (get) things right inside the organisation while also coping with a competitive labour market for talented people, and responding to the changing demands of customers and clients. (Purcell et al., 2000: 32)

Achieving fit is notoriously problematic. This is particularly the case in multidivisional organisations where business strategies, management styles and actions and workplace cultures tend to differ across strategic business units. In trying to respond sensitively to local needs HR policies and practices may lose identification with overarching corporate HR strategy. Both horizontal and vertical fit will suffer where each set of HR practices becomes increasingly insular within its particular SBU, and in so doing also loses alignment with corporate goals (Miller, 1987; Ahlstrand and Purcell, 1988; Legge, 1995).

Becker and Gerhart in their research found no evidence of any 'best practice magic bullet' to resolve the difficulties of fit, but they warned against an approach that focuses overmuch on improvements at individual or unit level while failing to align adequately with corporate goals and needs:

> Both HR system and HR function must have as their principal focus a set of properly aligned HR policies that solve business problems and support the firm's operating and strategic initiatives ... A set of practices that have individual, positive effects on performance may be a necessary, but not sufficient, condition for a larger effect on firm performance. (Becker and Gerhart, 1996: 797)

Case example 2.1 further demonstrates the need for alignment.

Many research studies now show that the operation of mutually reinforcing systems of HR practice can directly improve company performance, mainly measured in financial terms (Caulkin, 2001). To take just one, in an ongoing research programme in the UK, David Guest has surveyed more than 1,000 chief executives and HR directors and found clear links between 18 key HR practices, employee attitudes and behaviour, and the financial performance of the business (Guest and Baron, 2000; Guest and King, 2001).

This 'bundling' approach involves the choice and use of sets of HR practices that best fit the needs, characteristics and core competencies of the business. Sets explored

Case example 2.1

Aligning SHRM with business needs

Company A is delayering and downsizing in order to become quicker and leaner in a tough competitive market. It needs a fast-adaptive workforce. The HR function can produce added value by producing and implementing policies related to harmonising pay and conditions, to disengagement and redeployment of people, and to the teambuilding and multiskilling needed to operate a new type of network or matrix structure where what matters is collaborative horizontal relationships and self-managing cross-functional teams instead of the traditional authoritarian vertical relationships. Those who have to manage that changed work organisation will need appraisal, training and development to acquire the task and behavioural competencies required. Recruitment and promotion policies will also have to change, as will the company's performance management process and its reward systems.

Company B is breaking into new markets in a turbulent environment where progress depends on rapidly responding to new and unfamiliar challenges. It has to be able to group and regroup its human, financial and physical resources, and produce new organisational capabilities that can respond quickly and innovatively to changing customer demands and can stimulate new customer wants. The HR function here can add value by helping to change and embed new organisational structure and culture, and to stimulate knowledge creation. That means that HR specialists will need to work with managers and team leaders to build a learning culture in the organisation, to form learning networks both within the organisation and across its boundaries, and to stimulate learning in the workplace that can lead to continuous improvement and also to radical innovation. Again, there will be implications here for HR policies to do with recruitment, promotion, rewards and performance management.

in research vary in their detail and through time, but those found to have the most powerful effects on organisational performance have individual and collective learning at their core, being concerned with (Guest and King, 2001):

- skills acquisition and development
- knowledge management
- commitment
- job design
- employee involvement.

However, research also indicates that less than 30% of organisations in the UK use more than two sets of skills, and that most of these are about improving individual competence rather than enhancing group-based, quality-based or broader types of skills that are vital to organisational performance. Similar research findings have been reported in America (Caulkin, 2001). The result of such a limited use of HR practices, focused so strongly on improving individual performance, is that individuals 'work harder but not smarter' (Stevens and Ashton, 1999: 31) – the very weakness against which Becker and Gerhart warned. This outcome is all the more surprising because new technology should be taking over the great majority of standard tasks, thereby freeing up increasing numbers of employees to use their brainpower in problem solving, improvement and innovation in the workplace.

It is not easy to choose and apply HR practices appropriate for organisations that confront a constantly changing business environment. The difficulty is compounded by current pressures on the employment relationship and on the organisation's HR investment.

PRESSURES ON THE EMPLOYMENT RELATIONSHIP

A differentiated workforce

In the current business landscape all occupational groups can expect some degree of change in their current roles and a reduction in job security. Cappelli (1995) found clear trends among organisations in countries as far apart as the United States (US), Britain, Australia and New Zealand to employ an increasingly differentiated workforce, often incorporating core full-time employees, contract, temporary, part-time and even voluntary workers, each group with its unique employment characteristics, needs and expectations. However, he found that trends to differentiation varied considerably across countries. He also failed to uncover any real evidence that trends to differentiation arose from a deliberate intent to build a flexible core and peripheral workforce. Rather they seem to have emerged in unplanned fashion through a number of years, as employers struggled to adjust in ad hoc ways to changing economic and labour market conditions and to pressures of short-termism. It therefore seems that at present there is a growth in differentiated workforces, but that this growth is relatively unplanned and varies in scale considerably from one country to the next.

A fractured psychological contract

An ESRC 2000 survey did, however, highlight across all sectors and levels in the UK a general reduction in employee morale and commitment (Taylor, 2002). In 2002 another survey, this time of over 360,000 employees world-wide, found lower levels of commitment expressed among British employees than by those in any other countries in the world's 10 largest economies except China and Japan (ISR, 2002). Such findings seem to echo another claim often made about the employment relationship: that the traditional psychological contract is in its death throes.

What is meant by the 'psychological contract'? It represents one aspect of the relationship that binds individual and organisation. That relationship is twofold. There is a legal contract that specifies duties, terms and conditions, and material rewards. There is also a psychological contract consisting of felt and perceived expectations, wants and rights. It comprises a dynamic and reciprocal deal, with new expectations being added over time. It concerns the social and emotional aspects of the exchange between employer and employee (Sparrow, 1999: 420), constituting:

> an implicit agreement between parties concerning what each party gives and gets in a relationship. It embodies the parties' assumptions regarding the 'rules of the game' by which they will fulfil obligations to one another. (Bowen et al., 1999)

In the past it was common for employers to offer employees relatively long-term job security and HR practices favourable to their up-skilling and continuous development, in return for their commitment and competent performance. Now, however, employers who are incorporating an increased cost-cutting drive into their business strategies are tempted to shift more of the social costs of employment onto the external market. According to Harrell-Cook and Ferris (1997) HR tactics here include:

- investing less in training programmes and developmental activity
- buying in more talent through the external labour market
- driving down bottom-line costs by downsizing
- making greater use of variable compensation schemes throughout the firm
- using more temporary and contract workers.

Again, though, we have to put the situation into perspective. In the UK, the ESRC survey to which we have already referred revealed that in 2000 90% of workers had permanent employment contracts, and those workers were remaining with the same employer for an average of seven years and four months. In Japan, despite some widely reported incursions made into long-term internal employment security by the sustained recession experienced during the 1990s, the employment system's three main principles – lifetime employment, company unions and seniority pay – remain so deeply inbuilt into the economy that 'lifetime employment does (still) apply to regular employees who would only be dismissed in extreme circumstances' (Ray, 2002: 108).

Still, where management chooses to shift the social costs of labour onto the external market in any of the ways mentioned above, individuals are likely to feel that their psychological contract with the employer is under threat. They become more vulnerable and need to take on a more active role than hitherto in managing their own learning and careers if they are to achieve continuing employability in the labour market. In a knowledge economy, those who are best equipped to do that, and who also have the most powerful employee voice to obtain support for their development plans, are the knowledge workers to whom we referred in Chapter 1. Those who are least equipped and who also have the weakest voice are – as they have always been – the non-knowledge workers, especially the poorly educated and semi- or unskilled, the young and poorly paid, and various minority groups. A quick-fix approach that favours short-term training in company-specific skills that have little value in the external labour market further disadvantages such employees.

A quick-fix approach in HRM focuses on intensive short-term utilisation of the organisation's human capital. Employee commitment, however, depends on development of social capital also – and the building and sustaining of productive human relationships in an organisation needs a strategic, rather than a tactical, response to the complexities of today's employment relationship. Where there is a reduction in employees' belief in a 'felt fair' employment relationship, and a consequent erosion of their trust in that relationship, the consequences for the organisation can be grave. In the changing economic and employment landscape, organisations need to develop HR strategies that forge a durable psychological contract between employer and employees. Without that, management will have to struggle increasingly with the costs of operating with a low-trust workforce in a world of increasingly high-risk, high-trust business relationships (Mohrman and Lawler III, 1999: 438–9). Such costs bring obvious risks to relationships within the organisation. They can also lead to failures in crucial, and increasingly common, inter-firm partnerships such as joint ventures, strategic alliances and other collaborative arrangements, thus directly affecting the business performance of the firm (Sparrow, 1999: 430).

There is also an important issue of ownership here. The value that employees set on their expertise and commitment to the organisation, and the expectations they have about how that value should be recognised by the employer, go to the heart of the psychological contract. Where corporate values clash with the collective values of employees, there will be disagreement on the ends as well as the means that the employment relationship should serve (Kamoche, 1996: 224). This disagreement is likely to be acute in the case of knowledge workers. As we will detail in Chapter 3, in the knowledge-intensive firms where they are key players they choose 'what kind of clients to work with, what kind of projects to undertake, which methods to use' (Kirjavainen, 2001: 175). So the psychological contract has to recognise their strategic role as well as their unique knowledge-based abilities.

However, in any organisation where knowledge creation is an essential part of adding value, the willing involvement of all employees in that task is vital. All have knowledge that can be utilised in continuous improvement and radical innovation in the workplace, but none can be forced to use it. Collaboration, trust, ethical behaviour and mutual endeavour are therefore crucial drivers in such organisations. It is in that context that Ghoshal and Bartlett (1995, quoted in Sparrow, 1999) have called for a new moral contract in HRM for all employees, to be focused on the development of work methods and the redesign of work processes that foster the creation of continuous self-development.

Summary

The conclusions suggested by our discussion thus far are that:

- an organisation needs to produce uniquely valuable internal capabilities if it is to exploit opportunities and reduce threats in its external environment
- the HR base of the organisation has the potential to produce such capabilities, and as such is key to the organisation's competitive advantage
- it is therefore in management's interest to make investment in its people a strategic competitive priority for the organisation.

Yet corporate management in many organisations does not follow the logic of this argument. Rather than invest, it divests. Why should this be?

Reflection

- What is meant by the 'psychological contract'?
- Try to identify the range of key HR practices that dominate in your organisation (or one with which you are familiar). Are they primarily to do with a short-term investment in people, or are they significantly focused on long-term commitment?

CALCULATING THE HR INVESTMENT

In today's business environment the pressures on corporate management in relation to its HR investment are considerable. They can include the following:

Pressures for short-termism

Stockholder influence

While competition across the world shows no sign of abating and prices continue to tumble, the virtual death of inflation in countries such as the UK means that much of the driving force of traditional economies in a capitalist society has been lost. There is a growing demand by stockholders for short-term financial returns as the stock market demonstrates increasing liquidity and volatility (Bowman et al., 2002). This volatility is underscored by the rapid rise and fall of Internet firms and high-tech companies such as Vodaphone, whose share price had fallen by mid-April 2002 to its lowest level since October 1999, marking a two-year downward spiral from a high of 399p to 111½p.

Stockholders have great power over companies because of their control over financial resource flow. Much stock is now held by institutions in investment funds such as public and educational employee pension funds that are tax exempt. If quarterly earnings are down, the institutional investor may sell. Frequent trading contributes to the liquidity of the stock market and this in turn attracts corporate raiders to take advantage of the undervalued stock to gain control of the company and sell off its assets for profit (Bowman et al., 2002: 34). In the UK, by January 1999, six fund managers between them controlled £200 billion of British shares and were forcing changes in boardrooms in order to enhance shareholder value (Waples, 1999).

Executive reward strategies

Pressures on executives are intensified when their pay is tied to short-term financial performance in order to transfer risk to them from owners and investors. Chief executives have to weigh up the risks of making a strategic investment in employees in order to aid long-term organisational viability. The returns on such investment are speculative and not financially quantifiable, whereas focusing on short-term strategies can provide investors with regular streams of cash flow even though it may weaken the organisation in other ways (Bowman et al., 2002: 34).

Pressures for human capital investment

Of course there are counter-pressures. Employees have 'voice and exit' power. However, exit power only works when the employees in question have unique skills and knowledge that the organisation needs, and the generalised power of voice is reducing, especially with the weakened influence of the unions over organisations' human resource policies. There are, though, other sources of counter-pressure.

Legislative and statutory constraints

These come from both national and international sources, and the latter create some of the greatest tensions for the employer. The European Social Chapter and human rights legislation protect individual employees to the point where many organisations struggle to achieve both compliance and the productivity targets that are necessary to achieve profitability. These constraints are now beginning to backfire, adding to many employees' vulnerability as employers opt for more contracting-out of work in order to avoid the high social costs that full-time and temporary workers involve (Cappelli, 1995).

Institutional pressures

These are the pressures exerted on the organisation by others occupying the same professional, sectoral or other territory. Organisations within an institutional network develop social and professional rules, norms and standards that can exert considerable influence over other network members (Huff, 1982; Child, 1988; Spender, 1994). Those that respond positively to such pressures do so in recognition of shared values and because of perceived benefits to be gained from their peers, in the form of shared resources, prestige, trust and acceptability. Compliance – for example by achieving nationally or internationally recognised quality standards – can also be useful when it reduces the scrutiny that external bodies would otherwise exert over the organisation's conduct of its affairs. The acquisition of such standards also sends out a positive signal to clients and customers about the level of product and service that the organisation is likely to provide (Harrell-Cook and Ferris, 1997).

New meta standards are now influencing HR practice by adopting multiple stakeholder strategic performance control systems. The Norton-Kaplan Balanced scorecard mode, for example, views strategic objectives from four perspectives: financial, customers, internal processes and organisational learning. It is now adopted by 60% of the top 100 US companies and is widely used in the UK. Sparrow (1999) believes that such standards are conducive to long-term investment in the organisation's HR base to the extent that through having to use them, managers in such organisations are coming to understand the need for a broader view of strategic and competitive performance.

Customer and client expectations

Customer and client values and expectations can exert a major influence on corporate values, and thence on HR strategy. The move by many organisations to total quality management and the consequent drive for the HR policies that will build a total quality culture, is only one example of this. When the customer is king and is also highly sceptical about corporate behaviour, there is a clear need for HR policies that help to build a customer-focused, flexible, high-calibre workforce, and that encompass corporate management and senior executives as well as other organisational members.

The agency theory perspective

What finally decides the kind of investment that an organisation makes in its workforce? Agency theory and transaction cost analysis provide a useful gateway into our discussion here. These approaches to examining the problems of human exchange derive from the fields of finance and economics but they are often applied to the study of SHRM (Harrell-Cook and Ferris, 1997).

Agency theory is concerned with issues related to the ownership of the firm when that ownership is separated from the day to day running of the organisation. It assumes that in all but owner-managed organisations the owner or owners (known in agency theory as 'the principal') of an organisation must vest authority in an 'agent' – corporate management – to act on their behalf. The principal recognises the risk here and acts on the assumption that any agent will look to serve its own as well as the principal's interests as it fulfils its contract with that principal. In other words, all agents are perceived to be opportunistic (Williamson, 1985; Seth and Thomas, 1994).

Given this perception, the principal feels unable to predict an agent's behaviour in any given situation and so brings into play various measures to do with incentives, monitoring, control and risk-sharing. Such measures, because they are part of an attempt to establish an efficient contract between the parties, are described as 'agency costs' (Jensen and Meckling, 1976). The costs incurred in the process whereby that contract is negotiated and ultimately enforced are known as 'transaction costs' (Jones, 1984). When it comes to dealing with the workforce, corporate management becomes 'principal' and employees are the 'agents', likewise assumed to be opportunistic. The employees' bargaining counters are their firm-specific skills and knowledge and their power of 'voice or exit'.

Thus agency theory concludes that corporate management, whether acting as agent or as principal, will behave opportunistically and should expect others to do so. In this view, HR strategy will act primarily (Kamoche, 1996):

■ as a tool of managerial direction and control to achieve the kind of HR practices that will create added value for the organisation

and/or

■ as an approach to mediate the employment contract. Elements of HR strategy (especially those to do with rewards and retention) can offer a way of ensuring an efficient transaction process that produces a mutually acceptable wage–work bargain.

In the next section we question the assumptions that underpin agency theory. However, it is clear from any viewpoint that in making final decisions about its HR investment, corporate management will be particularly influenced by whichever stakeholder group can exercise the most power over resource flows – especially financial. This is because when key resource flows are threatened, so too is the viability of the business.

Reflection

■ What are some of the internal and external pressures that seem to complicate the decisions that top management in your own organisation has to take about its human resource investment?
■ What are the *main* standards by which strategic performance seems to be judged in your own organisation, and how far do they appear to encourage or inhibit a long-term investment in the organisation's human resource base?

TESTING ASSUMPTIONS

The arguments that we have been pursuing thus far rest on a number of assumptions:

■ that the competitive drive dominates business strategy
■ that 'strategy' is a product, chosen, designed and implemented according to a rational decision-making process where top management is the dominating player
■ that human behaviour in organisations is self-serving.

But how soundly based are these assumptions? We need now to look at them with a critical eye.

The competitive drive

We have already noted the preoccupation in the literature of strategy and of HRM with the competitive driver. This is unsurprising when the influential literature of the resource-based view of the firm focuses mainly on highly competitive companies and draws primarily on North American and European writers. RBV research is characterised by many small-scale case studies produced at a particular point in time, and located in a relatively small number of private sector organisations. A high proportion of those organisations are large multinational/multidivisionals in the manufacturing sector, or are in the high-tech sector (for example Bettis and Hitt, 1995).

Findings from such research can provide only a partial view of the many influences that shape business and HR strategies. The search for competitive advantage is powerful, but it is not the only strategic driving force. We have noted earlier in the chapter that national differences help to explain differences in the focus and content of HR strategies across countries even when the major HR challenges faced by organisations are broadly similar:

> Recent research on the variation in governance arrangements across different societies ... divergent forms of capitalism throughout the world ... and new forms of organizing in Europe and Japan ... indicate how and why national cultures and institutions can shape the strategy and behaviour of corporations. (Pettigrew et al., 2002a: 15)

So geographical spread, particularly into Asia and Eastern European countries, 'presents new challenges in managing human resources in diverse cultures and societies where laws, customs and prevailing social values are quite different from those at home' (Sparrow and Hiltrop, 1994: 199). But even at local level and within particular

---

Case example 2.2

Hutton Borough Council, UK

'Hutton' was the pseudonym given to a labour-dominated metropolitan borough council in a deprived urban area of the North East of England in a case study by Malloch in the early 1990s. At Hutton, new top managers had arrived in the early 1980s who saw the council's environment as a community to be served. The council's corporate mission was summarised by the phrase 'to build the community'.

They did not see their environment as a set of product and labour markets to be exploited. They saw the poor economic and social conditions in Hutton as an environment to be improved. The main point is that organizations can and do have the power to define the environment in which they operate. (Malloch, 1992: 134)

The council's HR mission and policies were driven by the same values that had produced the corporate mission. There was a tactical approach to tendering, aimed at ensuring that few if any outside contractors won council tenders; and there was a policy of redeployment which had a clear economic rationale – it increased the utilisation of human resource capacity; it transferred employees' learning and skills between locations; and it permitted a greater range of work to be done with the existing workforce. But for the policy-makers its most powerful rationale was that it honoured the council's commitment to internal employment security. Moral, rather than economic, values shaped HR strategy and policies at Hutton, just as they shaped its corporate mission and goals.

Source: Malloch, 1992, 1992a

sectors, HR strategies can vary significantly from one organisation to the next, often for reasons that have little to do with any competitive drive. Case example 2.2 is set in the public sector in the UK. It illustrates some non-economic strategic drivers.

Malloch also carried out research in a National Health Service hospital, a brewery and two large multinational chemical producers (1990). In each context he found that unique management values drove the employment system both directly and indirectly. They worked directly by defining certain HR policies as being appropriate on grounds of morality, personal interest or tradition. They worked indirectly by shaping decisions on technology, work organisation, how costs were to be reduced and changing definitions of market domains. Malloch concluded that there are many private sector as well as public sector organisations that partly define their environment as a community and are driven by more than purely economic values in strategic decision-making.

Strategy: product or process?

The strategy field is fragmented by the number of schools of thought it contains, and by wide-ranging differences in their underlying theoretical dimensions and research methodologies (Elfring and Volberda, 2001: 8). The RBV literature that has dominated the field for some years lacks a strong grounding in longitudinal studies. Much of it is preoccupied with strategy as a product intended to respond to forces in the competitive market, with far less attention being given to the ongoing outcomes of strategic decisions taken at particular points in time.

There is, however, another view of strategy. It draws particularly on thinking in the behavioural and organisational sciences. It is of strategy as a process, more spontaneous than it is formalised, and representing a pattern in a stream of actions through time (Mintzberg and Waters, 1985). In this view there is a difference between intended, emergent and realised strategy: the strategy process continually changes as a result of ongoing learning and action across the organisation (Lindblom, 1959; Quinn, 1980). Seen in this light, strategy as process is powerfully influenced by individual and collective cognitions and by the interplay of power and politics at every organisational level (Pettigrew, 1973). It is enacted in an environment that is constantly throwing up new and often unfamiliar pressures, challenges and opportunities, and in a context where the boundaries between organisation and environment are fluid and dynamic. It is influenced by values that different actors within and outside the organisation believe to 'matter', whether or not they are to do with market competition (Silverman, 1970).

In a knowledge economy, it is more appropriate to treat strategy as a process than as a product. In such an economy, organisations have only short periods in which they can maintain competitive advantage before strategic recipes and assets lose their relevance. Regular structural reconfiguration of the firm must therefore be integrated with continuing changes in strategy as current stocks and resources within the firm need to be redeployed and/or new ones must be acquired (Pettigrew et al., 2002a: 17). The firm has also increasingly to interact with the customer in order to 'co-create' value. Prahalad and Ramaswamy quote the case of the Saturn Corporation, launched by General Motors in 1985 as not just a new car company, but a 'community':

> Saturn works with its customers in the design, manufacturing and sales processes, and it engages Saturn owners to help continuously innovate and improve its cars. (Prahalad and Ramaswamy, 2002: 5)

Therefore HR policies and practices too must continuously innovate and adapt in order to fit a variety of organisational configurations, meet the needs of a 'shifting array of workforces' (Pettigrew et al., 2002a: 17), and help employees acquire new skills, knowledge and customer-focused attitudes. For organisations in a knowledge economy, what matters most is not 'strategy' and 'organisation' but continuous 'strategizing' and 'organizing' (ibid: 16). That is as true for SHRM as for all other business functions.

In the SHRM field, however, there are enduring problems. Research shows 'a major "disconnect"' evident between what studies say firms should do about their HR strategy, and what happens in reality (Becker and Gerhart, 1996). John Storey (1992: 17), in his groundbreaking HRM research in the UK during the 1980s, visited companies identified in the literature as having made radical innovations, 'only to discover that the "breakthrough" was viewed as a peripheral trial, was hardly recognizable to the participants on the ground, or had been abandoned altogether'. Such observations are not unusual (Truss and Gratton, 1994; Pettigrew et al., 2002).

One of the reasons for the difference between the espoused and the real in organisations may be that it is their *intended* HR strategy that management attempts to relate to business strategy, not their *realised* strategy – that is to say, strategy as it is implemented from day to day in the workplace (Truss and Gratton, 1994: 681). Another is that HR strategies, like business strategies, can sometimes be an illusion. Action may have preceded thought, rather than the reverse, so that what are retrospectively claimed to be intended strategies are in truth no more than 'reconstructions after the fact' (Pettigrew et al., 2002a: 12).

Such reasoning fits well with the view of strategy as process rather than product. Written plans, reports and other company documentation may paint a picture of life proceeding in the orderly fashion that strategic management originally intended. In reality, however, the HR strategy process like any other is continuously affected by context. It is influenced especially by the interplay of organisational actors who use their power to impose their definition of the situation on others, and by individual and collective learning that leads to changing perceptions of outcomes being achieved and of issues that demand action. Repeatedly, therefore, HR strategy moves in unexpected directions, and has unexpected results on the ground. The product may state what is intended. Only the process can show whether, and when, intention becomes reality.

Self-interest or co-operation?

We have noted in an earlier section the assumption underpinning agency theory that human behaviour in organisations is dominated by opportunism. In this view, 'conflict among disparate subunit goals is seen as pervasive, and incentives and fiat are viewed as the key mechanisms for achieving cooperation' (Ghoshal and Bartlett, 1994: 109).

This is a disputed assumption. In their longitudinal study of Semco (the pseudonym given to an electronics-based industrial products company owned by a diversified group), Ghoshal and Bartlett (1994) found that management actions at all organisational levels that emphasised discipline, stretch, trust and support were critical in explaining high levels of individual initiative, mutual co-operation and collective learning across the whole workforce. Such a belief in the importance of context as a primary determinant of human behaviour is consistent with notions about the values needed in organisations operating in a knowledge economy. As we will show in Chapter 3, the impact of that economy is causing radical changes in organisational structures so that they increasingly resemble networks of small organisations with fluid boundaries. In such structures there is a clear need to 'inspire cooperative personal decisions by creating ... faith in the integrity of common purpose' (Barnard, 1938: 259).

Assignment 1 for Chapter 2 is provided in Appendix 1 to help readers interested in developing their skills in researching the HR strategy process and its goals in their organisation. Before doing so, it may be helpful to reflect on the following points:

Reflection

■ 'Strategy is a process, not a product.' How far do you agree or disagree with the statement, and for what reasons?

■ How far do you believe that the competitive drive is the only one that matters, strategically, in an organisation? And how far does it matter in your own?

Qualifying our assumptions

Looking back on the assumptions underlining contemporary theories about strategic management and HR strategy that we have reviewed in these two sections, we can now see that they are unsound:

■ It cannot be assumed that the sole strategic driver in all organisations is one of competition. In many organisations, and across different sectoral, national and international boundaries and cultures there are other compelling drivers, underpinned by non-economic values.

■ Strategy is essentially a process, not a product. It involves the interaction of sociopolitical forces and of individual and collective knowledge, learning and action within and across organisations. In a fast-moving knowledge economy where no advantage obtained by one organisation can be sustained for long and where organisational boundaries are fluid and dynamic, it is not 'strategy' and 'organisation' that count, but 'strategising' and 'organising'.

■ Human behaviour in organisations is fuelled by more than economic self-interest – and must be, if the high level of co-operative endeavour and the rapid collective learning and unlearning that is needed by organisations operating in a knowledge economy are to be achieved and sustained.

DO WE NEED A NEW HR PARADIGM?

There is one final assumption, core to all those reviewed in the previous section, that now needs to be questioned. It is that in every organisation the achievement of economic advantage can be taken for granted as the dominating goal. This assumption underpins much of the contemporary literature of strategy and SHRM. It leaves only the means to corporate goals, not the goals themselves, open for debate, and it rests on what Brewster (1999) calls the 'universalist paradigm'. By this he means, essentially, an ingrained way of thinking about the organisation and the HR function's contribution to it that sees SHRM's universal purpose to be the integration of HR goals and practices with business strategy in order to aid the organisation's (financial) performance.

The unitary perspective

Hard and soft SHRM models

The unitary approach has been popularised by SHRM models focused on a set of generic goals that link HRM and the financial and competitive performance of the organisation through a set of key HR outcomes. There are two types of model here: hard and soft. The 'hard' tight-coupled models come predominantly from the Michigan School of business management theory in the US (for example, Galbraith and Nathanson, 1978; Fombrun et al., 1984). They take it for granted that every firm has, or can produce, a detailed business strategy that is agreed by all the parties, that consistently guides action throughout the organisation, and to which each HR process (recruitment, training, rewards and so on) can be closely fitted. In the current turbulent business environment, such a highly engineered approach has been dismissed by many as 'a fantastically idealized picture: in reality achieving it is extremely rare' (Mabey and Salaman, 1995: 46).

On the other hand, a 'soft' HR approach, typified by the Harvard School's 'mutuality' model, has many supporters. Its purpose is to build mutuality of interest through HR practices that make an impact on corporate goals through an interaction between their behavioural outcomes (in terms of enhanced employee motivation, co-operation and involvement) and their HR outcomes (in terms of enhanced commitment, quality and flexibility). This high-commitment model requires organisational leaders who are willing to make a high level of investment in human resources over a long rather than short time span, and is presented as relevant for all organisations seeking to obtain a leading edge in their field (Guest, 1987, 1997).

An emphasis on outcomes to do with co-operation, commitment and flexibility has clear relevance for organisations operating in a knowledge economy. Furthermore, as we have already seen, research on 'bundling' does now indicate that the operation of mutually reinforcing systems of HR practice can improve companies' financial performance. However, analysis of the high-commitment model reveals considerable inconsistency among its elements (Legge, 1989, 1995). Its research base is also beset by methodological weaknesses, including a tendency to rely on data collected at head office as a basis for company-wide statements about HR practices (Guest, 1990, 1997) and a primary interest in company performance as measured by financial indices. Such indices exclude from consideration issues that can be of profound importance to many organisational members, and that can damage employees in a variety of ways that may ultimately threaten the employment relationship. Importantly, Guest and Hoque (1994) found significant data showing HR practices in some organisations as 'good' when assessed by their impact on those indices, yet 'ugly' in terms of their impact on employee relations and the overall treatment of the workforce.

Unitary systems

Both hard and soft 'universalist' models treat organisations as unitary systems – that is to say, as systems that seek to adapt to their environment through rational behaviour in the pursuit of unifying organisational goals. In the unitary view, 'common purpose' must be achieved by either avoiding conflict or by subjecting it closely to managerial control. The assumption is that conflict is dangerous and should be suppressed where it occurs. Guest (1987) typified this stance when he explained that the high-commitment approach works best on greenfield sites where there is either no union presence or a management–union relationship where management is the dominating party.

The pluralist perspective

A quite different, pluralist view of the organisation figures in what Brewster (1999) calls the 'contextualist' paradigm. In this perspective, organisations shape, as well as are shaped by, the environment, and the boundaries between them and their environment are fluid. Goals are multiple and operate at many organisational levels. They are not dominated by any common logic but are the outcome of various non-economic as well as economic interests. Human beings are motivated by many different interests but will tend to respond positively to organisational strategies that can 'inspire cooperative personal decisions by creating ... faith in the integrity of common purpose' (Barnard, 1938: 259).

In this view, all value systems matter. Since the concern is to build social as well as human capital in the organisation, it is vital to explore the implications of different kinds of goals for 'individuals within the organization, for the long-term health of the organization and for the community and country within which the organization operates' (Brewster, 1999). Organisational goals must be the outcome of collective decision-making, and although in that process conflict is bound to occur, it should not be viewed as a negative force. It is a natural phenomenon, born of inevitable tensions between different value systems. It can have negative or positive results for the organisation, but it will tend to have a positive value when it challenges irrelevant old learning, thereby unblocking creative processes and stimulating new thinking.

The pluralist perspective sees competitive forces as only one aspect of the context in which an organisation has to operate. That is why the paradigm associated with it is called 'contextualist'. In this view every organisation operates in a context that is to a greater or lesser degree unique to itself. The contextualist paradigm also embraces ethics. Once all values are accepted as worthy of discussion, not just the values of a capitalist society, then questions can be asked about ethical issues upon which a clear economic value cannot be placed but which in other terms may still have great significance (Carter and Jackson, 1990: 226). In Chapter 11 we discuss the crucial ethical dimension related to organisations in a knowledge economy.

The pluralist perspective is highly appropriate for organisations operating in a knowledge economy where trust, collaboration and creative capability are crucial features to promote organisations' knowledge processes. However Brewster (1999) urges complementarity, since there are features in both pluralist and unitary paradigms that work well in combination.

Reflection

- What assumption underpins the unitary view of organisations?
- In what ways does the pluralist perspective differ from the unitary perspective, and which viewpoint seems mainly to prevail in your own organisation?

Assignment 2 for this chapter is provided in Appendix 1 for readers who wish at this point to develop their consultancy skills related to analysing HR strategy issues.

CONCLUSION

At the start of this chapter we argued that it is essential to understand an organisation's business environment, strategic management process and general HR policies and practices in order to produce relevant and feasible HRD processes and activity. In the chapter we have sought to demonstrate the importance and meaning of a strategic approach to human resources in order to create value for organisations, especially those operating in a knowledge economy.

In today's organisations, competitive advantage depends not merely on the acquisition and development of superior human resources, but on the way in which human and social capital are organised, developed and sustained through time and space. The new tasks for HR practitioners in a knowledge-based environment require an ongoing coupling of HR strategy and practices to corporate, business unit, individual and environmental demands, and therefore a mastery of strategy as process. They call for the kind of political, cultural, strategic and relational expertise that those used to 'traditional HRM' may find hard to acquire. They also require a sophisticated understanding of an employment relationship that is being subjected to increasingly complex pressures.

We have argued that strategic HRM is an essential but also a problematic process in such organisations. No matter how clear it may seem that it is in the interests of the business to prioritise a strategic investment in its people, in practice this often fails to happen. Pressures of short-termism conflict with a variety of counter-pulls to muddy the waters of strategic decision-making. Such conflicting pressures are poorly understood by those who treat the organisation as a unitary system characterised by unifying economic goals and rational behaviour of all stakeholders. A pluralist perspective, by contrast, sees human behaviour in organisations driven by goals that, operating at many organisational levels, are not necessarily dominated by any common logic, shared values or compatibility of interests, although they are powerfully shaped by external and internal organisational context. It recognises the value of social capital and therefore the need for investment in long-term learning and development processes that can enhance trust across the organisation and build knowledge-productive relationships. As such, it also has a distinctive ethical dimension.

The research that we have reviewed in this chapter suggests that SHRM is still in transition. The main implication of our conclusions for the HRD field is that if the HRD process is to be effective, it, like other HR processes, must be able to respond flexibly to the unique needs of its organisation. HRD professionals should work in business partnerships with organisational leaders, HR colleagues and other stakeholders to create a culture favourable to learning that will fuel continuous improvement and radical innovation. They should place a premium on inclusive processes that will build a genuine learning community in both traditional and new organisational forms. It is to those new forms that we turn in the next chapter.

... and Organising

INTRODUCTION

Drucker (1974) defined structure as a means for attaining the objective and goals of an institution. Child (1977: 8–9) identified its main components as basic structure, which formally allocates people and resources to tasks, operating mechanisms, which indicate clearly what is expected of people, and decision mechanisms, which aid decision-making and related information processing.

Such definitions are useful to open a discussion about organisational design. However, it is our aim in this chapter to show that they offer insufficient insights into how to respond to those new environmental demands that, by the early 1990s, were already driving some of the most radical changes in strategy, structure and management since the post-War managerial revolution (Bartlett and Ghoshal, 1993: 24). There are no clear answers, either in the literature or in the field, to the most problematic questions related to organisational design, nor can we provide them. 'We are still in the experimental stages with different organizational forms to understand how they function as mechanisms for expertise leverage' (Venkatraman and Subramaniam, 2002: 471). It is for this reason that throughout the chapter we focus on the innovative and the speculative, seeking to identify and explore the questions they raise and the skills that they highlight.

In the chapter we first examine a variety of perspectives on structure, and explain the difference between 'organisation' and 'organising'. We then review a body of research into some of the new organisational forms that are emerging at the time of writing and identify those that seem appropriate for knowledge-creating enterprises. Finally, we provide a case study that illustrates key issues in the chapter, and outline some major human resource (HR) implications of new ways of aligning people, systems, tasks and processes to the purpose of the organisation.

At this point we have produced the chapter's first assignment, in Appendix 1. It will also act as an aid to reflection as you read through the rest of the chapter.

Reflection

- We have just claimed that Drucker's and Child's types of definition of organisation structure offer insufficient insights into how to respond to new environmental demands. What kind of environmental demands do you think put pressure on organisation structure – and how?

PERSPECTIVES ON STRUCTURE

Changing organisational forms

Since the mid-1990s organisations operating in a knowledge economy have been turning away increasingly from operating as discrete business units to horizontal and cross-boundary restructuring that incorporates webs of alliances, partnerships, supply chains and joint ventures (Whittington et al., 2002: 483). The resource and knowledge that reside in such networks are far greater than that to which the organisation would otherwise have access, and enable the expansion of the capacity for continuous improvement and innovation upon which competitive capability depends.

Currently many types of organisational form coexist. There are no generalised prescriptions. As Roberts and Grabowski (1999) observe, environmental, organisational and individual influences all have a part to play in shaping organisation structure. Environmental effects such as national character are particularly influential, as can be seen from the unique organising principles embodied in the *keiretsu* (Japan), the *chaebol* (Korea) and the family networks of Chinese business (Whitley, 1999). Structures are also influenced externally by local character, changes in the business environment, and characteristics of specific industries. Internally, structure is shaped by, and helps to shape, the characteristics of jobs, tasks, technology and the organisation as a whole.

Structure as policy

Until the closing decades of the 20th century structure tended to be a static concept, primarily conceived of as policy – that is to say, the outcome of formal strategic decisions made at specific points in time. In this view, structure follows strategy and the key issue in organisational design is to establish which structures are most effective in terms of performance, both generally and in 'fit' with different strategies (Whittington 2002).

Early theories focused on the formal, documented structure of the organisation and its effectiveness in co-ordinating tasks and controlling workers in order to achieve the organisation's goals. The two dominating schools of thought up to the 1950s were the Classical School and Scientific Management. We discuss these in Chapter 7, where we also outline the work of systems theorists who focus on the dynamic interaction between the organisation and its environment. It was, however, Chandler's 1962 study of General Electric in the US that marked the most profound turning point into research on structure, influencing the entire field for the following two decades or more. Chandler defined structure as 'the design of organization through which the enterprise is administered' (1962: 14) and identified its two key components as the lines of authority and communication, and the information and data that flow through these lines. His full definition is illuminating because it 'includes both the formal and the informal', and identifies 'not just what is connected but the content of what flows through the connections; financial and physical assets, but also the knowledge assets incorporated in the skills of its people' (Whittington, 2002: 117–18).

Chandler's concern was with the large corporations that had arisen from the technological and managerial revolutions of the late 19th and early 20th centuries. He argued that for companies driven by market growth and technological change, the multidivisional or 'M-form' structure is essential to the efficient management of strategies to develop greater diversity in products and markets. The M-form philosophy revolves around the devolution of assets and accountability from corporate level to strategic business units (Whittington, 2002: 115).

The configurational perspective

Through the next two or three decades the many spin-offs of Chandler's foundational work continued to focus on structure as policy. The policy literature of that time is marked by a strong interest in configuration, similar to the current preoccupation in the HR strategy literature with the bundling of HR practices that best fit the strategy and context of the business (see Chapter 2). Configuration theory assumes that organisations function effectively not because of the specific structural design that they choose, but because they combine different organisational characteristics, including structure, in complementary ways (Elfring and Volberda, 2001a: 274).

Recent configuration studies have featured designs that, with their emphasis on dynamism and knowledge development, have particular relevance for organisations operating in a knowledge economy. Elfring and Volberda (2001a: 282) include in their list:

- the virtual corporation (Davidow and Malone, 1992: Sun Microsystems)
- the dynamic network form (Miles and Snow, 1986: Dell Computers)
- the cellular organisation (Miles et al., 1997: Acer)
- the platform organisation (Ciborra, 1996: Olivetti)
- the electronic shamrock organisation (Handy, 1995: F International).

These are all types of flexible organisation that create sufficient structure to maintain basic order, while also allowing the development of internal processes to unleash improvisation, self-organising, and emergent strategies. As we show later in this chapter, such forms are characterised by new management and organising logics founded on principles of self-organising and trust in bottom-up processes (Elfring and Volberda, 2001a: 282).

Structure as process

Use of the term 'organising' marks a growing preoccupation in research with structure, like strategy, as process (Roberts and Grabowski, 1999). Pettigrew's 1985 and 1987 studies of transformation at ICI in the UK provided an influential example of this approach. He found that change at ICI was episodic, meaning that it was part of a continuing organising process punctuated periodically by radical eras of transformation that featured substantial ideological, structural and business strategy change. Many studies have subsequently clarified organising as a process that requires the capability for ongoing structural combination and recombination of the firm's resources. They also lend support to the view that large organisations are more typically characterised by structural continuities than by clean breaks (Brickley and Van Drunen, 1990). In a knowledge economy, the periods of structural continuities become ever shorter, highlighting the need for flexibility:

> In a world of rapid change, the achievement of any sort of order depends in part upon the capacity for constant micro-adjustments and flexibility ... The rise of knowledge-intensive firms and the importance of innovation make this appreciation of continuous change still more important. (Whittington, 2002: 130)

Research into smaller enterprises confirms the utility of the processual view. For example, studies of professional partnerships show that organising is 'not the apparently clean-cut decision-making process but a consensual, non-analytical process'. In such firms structure emerges as 'a deeply embedded part of the organizational whole' rather than as a discrete variable, and as a continuous organising process rather than a fixed organisational state (Whittington, 2002: 121).

We referred earlier to Chandler's classic definition of structure. A processual definition yields different insights. Drawing particularly on Pennings (2001) and Venkatraman and Subramaniam (2002), we define structure as:

> an organising process, both proactive and reactive, whose aim is to achieve a continuous alignment of people, other resources, tasks and routines with strategic requirements in order to maximise current performance and generate options whereby to best position the organisation for the future.

The primary resources for structure as a process are hard-to-copy technologies, organisational routines (such as budgeting, research and development arrangements, templates for organising work and control and planning routines), culture and socialisation processes, and relational competencies that allow the organisation to combine its unique resource with those of other firms, particularly those belonging to its value chain (Pennings, 2001: 241).

Reflection

■ What do you see to be the main differences between the concept of structure as policy and structure as process?

■ If you were conducting organisational research into strategy from a processual perspective, what would be your main focal points of enquiry, and why?

Different perspectives on organising

Lorenz (1994) commented that 'the arrival of the single European market has combined with recession and greater global competition to force company after company to reconfigure its network of activities'. He concluded that it is the demands being made by the new knowledge economy that are now having the biggest impact on theories of structure. New thinking here has been stimulated by the expansion of many traditional Western companies into new regions where they are directly exposed to alternative business models, and by the transformation of advanced nations into increasingly diverse and service-oriented economies (Whittington, 2002: 116).

In an economy where managing knowledge and learning is a key strategic task, the organisation can be viewed in a number of different but complementary ways:

- as a reservoir of knowledge (Hedlund, 1994; Kogut and Zander, 1996; Whittington, 2002)
- as a portfolio of dynamic capabilities (Teece et al., 1997)
- as a network of relationships (Quinn, 1992; Miles and Snow, 1995; Baum et al., 2000; Venkatraman and Subramaniam, 2002).

In the next three sections we explore organising principles relevant to each of these perspectives. Although we treat the viewpoints separately, in reality organisations are increasingly seeking to achieve all three of the purposes that they embody: to create knowledge, to develop dynamic capabilities, and to form and manage complex knowledge networks.

ORGANISING FOR KNOWLEDGE CREATION

The firm as a reservoir of knowledge

Knowledge is held by individuals and is also embedded in the organising principles that bring people together to co-operate in an organisational context. The creation of new knowledge, however, depends on existing organisational structure and capabilities. This is because the knowledge of the firm is 'path dependent': new knowledge follows a historical curve. It evolves through the replication and recombination of current knowledge and organisational routines, encoding inferences from history and guiding individual and group behaviour (Cyert and March, 1963; Kogut and Zander, 1992).

The firm in this sense has been called a 'repository of knowledge' (Nelson and Winter, 1982) whose past and current ways of organising stimulate or inhibit knowledge creation. McDonald's operating manuals or KLM's directives, policies and procedures for aircraft maintenance typify specialised routines based on static control and on static models of competition. Their function is to provide a memory for handling standard situations. They are limited to competitive changes which can be anticipated and to which an appropriate response can be identified (Elfring and Volberda, 2001a: 268). Like the training that supports them, they can improve current performance but can prevent knowledge creativity.

The kind of routines and processes that are needed for knowledge creation are those that can develop 'absorptive capacity' (Cohen and Levinthal, 1990) – that is to say, can help organisational members to recognise the value of external information, assimilate it and apply it to new ends. This capacity too is path dependent. It is determined primarily by the types of internal channels of communication that have already developed in the firm, by the distribution, type and level of knowledge current in the firm and its environment, and by the organisation's past research and development investment decisions (Eisenhardt and Santos, 2002: 142). Identifying the level a particular business or process has reached is another key issue for knowledge-creating organisations, since the level of existing knowledge determines how a process can be controlled, whether and how it can be automated, the key tasks of the workforce, and other major aspects of its management (Bohn, 1994: 61).

Types of knowledge

The knowledge-creating firm is heavily dependent on tacit knowledge (that which is not formalised but is deeply embedded in individuals). Unique combinations of tacit and explicit knowledge (that which has been articulated in procedures, routines, manuals and so on) can stimulate both continuous improvement and radical innovation. As we shall see in Chapters 7 and 8, valuable tacit knowledge is widely distributed among dispersed organisational participants whose learning processes are grounded in daily work, with new knowledge emerging from human interactions in the workplace. It was in this sense that Brown and Duguid (1991) described organisations as multiple communities of practice, each of which is continually engaging in experimental and interpretative activities in a workplace environment from which sense-making emerges. 'Organizations thus evolve based on the competing perspectives of different communities of practice' (ibid: 42).

A major decision in organisational design is how much to regulate by formal procedures and how much to leave to the knowledge-creating processes of workplace communities of practice. Organising for knowledge creation involves finding ways of integrating the specialised and tacit knowledge of individuals, and ensuring its dissemination so that it can be developed to produce strategically valuable knowledge. Internal and external networks have a key role here. We explore such ways in Part II of this book.

Barriers and aids to knowledge creation

Other crucial managerial decisions include those relating to modes and methods of decision-making, problem solving and training, since all of these learning processes can either block or help knowledge creation.

Learning that is grounded in communities of practice is not always productive for the organisation. Such learning and the initial success that it may bring can produce 'simplicity' – meaning narrowness and rigidity in the ways in which organisational members see their world and make decisions about it (Miller, 1993; Bohn, 1994). This can foster what Argyris (1996) called 'skilled incompetence', whereby successful organisations come to concentrate only on certain skills, losing important secondary skills and causing strategies and behavioural patterns to become increasingly constrained. Defensive routines can spread across the organisation, developing a culture that avoids confrontation and cannot test assumptions (ibid). Ultimately the organisation becomes proficient only in one or a few methods of learning, assumes there is nothing more to learn, and 'locks in' present methods by specifying rigid procedures that can deskill the workforce and inhibit innovation (Bohn, 1994: 71–2). Relying on 'best practice', whether internal or external, may bring short-term gains but longer-term losses as other firms seize the competitive edge (ibid). Sharp was able to develop dynamic capabilities in the electronic calculator industry while Texas Instruments failed to do so because, unlike Sharp, it was dominated by managerial mindsets that were narrowly focused on the familiar semiconductor market (Elfring and Volberda, 2001a: 269).

Structural inertia can be particularly damaging when it concentrates power in a single group, focusing the organisation's strategy ever more tightly on the values and ways of thinking of that dominant coalition whose mindset regarding the business and the tools and structure needed to achieve successful performance can become dangerously closed to new learning (Miller, 1993; Bettis and Prahalad, 1995). Case example 3.1 is a case in point, although with a hopeful ending.

Case example 3.1

Product development in Ford of Europe in the 1980s and 90s

Starkey and McKinlay (1996: 216) point out in their account of product development at Ford Europe in the 1980s and 90s that Ford, throughout most of the 20th century, was Mintzberg's (1983) typical 'machine bureaucracy': organised functionally with top-down decision-making and cost reduction, sacrificing innovation in favour of efficiency. Product Development at Ford in the 1980s covered product planning, car engineering and design. The process was controlled by a centralised industrial research organisation, with Ford's finance staff ultimately determining investment decisions. The product and the customer were lost in preoccupation with internal control.

The first reorganisation attempt

Starkey and McKinlay explain (ibid: 224) that market failures in 1984 led to a sweeping examination of the company's strategic vision. A project team talked to people within Ford and in product development in other companies, particularly Mazda in which Ford held a 25% equity stake. At Mazda employees made decisions through consensus and top management delegated decision-making to relevant teams. It had an environment of harmony contrasting with Ford's environment of competition. The Japanese managers worked in flexible and transient project-based teams. Each programme director worked with the functional area to agree on who would contribute what at each point of the programme. He acted as catalyst but with no direct power. His task was to keep channels of communication open.

Reflecting on these organising principles, Product Development at Ford proposed a form of matrix management in which the key unit was product development programme teams and a radical devolution of responsibility by top management. The proposed system foundered because of major tensions between programme managers and functional managers, lack of a pool of experienced programme managers, and staff turnover.

Successful reorganisation

In 1989 there was another, and this time successful, attempt at restructuring. It took the form of simultaneous engineering: structural integration of the previously separate functional groups of Product Development and Manufacturing. The aim was to ensure continuous co-operation and communication between them from initial customer requirements through to delivery of vehicle.

Mazda had separate Product Development and Manufacturing Engineering divisions, but achieved integration through a company culture of teamwork, dedication, personal relationships and customer-driven activity, and through cross-divisional programme management teams. Cross-functional training supported this culture by aiming at character building, knowledge acquisition and skill learning. It emphasised the need for involvement of senior employees, and for their guidance of subordinates and junior workers in their workplaces.

In its own restructuring, Ford introduced separate vehicle programmes to become the means of providing strong, company-wide, product-focused leadership to the Vehicle and Powertrain Divisions, which were to be integrated through a new matrix structure.

Outcomes

Starkey and McKinlay make clear that at Ford, a new willingness to be self-critical and to innovate grew slowly during the 1980s and 90s. It was becoming recognised that the balance of strategic thinking must move from cost cutting as an end in itself to cost cutting in relation to the defined output. Efficiency and innovation must be interrelated rather than being mutually opposed. With a move to managing across levels and tasks there must be a fundamental shift in organisational values, focused on open communication and sharing of information. A senior Ford manager was quoted as saying:

Case example 3.1 *(cont'd)*

For the first time (product development study teams) used our stars, our best individuals. For thirty years study teams were used as dumping grounds for under-performers and people about to retire. (Starkey and McKinlay, 1996: 228)

There had to be a new way of thinking about products – the car as a totality rather than a collection of individual components.

Source: Starkey and McKinlay, 1996

In such organisations as Ford, it can take a long time to achieve a 'clean break' with the past and expand innovative capacity. This points to the difference between intended and realised strategy, and to the role of top management in building values and organisational forms that can produce a productive balance between formal regulation and self-managed work and learning in order to build innovative capacity.

The strategy process

The Ford case was about strategising as well as organising, and this raises the issue of how best to build an effective strategy process. Much has been written on this, but the main point we make here is simply that an organisation's strategy-making process modes have a direct influence on the structural arrangements that are chosen: strategising and organising processes are dynamically interactive. In conflictual situations the modes used can determine the firm's ability to resolve disputes regarding selection of strategic assets for competitive advantage and to choose an appropriate organisational design whereby to develop and deploy such assets.

Choice of strategy process modes can thus directly affect the performance of the firm (Hart and Banbury, 1994). Heterogeneous groups can often produce better quality in strategic decision-making than homogeneous groups, because a narrowly based top-level oriented strategic management mode cannot utilise the full range of cognitive functions and so may not be able to promote innovative strategies (Hurst et al., 1996: 407. See also Hart and Banbury, 1994). A strategy process that utilises a wide range of human potential can help to develop that absorptive capacity that emerged as so crucial in our discussion of the firm as a reservoir of knowledge. In Chapter 5 we return to this issue in order to explore ways in which the HRD function can help to improve an organisation's strategy process.

Promoting the knowledge process

In their review of research into structure and knowledge creation, Eisenhardt and Santos (2002: 158) examined ways of organising to achieve and preserve key processes of knowledge sourcing, transfer and integration. In some studies structures impeded knowledge flow, but in others designs that featured teams, liaisons and meetings improved it within and outside the organisation. Loosely linked structure seemed to relate positively to innovative knowledge flows and adaptive organisational outcomes.

Hedlund (1994) proposed a model of knowledge management, building on the interplay between explicit and tacit knowledge at four levels: the individual, the small group, the organisation, and the interorganisational (see Table 3.1). As he explained,

Table 3.1   *N-form vs. M-form*

	N-form	M-form
Technological interdependence	Combination	Division
People interdependence	Temporary constellations, given pool of people	Permanent structures, changing pool of people
Critical organizational level	Middle	Top
Communication network	Lateral	Vertical
Top management role	Catalyst, architect, protector	Monitor, allocator
Competitive scope	Focus, economies of depth, combinable parts	Diversification, economies of scale and scope, semi-independent parts
Basic organizational form	Heterarchy	Hierarchy

Source: Hedlund, 1994, p. 83. Reproduced with permission of John Wiley & Sons Ltd

his new N-form organisation structure prioritises combination of knowledge through a horizontal communication network and shifting groupings of people in temporary multifunctional, multinational, multidivisional projects. It relies on a high degree of permanence in the personnel pool in order to achieve sustained commonality of purpose and stable communities of practice where tacit knowledge can be preserved, disseminated and integrated.

In the N-form, middle management stimulates, supports and co-ordinates knowledge activity across internal and external organisational boundaries. Whereas in the M-form top managers are monitors and allocators of resources, in the N-form they are knowledge catalysts, architects and protectors. Many of the N-form's principles can be seen in various emerging organisational forms, as we shall see in the case that concludes this chapter.

Knowledge-intensive firms

Knowledge-intensive firms (KIFs) are enterprises whose revenue depends on their ability to continuingly generate new knowledge and apply it successfully to clients' needs. Core to such firms are professional knowledge workers, and the firms include professional partnerships, consultancy firms and media organisations. Their structuring offers insights relevant to all organisations where knowledge creation is a vital task.

Strategy in KIFs is typically emergent. As we have noted in Chapter 2, top management is not the sole strategic actor in these firms: knowledge workers are key players too. Their autonomous behaviour alters the KIF's pattern of action in small, incremental steps as firms' offerings are shaped by individuals' competence, client contacts and personal interests, and by their everyday learning through projects that create new knowledge (Kirjavainen, 2001: 175). While most KIFs may not have clearly defined strategies, they do seem to have umbrella strategies that provide guidelines for organisational behaviour that are often also rooted in the organisational culture (ibid: 176).

Case example 3.2 concerns a European KIF that has tackled difficult strategising and organising questions over a seven-year period. We have found of particular interest the ways in which the performance of this firm is measured and the core

Case example 3.2

The Learning Company

The Learning Company, an HRD consultancy established in 1977, consists of 30 HRD professionals working in a co-operative enterprise, with shared values and shared ownership. The core beliefs are that the key need is to develop scarce talent that will be recognised by clients as helping them to deal with challenges and related problems, and that when talent is successfully developed and utilised in this way, a healthy financial position for the firm will automatically follow. Financial targets are not the dominating ones and revenue is not primarily treated as return on financial investments, but as the resource to support the main goal: the development of scarce talent.

There are no formal managerial roles in the firm, because self-management is a crucial value. Employees set their salaries, based on the type of work they want to do, the amount of time they want to spend on work, the results of the previous year, and for a tariff that they deem acceptable for their clients and colleague project leaders. The salaries available equal 50% of the annual revenues on projects. Once the personal annual target is set, the salary is guaranteed, even when the target cannot be met. The generalised aim is to achieve around 50% chargeable hours, leaving around 50% of time available for study, research, internal work for The Learning Company and for relevant voluntary community-based projects.

The criteria used to determine what work to choose are mainly personal interest and type of learning opportunities offered. Project leaders, generally the more experienced staff, may also consider a project by reference to the extent to which it can provide learning opportunities for young or inexperienced consultants who have not yet developed their own accounts. The amount of paid work directly relates to the set salary. Voluntary work primarily serves additional learning opportunities.

The firm did not show any pattern of extreme growth in terms of revenue and employee development in the earlier years of rich market opportunities, as many consultancy firms did. On the other hand, the major recession of 2001 that hit so many of them badly left it unaffected. Prospects for 2002 showed continued steady growth.

Over the years the scope and complexity of projects have increased in terms of number of consultants involved per project, international activities (those in which various different countries or nationalities are involved), major political issues in client organisations, and amount of boardroom consulting. Employee turnover averages 8% per year. This is relatively high but is largely due to the fact that The Learning Company attracts many university graduates whose interest has often been raised initially by the firm's staff who hold part-time positions at various universities. These young professionals wish to explore the work of a learning consultant in an almost virtual company. However, some find it difficult to assimilate the regime of high-speed solo work, and miss the day to day social traffic of a conventional office. Those who prefer more traditional working conditions regularly find a job with the firm's clients and so may join the firm's wider knowledge network.

The Learning Company's services have become geared increasingly towards building learning capacity in individuals and teams. The process of knowledge construction and the development of favourable conditions for learning in the workplace are becoming the prime focus of its work with clients. These services are spread across industry, banking and insurance companies, the healthcare and education sector, as well as to government agencies. There has been a particularly marked increase in projects with vocational and higher education institutions.

values that bring together its knowledge workers in a community of practice. In this account we have changed the name of the firm to ensure anonymity, but other details are factual.

This case has a wider resonance. The first set of findings from a three-year study on the relationship between people management and business performance, sponsored by the UK Chartered Institute of Personnel and Development and carried out by the Work and Employment Research Centre (WERC) at the University of Bath School of Management (Swart et al., 2003), relate to performance in KIFs. The sector was chosen for early investigation because 'it reflects likely changes in the UK economy in the future' (ibid: vii). Data gathered from six UK-based research and technology organisations confirm insights suggested by both the Learning Company case and other research in this chapter: that knowledge-intensive work poses major challenges to widely held beliefs about how organisations in an emergent knowledge-based economy should be structured and managed. The Bath University researchers point to what they find to be a 'new model of people management', in which three factors are critical:

- developing individual knowledge and skills
- sharing and developing this knowledge within the organisation
- sharing and developing this knowledge with clients and other parties in the network. (Swart et al., 2003: ix)

Knowledge workers formed a high proportion of employees in the six firms involved in the first stage of the WERC study, and they were uniquely important to the success of those firms. However, there was a real tension between those workers' individual needs and the requirement to share their knowledge within and beyond the organisation. Knowledge workers 'will want to work on interesting projects which make good use of their high-level knowledge and skills' (ibid: 69). Because of the importance of these workers to KIFs, special care must be devoted to crafting HR policies to do with their recruitment, development, reward and retention. At the same time, ways must be found of facilitating the transfer of knowledge between separate project teams, and of resolving the 'potential tension between various competing loyalties or identities – the team, organisation, profession and client' (ibid: 71).

The WERC researchers concluded that while people management practices are key in overcoming barriers to integration in KIFs, they are likely to work best 'when they have been allowed to develop inductively rather than from the top down'. This should ensure that they become 'embedded in the organisational routines and ways of working' (ibid: 7). This conclusion lends a special importance to one of the most interesting features of The Learning Company in Case example 3.2: the abandonment of formal management roles in favour of self-management. Such an approach is of course far easier for small than for larger firms, but it does underline the need to consider with particular care the form the management process should take in organisations operating in a knowledge economy. 'Management', after all, was the product of the Industrial Revolution. In a new kind of economy where knowledge is the key asset, we have to ask whether some new conceptualisation should replace the old. We will return to this issue later in this chapter, and thereafter in Chapters 5 and 6.

Summary

Research reviewed in this section has had a wide scope. It has covered the firm as a reservoir of knowledge, types of knowledge, barriers and aids to knowledge creation, the dynamic interaction between strategising and organising, the promotion of the knowledge process, and organising principles in knowledge-intensive firms. It points to two general conclusions:

■ that all knowledge-creating enterprises face similar design questions. These are to do with the kinds of structure, routines and processes that can facilitate knowledge construction, transfer and integration, with how to ensure a productive interplay between explicit and tacit knowledge within and between organisations, and with how to organise for both routine and innovative activity in the organisation

■ that there are no general prescriptions for organising in an increasingly knowledge-based economy. Each firm must find its own structural response to the internal and external knowledge-creation issues that it confronts, and must ensure in so doing an effective interplay of organising and strategising processes.

Reflection

■ In what sense can learning produce 'simplicity' that inhibits organisational knowledge creation?

■ What examples of 'skilled incompetence' can you identify from your own experience or reading?

ORGANISING FOR INNOVATION

The firm as a portfolio of dynamic capabilities

In a turbulent knowledge-based environment competitive advantage depends on innovation in organisational and managerial processes, termed dynamic capabilities. These capabilities represent the firm's ability to integrate, build and reconfigure internal and external competencies (Nelson and Winter, 1982; Wheelwright and Clark, 1992; Miles and Snow, 1995; Teece et al., 1997). They enable the organisation to conceive and implement plans for new patterns of provision of services, for a quite different type of product, or for a radically new process (Eisenhardt and Santos, 2002: 143). In a knowledge economy where superior performance occurs by continuously creating temporary advantages, it is crucial to have the ability to learn quickly in order to alter the resource configuration in response to market change.

Elfring and Volberda (2001a) identify three types of capability development, and we use their typology in this section: the types are *cross hierarchical*, *cross functional* and *cross value*. In some organisations, capabilities are developed in all three modes. Nonaka (1994) cites Japanese firms such as Honda, Canon and Toyota here. It was for such organisations that Hedlund (Table 3.1) advocated a structure that could achieve a balance between facilitating self-organising team activities that are valuable for generating new capabilities through intensive, focused research (where heterarchy with its flexible organising principles is relevant), and enabling the exploitation of capabilities (where hierarchy can be more efficient).

Cross-hierarchical (vertical) capability development

Capability development can be a top-down process, emerging from fundamentally new insights at corporate management level, with exploitation of these capabilities taking place at business unit or lower levels. An example is CEO Jack Welsh's corporate revitalisation of General Electric (Elfring and Volberda, 2001a: 271). Capabilities can also emerge from autonomous strategic behaviour of individuals and small groups lower down the organisation. Finally, capability development can be bottom-up, with top management as the creator of purpose and challenger of the status quo. This is the process advocated by Bartlett and Ghoshal (1993), and by Hamel and Prahalad in their 'strategy as stretch' model (1993), where new capabilities derive from front-line managers who have the most current knowledge and expertise and are closest to sources of information critical to new capabilities. We illustrate the process in our concluding case example for this chapter (Case example 3.3).

Cross-functional (horizontal) capability development

This refers to more participative forms of development that may be explicitly designed – as in teams, projects or task forces – but may also emerge out of an inter-active process. Toyota's principles of decentralised authority and lateral communi-cation across functions, buyers and suppliers provided the cross-functional capabilities to generate speed and flexibility (Elfring and Volberda, 2001a: 272).

As Case example 3.3 will show, effective cross-functional capability develop-ment depends on appropriate managerial and organisational support for self-co-ordination among experts across functional and organisational boundaries. This kind of development can easily be disrupted by managerial meddling (Elfring and Volberda, 2001a: 272). For example, team-based financial incentive systems can tend to divide instead of draw together workplace communities of practice and inhibit collective learning.

Cross-value capability development

This relates to the capability to produce a shared ideology, emerging from a core organisational identity, in which there is a coherent set of shared beliefs, values and language (Elfring and Volberda, 2001a: 273). In firms with this capability, every member identifies strongly with, and professes loyalty to, the goal of preserving, extending or perfecting the organisation's mission. All employees can therefore be trusted to make decisions in the organisation's interests. Elfring and Volberda quote the attempts by Japanese companies such as Canon and Honda to enhance cross-value capabilities by facilitating dialogue, camp sessions and brainstorming seminars held outside the workplace.

There is an extensive literature on tools and techniques for innovation, but the most crucial need is to develop underlying 'capacities for action' that enable organisa-tional members to select and use those tools and techniques effectively. Such capaci-ties require a culture of working with customers, forming teams, solving problems creatively, applying technical potential to market needs, appreciating the relationships among functions and businesses well enough to shift them as necessary, and develop an ongoing sense of how well they are doing. In other words, they require high cross-value development (Dougherty, 1999: 186).

Bartlett and Ghoshal (1993: 45) argued that within any organisation, human behaviour is determined in part by the prior disposition of actors, and in part by context that is powerfully shaped by ongoing management action. They are of the view, commonly expressed in the literature, that management actions provide the key to creating a context that will induce organisational members to take initiative, co-operate and learn. This reflects a quite different notion of human behaviour to the opportunistic concept discussed in Chapter 2. It regards people as 'capable both of initiative and shirking, given to both collaboration and opportunism, and constrained by inertia but also capable of learning' (ibid). It is illustrated in the case study at the end of this chapter.

There is a consistent emphasis in the literature on the need for top management to provide the overall vision and co-ordination that drives the organisation forward. In so doing, it must organise in ways that achieve a balance between direction and standardisation of routine work on the one hand, and diversity and autonomy to ensure innovation on the other. It must ensure that strategic runners with the most potential for the firm are integrated into strategy, and are supported by organisational routines that will consistently deploy diverse value-adding knowledge resources (Kirjavainen, 2001: 189).

Other critical roles consistently identified in the literature (Tushman and Nadler, 1996) are:

- Idea generators, who creatively link diverse ideas and see new approaches
- Champions or internal entrepreneurs, who take creative ideas and produce tangible innovations
- Gatekeepers or boundary spanners, who link their more local colleagues to external information sources
- Sponsors, coaches or mentors – senior managers who provide informal support, access to resources, and protection as new ventures emerge.

Clearly, in organising for innovation, managers will have to take on roles and develop attitudes and skills that for many will contrast sharply with those to which they have become accustomed in more traditional organisational forms.

Summary

Research reviewed in this section reveals a need for organisations to acquire a deep knowledge base and variety of expertise if they are to organise effectively for innovation. Three main modes for the continuous development of dynamic capabilities are cross-hierarchical, cross-functional, and cross-value. No matter which mode or modes to be used, dynamic capabilities grow through the collaborative actions of employees at all organisational levels, working for a common purpose that is shaped and continuously reinforced by top management. This draws attention to the need to radically rethink traditional organising and management principles and the skills associated with them.

Reflection

- What forms of dynamic capability development can you identify in your own organisation?
- What kind of structural changes might be needed to improve their rate of development?

ORGANISING FOR ECONOMIES OF EXPERTISE

The firm as a network of relationships

In a knowledge economy, no one firm can have all the required capabilities within its corporate boundaries. Firms need to complement their internal capabilities with a wide array of external relationships and become proficient in achieving 'economies of expertise' (Venkatraman and Subramaniam, 2002: 466).

Partnership arrangements are flexible and important competitive tools but they involve tensions between co-operation and competition. Organising is a key process to ensure an effective partnership structure and the values and routines that will build and sustain commitment to a common purpose. Stiles (2001: 131) observes that:

- *From a co-operative perspective,* alliances can facilitate rapid upgrade in resources and create synergistic benefits from the pooling of resources/capabilities, help reduce costs and encourage efficiency through the transfer of knowledge and capabilities that might otherwise not be effectively transferable through the market system.
- *From a competitive perspective,* the alliance may result in a loss of core competencies and capabilities, encourage alliance dependency and loss of control, and introduce a form of development inertia into the industry that may ultimately have implications for the potential product life cycle and for the balance of future competition within the industry. Hamel's research (1991) has shown that it might also offer a competitor a unique means of assessing a partner's strengths and weaknesses.

Networks thus require special skills in strategising in order to achieve an effective risk–benefit balance, choice of appropriate partners and the establishment of relevant units. They require skilful organising, with particular attention to formal controls that will ensure adequate monitoring of the exchanges of competence or capital assets. This is necessary to reduce agency and transaction costs while maintaining co-operation and trust. 'A level of formalization ... avoids overextending trust and actually provides a basis for further trust-based developments' (Koenig and Van Wijk, 2001: 126).

Cellular organisations are one way of achieving economies of expertise, and we look at one such in Case example 3.3. Tushman and Nadler (1996: 145) identified corporate venturing or independent business units as other ways of organising along network lines that are particularly likely to suit organisations wanting to take advantage of internal expertise yet still produce major innovation. The units are small, separate from the core organisation, and comprise individuals from all key disciplines and functions. They are relatively low cost so the likelihood of frequent failure matters relatively little. Successes can be highly profitable and strategically important. Microsoft and Intel have used part of their venture funds as investments in a wide domain of expertise. They illustrate how corporate ventures and investments now constitute 'an important mechanism to create network centrality and consequently increase economies of expertise' (Venkatraman and Subramaniam, 2002: 469).

Summary

Research reviewed in this section shows that the issue for organisations operating through network principles goes far beyond systems and processes for managing knowledge and expertise inside the firm. 'It is about conceptualizing how a company develops superior strategy by understanding the knowledge flows in a complex network of relationships' (Venkatraman and Subramaniam, 2002: 467). Network forms require a superior organising process and special strategising skills if the agency and transaction costs of negotiating, setting up and operating such inter-organisational partnerships are to be recouped, and if the tensions that naturally arise in such complex arrangements are to be channelled in effective ways.

Assignment 2 for this chapter is contained in Appendix 1 for readers wishing to reflect further on network organisations.

CONCLUSIONS FROM RESEARCH

The non-prescriptive approach

In the previous three sections we have explored issues of structure and of organising in knowledge-creating organisations from three related perspectives: the firm as a reservoir of knowledge, as a portfolio of dynamic capabilities and as a network of relationships. In this section we report some generalised conclusions from research into the organising process in an emergent knowledge economy.

Research confirms that there are no universal structural prescriptions for such organisations (Whittington and Mayer, 2002). Context is a powerful determinant of what is appropriate, and the historical path that has been travelled by each organisation is of particular importance here. Levels and types of knowledge that already exist in the firm, its past record of innovation and innovatory design capability, and the unique challenges facing the firm at particular points in time must be carefully considered when deciding how best to organise for the future. So must the added value offered by different structural options.

Eisenhardt and Santos (2002) conclude tentatively from their comprehensive review of research-based literature that:

■ When knowledge is varied and changing, structures and cultural norms that make managers aware of knowledge transfer opportunities are effective, but incentives to collaborate do not seem to be so. They may also encourage managers to waste time and resources transferring non-strategic knowledge – an important cost–benefit consideration. Incentives focused on successful performance of the business unit instead of on the knowledge-creating activities of the individual seem more effective in promoting the development of strategically valuable knowledge.

■ Managers should concentrate on transferring only the most strategically valuable knowledge. Less knowledge transfer can be more effective than more, especially in high-velocity environments where management time is so limited – again, an important cost–benefit issue.

■ The degree to which specialised knowledge is integrated from different sources, whether to generate new knowledge or to apply that knowledge to the creation of new products and services, is significantly influenced by how individuals from different communities of practice share and integrate their specialised knowledge. Horizontal structures such as Hedlund's N-form are relevant here.

■ Concrete expressions of knowledge, especially through the process of tackling real problems, play an important part in achieving knowledge integration within and across firms. They help to overcome potential inhibitors to integration arising

from different knowledge, different modes of knowing, and different ways of expressing knowledge across communities of practice.
■ Organisational rules and routines have a powerful effect on knowledge integration, which they can either improve or impede.

Reviewing research and practice across contemporary Europe, Whittington and Mayer (2002) are equally tentative. Observing the lack of systematic enquiry into the organising process, they draw particularly on the work of Schoonhoven and Jelinek (1990) and Eisenhardt and Brown (1999) on rapidly reorganising high-tech American businesses and on Buchanan et al.'s (1999) survey of British managers' experience of managing change in the 1990s, as they explore various frameworks for organisations working in conditions of rapid change. Whittington and Mayer (2002: 26) identify from that survey the need for:

■ clear formal structures and reporting relationships
■ clear, standardised performance metrics across the organisation
■ consistent, standardised compensation policies across the organisation
■ propensity to organise in small, performance-oriented units
■ culture of change within the organisation.

They acknowledge the apparent contradiction between formal structures and an innovative drive, but explain that 'in some important dimensions, organisations need to be hard to be flexible. Too soft just adds to the confusion of change' (ibid). Above all, they stress the provisional nature of research findings:

> We need to know more about both what organisational designs and what organising processes deliver the most effective outcomes, and under what conditions ... The bias of existing knowledge is still towards organisation rather than organising, designs rather than designing. In a context of increasing change, practising managers ... will find the greatest gains from shifting the focus more from the *what* of organisation to the *how* of organising. (ibid: 31, italics in original)

An integrative case study

For our concluding case study we have chosen a well-known account by Bartlett and Ghoshal (1993). They took five years to study companies in complex and dynamic businesses in Europe and Japan. They found that large global corporations seemed to be creating a new organisational model that was significantly different from the M-form. To illustrate the model they chose the European corporation of Asea Brown Boveri, admitting to selectivity in their highlighting of those attributes of the organisation that were most relevant for their purpose.

We chose ABB for this major case study because it is a globalised organisation confronting some of the greatest challenges faced by firms operating in what ABB's chief executive officer described in 2000 as 'a new world where speed, flexibility and brain power are the keys to delivering value' (ABB website). ABB has consistently experimented with innovative organisational forms and radical business strategies in order to make its way in that world. In Case example 3.3 we first outline the ABB case as it was described by the researchers in 1993. We then update it in order to cast light on processes of strategising and organising at ABB over the years.

Case example 3.3

Asea Brown Boveri (ABB)

The company in 1993

Asea Brown Boveri (ABB) was formed in 1988 from a merger between the Swedish Asea AB – whose CEO, the young Percy Barnevik, had over a seven-year period turned it round from a failing company to a competitive leader – and the Swiss firm, BBC Brown Boveri. It was an international electrical engineering company manufacturing machinery and composite plants. In its early years it confronted challenges arising from slow growth and overcapacity, and also from the newness and fragility of its organisational structure and management processes.

The organising principles

Barnevik introduced a radically decentralised matrix organisation, designed as a federation of 1,300 companies. The corporation operated in four sectors and was structured as separate and distinct businesses. Each on average employed 200 people and in 1993 ABB's total workforce numbered around 200,000.

Barnevik's ABB model was based on a principle of 'proliferation and subsequent aggregation of small independent entrepreneurial units from the bottom up' (Bartlett and Ghoshal, 1993: 42). Resources were decentralised to the front-line units that operated with limited dependence on the corporate parent for technological, financial or human resources, but with considerable interdependence among themselves. In 1993 there was only one intermediate level between the ABB corporate executive committee and the managers of these companies, and the entire corporate headquarters numbered less than 100 people.

A focus on adding value led to the development of three core processes which remain critical in the company today. They are outlined below.

The entrepreneurial process (combining direction and control with initiative and flexibility)

Unlike in conglomerates, at ABB both middle and top managements remain involved in the operational realities of the business and contribute directly to the entrepreneurial process (ibid: 29). Human resources are recruited and developed at the level of the front-line companies, who also carry out most of the technology development and have responsibility for their own balance sheets. Middle-level managers coach and support the front-line manager. Top management develops a broad set of objectives and establishes stretched performance standards that front-line initiatives must meet (ibid: 29).

The integration process (creating a horizontal information processing capacity)

By radically decentralising, the aim has been to create an environment in which scarce knowledge can be developed and applied most appropriately. Middle-level managers are the horizontal integrators of strategy and capabilities, ensuring that the entire organisation benefits from the specialised resources and expertise developed in the entrepreneurial units. This is another major feature distinguishing the ABB model from the classic M-form.

The renewal process (ensuring organisational adaptability)

Barnevik did not hold the traditional view of an organisation as a scheme for dividing the overall corporate activities among a group of subunits. He and his management viewed it as a cluster of roles and their interrelationships whereby to generate, link and leverage unique capabilities (ibid: 41). The company's core value was articulated in its 'Statement of Values' as:

individuals and groups interacting with mutual confidence, respect and trust ... to eliminate the we/they attitude ... and to remain flexible, open and generous.

Top-level managers' role at ABB is to translate this core value into action through selecting and promoting those who reflect such behaviours, imposing sanctions against those violating the values, and through their own role modelling actions (ibid: 35).

Case example 3.3 (cont'd)

ABB: an update

In 1993 ABB was a 'vigorous and successful company' (ibid: 25) with an outstanding leader and a highly innovative cellular structure. In subsequent years there was a continuous process of reorganising punctuated by periods of radical structural change.

In 1996 there was operational and financial restructuring and job cutting. Organisational changes continued throughout 1997, building on past practice. A new Global Key Account Management corporate function was established at Zurich headquarters to provide large international corporations with a well-defined senior management interface with ABB and so strengthen its global sales efforts. There was also a new President and CEO – Goeran Lindahl, promoted from within. Barnevik remained ABB Chair.

Late in 1998 there was fundamental structural change. ABB's existing four market segments were divided into six, with the aim of promoting growth areas where ABB had technology advantages and unique capabilities, and ensuring greater responsiveness in local and globalised markets where deregulation and privatisation were opening up new opportunities. The Group Executive Committee was expanded and ABB's corporate regional structures in Europe, the Americas and Asia were dismantled.

1999 was a 'milestone year' for the company, by now one of the 'new global leaders'. It saw rapid change to ABB's business portfolio, more downsizing, and a continued shift to higher value-added, more knowledge-based businesses. ABB was named for the first time to the prestigious *Industry Week* magazine's annual list of 100 best-managed companies, judged by its innovative employee development programmes, its creative research in areas of high risk and high reward, and the support it gave to various community projects. Lindahl was named CEO of the Year, and praised particularly for the strategic changes he had introduced since early 1997, his drive to create and sustain synergies throughout the company, his efforts to create a truly multicultural corporation, and his commitment to provide greater opportunities for younger managers. Lindahl continued to strategically transform ABB during 2000.

By the start of 2001, however, Lindahl and the company had parted (news releases on the website do not identify why). Jorgen Centerman took over as President and CEO, and announced a radical restructuring to move from business to customer segments in order to grow faster by linking the value chain more directly from suppliers through manufacturers to end users.

By mid-2001 the fundamental reasons for restructuring became clear when Centerman, citing difficult markets, initiated another cost-reduction and downsizing programme. Standard & Poor's, the Web-based credit analysis system, subsequently revised downwards its outlook on ABB, influenced especially by the high degree of uncertainty regarding future developments in the US. However, it retained confidence in ABB as a leading player in all of its business segments, with a strong, fast-responsive management record and geographical and product diversity that should enable it to overcome the economic downturn. In November, 2001 Barnevik announced his resignation both as ABB Chairman and board member. A cryptic news release statement said little, quoting Barnevik's wish to 'take my share of responsibility for the less good performance of ABB in recent years'.

By March, 2002 ABB's employee headcount had fallen to around 152,000 as financial and organisational restructuring continued. The responsibilities of its board of directors were expanded but performance remained weak, with some divisions reporting favourable order books but others not.

The present

At the time of writing ABB retains its cellular structure and its concern for knowledge development, adding value and customer focus. One of is most recent restructuring innovations has been the introduction of the 'global factory' concept. This involves the group identifying a strategic location for producing a product that will cater for global demand, thereby cutting down operating expenses drastically and enabling a focused approach by individual companies or business units.

In 14 years ABB has moved from being an international engineering firm to a 'global leader in power and automation technologies that enable utility and industry customers to improve performance while lowering environmental impact' (ABB website). During that time its leadership has changed, its corporate governance has been expanded, its workforce has steadily reduced in size, and cost cutting and innovation have become bedfellows as the corporation has sought to work its way through an international recession and respond quickly to unpredictable market changes. At this stage the company's turbulent environment makes it impossible to predict ABB's likely future path: a continued financial deterioration, or a steady recovery benefiting from the fruits of a long-term strategy of knowledge creation, economies of expertise, and of a cellular organisational form.

Main sources: Bartlett and Ghoshal, 1993; ABB's website 'News Releases' at www.abb.com

Some human resource implications

Of course our updating of the ABB case is partial, and the opacity of some of the available information about the company in recent years highlights the difficulty encountered by all organisational researchers (noted in Chapter 2) as they try to establish from the outside what is *really* going on here. However, ABB's history through the years confirms the conclusion reached in recent research:

> Organisation and organising involves a web of complementary elements stretching through the organisation as a whole. Key responsibilities of human resource professionals are intimately involved, from recruitment and development processes to reward systems. (Whittington and Mayer (2002: 29)

The consequences for people of the kind of organising initiatives noted in the ABB case can be a mix of positive and negative. HR practitioners and other managers need to be able to handle especially unwanted consequences of career disruptions, fatigue, survivor guilt, vicious circles of change as one cycle of reorganisation sets off many more through time, and consequent performance dips as elements in the cycle take time to lock into a sufficiently tight system of mutual reinforcement – or fail to do so at all (Whittington and Mayer, 2002: 28). The ABB case example provides an interesting comparison with Pettigrew's accounts of ICI, discussed towards the start of this chapter, in that it too indicates an episodic organising process that has incorporated both incremental and revolutionary changes. However, ABB has had to rethink strategy and organisational form with increasing regularity, as the intervals between continuous improvement and radical change have been reducing in line with steady reduction in the timescales over which the company can maintain its competitive advantage – a trend also identified in Whittington and Mayer's research, where they found that big businesses are reorganising with increasing frequency. Unless HR strategies and organising practices are coupled together effectively, it can have a disruptive effect on the workforce that can undo the very benefits that structural change seeks to achieve.

At ABB, management actions have clearly played a crucial part in the use of three modes in combination to develop dynamic capabilities, and in their account Bartlett and Ghoshal (1993) stressed the centrality of top management's role in creating and sustaining common purpose and stimulating innovation at ABB. In Chapter 2, in our discussion of the universalist and contextualist paradigms, we noted Brewster's (1999) suggestion that a complementary rather than opposed use of many of their features could be of value. That seems to have been the case at ABB. Its company values concern the need for strong, directional leadership but also for supportive, facilitative management. They reflect goals to do not only with the economic motive, but also with trust, collaboration, individual development, respect for diversity, and wider community involvement of company members. It will be interesting to see whether the criteria used by *Industry Week* in 1999 to judge its 'best-managed companies' will become critical measures of performance more widely in knowledge-creating organisations.

CONCLUSION

We explained at the start of this chapter that our main aim was to reveal the limitations of traditional definitions of structure and explore innovative ways of organising in a knowledge economy. The chapter has shown that in such an economy organisation structure cannot be a fixed state. It must be a continuing process, supporting knowledge creation and the development of dynamic capabilities, and facilitating the acquisition and use of expertise across boundaries (Venkatraman and Subramaniam, 2002: 471). It must also be a reflective process. The path-dependent nature of knowledge creation raises a need to understand the historical roots of current structural arrangements and of learning and knowledge in the firm before deciding on how best to restructure in order to facilitate strategic change.

It is important not to make excessive claims here. The traditional structures that support control and efficiency of mass production and that strive for standardised performance still have meaning because such work still exists. On the other hand, organisations that must increasingly compete on the basis of quality improvement and innovation as well as of cost reduction require innovation in their organising principles. Like ABB at one end of the spectrum and The Learning Company at the other, they must not only achieve profitability but also respond to a range of customer expectations and of client values that increasingly include environmental responsibility, ethical business behaviour, integrity, trustworthiness and community service.

Cases we have quoted in this chapter demonstrate practical ways in which, in a number of organisations large and small, principles such as self-organising teams and knowledge partnerships are replacing more conventional structures. However, they also raise important questions to which we seek to respond in Part II of this book:

■ What kind of organisational forms can achieve an effective balance between a company's current operations and the innovatory actions needed to facilitate new capability development? And how can they be monitored and maintained?
■ In a knowledge-creating organisation, how should organisational performance be measured, and what kind of incentive and reward systems are appropriate for individuals and teams?
■ Since some of the most valuable knowledge emerges from workplace communities of practice, how can a productive balance be achieved between formal regulation and self-managed learning in order to maximise on that knowledge process?

- How should any stultifying effects of existing learning in the organisation be addressed in order to promote a culture of challenge and innovation?
- If dynamic capabilities are to emerge from all organisational levels, and also if organisations are to operate increasingly on network or cellular principles, what do such developments imply for managerial roles and skills? Or is 'management' in its traditional sense becoming an irrelevant concept for some knowledge-creating organisations?

We saw in Chapter 2 the ways in which senior HR professionals are playing a crucial role in organisations exposed to an increasingly globalised business environment. In this chapter it has become clear that in all knowledge-creating organisations those professionals have a major contribution to make to processes of organising. They need to take a proactive rather than a reactive stance, taking a lead in the planning and implementation of structural change and in complementing 'organising' by effective HR strategising. Whittington and Mayer (2002: 3–4) point to Dave Ulrich's observation (1998) that the HR function must take on a new mandate, as strategic partner in the organisational architecture and as agent in processes of continuous transformation. They conclude that 'new organisational designs will only succeed when the people dimensions are right too' (Whittington and Mayer, 2002: 29).

chapter four

HRD: Country Frameworks

INTRODUCTION

We have seen in Chapter 1 that across Western society the drive for lifelong learning to support the emerging knowledge economy has been articulated in a variety of policy measures that frame countries' national vocational education and training systems (NVETs). These systems are confronting increasingly common issues in a business environment that is becoming globalised, but their features vary from one country to the next. In this chapter our aim is to provide an overview of some major systems, and to explore some in more detail in order to understand the impact that NVET policies can have on workplace training and learning.

There is a wealth of official information available on NVETs, particularly stemming from the Brussels-based European Commission (EC), the Paris-based Organization for Economic Co-operation and Development (OECD), the Thessaloniki-based European Centre for the Development of Vocational Training (CEDEFOP), and professional institutions such as the UK's Chartered Institute of Personnel Development, now sponsoring several research projects into the impact of the knowledge economy on HRD and workplace learning across Europe. We draw heavily on such sources in this chapter. That said, comparisons of country NVETs remain difficult, not only because policies and practice are continually adjusting to economic, social and technological changes, but also because of the different ways in which databases are drawn up across countries. Methods of evaluating training constitute the only component of HRD to be assessed consistently in international and national statistics, but they too vary from one country to the next and:

> Common points of reference – such as systems for apprenticeship and initial training, provision for continuous training and funding arrangements – highlight very different principles in terms of the role of the state, the link between education and vocational training, the responsibility of organizations to fund training, the degree to which there is a training culture, and the depth of training provision. (Sparrow and Hiltrop,1994: 425)

All of this is unsurprising when countries have followed different paths of industrial development, face different challenges in the global economy and have cultural differences in education practices, work structuring and management styles. It means, however, that while official statistics abound, reliable and meaningful comparative data are hard to obtain.

We begin with a discussion of the lifelong learning policy drive that was referred to initially in Chapter 1 but now needs to be more critically examined. We continue with an outline of some key features in NVETs in Europe and beyond, and we then explore the systems of six countries in some depth: the Netherlands, Germany, France, the United Kingdom (UK), the United States (US) and Japan. An integrative case study from Singapore provides the conclusion to the chapter.

THE DRIVE FOR COMPETITIVE ADVANTAGE

Harnessing lifelong learning to the economic drive

The European Commission's range of social and economic public policy objectives are driven by the aim of improving European firms' competitive capability in the global market. EC policy on VET presents lifelong learning as the key to economic growth, to social cohesion, and to the fulfilment of individual potential. However, it is the economic driver that is uppermost. The dominant view that now frames VET policy across Europe – and more widely – is that global competition requires greater labour market flexibility and that lifelong learning is a key adaptive process to enable that flexibility to be achieved (Edwards, 1997: 27). The rationale is clear enough here, and indeed has emerged from our previous chapters: flexibility, continuous improvement and innovation are both driven by and help to drive an emerging knowledge economy. The high-level skills that this economy requires are technical, social, inter-personal and organisational (IPTS, 2000) and those skills need constant upgrading if they are not to become obsolescent in rapidly changing organisational and work settings. Initial education and training can only be a starting point here. Continuing education is viewed as the ideal vehicle whereby to achieve the necessary transformation across Europe of skills and qualifications because it 'fulfils individual needs for personal education strategies and fits in with the human resources development policies of companies and other organisations' (Commission of the European Communities, 1993: 20). OECD reforms that are focused on improved training opportunities for adults produce consequences to do with:

> improving the training of trainers, the integration of education and training and an emphasis on multiskilling and workplace assessment. This is reflected in developments such as the recognition of prior learning, competency-based standards for vocational and general education and the development of new models of formal education which link industry and education more closely. (Boud and Garrick, 1999: 4)

As Edwards observes in his analysis of the many issues involved in lifelong learning (1997), flexibility is the major aim of current lifelong learning policy across Europe, but in practice it has many meanings. For governments, labour market flexibility is a way of attracting capital investment as national economies compete in an increasingly tough marketplace. For organisations, 'flexibility' enables the mobilisation of workers around new workplace practices that will bring competitive advantage. For individuals 'flexibility' can take the form of multiskilling but also deskilling with associated loss of income. It can involve transfer of skills between organisational workplaces but also transfer from one job, profession or occupation to another, and movements in and out of employment as organisational restructuring and the ongoing reshaping of the labour market continue (Field, 2000: 76).

We explore the downside of flexibility in Chapter 11. Suffice to note here that although the close relationship in the EU between training and education policy and economic policy may promote flexibility, it will not achieve social cohesion until there is greater consistency in lifelong learning policy across countries and a firmer legislative base. Only then will there be the kind of equal access to employment and training opportunities that can break down the barriers between the privileged high-skilled primary labour market and the low-skilled, low-wage secondary labour market. At present, key reports show that the provision of learning opportunities for adults in many EU countries suffers from a lack of coherence in policy at national, regional and local levels that is a major barrier to provision, and that creates and sustains inequalities in access, participation and progression (FEU, 1992: 73, quoted in Edwards, 1997; Wouters, 1992). Field (2000: 85) concludes that the introduction of flexible forms of employment is more likely to increase competition between workers than to build trust.

However, as long as the primacy of the economic driver remains taken for granted policy direction will not change, and there is consensus about the current position 'across the political spectrum including by business and trade union organisations, as well as major political parties and international organisations, such as the European Commission, the Organization for Economic Co-operation and Development, the World Bank and International Monetary Fund' (Edwards, 1997: 41).

NVET SYSTEMS: SOME KEY FEATURES

In this section we make some general observations about NVETs in Europe (including the UK), the US, Singapore and Japan. We look at three key parameters: the link between education and training, funding and provision of training, and vocational standards and qualification frameworks. We do not attempt comprehensive analysis. Our aim is simply to identify some distinctive features across countries in order to indicate the variety of systems currently in use.

The link between education and training

A country's educational system can be either full-time or dual (Van der Klink and Mulder, 1995: 159). The UK system is basically of the former kind: vocational routes begin to open up in the school system from 14 years, and thereafter most vocational education takes place at a state (or independent) institution of study and least in-company, with a major emphasis on obtaining theoretical qualifications. The system broadly resembles that in the US, but it is severely weakened by 'disparities between academic and vocational pathways, poor standards, multiplicity of providers, resource constraints, tensions between forces of centralisation and decentralisation, and intractable "underclass" problems' (Harrison, 2002: 50). Although a vision of investment in human capital embedded in lifelong learning was endorsed in 1998 in a Green Paper, *The Learning Age*, as 'the foundation of success in the knowledge-based global economy of the 21st century' (Department for Education and Employment, 1998: 1), the realisation of that vision is hampered by many discrepancies in educational attainment. The question Peter Drucker posed in 1993 has never been more pertinent for policy-makers in the UK: in an increasingly knowledge-based society, how can those who are educationally disadvantaged join in fully, not only at work but also as a citizen? The government is looking to a radical overhaul of the primary and secondary educational system announced in 2001 to provide the necessary impetus.

Germany typifies the dual system more prevalent in Continental European countries. The German reverence for trade crafts is at the heart of its three-track high-school system, considered to be the best in the world. About one third of young people go on from gymnasium (high school) to university, the remaining two thirds to vocational and technical schools. The education system is flexible, allowing qualified vocational and technical students to switch to the gymnasium at any point, while on the other hand some gymnasium students enrol in vocational programmes even after getting into university. It is enshrined in law that no young person should begin their working life without vocational training and this is provided through a partnership approach in which that training takes place largely on the job with less, but complementary, provision in institutions of study away from the company. In this dual system the major emphasis is on the acquisition of practical competencies, with theoretical qualifications being primarily focused on the underpinning knowledge they require. However, Germany suffers from skills shortages because 16-year-olds are increasingly opting for an academic rather than a manual education. There is a major concern to reform the education system – and especially university education – to make it more oriented to market needs, and to spread cost and control more evenly between the state and the private sector.

In the Dutch dual system, school-based training is combined with learning in the workplace. This model has recently been expanded and incorporated into the higher vocational education system also, and is now beginning to be adopted in parts of the university system where there is a drive to integrate accredited workplace learning into educational programmes. This is a novel type of dual university training system for the Netherlands, and the University of Twente has produced a prototype focused on a competency-based curriculum that uses the workplace as a site of academic learning (Kessels et al., 2002).

Japan differs significantly from most Western countries in its education system. There is little pre-vocational or vocational training in schools. The system's purpose is to lay a broad, non-specialised foundation of knowledge and attitudes to underpin future training, and to set high standards of educational attainment upon which employers can then build with organisation-specific training and development. Full-time upper secondary education is almost universal, most of it being general and a decreasing proportion vocational. The Japanese education system has a rigidly structured, test-centred national curriculum that on the one hand 'is superb at producing a capable and efficient work force to keep production booming' (*Newsweek*, 1991), but on the other hand is very rigorous. It not only threatens the development of creative skills but is linked to high suicide levels of young people. Japan's advanced education system is uneven in quality, with universities failing to produce enough students in key disciplines such as computer software and biotechnology (Porter et al., 2000: 144).

The integration of work-based learning into a school or university curriculum is thus tackled in a variety of ways across countries, raising important questions about educational goals and outcomes, and about how to maintain academic standards when part of an educational programme takes place outside the schoolroom or campus. Many fear the demise of traditional academic values in a system incorporating vocational training. Others see in the historic development of quite distinct academic and vocational pathways, as in the UK, a major contributor to the formation and perpetuation of an educational underclass that remains seriously disadvantaged as it enters the labour market.

Funding and provision of training

In the US and the UK training is largely left to market forces, although in both countries recent legislation has endeavoured to stimulate more, and more relevant, training provision to better respond to market needs. In Germany, the Netherlands, Denmark and France, governments, unions and sectoral organisations, together with other public organisations, play a more central role. However, institutional structures account for variations in approaches. Provision in France is more highly centralised while in Germany, the Netherlands and Denmark it is largely determined by the actions of the social partners within a broader national framework (Ashton et al., 2001).

In Singapore, training strategy has always been underpinned by the national economic development strategy and direct intervention has been made within the context of a broader framework designed to encourage training (ibid). In Japanese companies employee development is well integrated with other human resource and business strategies, is driven by company goals and is dominated by a culture of 'company as family' (Ray, 2002).

In terms of funding, in France collective agreements usually link pay to vocational and technical qualifications and there is a compulsory training levy (Ashton et al., 2001). In Sweden the state pays for the integrated upper secondary school, and in Italy, France, Belgium, Luxembourg and the Netherlands the state pays for full-time training. NVET funding in Germany is shared between state and employers, who voluntarily bear the burden of most of the cost and effort involved. In the UK and the US funding is also split, with the state helping to resource external provision and the employer carrying the main responsibility for funding training in employment. In Singapore private-sector employers spend on average approximately 4% of payroll on training – a much higher spend than the 1% average in the USA and the 1.7–2% average across Continental European countries (ibid). In Japan, the costs are shared by the education system and the employer, with only limited state-sponsored public sector provision.

Vocational standards and qualification frameworks

In most European countries there is a major emphasis on standards and, as we shall see in Chapter 6, many are now committed to a competency-based approach to VET, although the meaning of competency differs between countries. There is also a general emphasis on independent control systems, with occupational training tied to the attainment of national standards and examinations being controlled by independent bodies or by partnership bodies of employers, unions and educationalists. In the UK, assessment is left to a multiplicity of providers and there is no independent national system of assessment of standards.

It is widely assumed across Europe that young people without a degree will be vocationally qualified and youth wages tend to be low until a significant level of vocational qualification has been achieved. In the UK however, wages are not tied to the acquisition of vocational qualifications and in consequence there is less incentive there than elsewhere for individuals or organisations to invest in those qualifications. In Germany, the aim has been that no one without a satisfactorily completed apprenticeship should enter the labour market. Even as long ago as 1984 over 90% of young German people had achieved that. It is also illegal in Germany to stop youth training before it has gone full term, or to stop the off-the-job element during the training period.

In Denmark the whole qualifications system is heavily institutionalised, with qualifications determined and 'owned' at the skilled worker and semi-skilled worker level by the respective trade committees appointed by the employer and the employee organisations (Ashton et al., 2001). The Danish government reformed the system of vocational education in 2001 to provide a competence-based system for adult education that will provide accreditation at four levels of competencies acquired through formal education and training and workplace learning (Ashton et al., 2001: 41). In France the qualification system includes theoretical technical courses, applied technology courses and applied vocational courses. The coherent range of academic, technical and applied vocational courses in secondary schools means that 'practically the whole ability range can gain nationally recognized qualifications which are frequently rewarded by higher pay, since collective agreements in France usually link pay to vocational and technical qualifications' (Steedman, 1990). In Japan there is a national skill testing and qualification system. It is used mainly by smaller companies and provides a coherent structure for individuals to obtain appropriate training and recognised qualifications.

Reflection

■ In this section we have outlined similarities and differences across Europe, and more widely, related to three key features of country NVET systems. Reflecting on the information provided, what differences in approach to HRD within organisations would you expect to find characterise any TWO of those countries – and why?

In the next sections we look in some detail at the operation of NVETs in six countries: the Netherlands, Germany, France, the UK, the US and Japan. In each case we review the systems at three levels: the institutional/sectoral level, the company level, and the level of the workplace.

THE NETHERLANDS

[NOTE: The information in this section is a summary of the account provided in the Chartered Institute of Personnel and Development's report *Workplace Learning in Europe* (CIPD, 2001: 35–8). Available to download: www.cipd.co.uk]

Institutional level

The Netherlands shares with the UK a market-oriented environment and an economy dependent on exports. The strong consultative approach to decision-making in the Netherlands ensures that unions and employers have a considerable input into policy formulation, both for education and vocational training. Decisions relating to work-based training are influenced by collective agreements between employers and unions, and these agreements are legally binding. They have created sectoral training arrangements covering more than half of the country's workforce and 75% of private sector employees (CEDEFOP, 1996), the funding of which comes from a surcharge on employees' salaries. Twenty-three Dutch sectoral training councils are linked under an umbrella organisation called 'COLO' and work to ensure a close match between training provision and industrial needs. They provide support for workplace learning, but the form such support takes is determined by local negotiations (CIPD, 2001).

The whole Dutch NVET system is flexible and easily adapts to specific demands. It also provides support for the development of groups such as temporary workers, the unemployed and older workers.

Subsector and company levels

Detailed decisions relating to specific practices are made by employers and trade unions at the subsector level. For example, in the printing industry the collective agreement covers the design of jobs, entry to different occupations, the introduction of new technologies and the training and retraining of mature employees. Company networks are of considerable importance in influencing workplace learning, especially in the case of small and medium-sized enterprises (SMEs), which the sectoral organisations have not been so effective in reaching. These networks are capable of rapidly delivering new technical knowledge to dealers and can be developed around an industry, a product chain or a specific technology (Warmerdam and Tillaart, 1998). They all tend to share certain characteristics, including: a company-based training centre (which contains the latest technology and simulations relating to the specific sector), a contractual arrangement surrounding the analysis of training needs, attendance at specific courses, and a system for monitoring quality.

Learning in the workplace

In the Netherlands the importance of sectoral organisations and other networks for the delivery of training largely explains why there has not been a perceived need for any national initiative aimed at encouraging workplace learning. Employers are introducing new ways of organising work, and because learning is regarded as an integrated component of these new forms, reflection-in-action has now become essential to the effectiveness of many production jobs. Dutch managers have a strong interest in the principles of self-managed workteams and of workplace learning (Mulder and Tjepkema, 1999) and employers are part-funding a number of major research projects into the process of learning at work. Some of these will be discussed in Chapters 9 and 10.

GERMANY

Institutional/sectoral levels

In Germany's partnership approach to NVET the federal government is responsible for training regulations, the 11 Lander governments are responsible for schools, regional chambers of commerce and industry are responsible for overseeing the dual system, and employers are obliged to belong to these bodies. At present the high-quality but inflexible NVET system is under severe strain, its high costs proving increasingly unaffordable as the German economy remains in downturn, with 4 million jobless, failed reunification policies pursued by both of Germany's main political parties, and a dearth of job-creating investment. Overall, 'the so-called German Model is now perceived by some experts to be unravelling amid multiple bankruptcies, a falling growth rate and an accelerating flight of capital abroad' (Campbell, 2002). There are formidable barriers to overcome, of which the dual system is but one, if Germany is to achieve the ability to compete effectively in a knowledge-based and increasingly globalised economy.

Company level

Employers collaborate with unions and the authorities to provide a high-quality, rigorously administered and controlled dual system, in which initial vocational training is closely regulated. Businesses see it as their responsibility to train young people in order to develop a national pool of labour. Unions have always played an active role in helping to decide on the structure and content of training provision, and on manpower plans. They are politically neutral and have the power to withdraw from firms the right to undertake initial training (Ashton et al., 2001). In Germany's present economic condition the partnership between union and employers is weakening, with unions demanding shorter hours, better conditions and higher pay, despite the already high hourly labour costs involved in operating a dual system that is no longer providing commensurate productivity gains.

Learning in the workplace

In Germany there is no clear framework for dealing with workplace learning outside the context of the dual system. That system has for some time been criticised for its inflexibility, length, its over-theoretical nature and a lack of co-ordination between examining bodies (Incomes Data Services, 1993: 64). A major weakness is its failure to meet the growing demand for workers with non-traditional skills in the high-tech sector. Many of the existing institutions have a vested interest in maintaining the occupational specialisation that has characterised the German labour market. In practice it falls to the employers to develop the use of the workplace as a source of learning, with private training providers and chambers of commerce playing a relatively minor although still important role here (Ashton et al., 2001). There is a tendency to encourage employees to undertake this training outside work hours or as part of 'work-integrated learning' in the enterprise. This means that unions have no influence over the shape this learning takes (Grünewald and Moraal 2000, reported by Ashton et al., 2001: 42).

However, in Germany, continuing education and development have long comprised a fundamental approach to coping with ever-changing work demands. Adult Education Centres dating back to the end of the 19th century are seen as part of an overall system of further education. They are usually operated communally or by local governments or registered associations, with the Lander contributing funds. This historic commitment to continuing education and training, together with a focus on high-quality and technical expertise, no doubt helps to explain many of the innovative attempts that are being made to upgrade the dual system to meet the demands of new forms of work organisation. One such is that of 'learning islands' (see Research example 4.1).

Ashton et al. (2001) observed that while new working practices associated with high performance working have been among the main drivers of enhanced workplace learning in other countries, the evidence from Germany is mixed. Crouch et al. (1999: 146), for example, found that in recent years in-service training has become increasingly important and suggested that companies are trying to solve the problem of further training by using in-company schemes to retrain relatively small parts of their labour force. Ashton and his colleagues concluded that the dual system is still seen by many as providing all the practical and theoretical foundations required for a lifetime's work, and that major innovation is most likely to come from within specific firms rather than emerge at institutional levels.

Research example 4.1

'Learning islands' in German companies

Dehnbostel and Molzberger (2001) described how 'learning islands' were originally initiated by large enterprises such as VW and Mercedes Benz AG in association with the Federal Institute of Vocational Training and Education (BIBB) to provide the opportunity of training trainees within the real work environment, while the trainees continued to work and learn as a team on 'real job orders' (Dybowski 1998: 129). They were at first developed for initial training, but following their success they were developed for use in the continuing training of current employees and induction training for new employees.

The success of the 'learning islands' lies in the fact that they integrate formal and informal learning, situated as they are within the enterprise, and enable the employees to work on real orders. While the trainees are part of the production process, time is allocated to ensure that teams can work together to 'plan, execute, and evaluate or improve this work'. This enables not only the individual trainee, but also the whole team, to 'autonomously organise its work processes' and to reflect together on progress. Indeed, training within the learning islands is not only beneficial to the trainees, but equally for the trainers, who are encouraged to reflect critically, in teams, on the skills necessary to be able to work (and to keep abreast of change in the industry) on the island with the trainees.

This new method of training requires not only a high level of skill and knowledge of the work carried out on the islands, but also a broad knowledge of the place of this learning and training within the 'overall technical system' (Dybowski 1998: 130). Dehnbostel and Molzberger (2001) point out that the training method enables the trainees to integrate the acquisition of the new 'key' skills such as teamworking and self-directed working with the acquisition of technical skills.

Reproduced with permission from: Chartered Institute of Personnel and Development. (2001) *Workplace Learning in Europe.* London: CIPD, p. 43. Available to download: www.cipd.co.uk

Reflection

- In what ways does the German dual system militate against a strong focus on workplace learning?
- Reflecting on information so far in this chapter, what kind of changes do you think are needed if German companies are to be able to compete in the emerging knowledge economy?

FRANCE

Institutional level

In France, training has to be seen in the context of social democratic legislation that since 1971 has profoundly shaped its focus and investment. In that year the 'Delors' law, following the social upheavals of 1968, was 'formulated very much in the spirit of encouraging maximum social dialogue between the main actors in industrial relations and hastening social mobility within the firm' (Jenkins, 1992: 1). It introduced a training tax or levy that has created a highly regulated system of formal training within the organisation's internal labour market and that emphasises co-operation between the state and social partners. The 1987 Riboud Report, commissioned by the Premier Ministre, stressed the need to change from treating training as a cost to the business to focusing on training as an essential social investment in skills and intelligence of all workers for the future. This has typified the national policy approach to training that has developed subsequently. It has also characterised much management practice in French firms, although there the main practical concern is to develop the human resource strategies and the skills needed to ensure the success of new forms of production system in the workplace (Jenkins, 1992: 6). The levy system and other legislation explains the continuous growth in public and private spending on initial and continuing vocational training since 1971. However, it is mainly invested in formal learning activity.

The educational system in France is dominated by education ministries and the French training system is likewise highly centralised with a strong tendency towards more general education. Vocational preparation in the education system takes place primarily through the *Baccalauréat Professionnelle* and the *Baccalauréat Technologique*. Once in the labour market, the framework for workplace learning is governed by the *Formation Professionnelle Continué*, or continuing vocational training (CVT). Together, these two forms of provision constitute a commitment by the French government, public institutions, organisations and the social partners to lifelong vocational training (Ashton et al., 2001).

Company level

Broadly speaking, training in French firms is concerned with *mobilisation* of workers and work around new high performance work priorities, *anticipation* through knowledge building (often helped by outside agencies) in order to develop flexibility and fast-responsiveness in a world where the future offers no clear picture of how jobs and organisation will evolve, and *targeting* of specific jobs, functions and individuals to meet changes that can be predicted (Méhaut, 1989, in Jenkins, 1992: 6). The interaction of these trends means that training becomes 'more completely integrated into everyday working life' (Jenkins, 1992: 6).

While unions and employers agree on the importance of training to achieve social and technical modernisation, 'they often part company over detail, both at the level of national negotiations and at the level of the firm' (Jenkins, 1992: 7). As in Germany, they work with the authorities to determine the content of training. They also collaborate in the trade testing procedures in the apprenticeship system, which was overhauled in 1992 through a national collective agreement and legislation (Incomes Data Services, 1993: 37). Apprenticeship is results-oriented, with vocational certificates entitling the young person to the wages of a basic-level skilled worker. Unions have the right to negotiate at company level over further skill-creation provision and encourage co-investment by company and individuals in training. Individual employee interests are protected through the legal right to paid training leave (the CIF).

Ashton et al. (2001) found that the strong emphasis on formal training provision tends to favour managers and the well educated over the semi-skilled and unskilled. Within large organisations continuous training is considered an important part of company strategy for dealing with both long-term and short-term competition in the product market, but smaller companies have traditionally been seen as paying the levy rather than providing the training.

Learning in the workplace

Although many companies have started to take an interest in on-the-job learning and the development of competencies (CEDEFOP 1997), recent research has revealed few examples of developments in workplace learning, a weakness probably linked both to the levy system's focus and to the strong hierarchical character of many French organisations (Ashton et al., 2001). A fundamental reason for differences between French and German firms in their approach to training decisions, and to training and career management procedures, is that in France 'large firms do not produce their own legitimate top managerial authority' (Bournois et al., 1994: 125). Overall, while HR policies in countries such as the UK, Germany and Italy seem to be converging, France appears to tread a rather different path, not least because of its strong family-owner tradition and its paternalistic attitudes to personnel management (Sparrow and Hiltrop, 1994). Some French commentators fear that the inheritance in French firms of manager–worker mistrust from 'an all too tenacious Taylorist past', and historically rigid functional demarcations within management and on the shop floor, will impede the progress of the 'social democratic' consensus on education and training that the state has done so much to consolidate (Jenkins, 1992: 9).

To conclude: in France, heavy reliance on a training tax has produced a number of beneficial results, including collective agreements at both the sectoral and multi-sectoral level that have had a major impact on skill formation (Ashton et al., 2001: 47). It has also attracted many criticisms, similar in kind to those which led to the demise of the UK's levy/grant system, established in the early 1960s to improve the amount and relevance of training provision in companies. One of the main challenges for the French training system in an emerging knowledge economy is how best to adapt or change a system that tends to a preoccupation with training to one with a stronger focus on the use of the workplace as a source of knowledge creation.

Reflection

- What were the main drivers behind the introduction of the French levy system in 1971?
- How do you think that system has shaped the training investment in French companies subsequently and for what reasons would you defend, or oppose, its continued existence?

THE UNITED KINGDOM

Institutional level

NVET in the UK is basically market-driven although government is increasingly attempting to stimulate that provision with various funded forms of involvement to improve the business focus of company training (the Investors in People – IiP – award), to revitalise the apprenticeship system (Modern Apprenticeships), and to help the unemployed to enter or return to the labour market (the New Deal welfare-to-work programme, introduced in 1998). This approach leaves employers relatively free from legal constraints to provide training.

There is a separation of VET roles in the system as between the state, employers and educational establishments, with the input from the state coming largely through an education system that is being radically overhauled to place more emphasis on the vocational route into the labour market (Harrison, 2002: 39–42). In 2001 the government introduced a reorganised NVET system whose cornerstone is a single public body called the National Learning and Skills Council (NLSC), with 47 local operating arms known as Learning and Skills Councils (LSCs). The NLSC has responsibility for the funding, planning, quality assurance and delivery of all post-16 education and training, excluding higher education. Sector Skills Councils identify specific skills shortages and deliver action plans.

This new system aims to produce an effective partnership with employers in order to ensure relevance of learning and training to local as well as national skills needs and to maximise the contribution of education and training to economic performance. Whether it will do so is open to question, since the roots of the UK's severe skills gap problem lie in two systemic features: a 'low-wage/low-skill economy' (Hendry, 1994: 102) in which, despite pockets of high-skill development, a high proportion of the workforce tends to be trapped by rigid division of labour and high demand for a low level of skills; and an educational system that produces relatively low levels of accredited educational attainment, and leads to far fewer numbers and proportions achieving craft-level qualifications and technical qualifications than in most competitor countries. Across British companies there is a very uneven pattern of occupational training coverage, privileging managers, professionals and those with a degree, and threatening serious shortage of skills in the middle and lower ranks of workforces. In sectors where low-paid workers form substantial elements of the workforce, training is particularly inadequate despite skills gaps in areas vital to the national economy (Whitehead, 1999). Training for manual workers is almost entirely in the form of apprenticeships, with the cost historically carried by employers. This pattern of coverage impedes progress in implementing technological change and more flexible work patterns (Westwood, 2001: 19).

Company level

As already noted, responsibility in the UK for workforce training and development is firmly located with the employers and the individual. Although the IiP scheme has had some very positive outcomes (Ashton et al., 2001: 55), and is now being used as a benchmark in the Netherlands, its coverage of organisations in the UK remains limited. Hope for an improved, better-focused and more inclusive training provision across companies lies more in the increased training role of unions. Since 2000 they have been able to become education and training providers in their own right, and government is now strengthening the role of learning representatives (set up in 1998 to stimulate individuals' learning and access to new skills) by measures to ensure that union-provided training can lead to formal accreditation. British Telecom is one of many large companies that are using unions as in-house training providers and finding them to be highly cost effective (Roberts, 2002).

Learning in the workplace

The UK emerges particularly badly from cross-national comparisons in relation to the readiness of workers for continuing training and learning in the workplace and to the organisation and management of workplace training (Stern and Sommerlad, 1999: 79). High performance working practices are only being systematically and comprehensively applied in a small proportion of establishments but many have introduced at least some, and this appears to be leading to an increasing use of the workplace as a source of learning (Ashton et al., 2001: 54). Nevertheless, national surveys continue to reveal little innovation here, with most trainers using traditional face-to-face methods rather than incorporating more learner-centred electronically based approaches (CIPD, 2002) – an issue we will explore further in Chapters 6 and 10.

Three of the most hopeful levers to improve workplace learning are the increasing involvement of unions, new state-funded initiatives to improve management of training and education in the workplace (see Chapter 6), and the opening up of electronically based learning, for example through the 'University for Industry' (UfI) initiative. This broker organisation, introduced in 1999, operates through a network of 'learning centres' run by consortia of bodies in accessible locations. It aims to link businesses and individuals to information technology-based education and training offered by a variety of providers across the country. Its funding lies in the NLSC's hands and it remains to be seen how adequate and well targeted that funding will prove to be. However, it represents a bold step forward in carrying high-quality networked learning and information services to users at all learning levels at low cost (Harrison, 2002).

Despite the many changes that have taken place over the past decade in the UK's NVET system, many believe that it remains in crisis (Evans et al., 1997; Westwood, 2001: 19). They urge a radically new vision, policy and system in order to avoid a repetition of the 'jumble of traditional skills supply initiatives that were still around when the new century dawned' (Keep, 2001: 25). Without stronger incentives for employers, the economy will lack the improved capacity that is needed to secure competitive advantage and the innovation essential to growth, and those in lower-level jobs will find it difficult to improve their skills and enhance their wage-earning potential.

Reflection

■ Looking at key differences between NVET in the UK and in other countries reviewed thus far, what are the main lessons that emerge for the UK, both at national and company levels?

THE USA

[NOTE: Most of the information in this section is a summary of the account provided in the Chartered Institute of Personnel and Development's report *Workplace Learning in Europe* (CIPD, 2001: 48–53). Available to download: www.cipd.co.uk]

Institutional level

As in the UK, training provision in the US is essentially market-driven. Traditionally, the US Federal Government has refrained from intervening in any major way in employers' training practices, limiting its programmes to instances of market failure for specified groups such as the unemployed or the disadvantaged. However, the Workforce Investment Act (WIA) 1998 represents an attempt by the federal state to ensure that all public training and HR programmes are responsive to the needs of the market place. Under the Act, governors in each state are required to establish a State Workforce Investment Board. These boards have replaced the private Industry Councils on which the UK's Training and Enterprise system was largely modelled. If successfully implemented, the Act could help create the framework necessary for the training and development of the entire US workforce (ASTD 1999, referred to in Ashton et al., 2001: 49).

The WIA is intended to centralise many of the activities formerly carried out by different institutions. It provides states with the flexibility to develop streamlined universal workforce development systems in partnership with local governments, and incorporates 'One-Stop Centers' (similar to the UK's 'Business Links' which deliver the IiP scheme) to provide readily accessible information on development opportunities that are available for both employees and employers. The WIA also seeks to improve provision by involving stakeholders in the formulation and implementation of policy, thus enhancing the accountability and responsiveness of the system.

Company level

In the US, major companies see training and development as a key to longer term competitive performance, encompassing all sections of their labour forces. This can be seen as a national vision which explains much of the drive for, and commitment to, education and training in the US (Hayes et al., 1984). Collaborative arrangements between employers and labour unions play an important role in supporting learning inside and outside the workplace (see Case example 4.1), and this is likely to be further facilitated by the WIA. Unions in the USA have a long history of supporting the training and continual development of their members, both through negotiations at the bargaining table and by providing development activities themselves (Ashton et al., 2001).

The traditional American ethos of individual initiative and of the innate value of education and training means that individuals invest highly in training and companies give support where needed. The pressure on employers comes more from individuals wanting training or prepared to undertake it on their own initiative (Hayes et al., 1984).

Case example 4.1

Employer/union partnership in training, USA

One example of an employer/union partnership is the case of the Communication Workers of America, the International Brotherhood of Electrical Workers, and the companies AT&T and Lucent Technologies, who formed an alliance for promoting employee growth and development. The partnership established a joint training trust under which 200 joint labour-management committees were set up to identify employee education needs and to formulate a subsequent plan for their on going development.

All participating employees can receive their instruction via the Internet. The employees are also offered the opportunity to attend accredited training programmes, which are delivered by their employers in collaboration with local education institutions. Using this approach, the partners aim to provide employees with customised training, enabling them to update their skills for evolving positions in their company.

Reproduced with permission from: Chartered Institute of Personnel and Development (2001) *Workplace Learning in Europe*. London: CIPD, p. 50. Available to download: www.cipd.co.uk

Learning in the workplace

In the absence of government support, employers are essentially left to their own devices to improve the use of the workplace as a source of learning, yet the US is a significant leader in the field here. This has been spearheaded in two ways: first through partnership arrangements between employers and unions, and second through the practices of leading-edge companies introducing forms of high perform- ance working that have stimulated numerous innovations in the use of the workplace as a source of learning. These include job enrichment, self-managed work teams and quality circles, the decline in the use of formal classroom-based instruction and the increasing use of techniques designed to capitalise on the use of the workplace as a source of learning (Ashton et al., 2001: 48).

JAPAN

Economic context

Japan has long been a benchmark for knowledge-creation capability (Nonaka, 1991; Nonaka and Takeuchi, 1995), total quality management and management expertise (Sawyers, 1986), and the unique interrelationships between Japanese economic struc- tures, economic systems, organisational units and employment practices largely explain the country's past economic success (Dore, 1987; Ackroyd et al., 1988). Currently, however, Japan is the world's weakest economy and its future to some looks bleak. It is for this unusual mix of features that we give rather more space to the Japanese case than to those of other countries discussed in this chapter.

As developing countries with cheap labour costs have moved into the global labour market, Japan has focused on developing and retaining a higher value-added manu- facturing base, taking advantage of new technologies (Nakamoto, 1995). 'It has become the world's second largest economy, having moved from competing mainly as a low-wage, low-cost supplier of goods that imitated Western designs to a country that epitomizes high-quality, high-reliability products' (Ray, 2002: 102). But for over a decade Japan has been fighting a recession that has led to major restructuring of many of its companies. Its manufacturers have been forced to relocate production overseas, while manufacturing costs at home have suffered particularly from a rigidly structured internal labour market within most large companies. By September 2002, Japan's Nikkei index was at its lowest for 19 years, its reliance on the US economy – itself in a prolonged downturn since 11 September 2001 – further weakening its condition. Currently it has the highest debt burden of any of the major economies and a gross domestic product of only 1.6%.

Some believe that it is the very interrelationships that gave Japan its past success that are now contributing most to its problems. Yet the country has a proven capa- bility in restructuring and has notable strengths in a well-educated workforce, deep financial reserves built up over time, good technology and some high-quality senior management. As Ray (2002) explains in his account of contemporary Japanese know- ledge creation, Japan's version of 'co-ordinated capitalism' was well established by the First World War, with *zaibatsu* (groups of companies owned and operated by a single family) gaining great power as Japan supplied the allies with munitions and other goods. In the 1950s the Ministry of International Trade and Industry 'exploited its links with industry to bring about horizontal *keiretsu* groupings based on banks, with the four largest *zaibatsu* re-emerging amongst the "big six" keiretsu' (Ray, 2002: 107).

Some see the Japanese economy as a 'catastrophe' that cannot get better, with 'spectacular corporate failures' waiting in the wings (Ian Shepherdson, chief US economist at High Frequency Economics, New York State, quoted in the *Guardian*, 10 September 2002: 7). Ray, however, believes that 'in circumstances where Western firms might simply go out of business and produce nothing, Japan's stable economic structure tends to remain intact and is poised for rapid recovery when the upturn comes' (Ray, 2002: 107).

Institutional level

In Japan there is an unusually tight integration between its NVET system and the economy on the one hand, and companies' employee development practice on the other. In most Japanese organisations, except the very small (that is, those employing less than 25 people), the preferred strategy is to recruit well-educated workers, offering them relatively long-term security and an internal career system, together with continuous development and improvement of their skills, knowledge and experience (Koike, 1988). Although lifetime employment is by no means universal, it has added to the high cost structure of Japanese industry. In 1994 Toyota announced the introduction of one-year contracts for white-collar workers, and this, in such an old, conservative company, signified a fundamental shift in practice in Japan. As is typical in Japanese companies, however, Toyota preferred redeployment to downsizing. It moved 20% of its 4,000 white-collar workers to new project divisions where the business had greater need of their skills (Gurdon, 1994). Rather than loss of human and social capital, the move resulted in more flexibility of staff levels to match pressures in the external environment.

The price that Japanese employees pay for long-term employment is quite high. Rewards in terms of money and promotion are accumulated slowly through time, and only in return for the sustained achievement of very demanding standards of job performance. Because Japanese workers are brought up in a culture which emphasises organisational affiliation, trust and 'company as family' (Ray, 2002), and firmly separates personal emotions from work behaviour, they stay with one employer for as long as they can, enduring work conditions, levels of effort and rigorous regular assessment processes that would be unacceptable to many in the West (Briggs, 1991). In a recent survey of 360,000 employees from the world's ten largest economies (ISR, 2002), only 50% of Japanese employees said that they viewed their employer favourably – the lowest level of commitment reported in any country, and significantly less than the other two lowest-ranking countries, China (57%) and the UK (59%).

Company level

In Japanese companies there is a uniquely tight and pragmatic integration of all business strategies and their subordination to a single overriding strategic goal (Reitsperger, 1986; Miller, 1991; Storey, 1991). Within HR strategy there is a similar approach, with strong consistency and coherence between human resource planning, recruitment, selection, training, appraisal, development, reward systems and the organisation and deployment of personnel (Ackroyd et al., 1988; Storey, 1991). Employee development mirrors this: after a brief period of initial training, all workers (and there is little distinction between blue- and white-collar workers in Japan) are given as wide a range of experience as is feasible, involving a well-planned mix of off- and on-the-job training, continuing development and learning from experience.

Larger Japanese companies employ a wide-ranging developmental strategy that includes job rotation and transfer, multi-task working, and participation in quality circles and zero defect groups. They link quality checks to training for subcontractors and train and develop new recruits in their own training schools and on the job. All big Japanese firms have their own education and training colleges, and some of them – Hitachi and Nippon Telegraph and Telephone (NTT) – are international showpieces.

Learning in the workplace

Continuing development, together with a high level of basic education and encouragement to learn and use standard problem-solving techniques, means that Japanese employees quickly gain an intellectual understanding of the structure of the machines and products and of the production process. They can thus deal remarkably well with any changes that occur, and can usually themselves suggest and determine with their supervisor how to improve efficiency. Supervisors and managers are continuously developed and trained in the workplace on the basis of the twin aims of perfection and the ability to learn so as to assume any new work role successfully (Hayes et al., 1984). They pay meticulous attention to detail, and have the will to continuously improve in all that they do (Sawyers, 1986).

Given this approach to workplace learning, it is unsurprising that Japanese companies have had outstanding success in the kind of innovation that springs from continuous improvement. Ideas that have originated in one context are regularly learnt, adapted and effectively applied to another (Gleave and Oliver, 1990: 68). The Japanese culture of obligation to the group coupled with a work ethos of lifelong loyalty to the organisation, close relationships among colleagues and an unfaltering focus on the company's strategic goals all promote 'steady state organizational knowledge creation' whereby 'employees re-use and adapt individual skills and collective competencies to generate new knowledge' (Ray, 2002: 102).

In many countries, the critical barrier to adequate knowledge creation lies in NVETs that produce insufficient emphasis on workplace learning. Paradoxically, in Japan the very preoccupation with that process could impede the degree of radical innovation that is needed if companies are to respond speedily enough to the increasingly rapid pace of change in the emergent knowledge economy. However, Japan's Institute of Physical and Chemical Research or RIKEN, established in 1917, has been extremely successful in encouraging creative research to support economic development and make Japan less dependent on Western science (Ray, 2002: 115). The greater question facing Japan is whether it will be able to climb out of its present severe economic straits, with GDP, share prices and inflation levels all combining to form a continuing recessionary spiral.

THE WAY FORWARD

Refocusing NVET systems

The major challenge in a knowledge-based economy is to find ways of enhancing knowledge creation through the successful adaptation of education and training systems at institutional, sectoral and company levels. This chapter has shown that within countries, distinctive features at macro level combine to influence the generalised focus of HRD within organisations.

Van der Klink and Mulder (1995) explain that the absence of a comprehensive NVET system – as in the UK – reinforces the division of labour found within companies. Where there is less perceived need for qualified staff – as again in the UK – then 'contacts between vocational training institutions and employers organisations are less well developed' (ibid: 168). By contrast, 'competencies provided by vocational training enable companies to reduce the rigidity of division of labour' (ibid) facilitating flexible organisation of the production process. These business innovations in turn encourage investments in vocational education and in-company training, and we have seen how that pattern occurs in countries such as the Netherlands and the US, where the introduction of high performance work practices is leading to a major focus on workplace learning.

Another essential for an effective NVET system is policy coherence. Without that, there are no clear boundaries for the field of VET and this impedes its rational management (Edwards, 1997: 88). Key reports show that the provision of learning opportunities for adults in many EU countries suffers from lack of a firm legislative base and a lack of policy coherence at national, regional and local levels that is a major barrier to provision, and that creates and sustains inequalities in access, participation and progression (Wouters, 1992, quoted in Edwards, 1997). Countries with particularly diverse and unco-ordinated provision appear to be France, Germany, Italy and the Netherlands (FEU, 1992: 73).

Edwards (1997) noted a general shifting of responsibility from state to market across Europe also, even if not in such an extreme form as in the US and the UK, where there is a reliance mainly on centrally established funding and quality criteria together with selective support for areas of failure to achieve policy goals. He attributes this shift in part to a reconceptualisation of national governments' function in an increasingly globalised society: a function of monitoring and specialised support, with a focus on competency-based national qualification structures, rather than of any more active interventionist activity.

Singapore is unique in its integrative NVET system. As in most Continental European countries, learning at work involves a partnership approach, but where Singapore differs from the rest is in a national policy framework that has a long-term 'developmental' outlook and is strategic in nature. One characteristic feature is the constant upgrading and refocusing of Singapore's training agenda in line with the changed requirements of

---

Case example 4.2

Lifelong learning: the Singaporean approach

The Singaporean 'system' has four infrastructural pillars: the Ministry of Trade and Industry, the Economic Development Board, the Council for Professional and Technical Education and the Productivity and Standards Board. Together these institutions provide a strong 'top down' influence on employers and national skill formation.

Although Singapore had a strong education and skills programme in place before, it was not until 1993 that it began to strengthen workplace learning practice with its first national plan for structured on-the-job learning: the OJT 2000 Plan. The objective was to improve the quality of 'sitting by Nellie' learning by provid-

Case example 4.2 *(cont'd)*

ing a structure for the on-the-job training of 100,000 employees.

The OJT system was organised sectorally and incorporated learning based on perceived best practice. The success of the system can in part be gauged by the fact that by the year 2000 Singapore had trained more than 330,000 employees and introduced structured on-the-job training in more than 60 per cent of companies.

A second plan was launched in 2000: OJT 21 aims to provide training for 500,000 employees by 2005. Reflecting the rapidity of change and the impact and growth of the knowledge economy, a new focus covers both the content of on-the-job learning and the underpinning of knowledge and the certification of skills to facilitate labour market flexibility and transfer of skills. Certification is provided by a new National Skills Recognition System.

These changes have been introduced because too many companies have concentrated on the development of functional skills but ignored associated under-pinning knowledge. Employees have known what to do but not why they are doing it in a particular way.

They also found it difficult to transfer their knowledge to new situations, products and processes.

Over time, the infrastructure has developed. Workplace learning in the form of structured on-the-job training is now part of an integrated skill system that includes two other major national initiatives: one is the People Developer Standard and the other has to do with work redesign. The People Developer Standard takes an organisational approach to skills development, looking at the linkages between strategy and learning. The work redesign initiative aims proactively to stimulate the regeneration and raising of learning needs by continuous reviews of work processes and job design in order to increase their value-added content. This has been described as a 'paradigm shift' in skills development, moving the emphasis from 'learning inputs' to 'organisational contribution'.

Reproduced with permission from: Chartered Institute of Personnel and Development. (2001) *Workplace Learning in Europe*. London: CIPD, p. 10. Available to download: www.cipd.co.uk

economic development, as Case example 4.2 demonstrates. In 2001 the government once again revised and restructured its training strategy to focus directly on lifetime learning in preparation for the next phase of growth, the emergence of 'a knowledge-based economy'. Many components within the training framework are integrated so that the various elements of learning at work are co-operating towards a single goal, namely that of 'lifelong employability' (Ashton et al., 2001). Singapore's particular form of government/industry alliance would be difficult, if not impossible, to replicate in other countries. However, it provides a powerful illustration, and is therefore used to conclude this chapter.

At this point we have provided an assignment in Appendix 1 that you may wish to tackle in order to consolidate learning related to this chapter and relate it to your own country context.

CONCLUSION

In this chapter we have discussed some major NVET systems in order to enhance understanding of the external policies and practices that influence the practice of HRD within organisations. Table 4.1 summarises some key findings.

Table 4.1   *A comparison of country NVET systems*

Country	VET system and funding	Training provision	Workplace learning
The Netherlands	Dual. Funding shared between state and employers.	Partnership approach between state, employers and unions. Sectoral, sub-sectoral and company networks stimulate and help to deliver training.	Integral part of new ways of organising work. Managers are committed to and strongly interested in workplace learning.
Germany	Dual. Funding shared between state and employers. The university system is being reformed to make it more responsive to the market and to share funding more equally between state and private sectors.	The dual system provides the framework for training and development at company level, and training provision is overseen by regional chambers of commerce and industry.	No particular emphasis on workplace learning as a separate system. Employers have to take most of the initiative, and a focus on informal workplace learning processes is hampered by rigidity of the dual system.
France	Dual, but highly centralised. Funded by a training tax. Mutual funds at sectoral and multi-sectoral levels help training to meet specific industrial and cross-industrial needs.	Strong emphasis on partnership between state, empoyers and unions. Social partners specify training priorities and negotiate collectively for use of funds and advice from official agencies.	Strong emphasis on formal courses and vocational training. Other forms of work-place learning need more focus but this is impeded by operation of the levy system and probably also by unique organisation and management of French firms.
US	Market-driven system with federal funding to aid special groups. Recent federal legislation has attempted to stimulate training to better meet market needs.	Partnership between state-funded Workforce Investment Boards and local governments at federal state level, and between employers and labour unions at company level.	Left to initiative of employers, but high performance working practices and a historic culture of self-development stimulate innovation and some world-class best practice.

Table 4.1 *cont'd*

Country	VET system and funding	Training provision	Workplace learning
UK	Market-driven system with state funding to aid special groups. Recent legislation has attempted to stimulate training to better meet market needs.	New attempt at partnership between state-funded Learning and Skills Council, employers, unions, educationalists and regional development agencies. Within companies, basically determined by employers, although unions have begun to claim a role.	Responsibility lies with employer and individuals. Emphasis has tended to focus on formal training and education and accredited competency schemes, whose quality and management national funding and standards are now trying to improve. The introduction of some high performance working practices in organisations is leading to greater interest in work-based learning processes.
Japan	The heavily centralised state educational system sets high standards of broad-based educational attainment upon which employers can build training and development tailored to company needs and goals.	Line management, not the training function, is the major partner in employee development. Japanese companies are nested in broader economic, structural and cultural systems. They are characterised internally by integration of all business and HR strategies and their subordination to a single corporate strategic goal. The preferred strategy is to recruit well-educated workers and develop an internal labour market and career system. Japan's deep economic recession now threatens that model.	Managers are responsible for creating a learning culture and employees are expected to be active in their own development (Tjepkema et al., 2002a:18). Strong emphasis on continuing training, and strategically focused group learning and knowledge creation as integral part of everyday work. 'Nested stability and the lack of labour mobility means that organizations are effective "social containers" for accumulated individual and collective tacit knowledge.' (Ray, 2002: 102–3)

Some countries – notably the Netherlands and Japan – seem uniquely well fitted by their national history and culture and their partnership approach to succeed in adapting their NVET systems to the needs of an emerging knowledge economy. Some, such as Germany and France, are encountering difficulty because of the rigidity of a NVET system that no longer meets the country's labour market needs. The UK seems less well equipped than any of its competitor countries to cope with new challenges, struggling as it does with systemic weaknesses in its education and training systems and a persistent and serious skills gap.

However, we need to put NVET systems in their wider context. The superiority of Japanese management, employee development and workplace learning practices struggles to make an impact in an economy in deep and continuing recession. On the other hand, in the UK, despite the weaknesses in its NVET system, the economy is strong and labour market flexibility and low cost are envied in countries such as Germany. There, the high price paid for the dual system is not being offset by any commensurate productivity gains, and economic prospects are extremely gloomy. Forecasts for the US are divided, with some commentators expecting a 'double dip' recession, others more hopeful about its chances of coming out of a downturn that by late 2002 still engulfed the globe (*Guardian*, 2002; Teather and Elliott, 2002).

At present, with mixed predictions about prospects for a truly global economy and with Europe in particular failing to push strongly towards global growth, most companies face tensions between the need on the one hand to achieve cost efficiency and high immediate productivity and, on the other, to develop skills and competencies for the future. However, while investment in HRD within organisations is undoubtedly influenced by a mesh of external forces, it remains most directly shaped by company leadership, by human resource strategies and practice in the workplace, and by the expertise and business credibility of HRD practitioners. It is these internal factors that we examine in Chapters 5 and 6, in order to assess the current state of play of HRD at organisational level.

chapter five

HRD: Emerging Challenges

INTRODUCTION

In this and the following chapter, our aim is to assess the present state of the human resource development (HRD) function in organisations by exploring the challenges that it currently faces, and its scope and practice in a variety of country contexts. In these chapters we make considerable use of the research findings reported in 2002 by Tjepkema et al. (hereafter referred to as 'the 2002 European HRD research project'). They surveyed HRD practice in just under 200 'learning-oriented' organisations (most employing upwards of 1,000 employees) in seven European countries: Belgium, Finland, France, Germany, Italy, the Netherlands and the UK. Of those organisations, 28 were covered by case study analysis, mainly undertaken in organisations employing between 500 and 1,000 people. A further 165 organisations, 38% employing over 500 people and 34% employing over 5,000, were covered by a questionnaire survey. In the terminology of the project, 'learning-oriented' organisations are those that (Tjepkema and Wognum, 1996):

■ create facilities for employee learning
■ stimulate employees not only to attain new knowledge and skills, but also to acquire skills in the field of learning and problem solving, and thus develop their capacity for future learning.

Unlike these researchers, however, we do not confine our review of the state of play in the HRD field to 'good' examples of learning-oriented organisations with a pro-active HRD function. They justified their sampling frame on the ground that 'it is from such examples that the most interesting lessons can be learnt'. Their findings have a unique value, but it is also essential to review organisations more widely since how otherwise can we understand why HRD receives so little attention in many firms, and why – in a turbulent environment calling for high-level organisational learning capability – a 'learning orientation' is not universally adopted? In similar fashion, Inkpen and Choudhury (1995) regretted that strategy researchers so rarely investigate situations where business strategy is expected to exist yet does not:

Absence is often used as a cue for investigation and as a subject of study in many areas of research. For example, Fleming's discovery of penicillin was instigated by the absence of bacterial growth in some parts of the laboratory culture. (Inkpen and Choudhury, 1995)

As they observed, the mere presence of strategy does not necessarily mean that business performance will be 'good or successful', nor does its absence invariably lead to failure of the business. Honda began its American experience with an absence of strategy that was instrumental in its subsequent success because it provoked the exploration of many options and produced innovative solutions to the question of how best to achieve competitive advantage.

We also draw on the three-year Price Waterhouse-Cranfield international comparative survey of organisational policies and practices in human resource management across Europe, reported in 1994 (Brewster and Hegewisch, 1994). It has some key similarities to the 2002 European HRD research project: its coverage included five of the countries also researched by Tjepkema et al. (2002) (it did not cover Belgium and Italy) and took in employing organisations across production, public and service sectors, with a quarter of organisations surveyed employing 500 to 999 people, and 1 in 10 employing 5,000 or more. None employed less than 200. However, it reviewed all the key fields of HRM, not just HRD, it was conducted purely on a questionnaire basis, and it yielded responses from personnel specialists at the corporate head of nearly 4,500 organisations in 13 European states. We refer to this research as 'the 1994 Cranfield HRM survey'.

We begin this chapter with an overview of the HRD field, exploring confusion about its identity and purpose in an attempt to clarify the meaning of HRD as an organisational process. We then examine four major HRD challenges in today's business environment: achieving strategic thrust, building a learning culture, promoting workplace learning and developing managerial and leadership capability. We conclude the chapter by identifying the agenda for discussion in Chapter 6.

Reflection

- ■ What does the term 'learning orientation' mean when applied to an organisation?
- ■ Can you identify any organisations you know of that deserve that description? If so, why have they become learning oriented, and what kinds of benefits does that orientation seem to bring to employees generally?

CLARIFYING THE HRD FIELD

Terminology and meanings

HRD has a complex interdisciplinary base that has developed differentially across countries, workplaces and in academia, and confusion still surrounds the field. Some argue that 'the role of the HRD practitioner lacks precision because it has not yet found its discipline' (Grieves and Redman, 1999: 81). Others claim that consensus is growing and that:

HRD encompasses adult learning at the workplace, training and development, organisational development and change, organisational learning, knowledge management,

management development, coaching, performance improvement, competence development and strategic human resource development. Instead of being a sub-discipline of
Human Resources Management, HRD is becoming a 'multidisciplinary' or 'transdiscipli-
nary' field in its own right. (Groupe Esc Toulouse, 2002)

Much ambiguity derives from a failure to distinguish between 'training' and the
wider HRD process. Some trainers who regard themselves as HRD specialists are not in
reality involved widely in that field. Likewise, some who hold the 'HRD' title are in
reality training practitioners. The 2002 European HRD research project indicated that
the term 'HRD' is rarely encountered in the workplace and that it is little used by
managers either in describing the specialist function or in referring to training and
development processes. Even when the term is used, the function it describes
frequently covers little more than training activity (Sambrook and Stewart, 2002).

The ambiguity extends to academia, where in many mainstream HRM texts and
reports discussion of 'HRD' regularly boils down to no more than a concern with
'training and development' (Beardwell and Holden, 1995; Mabey and Salaman, 1995;
Purcell, 1995), often with a particular preoccupation with management development
(Storey, 1995). Stewart and Tansley (2002), by contrast, use the terminology of
'training', 'training and development' and 'employee development' to discuss not
only training issues but also the organisation of work and individual and organisational learning that have important implications for HRD and its practitioners.

Use of training rather than HRD terminology is sometimes a presentational tactic,
prompted by need of authors to talk the language of their audience even when that
language is not the one that they themselves prefer. Often, however, it suggests an
uncertainty about the meaning and scope of HRD. Walton (1999) reflected this in his
survey of the constituents of HRD, noting that they are no longer restricted to individuals operating as employees within a given organisation, but can incorporate non-
employees also. He concluded that 'learning', 'knowledge' and 'development', while
all encompassed by the HRD process, are 'big themes' that are not easily contained
within a single definition.

In real life, stakeholders have little patience with HRD professionals who are
confused about the function yet claim it to be crucial to their organisation's success.
Stewart and McGoldrick take a pragmatic line in their definition:

The term (HRD) assumes that organisations can be constructively conceived of as
learning entities, and that the learning processes of both organisations and individuals
are capable of influence and direction through deliberate and planned interventions.
Thus, HRD is constituted by planned interventions in organisational and individual
learning processes. (Stewart and McGoldrick, 1996: 1)

Such definitions place a welcome emphasis on HRD as a field to do with learning
processes, but they do not clarify that field's organisational purpose. At the practical
level, that clarity is essential, and matters more than agreement on title. In the UK, as
elsewhere, titles change through time. At present, that most favoured to describe the
HRD field is 'Learning and Development', adopted after a country-wide consultative
process within the profession by both the body that has produced revised national
occupational standards (these can be viewed and downloaded at www.empnto.co.uk)
and by the Chartered Institute of Personnel and Development in its new professional
standards (CIPD, 2001a, and can be downloaded from www.cipd.co.uk). We discuss
both sets of standards briefly at a later point in this chapter.

Reflection

- How would you define 'HRD' at this early point in the chapter?
- What purpose does the HRD function appear to have in your own organisation, and to what extent is there agreement about its identity there?

Focusing the HRD process

Stewart argues that HRD should not necessarily be bound up with achieving 'organisation objectives which are either pre-determined by the economic system or which are determined solely by specified groups such as boards of directors or senior management teams':

> Behaviour directed towards formulating and agreeing objectives can and does change, and the direction of change can be influenced through interventions in the learning process. HRD therefore … can also have the purpose of changing established objectives and objective-setting processes. (Stewart, 1999: 19)

It is of course undeniable that the outcomes of HRD activity can lead to changes in established objectives, objective-setting processes, and individual and collective behaviour. Sometimes such changes occur purely by chance. Sometimes they are 'helped' by HRD practitioners. Often they prove to be highly beneficial to the organisation and to its employees. However, it seems self-evident that if HRD as an organisational process is to gain any kind of foothold in the business, let alone achieve a strategic role, its formal purpose must be aligned with corporate goals of the business. How else can it can convince an often sceptical, sometimes ignorant, audience of the business relevance of its intent, and win the resource base it needs for its proposed strategies?

Resources are the key. If those who control resource flow decide that HRD processes and activity will not add sufficient value to the business, then they will reduce or withhold resource. As noted in Chapter 2 in our discussion of pressures on the employment relationship, many organisations are now restricting their investment to only immediately needed training, because wider HRD activity is regarded as too long-term and speculative.

The performance–learning debate

In the US, the discipline of economics has exercised a powerful influence on the focus of HRD. It continues to do so, as can be seen in the preoccupation of a body of HRD researchers, there and in Europe, with performance improvement. The stance is typified by the following statement by a leading member of the Academy of Human Resource Development:

> HRD is a process for developing and unleashing human expertise through organizational development and personnel training and development for the purpose of improving performance. (Swanson, 1995: 208)

Learning-oriented researchers, on the other hand, emphasise a more long-term strategic focus. A typical definition embodying this view is:

HRD is the field of study and practice responsible for the fostering of a long-term work-related learning capacity at the individual, group, and organizational level of organizations. (Watkins, 1989: 427)

The assumption that HRD should be focused primarily on improving performance rests on three further assumptions:

- that in all situations a desired level of performance can be clearly described
- that the situation in which that performance must be achieved can be fully analysed and understood
- that the required interventions can then be accurately identified through gap analysis.

In Chapter 3 we noted the need for organisations operating in a knowledge economy to produce a regular stream of dynamic capabilities, and their reliance in this task on continuous learning and knowledge-construction processes. The logic of gap analysis has little relevance here. It fits well with stable situations and predictable environments, when the desired outcome is to achieve standardisation, repetitive routines and fixed procedures. It sits uncomfortably, however, with aims to achieve enhanced long-term flexibility, the ability to operate in dynamic environments, and raised levels of strategic awareness and creativity across a workforce. In that scenario management must still set targets related to increasing turnover, to reducing complaints, to expanding market share, to lowering costs and raising profits per employee. The operational task of training to improve current performance remains an important one. However, there is a further and crucial strategic task for HRD. It is to promote across the workforce knowledge development that will lead to continuous improvement and radical innovation. Here, as we saw at various points in Chapter 3, management's role is to provide generalised direction and support, not close monitoring and control. Outstanding performance remains the desired outcome, but performance of a longer-term, more open-ended nature.

Therefore, in our view, a knowledge economy calls not for an opposition but for an integration of the performance–learning perspectives. When individuals and teams are having to deal daily with challenges whose precise nature cannot be anticipated in advance, then working and learning together in order to find the best way to proceed become crucial. A focus on continuing learning and development signals a strategic response from the HRD function to the challenges of adaptability and innovation posed by the operation of a knowledge economy. Protracted confusion about the focus of a field that is of such importance in today's organisations can only be damaging to its practice. Current debate exemplifies the confusion while doing little thus far to resolve it.

Building human and social capital

Underlying the performance–learning debate are two distinctive theories that we introduced in Chapter 1. They concern human and social capital. Human capital theory (Schultz, 1961) became widely known in the US in the 1970s, largely due to the writings of the economist/sociologist, Becker (1975). It views people as organisational assets whose economic value derives from their skills, competence, knowledge and experience. Intangibles such as intellectual property and customer equity are all derived from human capital and are regarded as the ultimate source of competitive advantage, generating earnings that are powerful drivers of stock returns. In sum:

> Human capital is the foundation upon which value is created through physical, financial, and intangible assets. (Schmidt and Lines, 2002: 32)

Much research is now being undertaken into ways of measuring the impact that distinctive HR initiatives can have on earnings growth (Mayo, 2001; Hurwitz et al., 2002; Schmidt, 2002). The US federal government's Office of Management and Budget insists that agencies include human capital management in their performance plans (Brown, 2002). This approach to the valuing of the human factor is welcomed by many who have hitherto been frustrated by an inability to express HR outcomes in terms that business unit leaders can readily understand.

An emphasis on human capital leads naturally to a perception of training and job-related education as the key value-adding HRD processes for both the business and its employees, since they improve individual skills and knowledge whereby workforce productivity can be increased. The concept of social capital, on the other hand, stresses the asset value of human relationships. It focuses on:

> networks together with shared norms, values and understandings that facilitate co-operation within or among groups. (OECD, 2001)

The concept is thus concerned with those social networks in the workplace through which powerful learning takes place and that, when harnessed to organisational purpose, can produce uniquely valuable knowledge. It draws attention to HRD's role in building and sustaining a learning community. Robert Putnam (2000), Professor of Public Policy at Harvard University, emphasised the dangers confronting a society in which the sum of social capital shrinks: communities fragment, trust and mutual commitment are lost, commonality of purpose disappears and society itself begins to break down. There are obvious parallels with organisations where HRD is focused on building human capital but ignores the task of enhancing social capital.

Ignoring that task can breed serious negative outcomes. Left to itself, the learning that resides in communities of practice can become strategically irrelevant, thereby pulling the organisation back instead of driving it forward. We are talking here about that 'skilled incompetence' to which we referred in our discussion of 'organising for knowledge creation' in Chapter 3, that can occur when old routines, processes and networks are allowed to continue unchanged, impeding innovation and progress. While it is true that in a knowledge economy HRD practitioners should become 'learning architects' (University Forum, 1998), it is essential that they perform that role in ways that do not build an 'architecture of simplicity' (Miller, 1993). They need to raise awareness in the organisation of the asset value of social as well as of human capital, and to take a lead in proposing and helping to implement processes and measures that will realise that value.

Reflection

■ In an organisation concerned with building social capital through the HRD process, what kinds of HRD activity do you think might be relevant in the workplace – and why?

■ In what ways might social capital impede continuous improvement and innovation in an organisation?

To conclude this section: academic debate is valuable in stimulating challenge and enquiry. Where, however, the debate becomes protracted and spreads inconclusively into the organisational arena it can be damaging. Ambiguity about HRD's meaning and focus has surrounded the function for many years and has become increasingly unproductive at the practical level. In the UK, a survey commissioned in 1998 by the Institute of Personnel and Development found that training and development practitioners were:

> affected by the confusion of meanings and boundaries between such terms as human resource management, human resource development, training, learning and development. (Darling et al., 1999: xii)

Our definition of HRD, given in Chapter 1 and repeated here, focuses on the purpose of the HRD field (under whatever title), emphasising the outcomes that the process can achieve for the organisation and its members, especially through its stimulation of knowledge creation:

> HRD as an organisational process comprises the skilful planning and facilitation of a variety of formal and informal learning and knowledge processes and experiences, primarily but not exclusively in the workplace, in order that organisational progress and individual potential can be enhanced through the competence, adaptability, commitment and knowledge-creating activity of all who work for the organisation.

However, what matters within the particular organisation is not any general definition of HRD. It is that there should be a shared understanding of the role, purpose and focus of that function *for that organisation*. Without that clarity, the function's business rationale as well as its utility for individuals will be constantly in doubt and the tasks and operations of its practitioners may be undermined as a result. Agreeing with stakeholders on the identity and value-adding potential of the HRD function is therefore one of the first challenges to which HRD practitioners need to respond. Demonstrating that potential in their activity thereafter is the challenge that they must then continually confront.

ACHIEVING STRATEGIC THRUST THROUGH INTEGRATION

Issues of 'fit'

We explained in Chapter 2 that a strategic approach to human resource management requires an integrative approach that achieves horizontal fit across all HR processes, and vertical fit of HR strategies with business goals and with external conditions.

The same approach is needed for HRD if it is to have strategic thrust. Looking first at horizontal fit, Sparrow and Hiltrop (1994: 423) in their review of tasks for HRD in internationalised organisations claimed that the function could 'improve stagnant productivity, speed up the incorporation of new technologies and adaptation to new competitors, inform long-term manpower planning, help develop more future orientated skills, substitute the need to recruit externally, modify management styles and develop new attitudes and improve the communication process'. They observed that this presupposes a high interrelationship between employee training and development (ETD) and other areas of HRM, and concluded that:

It (ETD) is best approached as part of a wider organizational strategy. ETD is one topic within the overall concept of employee resourcing. (Sparrow and Hiltrop, 1994: 423)

The principle is about linking all HR processes in a 'virtuous circle of best practice human resources, that is sustained over the long term and is self-reinforcing' (Sloman, 2002: 44), with learning and development integral to the whole. The viewpoint of the UK's University Forum for HRD is of interest here. The Forum was established by HRD academics to promote HRD-related research and practice. It has partnership links to similar institutions in the US (Academy of Human Resource Development) and in Europe (EURESFORM). According to the Forum, HRD has a unique organisational and strategic identity because of its close relationship with the learning process:

It is not helpful to think of HRD as a sub set of HRM, either in structural or functional terms. As the strategic significance of organisational learning as a source of competitive advantage gains recognition, a strategic need arises for appropriately positioned 'learning architects' with the distinctive competencies to orchestrate learning initiatives on behalf of organisations. (University Forum for HRD, 1998, quoted in Walton, 1999: 67)

The authors of a recent report on the role of training in a knowledge economy made a similar point when, discussing the need for trainers both to take a leading role in the knowledge management (KM) field and to work more closely with operational managers and employees across the business, they concluded:

Training has traditionally been located as part of personnel in organisational structures. More recent trends would suggest that training is increasingly recognised as vital to KM and therefore new structural relationships are being adopted. (Stewart and Tansley, 2002: 33)

There is indeed a need for trainers and others in the HRD arena to become active in a field commonly called 'knowledge management'. We will discuss this further in Chapter 10. However, the real issue when considering the relationship between HRM and HRD is not to do with structural positioning, or with the subordination of any one specialist function to another. It is to do with integration and collaboration. If HRD is not to be impeded by barriers of human resource practice and policy as it strives to provide a strategically focused response at all organisational levels to the challenges of a more knowledge-based economy, then HRD practitioners must work in close partnership with their other HR colleagues. This is particularly vital at a time when all HR practitioners are being required to generate increasingly innovative responses to a variety of major and unfamiliar challenges. As a leading HRD professional remarks:

We must be prepared to approach our jobs in a different way, deploying our skills in new directions. One inevitable consequence is that we will be effective only if we are integrated with the overall human resource function. We can no longer operate in a silo. (Sloman, 2002: 43)

In Chapter 3 it became clear that the challenges facing organisations in an emerging and turbulent knowledge economy are to do with a need for superior speed, flexibility and knowledge creation. These challenges are organisationally focused and require HRD to have real strategic thrust. Short-term training interventions have their part to play here, but only a part. The greater need is for HRD strategies that, while being well integrated with current business and HR strategies, are also focused on embedding a fast-responsive learning culture that will help to build organisational capacity for the future.

Reflection

- Can you identify any HR barriers or aids to the success in your workplace of HRD processes such as mentoring, coaching, on-the-job training and team learning? If so, how might such barriers be tackled?
- If your organisation employs specialist HR staff, to what extent do its HRD practitioners work collaboratively with other HR staff? If there are problems here, what seem to be their causes and how might they be resolved?

BUILDING A LEARNING CULTURE

Challenges in changing culture

Contributing to culture change is a key task for HR practitioners in today's organisations where new organisational forms, new patterns of work, high performance work practices and the increased need for flexibility and knowledge creation call for new values and behaviours as well as new skills in the workplace.

Culture has been described as 'the shared meanings, hidden assumptions and unwritten rules across countries or organizations (that) provide the real energy that will either progress or impede change' (Sparrow and Hiltrop, 1994: 247). Nonaka (1996: 19) commented in a similar way that if organisations are to become knowledge-creative, there must be 'a shared understanding of what the company stands for, where it is going, what kind of world it wants to live in, and … how to make that world a reality'.

Schein (1985) produced one of the most well-known typologies of culture, identifying its existence at three levels:

- *Level 1: 'Artifacts and creations'*. This is the most visible level of culture, and is to do with its 'constructed physical and social environment' (ibid: 14). It incorporates technology, art, behavioural patterns, all of which are 'visible but often not decipherable' (ibid).
- *Level 2: 'Values'*. This is the intermediate level. It is about people's 'sense of what "ought" to be, as distinct from what is' (ibid: 15). Schein explains that some of these cultural values are testable in the physical environment, but others are testable only by social consensus.
- *'Basic underlying assumptions'*. These are to do with assumptions that actually guide behaviour and 'tell group members how to perceive, think about, and feel about things' (ibid: 18). Many such assumptions are shaped in part by national and local cultures. Because they are so deeply embedded in the unconscious, they are difficult if not impossible to confront or to debate. Schein contends that they therefore make the process of double-loop learning intrinsically difficult. As such, they constitute the level of culture in a workplace that is likely to be the most resistant to change.

Another way of describing culture is as a kind of 'tool kit' of material such as symbols, stories, procedures, habits and skills that become a set of general cultural 'capacities', influencing people in the decisions they make and in the actions they perform (Swidler, 1986, discussed by Dougherty, 1999: 182). Country context, the business environment and sector, role of the founder, size and geographic dispersion of the organisation, and its HR practices, all influence organisational cultures.

It is a common theme in the literature that leaders have a key responsibility for building and sustaining organisation culture, but that unless culture, structure, systems and jobs of the organisations are 'aligned', culture is likely to regress. Hendry (1995: 129–31) explains that typical recommendations are to do with applying a series of 'levers' to culture change:

- identify the behavioural requirements for effective performance
- then make those work behaviours central to the organisation's selection, training, development, rewards and appraisal systems (Parker et al., 1994: 2)
- then reinforce those behaviours in a set of values that typify the work environment.

Such an approach is often associated with developing competency frameworks that can help build and embed the required new behaviours.

However, any purely rational, systematic approach to tackling culture change has to be treated with caution, given the rootedness of culture at its deepest level in largely inaccessible cognitive structures (we will discuss such structures in Chapter 7). Sparrow and Hiltrop agreed that recruitment, induction and initial training can help to shape a workforce culturally, and that further cohesion can be promoted by financial and non-financial reward and development systems; but they emphasised the limits to what can be achieved. The outcome is at best likely to be a gradual steering of cultural change. Attempts to change culture can also have perverse effects. Some interventions may encourage behaviours that result in an improved organisational ability to respond to current challenges, but at the same time may lead to the 'skilled incompetence' to which we referred in our discussion of barriers and aids to knowledge creation in Chapter 3, thereby reducing ability to adapt rapidly to unpredictable external changes. In sum:

> Organizational culture is manageable, but only with extreme difficulty. (Sparrow and Hiltrop, 1994: 248)

The Global Practice Leader at the Gallup (polling) Organisation used blunt language about HRD and culture change:

> Almost all the money that organisations invest in leadership and management training is wasted. (Buckingham, 2001)

Between 1999 and 2001 Gallup had conducted research into the views of 1.7 million employees in 195 countries across the world about factors they felt most affected their productivity. The findings indicated that no organisation – not Marks & Spencer, not Shell, not the Disney Corporation, not Virgin – has a coherent culture. Rather, organisations 'contain as many cultures as they do work groups'. The survey suggested that training to embed or change culture is generally wasted, since it does not create, in every local work group across the organisation, the kind of conditions that stimulate productivity:

You cannot impose a productive culture from the centre. All you can do is try to teach leaders, managers and supervisors how to engage employees and then measure the results. (Buckingham, 2001: 40)

Findings emerging from opinion surveys and other diagnostic instruments that rest mainly on self-definition need to be treated with caution. A particular problem has been identified in researching training and development, where 'there seems to be a persistent discrepancy between what organisations say they are doing on training and the actual training efforts that can be observed on the ground' (Brewster et al., 1994: 234). That point is often made in the HRD literature. Certainly the true outcomes of 'shaping' can be hard to determine. Even where the appearance of a 'unifying culture' does exist, the reality may be a compliant but low-morale workforce, or an uneasy state of truce while the parties regroup (Gouldner, 1965). That kind of reality is frequently the outcome of a fractured psychological contract between employer and employees such as we discussed in Chapter 2.

However, strong subcultures do exist within organisations, often reflecting functions and hierarchies such as managerial, sales and marketing and professional, technical and scientific groups (Sparrow and Hiltrop, 1994: 247). Cultural 'capacities' can thus vary across the organisation, determining the extent to which there is, or is not, shared understanding of what the company stands for and often leading to the problems of culture change to which Buckingham (2001) referred.

What is really at issue is a failure to prepare for culture change. Many research studies demonstrate the importance of context. One such was reported by two UK researchers, Terry and Purcell (see Research example 5.1).

What is significant in Terry and Purcell's research is that, in each of the seven organisations they studied, the new HR practices were applied differently in order to respond to each organisation's unique needs and situation. They interacted with other elements of organisational context to produce gradual culture change in the workplace. The key elements of organisational context to which they had to adapt were:

- top management's vision of the organisation
- the way that vision is communicated and reinforced
- management style and actions across the organisation.

Research repeatedly shows the importance of these three factors in determining the impact of HR practices on culture (Hendry, 1995; Patterson et al., 1997). The effectiveness of HRD in contributing to culture change thus rests on HRD practitioners' alertness and responsiveness to new needs in the workplace, on their ability to raise awareness of the need for a culture of learning and what that means in practice for managers and other employees, and on their production of relevant interventions that can form part of culture's new context. To do this, they require a deep knowledge of culture, its roots and type of impact on workplace behaviours and performance. They must be able to identify any aspects of organisational context (including HR practices) that may interact negatively with HRD interventions proposed in order to change culture. They must be effective business partners, skilled communicators, and proposers of strategies to increase motivation to learn across the organisation.

To summarise: culture's roots go deep and wide. They are embedded in history as well as in current practices, and are shaped by powerful forces both within and

Research example 5.1

Seven organisations seeking 'leanness'

During the 1990s Terry and Purcell studied seven organisations in the UK that were restructuring in order to become more competitive by achieving greater leanness, knowledge creativity and flexibility. They found that the values of 'leanness' and 'responsiveness' were key elements of an organisational vision that it was essential for all employees to share, if the organisations were to make progress in increasingly challenging business environments. However, they also found that the style and actions of some of the line managers and team leaders were inconsistent with that vision. In some cases this was because they were inadequately trained for their new responsibilities, in others because those responsibilities were not clearly identified.

To resolve this problem, seven key HRM practices had to be put in place:

- communication processes to explain the strategic purpose behind restructuring
- team structures and technology to spread knowledge across the organisation
- competency frameworks to identify and foster behaviour needed
- career structures to provide life-skills and employability
- reward systems, often group-based
- systems for monitoring and measuring performance, including appraisal
- training interventions, especially for team leaders, to equip them with the skills

needed to manage team members as well as products.

These HR practices made new responsibilities and structure transparent, and provided appropriate support mechanisms for them. However, what proved crucial to success was a positive interaction between leadership's vision, management's style and actions in the seven organisations, and the HR policies and practices that were introduced. Through this interaction the organisations were able to 'invent responsiveness for themselves – from within the history and culture of the organisation' (Terry and Purcell, 1997: 46, 47). That interaction produced a workplace context that influenced people's attitudes, performance and learning there through time and so shaped the development of a new culture.

In each firm, organisational context manifested itself structurally through human resource policies and the employment system: for example through job descriptions, through planning and information systems and networks, and through performance and reward management, training and development processes. It manifested itself culturally in a set of developing norms, values, narratives and practices that increasingly grew to typify the daily work environment.

Source: Terry and Purcell, 1997

beyond the organisation that can be highly resistant to planned change interventions. The processes most likely to stimulate change are those that act indirectly on the context that has shaped, and continues to shape, workplace culture.

The Learning Organisation concept

While aiding culture change has long been a key task for many HRD functions, it is the building of a learning culture that, as we have seen in previous chapters, is one of the main challenges facing the HRD function in a more knowledge-based economy. In Part II of the book we will explore this challenge in detail. Here, it is relevant to briefly discuss the concept of the 'learning organisation' (LO), since it focuses strongly on how to build a workplace environment focused on learning (Senge, 1990). It emphasises the value of work-based learning in developing individual and collective learning capability, and provides guidelines, or building blocks, to develop a climate of trust, openness and challenge to facilitate that task. The guidelines identify tasks for, and resources needed by, managers, trainers and learners in this endeavour (Pedler et al., 1991; Burgoyne, 1999). Action learning is one approach within the LO concept (Revans, 1969; Morris, 1991).

The LO concept and attempts to implement it in practice have been much debated (see Coopey, 1995; Argyris and Schon, 1996; Harrison, 1996, 2002: 386–9). Here, it is relevant simply to observe that evidence of the existence of learning organisations is hard to find (Tjepkema et al., 2002), and the concept is perhaps best treated as an aspirational vision. At a more fundamental level, the practitioner literature is vulnerable to the charge that it focuses on learning and problem solving to the virtual exclusion of knowledge as a linked but distinctive process. When knowledge is treated only as a commodity, with its processual nature ignored or underplayed, the complex and often problematic relationship between learning and organisationally valuable knowledge creation is also ignored. Yet as we will show in Chapters 7 and 8, that relationship lies at the heart of so called 'organisational learning'.

The LO concept has many advocates in the field, and has a proven value in arousing interest in the idea of a learning culture. Its practical guidelines offer a starting point to managers and their teams in developing a shared language of learning and common ownership of the learning process. However, a number of scholarly commentators agree that:

> To the extent that the idea of 'organisational learning' remains problematic, the idea of 'learning organisations' cannot be said to be capable of operationalisation in any meaningful sense. (Sambrook and Stewart, 2002: 183)

At this point we have produced an assignment in Appendix 1 that you may like to tackle. Before doing so, the following reflection should be helpful.

Reflection

- It is common to focus culture change programmes on leadership development and on cross-functional training and development. What do you think is the rationale for such a focus?
- What other approaches to building a new learning culture in the workplace would you suggest, and why?

PROMOTING WORKPLACE LEARNING

Workplace learning as competitive resource

In a knowledge economy, workplace learning that is embedded in the process of production and is integral to the way in which work is organised has been memorably described as:

the new form of labor because it enables an organisation to achieve the expansion of knowledge that is one of its principal purposes [and resides] at the core of what it means to be productive. (Zuboff, 1988: 395)

As Stevens explains (2001: 1), workplace learning has a long history. As we saw in Chapter 4, what is new is the extent to which it is becoming recognised as a crucial source of competitive advantage that can produce the higher levels of innovation and customisation needed as customers become more discriminating and as competition becomes increasingly globalised. The management and development of people needs to place particular emphasis on technical competence and closeness to the customers in organisational scenarios where computerisation facilitates large increases in productivity, autonomous teamworking, flatter structures and more accessible knowledge management and learning systems (ibid).

We explore in detail notions of knowledge-productive learning in Part II of this book, and examine the impact of new technology on learning processes and on the HRD function in Chapter 10. At this point, it is relevant only to briefly introduce the kinds of learning most likely to lead to the two outcomes that, throughout this book, we stress as key determinants of organisational capability in a knowledge economy: continuous improvement and radical innovation.

Engestrom's (1995) typology (or classification system) of learning is well known. It distinguishes between adaptive, investigative and expansive learning, each presupposing a different type of relationship between learner and context. Its adaptation by Guile and Young (1999) is pertinent here because they added two further dimensions that draw attention to the importance of work-based learning. The first is the negotiated character of learning as a form of social practice, and the way in which 'opportunities to participate within workplace cultures influence whether and how we learn'

Table 5.1   *Typology of learning to support the development of learning organisations*

Type of learning	Focus of learning	Mode of learning	Outcome of learning
'adaptive'	acquired previously	formal HRD programmes 'mastery' of new unknown concepts or ideas tertiary or higher education access to Web sites/multi-media/books.manuals etc	concepts/ideas motivation to apply concepts/ideas to practice
'investigative'	collaborative activity/ risk-taking	participation in workplace 'community of practice' participation in 'distributed communities of practice'	shared understanding of concerns development of 'knowledgeability' continuous evolution of practice
'reflexive'	critique of context and practice	participation in 'communities of practice' using external resources to critically interrogate context and practice	production of new knowledge production of new knowledgeability transformation of social and material practice

Source: Guile and Young, 1999, pp. 15–16. Reproduced with permission

(an issue we will discuss in Chapters 7 and 8). The second is the resources needed in order to support such learning.

Guile and Young use the term 'reflexive learning' to indicate organisations' capacity to ask fundamental questions about 'their own internal relationships as well as their relationship with their environment, other organisations, and society as a whole' (ibid). They contrast this kind of learning with adaptive learning that does not change existing conventions or paradigms, and that therefore leads to continuous improvement rather than to radical innovation. Their typology focuses on the workplace as a site where social as well as human capital can be developed (see Table 5.1).

We have seen in Chapter 4 that across countries much of the attention of funding providers, managers and trainers is on formally planned learning in or adjacent to the workplace. There is an urgent need for a stronger focus on informal learning processes and outcomes, and, as Guile and Young's work shows, on integrating informal learning with planned training and off-the-job vocational education in order to maximise the value of all modes for both the organisation and individuals. In a knowledge economy workplace learning is becoming a complex and demanding area of concern that presents another key challenge to the HRD function and its practitioners.

Reflection

■ What is meant by 'informal workplace learning', and how does it differ from learning acquired through training or educational programmes?

■ What kind of attention is paid to informal learning in your own organisation? How far, if at all, is it recognised as contributing to organisational performance or to competitive advantage?

DEVELOPING MANAGERIAL AND LEADERSHIP CAPABILITY

In Chapter 3 many questions were raised about the validity of the whole concept of 'management' in a knowledge economy. That is something to which we return in Chapters 8 and 9. At this point we restrict ourselves to reflecting on the management development implications of the strategising, organising and HRD processes discussed thus far in the book.

Improving the strategising process

It has long been argued in the literature that if an organisation's strategy-making process is to realise its potential to give unique competitive advantage then management training and development (MTD) should be used as a strategic tool to link management capability with the strategies of that organisation (Wissema et al., 1981; Sisson and Storey, 1988; Hart and Banbury, 1994). Strategising, as we saw in Chapter 2, represents a dynamic learning process that operates at all organisational levels. MTD interventions can have multiple levels of impact on that learning process.

We have emphasised in our discussion of strategising the need to develop an inclusive process that draws on a wide range of human potential in order to overcome organisational inertia and negative outcomes of internal dispute, and to ensure wide-ranging knowledge and challenges to accepted norms. The learning population encompassed by MTD must therefore comprise a critical mass of those who give the firm its strategic capability. Across most of today's flatter and reengineered organisations it is the management team rather than the chief executive that most affects the quality and outcomes of strategic management (Bates and Dillard, 1993). However, we are not just discussing here the formal strategic decision-making process. The Asea Brown Boveri case study (Case example 3.3) that concluded Chapter 3 showed the vital contribution of the strategic roles carried by middle management and team leaders to tasks of knowledge creation, innovation and increased market sensitivity. In an emerging knowledge economy the capability of these personnel needs particular attention, since it connects vertically and horizontally with the knowledge structure and strategic management of the firm.

Many contextual factors have a direct impact on the strategising process. Culture is of primary importance here, and other factors with direct implications for the skills and the disposition needed by strategic managers and leaders at all levels include the strategic goals and type of firm (Goold and Campbell, 1987; Floyd and Wooldridge, 1992, 1994), its stage of growth, and the degree of turbulence in its environment (Ansoff and Sullivan, 1993). Because the precise nature of the strategising task in changing organisational forms is hard to define and organisational contexts vary so widely, there is great uncertainty about the nature of strategic management skills and therefore about the most appropriate focus and content for MTD interventions. It is not the acquisition of operational competence that is at issue here, but the development of those broader, higher level capacities that are involved in strategising. There is no consensus in the literature as to how they form, interact, or can be measured (Marsick, 1994; Mintzberg, 1994, 1994a). A reliance on simple lists of attributes or competences is dangerous because it can oversimplify the innately integrated work of managing (Mintzberg, 1994).

An illustration here relates to the oft mentioned capacity to 'think strategically' – a term that refers to the continuous process of synthesising of hard data with soft insights, of intuition and creativity. Mintzberg (1994a: 107, 108) sees the outcome of this process as 'an integrated perspective of the enterprise, a not-too-precisely articulated vision of direction'. However, how to express the process clearly enough to enable clear targeting in MTD remains unclear. While few question the importance of the exercise of judgement, intuition, mental elasticity, abstract thinking, tolerance of risk and ambiguity and other holistic skills, there is a continuing and inconclusive debate about the extent to which these are discrete skills or interrelated synergistic capacities – and about how to generate the mindsets and disposition to use them in a strategic context. This latter point is particularly important because success as an operational manager or the mere attainment of a senior position do not of themselves guarantee strategic ability. Even those individuals who do show potential may not have the disposition to develop or use their skills (Bates and Dillard, 1993). What is needed is an approach to learning and development that achieves an effective combination of competence and disposition in those who have to exercise strategic roles at different organisational levels.

When discussing barriers and aids to knowledge creation in Chapter 3, we noted that one important lesson from research is that while managerial learning can be a powerful stimulus to performance in the short term, it becomes dysfunctional when it results in a skilled incompetence. Such 'simplicity' prevents the generation of radically different strategies to guide the firm for the future (Argyris and Schon, 1978;

Levinthal and March, 1994; Inkpen and Choudhury, 1995). One clear essential is to equip managers and leaders across the organisation with a future-oriented set of competencies:

> As cost and quality advantages have lost their potency and the life cycle of technical skills continues to shorten, then the importance of effective (HRD) systems that can reduce the time to develop managers and resource organizations with managers who have a set of capabilities that are both flexible and attuned to the strategic pressures facing the organization becomes paramount. (Sparrow and Hiltrop, 1994: 426)

Perhaps the most important lesson from strategy research, however, is that strategising is a dynamic multi-level process that is not only influenced by context but also itself shapes that context:

> What occurs at one level affects and is affected by what occurs at the other levels ... The purpose, management systems and informal organization of the firm are influenced by the outcomes from the very actions and decisions that they seek to influence. (Chakravarthy and White, 2002: 198)

Since members of an organisation both individually and collectively make decisions at all organisational levels that affect strategy's ongoing outcomes, and since these decisions are not just rational but are also driven by intuition and emotion – an area that is under-researched – then in that fundamental sense all organisation members have a formative influence on the strategy process (ibid: 199). Training and development that seek to improve 'strategising' only by interventions aimed at formal managers and leaders in the organisation, rather than also by some collective developmental processes, will not achieve their desired ends. Nor will interventions focused only on the rational, excluding the emotional and intuitive realm.

Improving the organising process

We saw in Chapter 3 that as new structural forms are introduced there are important consequences for the organising skills needed by managers. The pressures that lead to restructuring include 'increased market and competitive pressure equalizing the number of management layers in organizations, a requirement for higher levels of workforce commitment, higher levels of communication, consultation and empowerment associated with redesigned business processes, and a requirement for more collaborative organizational cultures' (Sparrow and Hiltrop, 1994: 313). As structural complexity increases, as new management networks develop, and as organisational boundaries become more blurred:

> The paradigms that managers are using to make decisions about the organization structure are shifting markedly. The levels of structural tension within organizations and the levels of change and uncertainty are rising. This is creating the need to resource organizations with different sets of skills and competencies. (Sparrow and Hiltrop, 1994: 314)

Stress on the importance of organising skills is a central feature of Whittington and Mayer's extensive review of research and practice in organising for a knowledge economy (2002). They found that while about 20% of the top 50 UK firms were

Case example 5.1

Reorganising at Procter & Gamble

With (the increasing) pace of change, organising becomes a critical skill and capability for the enterprise. There is a lot at stake ... The upside of reorganising can be very substantial. But the costs and risks are high too. In 1999, the new Chief Executive of Procter & Gamble, Durk Jager, launched a new more globally integrated structure labelled Organisation 2005. Full implemen-

tation of Organisation 2005 was expected to take six years and cost $1.9 billion ...

By the summer of 2000 the reorganisation was seen as a failure and Durk Jager had lost his job. Organising skills and capabilities were something that Procter & Gamble under Durk Jager seemed to lack.

Extract from: Whittington and Mayer, 2002: 3

engaging in large-scale reorganisations every year in the early 1990s, between 1995 and 2000 the average had climbed to above 30%. 'The average big business today can expect to reorganise in a major way roughly once every three years' (Whittington and Mayer, 2002: 3). While emphasising formal structure's potential as a major value-adding feature, they note the downside: destruction of value where there is a lack of organising skills and capabilities (see Case example 5.1).

Whittington and Mayer conclude that only when organising initiatives are launched in the right context, and are supported by appropriate capabilities and conduct, can successful consequences be expected. This means that current and potential managers and team leaders need to understand the historical roots of current structural arrangements and of learning and knowledge in the firm before deciding how best to organise for the future, or how to implement organising decisions in the workplace. As the Asea Brown Boveri case (Case example 3.3) demonstrated in Chapter 3, top management must be the creators of vision and the stimulators of organisational renewal, working with middle managers on the entrepreneurial activity that will produce new dynamic capabilities for the business. In decentralised organisations where entrepreneurial success depends on the efforts and expertise of front-line teams and individuals, middle managers must also be skilled horizontal integrators of strategies and capabilities.

Improving the HRD process

Many managers in decentralised organisations have to take on significant HRD responsibilities and should be building and sustaining 'learning cultures' in their workplaces. It is not enough for HRD professionals to help these personnel to acquire the skills that they need. They must also know how to stimulate their motivation and give them continuing support in carrying out what can often seem to those pressured by a target-driven daily work routine to be irrelevant tasks that do not add value. The acquisition of HRD skills without the willingness or disposition to perform them will not produce an effective delegation of HRD responsibilities to the line.

Formal or experiential learning?

There has always been debate about the relevance of formal off-the-job programmes in the development of managers, especially those holding or preparing to take on strategic roles (Taylor, 1991). Business strategy, whether at corporate or divisional level, is so shaped by internal and external context that many argue for MTD to be organisation-based and grounded in managers' ongoing strategic tasks. Research into learning processes undergone by successful directors of businesses has highlighted the superior contribution to their own development that many of them claim for on-the-job experience and powerful role models as compared to formal learning (Mumford et al., 1987). Further weight has been given to that argument by those who identify the core of managers' work as an incremental, often intuitive activity characterised by 'messy processes of informal learning' that are carried out by people who are 'deeply involved with the issues at hand', and from which strategies vital to the business can emerge (Mintzberg, 1994a: 107,108). There needs to be a guided apprenticeship in such work since:

> much of the time, organizational events and processes are so complex, scattered and uncoordinated that no one can fully understand – let alone control – what is happening. (Bolman and Deal, 1991)

There is also doubt about whether formal programmes can achieve the fundamental shifts in mindsets that are needed by managers and leaders who are new to their role or who are moving to a higher level, especially when there is evidence to show that radical change in mindsets may emerge spontaneously rather than by being caused in a direct, linear way by a given intervention (Tosey, 1993: 188; see also Levy, 1994 and Von Krogh et al., 1994). This takes us back to the uncertainties still surrounding the nature of knowledge structures and cognitive processes – an area we will explore further in Chapters 7 and 8. Some argue that formal MTD programmes cannot make any significant impact on the higher level and contextualised skills that managers need as they move into increasingly complex organisational roles (Taylor, 1991: 277).

However, the powerful impact of the firm's dominant managerial logic on managers and team leaders at all organisational levels suggests, in our view, a unique role for formal programmes. When carefully designed and imaginatively delivered, they can aid unlearning and new learning. They can help to stimulate radical breaks in managerial routines and mindsets that can promote innovation in thinking and in action. Such programmes should focus on the corporate goals, strategies and strategic management processes of the organisation. They should incorporate both adaptive and reflexive learning (see Table 5.1) in order to help managers and team leaders to understand not only the present context of their roles, but also how to evaluate the relevance of current organisational goals and strategy given any major new external challenges (Harrison and Miller, 1999).

We conclude that:

■ In today's newer organisational forms, formal planning skills are needed by most managers and team leaders across the organisation. These and other skills that relate to discrete operational tasks can be quite clearly defined and targeted in formal MTD programmes, and can be continuously developed in the workplace through exposure to new business processes and routines, and through HRD processes including mentoring, coaching and action learning.

- There is much still to be determined about the precise nature of the higher level, holistic and synergistic capacities involved in strategic management work, and about the processes that link managerial learning, dominant logic and organisational intelligence to strategic management capability. However, the dominant logic or mindset of the firm, which is to do with the way in which leading managers conceptualise the business and make critical allocation decisions, has a very significant influence on management attitudes and behaviour across the organisation (Prahahlad and Bettis, 1986). The culture and strategic type of the firm, together with its stage of growth and the degree of turbulence in its environment, also strongly condition the nature and direction of strategic managers' work, especially at unit level.

- The key contribution made by higher level, holistic and integrative skills to the effective performance of those carrying strategic roles at any organisational level, coupled with the embeddedness of those skills and roles in organisational context, produces a powerful argument for focusing the development of current and potential managers and team leaders primarily on on-the-job experience, coaching, counselling and role modelling.

- However, formal programmes can make a unique contribution to the development of strategic capability at all organisational levels. They can provide a complementary educative process to programme participants' ongoing development through their organisational experiences and routines. They can also utilise the very distance that they provide between those participants and their organisational context to stimulate critical reflection and the development of new insights and knowledge.

Summary

In this section on the management and leadership development challenges for the HRD function and its practitioners, we have suggested that managers and team leaders need to develop many new skills and attitudes if they are to master strategising, organising and HRD processes relevant to today's changing organisational forms, and that they can be helped by MTD that carefully integrates on- and off-the-job learning processes. At this point, with much still to consider in Part II of the book about management roles in a knowledge economy, we make tentative proposals only about their main developmental needs:

- an understanding of the strategy process that will stimulate the generation of new responses to new challenges, and produce challenges to dominant logics that have begun to stifle innovation and organisational progress
- skills to introduce and operate strategy process modes that are most relevant for their own organisation, and to monitor utilisation and outcomes
- a deep knowledge base and variety of expertise in order to devise appropriate responses to new challenges and opportunities 'out there'
- a high absorptive capacity for recognising the need to change. This involves recognising the value of new external information, assimilating it, and applying it to improvement and innovation in processes, products and services. This capacity can be developed particularly through social networks and boundary spanning and calls for high-level skills in those areas

■ the ability to work with their teams and with others across functions, organisational levels and increasingly across organisations themselves to increase the variety of their firm's dynamic capabilities by identifying and supporting new ideas rather than just exploiting existing routines. This involves double-loop learning skills and the political ability to successfully challenge current operating assumptions

■ the motivation and ability to work in partnership with all organisational members in developing a learning culture that will provide the knowledge needed to produce, apply and sustain those capabilities through time

■ the motivation and ability to handle effectively whatever HRD responsibilities they may be required to carry, especially in decentralised organisations and in new organisational forms.

At this point we have produced a second assignment in Appendix 1 that you may like to tackle. Before doing so, the following reflection should be helpful.

Reflection

■ Lack of effective strategy in an organisation can be due to many causes. Which cause seems to you to be the most fundamental one here, and why?

■ The process whereby strategy is developed and agreed, and the kinds and numbers of those involved in that process, have a decisive effect on strategy's quality and its practical outcomes. What kind of strategy process seems to predominate in your organisation, and how effective do you see it to be?

CONCLUSION

In this chapter our aim has been to identify some of the key challenges facing HRD in organisations operating in an increasingly internationalised and knowledge-based economy. We have found that, providing there is clarity within the organisation about HRD's role, meaning and focus, the key challenges then become:

■ achieving strategic thrust through integration of HRD strategies with current business and HR strategies, coupled with a focus on building future organisational capacity for superior speed, flexibility and knowledge creation

■ facilitating culture change and building a knowledge-productive learning culture

■ promoting high-quality workplace learning processes that will unleash the asset value not only of human but also of social capital

■ helping to develop managerial and leadership capability that will aid processes of strategising, organising and HRD in newer organisational forms.

These challenges therefore form the agenda for Chapter 6, where we explore how far they are being recognised by HRD practitioners and what kind of practice currently characterises the HRD function across countries.

chapter six

HRD: The State of Play

INTRODUCTION

In Chapter 5 we found that providing there is clarity within the organisation about HRD's role, meaning and focus, the key challenges for the HRD function then become:

- achieving strategic integration and thrust
- facilitating culture change and building a learning culture
- promoting workplace learning processes that build social as well as human capital
- developing managerial and leadership capability to operate in changing organisational forms.

These challenges form the agenda for this chapter, where our aim is to explore how far they are being recognised and tackled by HRD practitioners across countries. We take each challenge in turn and examine how far and in what ways HRD strategies and practices are being used to respond to it. We conclude by identifying the skills and roles that HRD practitioners need if they are to respond effectively to these challenges.

ACHIEVING STRATEGIC THRUST THROUGH INTEGRATION

Converging HRD strategies

We have seen in previous chapters that internationalisation and the increasing globalisation of businesses are leading to more convergence in organisations' business strategies. This is producing more convergence in HRD strategies also. Sparrow and Hiltrop found in 1994 that a higher level of foreign direct investment and the impact of mergers and acquisitions entail a need for longer-term training plans and often result in an increased training load as new strategic and business plans have to be communicated and new teams built. Radical changes in employment patterns emphasise the need for employee and work practice flexibility, and therefore for cross-functional training and enhanced management skills. HRD in international businesses, and in those entering or operating in international markets, is concerned less exclusively with management training and development, more with a broad-based coverage that is increasingly prioritised around the areas of people management, the accommodation of new technology and the management of change (Sparrow and Hiltrop, 1994: 362, 425). Figure 6.1 illustrates the forces at work here.

The 2002 European HRD research project also indicates that there are now more similarities than differences apparent in HRD strategies and practice across Europe, the US and Japan (Tjepkema et al., 2002). Changes in HRD professionals' roles seem also to be very similar across Europe and in the US, although rather different in Japan where line management, not a specialist HRD function, has always been the major partner in employee development (ibid).

The researchers identified four different types of HRD strategies in use – although not always in common use – in the 'learning-oriented' organisations that were surveyed:

■ Strategies supporting the business in general, or supporting specific current business objectives.

■ Strategies supporting informal learning and knowledge sharing, including examples of:

  ■ learning from each other (for example through mentoring, coaching, projects, learning groups and networks, secondments and benchmarking activity)

  ■ IT networks to support knowledge sharing

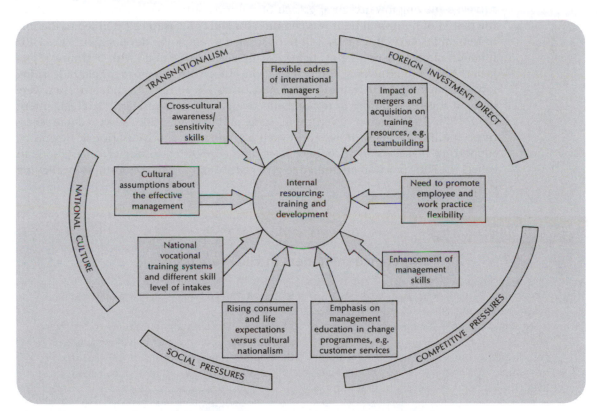

Figure 6.1   *The factors influencing change in training and development*

Source: Sparrow, P. and Hiltrop, J.-M. (1994) *European Human Resource Management in Transition*. Hemel Hempstead: Prentice Hall. Figure 10.1, p. 362. By permission of Pearson Education Limited

- fostering employee responsibility for learning through personal development plans, open learning centres and other ways of encouraging self-regulation and linking work and learning
- supporting team and 'organisational' learning.

- Strategies to provide training. These helped to develop a learning culture when used to ensure a foundation of competence and to stimulate motivation for learning.
- Strategies to change HRD practices and structures, including examples of:
  - decentralising the HRD function
  - supporting management in HRD tasks
  - increasing employees' responsibility for HRD
  - the professional development of HRD practitioners. Significantly, though, this strategy was identified in only one of the 28 companies in which case study work was carried out, and there was no evidence from the questionnaire survey of a further 165 companies that the professional development of HRD practitioners is a widely used change strategy in Europe (Tjepkema, 2002).

Strategic integration

Survey responses and case study data gathered by Tjepkema et al. (2002) thus revealed clear attempts by HRD professionals to ensure that the HRD function achieved both horizontal and vertical fit, with most of the 200 or so learning-oriented organisations surveyed moving towards an approach of full integration as a business function. On the matter of horizontal fit, it was common for HRD's focus to be extended to the role of human resources in general, not to be limited to employee development. The HRD function rarely bore that name, being usually given a title to do with 'training' (Tjepkema, 2002: 158). However, where it was concerned with the broader field of learning rather than only with training, HRD and other HR initiatives and processes were brought together in order to respond effectively to the organisation's strategic intent (ibid: 157). On the matter of vertical fit, some of the organisations surveyed had objectives specifically relevant to HRD such as enhancing organisational flexibility, supporting managers in their new roles, and supporting customer orientation. In others the HRD function attempted to give general support to the business by aligning

---

Research example 6.1

Competence managers in HRD functions

'Competence managers' is a term used to describe managers who work in an HRD capacity to support people managers in the business. They operate as a kind of internal job agency, ensuring each business project has the necessary employee competencies to fulfil its objectives. They support employees by ensuring that all have personal and career development plans. They are also responsible for analysing compe-

tencies that the organisation needs now and for the future.

Ericsson, the telecommunications company, uses three types of manager in its Research and Development division: competence managers, operational managers and process owners.

Source: Ter Horst and Tjepkema, 2002: 118–19

its activity with the thrust of business goals (ibid: 159). Research example 6.1 relates to the use of competence managers.

However, while the 2002 European HRD research project's data showed a definite move in most of the learning-oriented companies towards an integrative approach to HRD, the researchers found no evidence that such integration was being widely achieved. Although HRD professionals consistently identified that supporting business objectives was a key goal for them, in reality their involvement in that process did not seem great. The most significant findings to emerge here were that:

- The envisioned role for HRD in most of the companies surveyed was not ambitious and training was still a key task (Tjepkema, 2002: 171).
- Few HRD professionals evaluated their contribution to the organisation on a strategic level. Many evaluated the training courses that they provided, but few did more or were expected by their organisations to do more.

  This weakness is consistently identified in research into European organisations. While acknowledging the difficulty of measuring the effectiveness of HRD, especially in relation to informal learning processes, commentators regard this as one of the most important areas to tackle, given the increasing emphasis on training and learning in most European countries (Larsen, 1994).

- Many HRD professionals who might wish and know how to acquire a more strategic role were being constrained by too little time to update materials, and develop new initiatives, and by scarce resources (including staff) (Tjepkema, 2002: 171).

A future thrust

In discussing issues of 'fit' in Chapter 5 we noted the need for HRD to contribute to the building of organisational capacity for superior speed, strategic and co-ordination flexibility, and knowledge creation. The strategies in use in the learning-oriented organisations surveyed in the 2002 HRD project showed only a limited awareness of this need. When senior HRD professionals were asked what key challenges they saw to be facing them they identified (Tjepkema et al., 2002: 1–2):

- relating HRD to business objectives by linking it to corporate goals
- finding new ways to support work-based individual and collective learning process, paying less attention to training related to closing specific skill gaps, more to other types of learning intervention that are focused on continuous improvement and innovation for the long term
- creating learning partnerships in setting learning objectives and supporting learning processes as an ongoing and integrated part of daily organisational life.

While noting their emphasis on business-focused HRD, on promoting continuous improvement and innovation, and on a generalised support for workplace learning, the researchers uncovered few very innovative HRD practices dominated by new initiatives such as knowledge management networks, stimulating a learning climate in the workplace or a widescale use of new technology and blended learning in order to achieve greater rapidity and effectiveness of learning (an issue we will discuss in Chapter 10). There was a focus on knowledge sharing, but not on knowledge creation.

It is particularly worrying that the HRD professionals in general expressed no expectation that a significant change would occur between strategies they were using now in their organisations and those they would be using in the future. There was also a lack of clarity about what their future role might be, and a lack of awareness about the need for learning to be actively promoted in their organisations. The researchers concluded that in learning-oriented organisations across Europe:

> There is a need for HRD professionals to ensure the development of a strategic role, to clarify their functional role, develop the new skills required ... and more clearly demonstrate their value and contribution to organisational success. (Sambrook and Stewart, 2002: 187)

If this is the case in organisations that espouse a learning orientation, does it apply to organisations more widely? We cannot provide a definitive answer to that question, but other research does offer some important insights, as the next section shows.

Centralisation or decentralisation?

One crucial indicator of a fully integrated HRD function is ownership of HRD by line managers, with any HRD specialist staff playing a supporting, facilitating role. However, in the 2002 European HRD research project the data indicated a relatively high trend to centralise the HRD function (Tjepkema, 2002: 161). Yet almost a decade earlier, the 1994 Cranfield HRM survey (Brewster and Hegewisch, 1994) had revealed a marked trend across European organisations generally to decentralise HRD responsibility to line managers.

Has HRD become more centralised over time? Or do the differences in sampling frames and scope confuse the issue? The answer to the first question is uncertain, and to the second is probably 'yes', but there are two key points to make here. One is that generalised trends in any activity can hide 'very great differences' from one country to the next – and they did so in the Cranfield survey (Larsen, 1994: 118). The other is that in sampling any activity it is essential to measure start as well as finish points.

In the countries surveyed in the Cranfield survey, line management responsibility was found at the end of a three-year period to be at its highest level in the group of countries comprising Turkey, Portugal and the Nordic countries, and at its lowest level in France, the UK and the Netherlands (three of the seven countries subsequently included in the 2002 European project). But that picture changed when account was taken of the levels of line management responsibility for HRD across countries that had existed at the start of the three-year period. It then became clear that in both groups of countries the HRD function had undergone a marked devolution to the line over that period. The level of devolved responsibility was much lower in 1994 in France, the UK and the Netherlands than in the other group of countries only because it had been extremely low three years before (Larsen, 1994).

In a similar way, the data revealed that at the end of the three-year period line management responsibility for HRD training was lower than for the HR processes of pay, recruitment, health and safety, and workforce adjustments, but that a greater increase in devolution of training responsibility had taken place during those three years than of any other HR functional area. This seemed to be due at least in part to 'the closer link between performing a job and benefiting from the spin-off effect in terms of learning. As line management is traditionally responsible for monitoring job performance, they also have the key to experiential learning on the job' (Larsen, 1994:

119). Workplace learning, in other words, was becoming recognised by 1994 as an integral part of the line manager role, even though in absolute terms levels of centralisation of HRD remained quite high.

Larsen further observed that training and development was the highest ranking main objective of HRM in all countries covered by the Cranfield Survey except Finland, but that companies were experiencing difficulty in establishing a close link between business strategies and HR strategies because of an increasingly unpredictable environment. This was making business forecasting and therefore human resource planning difficult, especially in service and knowledge-based organisations with immaterial resources and products. Implementation and costing of training was also often problematic, typified by a non-systematic approach. Where HRD is seen to be increasingly vital to the success of the business, yet where it is also increasingly difficult to plan and organise at local organisational level for whatever reason, a trend to regain control of HRD by centralising rather than by continuing to decentralise would be logical.

It seems reasonable to conclude that the data gathered in the 1994 Cranfield European HRM survey indicated a generalised awareness of the need for full integration that would 'create a synergy between the training and development of the individual employee, development of business strategies and plans, and development of the organisation' (Larsen, 1994: 121). There was increased decentralisation of HRD to line management and the aim here seemed to be an increased integration at operational levels of the business. The data gathered in the 2002 European HRD research project may indicate that such integration had not been effective. If it had not, then this, coupled with corporate management's appreciation both of the increased importance of learning and development processes to competitive advantage and of the even more complex and uncertain business environment, could have led to the maintenance of quite high levels of centralisation of the HRD function in organisations across Europe.

Reflection

■ Four kinds of HRD strategy were identified in the European research project we have just discussed. What kind of HRD strategies can you identify in your own organisation?

■ How far are your organisation's HRD strategies likely to enhance its speed, flexibility and knowledge creation?

BUILDING A LEARNING CULTURE

Lack of learning cultures

We have already seen in Chapter 3 (and we will explore this further in Chapter 8) how 'the locus of innovation is found in networks of learning' (Leadbeater, 2000, in Stewart and Tansley, 2002: 19). We saw in Chapter 5 that a learning culture is crucial to build and operate such networks, and is therefore essential to an organisation's competitive capability. Contributing to the creation and maintenance of a learning culture is a key challenge for HRD professionals.

The 2002 European HRD research project findings showed that in the learning-oriented organisations that were surveyed, HRD professionals were involved in supporting a variety of culture change processes. However, few were actively helping to build learning cultures and there was a widespread lack of such a culture. This was manifested particularly in a general lack of motivation on the part of managers and/or employees to take on new learning tasks or engage actively in learning processes (Tjepkema, 2002: 172–4). Work pressures on employees and HRD professionals contributed to this situation but did not appear to be its fundamental cause.

A learning culture is a major source of support for the HRD function. Larsen (1994) found in his review of HRD practice across European countries that few weaknesses in HRD activity seem fatally to damage the function in organisations where there is a culture supportive of learning and development. He identified a worrying lack of ability to produce detailed future plans and a non-systematic approach to implementation and costing of training, yet he did not find evidence that these weaknesses significantly reduced the function's acceptance in such organisations. It is therefore all the more disturbing that in the 2002 research study, even in the very types of organisation where a high level of HRD expertise and proactivity should be expected, there seemed to be so little attention to building learning cultures.

Developing a learning culture

It is by no means clear from the research either of Larsen in 1994 or of the European HRD research team in 2002 how such a culture can be developed. The 2002 project revealed that while in theory the main rationale for all the organisations surveyed to become more learning-oriented was to achieve greater responsiveness to customer needs, in practice those that had adopted a learning culture seemed to have done so not as a result of the analysis of any objective body of evidence, but as an act of faith. Once a learning culture was established, that act of faith usually proved sufficient to overcome most obstacles of time or resource. Sambrook and Stewart (2002) detailed the case of Royal Mail in the UK, where time was made for scheduling learning events in work time and in the workplace despite strong pressures of shift work and daily targets.

There seems to be a conundrum here: it takes a learning culture to produce a learning culture! But on closer examination what is really at issue is context. What the 2002 European HRD research project uncovered was that a learning culture in the workplace tended mainly to develop where there was a combination of contextual factors that, in their interaction, began to work on culture at its various levels gradually, with a new culture emerging through time. Key contextual factors included (Tjepkema, 2002: 174–5):

■ a strong push to innovation in the workplace
■ new structures that provide employees with new possibilities for linking work and learning, for example through increased contact with customers, through team-working and through learning networks
■ top management that was active in establishing and communicating new organisational vision and values
■ clarity on HRD's new role related to learning, plus positive results of new HRD initiatives.

However, where this combination of factors had occurred it did not seem to have been the result of forethought and the researchers were not optimistic about the extent to which the HRD professionals surveyed were, as a body, prepared or preparing to play a key role in promoting and supporting lifelong learning (Sambrook and Stewart, 2002: 186). They tended to agree with Raper et al. (1997) who found in their own research that often the true motive for changes in HRD tasks and interventions seemed to be that of reducing training budgets and scaling down central training departments. Drivers for change in learning processes at work usually related more to product market and technological change than to conscious support for any new learning philosophy.

So there are three lessons for HRD practitioners here:

- They need to become deeply knowledgeable about the culture process and about the drivers of culture change.
- They must be able to work in partnership with other HR colleagues and with managers across the organisation to build an organisational context conducive to the development of a learning culture in the workplace.
- They need to be alert to internal and external changes that are likely to open the door naturally to a new culture of learning in the workplace, and must know how to utilise that opportunity to promote culture change.

Research example 6.2 is an illustration of the latter scenario.

Such examples show how once the work organisation changes in the workplace, old learning strategies and routines often become redundant. A new philosophy about

Research example 6.2

Knowledge-productive teams in the workplace, the Netherlands

In the Netherlands the impact of intensified global competition has led to downsizing, the increasing use of self-organised teams and an increase in the knowledge intensity of production (Mulder and Tjepkema, 1999). New ways of organising work have led to many shopfloor workers having to take greater responsibility for the control of work flow and work processes. There have been movements towards task group structures, task rotation in the group and adherence to stricter safety requirements, not to mention the increased drive towards quality. These are all changes with implications for the process of learning at work and they are covered by sectoral and often at sub-sectoral collective agreements that are moderated at company level. Research reported by CEDEFOP (1996) identified common trends across sectors that involve increased on-the-job learning, with supervisors acting as an instructor as well as workers learning from each other – similar trends to those identified in the UK by Raper et al. (1997), and exemplifying a 'learning to learn' culture.

As a result of these changes workers' responsibilities increase beyond their traditional boundaries and they start asking questions of each other and at the same time resolving problems with each other. This process enables employees to become 'an enquiry centre' for each other, and to provide information about specific issues when requested. Workers are provided with further incentives for learning since they become the individual owners of skills and knowledge. In this context, reflection-in-action has now become 'part and parcel' of many production jobs, while learning is being regarded as an integrated component of the modern organisation of work (Mulder and Tjepkema, 1999).

Reproduced with permission from: Chartered Institute of Personnel and Development. (2001) *Workplace Learning in Europe*. London: CIPD, pp. 36–7. Available to download: www.cipd.co.uk

learning may not have caused that redundancy, but once the redundancy becomes evident, such a philosophy is likely to emerge. Through time, and helped by skilful HRD interventions and facilitation, it can then inform the development and embedding of a new workplace learning culture.

PROMOTING WORKPLACE LEARNING

Practice across Europe

It will have already become clear from the research findings reviewed in this chapter and in Chapter 4 that in many countries, despite the strategic importance of informal workplace learning situated in communities of practice, the focus on that learning is wavering and insufficient. Research also shows the quality, relevance, coverage and impact of formal learning provision in the workplace to be very mixed, as Case example 6.1 demonstrates. It relates to practice in the UK, where in 2000

Case example 6.1

Improving workplace training and education in the UK

In the UK, the National Learning and Skills Council established in 2001 plans to deliver some £7 billion per year into workplace training and education. To qualify for a share, an organisation must demonstrate that it meets the qualifications and competency requirements that are a condition of funding. Currently, few are doing so. In 2002 employers across the UK were urged to reassess their work-based training after a report by the Adult Learning Inspectorate (ALI) revealed that six out of 10 providers are delivering an inadequate service. Only one of the 298 providers inspected was judged to be outstanding. Lack of funding was a contributory factor in some cases, but the report painted a damning picture of the quality of work-based training in the UK, detailing a catalogue of failure with only a third of participants completing a modern apprenticeship qualification. Leadership and management was criticised and 31 providers lost their contracts.

The Chartered Institute of Personnel and Development, in its 2001 professional standards, produced a revised Certificate of Training Practice and a new suite of professional 'learning and development' standards to improve the competence of those with responsibilities both for formal and informal learning and knowledge processes in the workplace (CIPD, 2001a, and can be downloaded from www.cipd.co.uk). The 2001 National Occupational Standards in Learning and Development have a strong focus on tasks related to formal workplace learning (these can be downloaded from www.empnto.co.uk). They cover:

■ managing the training and delivery process
■ planning and developing integrated programmes of work-based training
■ identifying trainees' abilities and needs in relation to programmes of work-based training
■ providing appropriate work-based training opportunities
■ supporting trainees and monitoring progress against an agreed training plan (for example through mentoring)
■ assessing trainees' achievements on work-based programmes
■ monitoring and evaluating effectiveness of work-based programmes
■ developing and monitoring professional competence.

Source: Harrison, 2002: 394–6

there were around 100,000 training practitioners engaged in formal workplace learning activity.

Stern and Sommerlad (1999) provide a thorough analysis of the state of informal and formal workplace learning in changing market conditions across the globe. Their review confirms the mixed quality of workplace learning processes and activity, although it also provides examples of innovative workplace learning practice that constitute helpful benchmarks for improvement.

The role of standards

It is common to many of the recent VET reforms across Europe that the content of VET courses, as well as workplace training and assessment, is based on occupational competency standards (Gonczi, 1999: 180). What differs across and within countries is how and by whom competency standards are conceptualised and developed, and how they inform educational curricula. In the UK, for example, both national occupational standards and professional standards cover the field of human resource development, but their conceptual and philosophical bases, the way in which they were generated, and their educational implications for those entering or already operating in the HRD field are significantly different (Harrison, 2002: 161–9).

The UK's national occupational standards in 'Learning and Development' that are referred to in Case example 6.1 derive from functional analysis. Their underpinning philosophy is that of the traditional systematic training cycle, where the core tasks are analysis of needs, planning, design, delivery and evaluation of training at different organisational levels. The standards relate to the existing spectrum of tasks considered by a broad body of training and personnel professionals and employers consulted between 1999 and 2001 to typify today's training and development activity (Harrison, 2002: 157–69). The CIPD standards, on the other hand, emerged from role analysis that incorporated perceptions not only of HRD practitioners but of others in their role sets about the present key activities of those practitioners and also about challenges anticipated in the future.

The national standards' focus on present rather than on future anticipated scenarios helps to explain why (unlike the CIPD's 2001 standards) they contain no explicit reference to tasks that are to do with the development or sharing of organisationally valuable knowledge. They emphasise workplace learning, but as the case example shows, the focus of attention there is on how training in the workplace is managed, co-ordinated and assessed in order to improve performance. This is a traditional perspective on workplace learning. It reflects a preoccupation with human rather than social capital, and with the achievement of the organisation's present goals rather than with building its future capacity.

There are two distinct views about the impact of standards on a field of practice. Some argue that an excessive reliance on them can encourage a compliant and backward-looking approach, stifling experimentation, innovation and challenges to prevailing norms. Others argue that, especially in a field like HRD that is characterised by much poor practice, standards are a vital aid to raising basic levels of competence, and depending on the way in which they are drawn up and applied, they need not do this at the expense of creativity and adaptability. Another point of relevance here is the importance of the process whereby standards are produced. This provides an opportunity for reflection on a field, and the discussions it involves constitute a vital attempt to move the whole profession forward. Therefore as many different stakeholders as possible should be part of the process.

Research example 6.3

Workplace learning: progress in Europe

The majority of European countries have begun to certificate learning taking place outside formal education and training institutions, including informal learning in the workplace. Portugal is developing a system based on agreement between the social partners that makes it possible for individuals lacking formal qualifications to have their actual competences assessed.

The UK's system of national vocational qualifications does this, though it tends to concentrate on hard skills. The French are gradually increasing the number qualifying on the basis of professional experience, experience-based degree courses and vocational assessment in the workplace. Traditionally, the French levy system has placed considerable emphasis on measurable learning inputs and these are almost inevitably course-based rather than on-the-job. However, a new law on the validation of professional experience was approved by the French Parliament in January 2001. The implementation of the law is still in its early stages but several experiments have been developed for different systems of certification.

No European governments have moved as far as that of Singapore in making the link between workplace learning and work organisation. However, evidence is emerging of major European employers, particularly multinationals, moving to develop workplace learning activities. Examples of these include Siemens across Europe and Statoil in Norway. Many of these initiatives focus on the delivery of learning content via the Internet and particularly through e-learning initiatives. Major areas of growth in the UK are to be found in professional, managerial and technical occupations – for knowledge workers – and in the development of high performance work practices, linking extensive formal and informal learning to teamworking, problem solving, continuous improvement, coaching and mentoring. In these cases it is clear that while techniques and theory can be learned off-the-job, the development of the soft skills associated with the management of the job need to be developed in the workplace.

Reproduced with permission from: Chartered Institute of Personnel and Development. (2001) *Workplace Learning in Europe*. London: CIPD, p. 11. Available to download: www.cipd.co.uk

Changing focus on workplace learning

In Chapter 4 we compared workplace learning philosophy and major trends in a number of countries across Europe, in the US, in Japan and in Singapore. At this point it is helpful to look at what Stevens (2001) writes in introducing the CIPD's 2001 report into workplace learning (see Research example 6.3). The passage shows that although much still needs to be done to promote workplace learning as a key source of continuous improvement and innovation, there is currently an increasing level of interest and experimentation that holds out a promise for advance in the field.

At this point we have provided an assignment in Appendix 1 that you may wish to tackle.

DEVELOPING MANAGERIAL AND LEADERSHIP CAPABILITY

Identifying trends

Sparrow and Hiltrop (1994) in their review of trends in European HRM practice found that a major trend in businesses entering or operating in international markets was a broad-based coverage around the areas of people management, the accommodation of new technology and the management of change, with a consequent reduction in the traditionally strong focus on management development. In the UK, management training and development in most companies seems to have the chief priority, with coverage of other groups suffering in consequence. As we saw in Chapter 4, in many other Western countries there is trend to a more inclusive workforce coverage as new, flatter forms of structure are introduced, work practices featuring teamwork and project management become a central part of new patterns of work organisation, and collaboration across and between organisations becomes more critical to the production and deployment of dynamic organisational capabilities. In Japan, as we also saw, broad-based coverage of employee development has always been a central feature of development strategy.

The 2002 European HRD research project found that in the learning-oriented organisations surveyed, change processes being utilised included those related to changing management styles and improving the strategy development process. Some HRD professionals also mentioned tasks of supporting managers in their new roles (Tjepkema, 2002: 158–9), the case of 'competence managers' being one example of this. Overall, the sets of HRD strategies identified in the study suggest a fairly inclusive approach focused on the development of teams and of collective learning.

Only a few companies seemed to be developing skills of managers in HRD processes. Cunningham and Hyman (1999: 18) also found managers lacked preparation for HRD roles, and Larsen (1994) identified a need in most European countries for 'training programmes and other types of development by which the (potential) line managers can become acquainted with the new role' (ibid: 121). He saw this to be vital so that, in the workplace, 'the job becomes a setting for learning, and a synergy is created between job design and learning/development of the individual and the organisation' (ibid: 108).

All these are generalised comments, because it is not possible to gain any clear picture from research studies about trends in the training and development of managers, whether in learning-oriented organisations or in organisations more widely. Bournois and colleagues (1994) attributed this difficulty to the wide variety of management models and practice across Europe. Research by Filella (1991) identified at least three cultural models of management there: the Latin model (France, Spain and Italy), the Central model (Germany, the UK, the Netherlands and Switzerland) and the Nordic model (Denmark, Sweden and Norway). Although there may now be more convergence in the challenges facing managers across countries, cultural differences are still powerful differentiators of management practice and of development strategies. Career development and management succession are universal preoccupations, and there is a general attempt to equip managers to respond to common challenges of flexibility, competitiveness and teambuilding. The emphasis, however, in how that response is achieved varies very widely between organisations and across countries.

Implications for HRD practitioners

Given the contingent nature of the management development process, it is unsurprising that one message emerges consistently from the literature: managers' training and development must be driven by a deep understanding of the challenges they face, and are likely to face, in their particular organisations, and of the driving forces of change in their environments. HRD practitioners cannot act alone here. Their management development strategies must mesh not only with other HRD strategies but also with HR processes of recruitment, deployment, reward and career development. They must also be aligned with organisational needs and context.

When considering options for management and leadership development at whatever organisational level, HRD practitioners therefore should reflect with care on the following points:

- Such development must be tailored to context and to specific needs. It should never rely on standardised packages or prescriptions.
- Training is not necessarily the most effective vehicle for equipping managers and leaders in new roles or with new skills. It has a part to play, but greater emphasis needs to be given to problem-centred learning, learning emerging from the development of new business processes and routine, coaching, mentoring, e-based learning and support both from HRD staff and from centralised policies and procedures.
- Since in newer organisational forms and in knowledge-based environments managers' roles are increasingly to do with horizontal facilitation, integration and co-ordination of entrepreneurial activity and knowledge creation, the development of managers needs to be integrated with the development of the teams to which they belong, which they support, or with which they interact.

Reflection

- Setting aside technical issues to do with training and development design, delivery and evaluation, what are the main issues that HRD practitioners should consider in developing managers in an organisation?
- How are managers developed in your organisation, and how far is management development restricted to current or identified potential managers, or expanded to include other sectors of the organisation?

THE STATE OF PLAY: KEY THEMES

New roles for HRD practitioners

The findings of a recent report on 'Training in the Knowledge Economy' (Stewart and Tansley, 2002), covering a wide range of studies in the UK and across Europe, suggest that although companies rely increasingly on knowledge creation in order to gain competitive advantage and to work effectively in various collaborative arrangements, there is no significant move by trainers from their traditional roles as instructors or training providers in the workplace to new and more relevant roles of learning facilitators and strategic partners.

The 2002 European HRD research project echoed these conclusions. Similar evidence has also emerged from extensive research into HR activities that contribute to competitive success, conducted in the UK by Luton University's National Centre for Competitiveness. Its 'Developing a corporate learning strategy' project revealed that training and development 'are not leading to an output of intellectual capital' (Coulson-Thomas, 2001). HR directors were ranked tenth out of 13 functional roles for playing a significant or very significant part in intellectual capital management. 'Existing knowledge is being shared, but new knowledge is not being created (and) crucial areas of knowledge are being overlooked' (Coulson-Thomas, 2001). Too many programmes are standardised instead of tailored to address specific and critical requirements of the organisation. Too many HR professionals are 'following fashion rather than thinking for themselves', failing to connect with the changing world around them and contribute to the creation of new knowledge (ibid).

New tasks for HRD practitioners

In Chapters 3 and 4 we proposed some new tasks for HRD practitioners working in changing organisational forms and in an emergent knowledge economy. In the light of our review in this and the previous chapter, we now need to rethink and expand on those tasks and the roles that they suggest.

It is quite widely agreed that HRD professionals need to become learning facilitators, learning architects who can promote strategically valuable knowledge, skilled business partners and thinking performers – that is to say, expert and proactive practitioners whose actions are continuously informed by reflection on the outcomes of their past activity, on the real nature of the needs to which they are being asked to respond, and on the likely consequences of various options open to them (CIPD, 2001a; Stewart and Tansley, 2002; Tjepkema et al., 2002). The specific skills they need in order to respond to present and emerging challenges identified in this and the previous chapter are to do with:

- identifying and investigating the specific implications for learning and development in their organisations of an emerging knowledge economy
- proposing and working in business partnerships to implement business processes and developmental activity that will equip managers and team leaders at all organisational levels to fulfil their strategising, organising and knowledge-creation roles
- raising awareness at all organisational levels of the need in turbulent and knowledge-oriented environments for a workplace learning culture that taps into, shares and utilises explicit and tacit knowledge of organisational members, and promotes the continuous improvement and innovation that is vital to organisational survival and progress
- producing well-contextualised processes and practical interventions that can help to transform the workplace into a learning environment conducive to the creation, dissemination and value-adding utilisation of knowledge
- working with HR and managerial colleagues to build a developmental performance management process that will encourage and reward knowledge-productive learning
- working with managers and team leaders to ensure an inclusive approach to learning in the workplace, in order to access and share knowledge embedded in the grass roots of the organisational community
- stimulating, facilitating and supporting self-managed learning activities of all organisational members
- ensuring that they themselves undertake the continuing professional development that is necessary if they are to fulfil their new roles and responsibilities.

In Part II of this book we will uncover further tasks for those HRD practitioners who work in organisations aspiring to be knowledge-productive. This list of tasks therefore is of an interim nature, to be reviewed and finalised at the book's conclusion.

At this point we have produced an assignment in Appendix 1 that you may wish to tackle.

CONCLUSION

Our aim in this chapter has been to assess how well equipped the HRD function and its practitioners appear to be in relation to the tasks currently facing them and to those emerging in a turbulent business environment. We conclude with both positive and negative comments.

On the one hand, considerable innovation in HRD practice is being reported now by researchers across countries, much of it providing benchmarks that can be tailored to specific contexts. Particularly illuminating information can be found in Sparrow and Hiltrop (1994), Stern and Sommerlad (1999), CIPD (2001), Drost et al. (2002), Stewart and Tansley (2002) and Tjepkema et al. (2002). On the other hand, there seems to be a generalised failure to promote a learning culture in the workplace, to achieve full strategic integration for HRD and evaluation of its organisational impact, and to promote high-quality workplace learning both in informal and formal modes. The position about management development is unclear because of wide variations in needs and practice across countries, but the tasks for HRD professionals here are clearly demanding. They are very much to do with integrating the training and development of managers with the development of the whole workforce in order to achieve higher levels of collective flexibility, adaptability and knowledge creation. Although knowledge creation is a key task in an emerging knowledge economy, most HRD practitioners, like their HR colleagues more widely, do not seem to be occupying even the low ground here.

The 2002 European HRD research project uncovered evidence of a particularly surprising lack of a learning culture in organisations that espouse a learning orientation. Context is a key issue here. Given a context where top management vision and values, management style, work practices and HR processes and activity interact positively to support learning in the workplace, then a culture of learning is likely to develop and be sustained. Where context is unfavourable or where HRD practitioners are passive, culture change interventions are unlikely to take root. For example, employees are unlikely to find credible any attempts by management to persuade or require them to take more control of their own learning and development if they are working in an organisation where the psychological contract between employer and employees is fractured. As we saw in Chapter 2, that condition is now quite common. Where it prevails, expecting employees to take charge of their learning runs the risk of being seen as abdication rather than delegation of responsibility – the same kind of ambiguity that is attached to attempts by top management to 'hand over HRD to the line' while at the same time stripping out specialist HRD expertise in the business and failing to support line managers in their new HRD role.

Overall, having reviewed practice in the HRD field across countries, we are forced to the conclusion that, even in organisations that espouse a learning orientation, the HRD function is not well equipped to meet current challenges. In Part II of the book we examine in detail what is needed to build and sustain knowledge-productive organisations, the new tasks involved for HRD practitioners here, and some frameworks and practices that can give them help in developing their expertise and in taking the HRD function forward in a knowledge economy.

part two

Building Knowledge-Productive Organisations

chapter seven

Notions of Knowledge

INTRODUCTION

In Part I of the book we focused on the changing world of work and learning. We looked at theories and processes of strategising, of organising, and of human resource management and development. We have seen that in a shifting competitive and employment landscape and an emerging knowledge economy many factors now combine to highlight the need for continuous improvement and radical innovation. Organisations have to be increasingly knowledge-productive to survive.

However, such statements disguise uncertainty. What exactly is knowledge? How does the knowledge process operate? How can the organisation's 'knowledge base' that we discussed at the start of Chapter 2 be developed or renewed? There are no clear-cut answers to such questions, nor any sharp boundaries between the various schools of thought. While information about 'knowledge' is plentiful there is still no agreement about how it forms, grows and changes in individuals or collectively. In Part II of the book we focus first on notions of knowledge, exploring a variety that explain some of the confusion surrounding knowledge management in organisations, and the challenges facing human resource (HR) professionals entering that field. We then propose ways of building and sustaining a knowledge-productive organisation, discuss current research approaches in this field and some of their outcomes, and conclude by reviewing innovations in the harnessing of new technology to workplace training and learning.

Our aims in this chapter are to explain some major theories about knowledge in its organisational context, and to identify the practical implications of each for approaches to what is loosely called 'knowledge management' (KM) in organisations and for HR policies related to KM initiatives. We discuss four linked yet discrete notions of knowledge:

- knowledge as control
- knowledge as intelligence
- knowledge as relationships
- knowledge as commodity.

We frame the notions in organisational metaphors, borrowed from Gareth Morgan whose rationale in this provides our own:

> The use of metaphor implies a *way of thinking* and *a way of seeing* that pervade how we understand our world generally … When we say 'the man is a lion' we use the image of a lion to draw attention to the lionlike aspects of the man. The metaphor frames our understanding of the man in a distinctive yet partial way. (Morgan, 1997: 4, italics in original)

Having examined the four notions and evaluated their theoretical bases, we provide a case study that helps to pull key issues together. We conclude by identifying tasks for human resource development (HRD) practitioners related to the knowledge process in their organisations.

Reflection

■ Given your own understanding of 'knowledge' at this point, how would you explain the concept to a child who has no precise understanding of the term? What metaphors might you use to help you here?

■ Use dictionaries and text books to identify two contrasting definitions of knowledge. What does each tell you about the concept, and in what fundamental ways do they differ?

KNOWLEDGE AS CONTROL

The organisation as machine

Imagine the organisation as a machine. Then picture knowledge as the engine that enables the machine to be controlled. The notion of knowledge as control is grounded in a belief that the possession and application of scientifically ascertained facts and formulae offer a way of avoiding arbitrary decision-making, inefficiency and incompetence. The assumption is that, given good information and communication processes, it is possible to acquire perfect knowledge and embody it in organisational design, roles and tasks that can then be used to regulate organisational life and human performance.

Scientific management

The notion of knowledge as control informed the classical theories of management and organisation that were developed from the late 19th century onwards. Those theories have exercised a profound influence over management theory and practice that is still apparent today.

Pioneering engineers of the Industrial Revolution, notably Taylor (1856–1915) Gilbreth (1869–1924) and Gantt (1861–1919) worked at the exhilarating onset of a scientific 'age of reason'. Their body of work on scientific management embraced the scientific process as a way of bringing under control the disorderliness and inefficiency that they often encountered in industrial organisations. Amongst the key processes to which they applied scientific principles and methodology were selection, training, rewards, job design and division of labour.

They looked to the new science of psychology (Watson, 1924) for the design of tests to select those with superior intellectual attributes – who could then be allocated to managerial roles – and those with superior manual skills, who could then be allocated to skilled and semi-skilled jobs. Taylor saw this basic division of labour into higher order functions of planning, organising, directing and controlling, and lower order operating functions to be logical and fair:

> Under scientific management, the 'initiative' of the workmen (that is, their hard work, their goodwill and their ingenuity) is obtained with absolute uniformity and to a greater extent than is possible under the old system (while) … 'the managers assume new burdens, new duties and responsibilities never dreamed of in the past'. (Taylor, in Pugh, 1971: 124)

To achieve an equally logical and fair system of work, 'objective' facts about every shop floor task and its elements were obtained by scientifically conducted observation and assessment of the performance of the most skilled workers. This information was then converted into 'a science for each element of a man's work, which replaces the old rule-of-thumb method' (ibid). Systematic training was used to 'insure all of the work being done (is) in accordance with the principles of the science which has been developed' (ibid). Financial rewards tied to the achievement of set performance targets acted as a further conditioning process.

Administration theory

The notion of knowledge as control also informs the writings of those who developed general design and operational principles to govern large complex organisations in public and private sectors – principles to do with line and staff relationships, span of control, functional specialisation and the management of professionals (Follett, 1941; Urwick, 1944; Weber, 1947; Fayol, 1949; Jaques, 1952). The principles were intended to eliminate barriers to effective and efficient performance at all organisational levels.

As an aside at this point, it is worth noting that Weber was unique among classical management theorists in having a radical humanist perspective on organisational life that is more characteristic of today's post-modern approaches than of those early theories. As a social scientist he was a concerned but sceptical observer of organisations, seeking to understand the principles that enabled large, complex human systems to conduct their business efficiently and to survive over the long term. He concluded that bureaucracy, of which he saw the Catholic Church as a prototype, came closest to fulfilling those requirements. He catalogued its features while making clear its shortcomings, given the inevitable diversity of people's needs, motives and behaviour. Much of his thinking is implicit in the relational approach to knowledge that we discuss later in this chapter.

In classical administration theory, organisation structure follows a pyramidical design in which all the core knowledge about the organisation is held at the peak, and authority to apply different areas of that knowledge is delegated downwards throughout the system along formal lines of authority. A key principle is of knowledge as a body of facts that, once captured and recorded in files, manuals and personnel procedures, controls all decision-making, all performance of roles and tasks and all interactions between positions, functions and levels. Knowledge in this sense is seen to offer a more impersonal and durable informational and regulatory system than could be achieved by other means. Its systematic application to selection, training and other personnel processes is intended to ensure objectivity and consistency of judgement through time and across functions. The central concept is that authority lies in the system, not the person, and is 'legalised' by being exercised strictly in accordance with knowledge that is codified and then stored in organisational memory.

Reflection

- Consider any bureaucratic organisation in which you have worked or that you know about.
- How far, and why, do you think that it is an effective organisation?
- What do you see to be its main weaknesses, and what are their fundamental causes?

Overview: knowledge as control

In the notion of knowledge as control there is the taken-for-granted assumption that all organisational members will become bound together in a shared concern to achieve the organisation's goals providing that all are controlled by clearly defined roles and tasks, by formal objectives, by logical procedures, and by incentives and rewards administered according to 'the rules'. The notion is rooted in that unitary frame of reference that we discussed at the end of Chapter 2 and that remains a powerful driver behind much theory and practice today, notably in the human resource management field. We can trace the influence of the notion of knowledge as control in processes of selection, deployment and assessment of staff that rely heavily on psychometric testing, in the application of the systematic training cycle methodology to the production of training standards and to the planning, design and delivery of training activity (see Chapters 5 and 6), and in reward systems that are dominated by individualised and task-related incentive schemes.

The writings of social scientists from the time of Elton Mayo (1933) onwards have revealed that the application of purely rationally based theory, underpinned by an exclusive focus on the economic goals of the business, has never been able to resolve – and indeed has often exacerbated – those many organisational problems that stem from the non-economic needs and motives of people at work. The elevation of the scientific process and its dominating influence over organisation and management theory throughout most of the 20th century have consistently downplayed its innate uncertainties and its vulnerability to human agency.

KNOWLEDGE AS INTELLIGENCE

Think now of the organisation as a brain or as an organism. Both metaphors suggest the notion of knowledge as intelligence that enables adaptation to environment. This notion derives particularly from cognitive theory and open systems theory.

The organisation as brain

If we imagine the organisation as a kind of collective brain, we can picture knowledge as the intelligence that enables it to make informed decisions about how to achieve its

Table 7.1   *The cognitivist view of knowledge*

The aim of knowledge: to solve problems presented by the outside world and so enable adaptation to it with increasing ease

---

■ Information processing produces in the individual sets of representations, or bodies of concepts, opinions, beliefs and remembered experiences about a particular object or domain (Codol, 1984).

■ They become the frames that the individual uses to interpret each new piece of information, each new situation and experience. They are stored in the individual's knowledge structure, where they become part of a unique 'cognitive map'.

■ Existing knowledge is applied to new situations, some similar, others not-so-similar, to those encountered in the past. In the process it is either confirmed, or becomes redundant as new knowledge develops.

■ 'Experts' help by showing how to apply knowledge collected in one context to another. Subject or technical experts, including trainers, are thus vital carriers and interpreters of knowledge.

---

primary task, given the nature of its environment. Researchers such as Simon (1956) and Cyert and March (1963), influenced by economics, by cybernetics theory and by cognitive psychology, were interested in exploring the organisation as an information processing system that could produce high-quality knowledge to fuel decision-making. Research has continued into the cognitive structures that help to explain the ways in which strategic decision-makers interpret and respond to their competitive environments (Gioai and Poole, 1984; Walsh et al., 1988; Porac et al., 1989; Harris, 1994; Hodgkinson and Johnson, 1994).

There are many cognitive theories, but in the early 'cognitivist' viewpoint the function of cognition is the creation in the individual, and in the organisation, through accurate information processing, of increasingly 'truthful' representations of the external world. In this view, knowledge is produced basically in the way pictured in Table 7.1.

As Table 7.1 makes clear, the traditional cognitivist portrays knowledge as 'abstract ... and oriented towards problem solving' (Von Krogh et al., 1994: 57). In early cognitivist theory, knowing and doing were assumed to be separate activities, and knowledge was thought to be formed and developed in essentially the same way collectively as in the individual: by the 'brain' using logic to produce the 'truth' about observed phenomena, building up an increasingly perfect base of knowledge through time.

The concept of bounded rationality

The early open systems theorists admitted that, in practice, information-processing, whether in the individual or collectively, does not function perfectly, and that decision-making processes can never be fully 'rational' (Simon, 1955, 1956; Cyert and March, 1963). Simon was one of the first authors to explain in detail the limitations to the concept of 'rational economic man' and to claim that decisions are not 'arrived at by a step by step process which is both logical and linear' (Miller et al., 1999: 44).

Such writers concede that in business organisations economic rationality repeatedly breaks down in the confusion caused by conflicting interests and by diverse perceptions as to 'what matters here' and how to tackle it. This 'bounded rationality' is attributed to ambiguous, excessive, incomplete or unreliable data, incompetent processing or communicating of information, pressures of time, and differences in individuals' cognitive processes, mental maps and reasoning capacity (Simon, 1955; Cyert and March, 1963). Decision-making is further limited by the complexity of modern organisations, and the power-play that goes on within and around them (Silverman, 1970). Because the strategic arena is the one in which unfamiliar, difficult and organisationally critical situations regularly occur, bringing with them a high price for players, it is there that 'rationality' can come under its greatest pressures (Miller et al., 1999: 45).

The organisation as organism

Early decision-making theory treated the organisation as a relatively closed system. Open systems theory draws heavily on biology and physics, and envisages the organisation as a type of organism that survives through successful interaction with its environment.

Socio-technical theory

Early systems researchers working in an organisational context such as Simon (1956), Katz and Kahn (1966), Perrow (1967), and Beer (1980) made connections between the ways in which living organisms functioned as a series of adaptations to an often hostile environment, and the behaviour of organisations as social systems. Those who drew particularly on psychology and economics, such as Trist and Bamforth (1951) and Emery and Trist (1960), saw the key to an organisation's success in achieving its primary task to lie in ensuring a productive balance between its social and its technical subsystems. They therefore stressed the need for management, personnel and work practices that would build good human relations in the workplace and the delegation of sufficient control to employees over their tasks to ensure satisfactory levels of motivation and performance.

Chaos theory

In later systems theory the influence of physics has focused attention on the organisation as a learning system that, in conditions of turbulence, can sometimes produce radically different knowledge from that used in the past, thereby enabling the organisation to transform itself. Levy (1994), whose work draws on the science of complexity and in particular on chaos theory, sees parallels – although imperfect ones – between the behaviour of business organisations and of physical systems. He finds it enlightening to conceptualise business organisations operating in flux (continuous and uncertain change) as chaotic systems. In such systems, history cannot repeat itself and therefore old routines and learning quickly become redundant.

However, such systems do trace repetitive patterns. They cannot be precisely predicted, but the conditions in which they are most likely to occur can be identified, as can their likely paths. Levy suggests that in a similar way, although organisational knowledge and the strategic recipes that it has produced become redundant in the face of unfamiliar and rapidly changing external conditions, useful lessons can still be learnt from history. They are lessons about the extent and nature of the organisation's past adaptive capability. Knowing what kind of coping strategies and learning processes the organisation has used successfully in response to unpredicted change can suggest generalised ways forward for the organisation now. This is essentially the point that was made in Chapter 3 where we discussed the extent to which an organisation's future 'absorptive capacity' and capability for knowledge creation are shaped by its current learning and knowledge processes and by their historical path.

In Levy's view, disorder can have a positive function in relation to knowledge creation. It should not be dismissed out of hand as the result of 'inertia, incompetence or ignorance' (ibid: 172). Others have expressed the same view, speculating that if some organisations that subsequently became commercially successful had not initially been 'able to "muddle through" without prematurely embracing any one type of strategy, they would not have succeeded in the long term' (Carroll, 1987, quoted in Starkey and McKinlay, 1993: 13). Turbulent conditions can prevent complacency and rigidity and can thereby work against the 'skilled incompetence' that stifles fresh thinking and the development of radically new skills and strategies in a hitherto protected or stable environment. In such an environment there is sometimes 'little conscious search for better methods of making decisions, however manifest the importance of the decision' (Cray et al., 1994: 203).

However, 'muddling through' produces human tensions. What may later prove to have been generally beneficial 'disorder' may be experienced at the time as intolerable uncertainty. In the view of the researchers of the Ford Europe case discussed in Chapter 3 (Case example 3.1), transformation at Ford was only achieved by the sustained vision and purpose of corporate leaders in ensuring the pursuit across Ford of 'often painful learning to undo existing patterns of thought and behaviour' (Starkey and McKinlay, 1993: 2).

Stacey (1995: 487), another writer influenced by chaos theory, likewise warns that human problems can be acute where 'disorderly dynamics of contradiction, conflict, tension and dialog provide the driving force for changeability'. In knowledge-intensive organisations especially, the pressure to continually innovate, the uncertainty of work patterns and routines, and the decentralisation of structure and decision-making carry with them the danger of loss of balance between operational and creative activity until strategic coherency breaks down and the firm's employment system becomes fractured. Negative human behaviours can then prevent the operation of the shared learning and knowledge processes on which the survival of both the organisation and its workforce may depend.

Reflection

■ What do you see to be the main difference/s between the view of human behaviour held by classical management theorists, and that held by systems theorists?

■ What kinds of HR policies do you think would be *unhelpful* for organisations operating in turbulent conditions where knowledge sharing and knowledge creation are essential tasks?

Overview: knowledge as intelligence

Early notions of knowledge as intelligence may seem to offer a less deterministic approach than that found in scientific management theory. However, they too emerged from what has been called a 'positivist' view of the world. They too are underpinned by the assumption that knowledge is 'out there', and can be captured by good information collection, processing and communication. The taken-for-granted importance of the economic driver and of a superordinate goal remain the same also, although approaches to the management of people and work differ. These early notions likewise yield important insights into the ways in which training and other human resource practices can be used to ensure the effective adaptation of employees to the goals and strategies of the business.

More recent theories about knowledge as intelligence, drawn from chaos theory, offer quite different insights. They suggest that conditions of external and internal 'disorder' do not necessarily inhibit organisationally valuable knowledge creation. In certain circumstances they can actually stimulate it. However, they indicate that for this to happen:

■ The organisation will need an 'absorptive capacity' that enables it to cope with uncertainty and to be adaptable in the face of high levels of turbulence. That capacity does not emerge overnight: it has to be consciously developed through time. It is a core competence for organisations that need to be highly knowledge creative in rapidly changing environments (Cohen and Levinthal, 1990).

■ As part of that capacity, those who work in and for the organisation will need to be skilled at 'learning to learn', and to have a particular mastery of the kind of investigative and reflexive learning that we discussed in Chapter 5 (Table 5.1).

■ Organisational leadership, a culture of openness combined with radical questioning, and conducive human resource policies will be needed to provide the drive, support and recognition that are essential for organisational members if stress levels are to be reduced in unstable situations. Without them, negative behaviours in the workplace are likely to put barriers in the way of organisationally valuable knowledge creation. Organisational context should be of a kind that encourages entrepreneurial behaviour while helping it to operate to the benefit of the collective whole.

These tentative conclusions are very much in line with those that emerged from our discussion of 'strategising and organising' in Chapters 2 and 3. They show a need for new approaches to the tasks of leadership, management and human resource professionals. They present a perspective on knowledge that associates it closely with collective as well as individual and group learning capability, and they indicate learning in the workplace as a crucial source of knowledge that can add value for the organisation. They are linked in many ways to the notion of knowledge that we discuss next: knowledge as a relational process.

At this point we have provided an assignment in Appendix 1 that you may wish to tackle. Before you do so, the following reflection should be helpful.

Reflection

■ Consider an organisation that you have worked in or read about that features a high level of knowledge work and that operates in a very competitive environment – for example a financial services firm, or a management consultancy. What signs of stress can you identify, and what outcomes do they appear to have for knowledge sharing and knowledge creation in the workplace?

KNOWLEDGE AS RELATIONSHIPS

The organisation as culture

Imagine the organisation as a culture, a society with its own identity and history whose values, norms and behaviour change through time. Then picture knowledge as a process strongly shaped by relationships within this society. This notion of knowledge stems from a view of the world as a socially constructed state (Vygotsky, 1978; Daft and Weick, 1984). In this so called 'constructivist' view there is no objective reality, nor is there any objective knowledge. Both reality and knowledge are socially created and are sustained and changed by social interactions (Von Krogh and Roos, 1995: 63; Von Krogh et al., 1998: 43).

A relational notion of knowledge draws attention to the ways in which people experience and make sense of organisational life through a process of 'knowing' and the influence over that process that is exercised by context. It highlights the learning that is situated in workplace 'communities of practice' (Brown and Duguid, 1991). This 'situated learning' is seen as the vital source of organisational knowledge (Lave and Wenger, 1991; also Knowles, 1970; Kolb, 1984). Research example 7.1 is an outline of a well-known research study that portrayed the existence and operation of such a community.

Research example 7.1

The photocopier technicians

Orr (1990, in Spender, 1994: 399) researched photocopier technicians who had to repair machines in customers' locations. They had been given detailed instructional manuals and training to enable them to perform their tasks. They could have worked simply as individuals, each developing an independent understanding of how the machine in use differed from the machine imagined in the instructional documentation. However, they did not. Instead, they worked as a team in what Brown and Duguid, reanalysing this research in 1991, described as a 'community of practice'.

The technicians had many problems to deal with when they went out to different locations to repair machines. It soon became clear to them that those who had designed those machines had not taken account of the many different ways in which people would use them from one workplace to the next. Studying all the facts that could explain the various problems they encountered, the repairers shared the experiences from which they had learnt through time, and called on their intuitive understanding of the machines and of different patterns of usage. Using this 'tacit' knowledge (knowledge embedded deep in the individual or collective subconscious, expressing itself in habitual or intuitive ways of doing things that are exercised without conscious thought or effort (Nonaka, 1991: 102)) as well as their formal, or explicit knowledge that they had learnt from their training courses and instruction manuals, they produced repair solutions that fitted the social, as well as mechanical and technical, context in which the machines were being operated. They made up for the limitations of their formal knowledge by going beyond the documentation and their training in order to produce new knowledge (Spender, 1994: 399).

They drew particularly on their common culture, exchanging stories of similar problems they had encountered in the past and recalling how they had resolved them. This shared language and history helped them to bring their tacit knowledge to the surface and reflect on it.

Uncertainty, and the need to know, ultimately produced in the group new collective knowledge that owed as much to their social interactions as to their intellectual grasp of technical or mechanical issues. The way in which they produced, shared and applied new knowledge was thus both social and cognitive. Their repair solutions changed through time with the impact of each new experience and each new period of reflection on it.

Source: Orr, 1990, in Spender, 1994

The self-productive knowledge process

Among the theories grouped under the general heading of 'knowledge as relational', one branch of cognitive theory – autopoiesis theory – is particularly powerful. *Autopoiesis* is Greek for 'self-production' and refers to a system that 'contains within its own boundaries the mechanisms and processes that enable it to produce and reproduce itself. The biological cell is (an) ... example of an autopoietic system (Von Krogh et al., 1998: 105).

We have seen earlier in the chapter that in the cognitivist approach cognitive processes are explained by reference to an input–output transaction with the environment. In the autopoiesic approach, cognitions are thought to be created and continuously recreated in a self-productive manner (Maturana and Varela, 1980; Luhmann, 1986). Table 7.2 shows how the knowledge process is assumed to work.

We can see by comparing Tables 7.1 and 7.2 that the self-productive view of the knowing process makes clear distinctions between data, information and knowledge that are not to be found in cognitivist notions of knowledge. In this view organisational materials such as books, papers, lectures, presentations, and memos are merely

Table 7.2   *The self-productive view of knowledge*

The aim of knowledge: to give meaning to people's ongoing experiences and to other information that they receive

- Data are the smallest elements that can be gathered and put together to produce information. They are not to be confused with either information or knowledge (Von Foerster, 1984).

- Information is an interpretive process that then puts data in form, and knowledge is the outcome of that process (Huemer et al., 1998: 137).

- As new knowledge is formed, it then determines the kind of data and information that the individual selects as meaningful thereafter. Knowledge is not produced from a fixed base of existing knowledge that is added to cumulatively in time. It emerges continuously and in a dynamic manner. Each new experience has an effect on how the individual views and makes sense of the world thereafter, and how he or she collects and analyses data.

- The development of knowledge is also heavily dependent on the individual's social relationships and the context in which he or she lives and works, relying significantly on a shared recall and interpretation between individuals of past experiences and of a current situation (Huemer et al., 1998:140).

- 'Knowing' is thus a dynamic social and emotional process as well as one shaped by the individual's internal cognitions and memory.

data, not information. They do not directly change people's knowledge or under-standing, since many data are rejected or go unnoticed. It is not until data are selected and assembled in particular ways by human agency that they become 'information'. The ways in which that information is then used – and by whom – decide whether, in the end, new knowledge develops. In the self-productive perspective, knowledge is thus both a process (of 'knowing') and the product of that process.

Concepts of 'truthfulness' and 'accuracy' that are central to notions of knowledge as control and to earlier notions of knowledge as intelligence have no similar meaning in the self-productive notion of knowledge, because 'truth' is not seen as an objective 'out there' reality but simply what people believe to be true at the time. In the same way actions are not seen to be determined by the possession of 'accurate' facts: they emerge from personal and social beliefs and from the interplay of relationships, emotions and cognitions in each particular situation.

Building knowledge connectivity

In the relational notion, the individual's knowledge is most likely to have an impact on others when it is expressed in ways that he or she can easily understand. Its sharing and development will be aided by the use of familiar language, signs and tools, by linking it to familiar organisational stories, and to workplace myths and proverbs, operating procedures and techniques (Von Krogh and Roos, 1995: 63–4). Orr's story of the photocopier technicians demonstrates the ways in which 'languaging' can operate in a community of practice. It involves both verbal and non-verbal forms of commu-nication that help to make new information understandable and acceptable to others in a work group or across an organisation.

Appropriate 'languaging', however, is not enough to produce and sustain new know-ledge. There also needs to be a culture that encourages a spirit of enquiry, of challenge to established ideas and customary ways of doing and behaving, and a structure and commonality of purpose that enable and encourage groups to come together to discuss and reflect on new information and ideas. This enables 'knowledge connectivity': the connection of new to current knowledge, and the sustaining of that connection through time (Von Krogh et al., 1994: 61). In Chapter 8 we propose a framework to achieve such connectivity.

Reflection

Von Krogh and his colleagues (1994, 1998) explained the role of 'self-descriptions' in promoting the knowledge process in an organisation. Self-descriptions include mission statements, strategy documents, written histories of the organisation, symbols and narratives that recall its purpose and its unique history. They give the organisation its unique identity. They also provide examples for organisational members of the kinds of information and knowledge that matter and should therefore be collected and shared across the organisation. They act as filters in the information process.

■ Reflect on some of your own organisation's 'self-descriptions'. How far do you think they are successful in producing a shared understanding of the organisation's iden-tity and purpose among organisational members?

■ How far do you think they identify the kind of knowledge that organisational mem-bers should co-operate with each other to develop and share?

Institutional knowledge processes

So far, we have explored the notion of knowledge as a relational process by reference to human interactions within an organisation. It can also be expanded to include institutional relationships. We have referred to these briefly in Chapter 2.

Organisations occupying the same professional, sectoral or other territory seem to be held together by shared aspects of cognitions, by common frames of reference and by a shared generalised culture (Huff, 1982; Scott, 1995; Bood, 1996). This can lead to problems. For example, professional and sectoral networks allow transfer of knowledge across sectors but they can also prevent or distort transfer (DiMaggio and Powell, 1991). In the same way, as we show in Case example 7.2 towards the end of this chapter, workplace communities of practice in a company can inhibit the creation and sharing of knowledge across their boundaries when they are not held together by a sufficiently strong organisational purpose.

Many research studies now indicate that collective knowledge develops at the institutional level in ways similar to those in which it develops at the organisational level (Bood, 1996: 7). Most shared understandings seem to be formed through individual sense making at a strategic level that takes place in a social context. They can be triggered by changes in situations confronting organisations that compete or collaborate in the same business environment, or by changes in organisational and institutional knowledge bases used to interpret and make sense of those situations. The latter types of change can emerge from contacts with new general theories, from discussions and reflections with others, or from being confronted with others' understandings of the particular organisation and its environment (Stjernberg and Werr, 2001: 262). Such contacts are promoted by learning events such as conferences and leadership and management educational programmes, as well as by horizontal and cross-boundary structural linkages of the kind discussed early in Chapter 3.

A modelling process often helps organisations to learn how to cope with problems encountered in a shared environment. This process can also increase their interactions so that they mentally grow further towards each other – although depending on the strength and thrust of competitive forces this does not invariably happen. Benchmarking, best practice activity, generic strategic recipes and the influence of meta standards such as those mentioned in Chapters 3 and 6 exemplify a modelling process.

Overview: knowledge as relationships

The notion of knowledge as relational derives from two primary sources: cognitive theory and the social sciences. Scholars have expressed concerns about its research base, that is limited by an emphasis on qualitative rather than on quantitative studies, using unstructured and semi-structured interviews, and with some key studies that are of an anecdotal and small-scale nature (Hodgkinson, 1996). Allard-Poesi (1996) found in her literature review that the cognitive perspective has focused on the individual level, from whence it has been uncritically applied to the group and organisational levels of analysis. What (she asked) does collective learning actually mean? How far and how much must be 'shared'? What exactly does an organisational knowledge structure consist of, and how is it constructed and made manifest? Is it stable or a dynamic? Similar questions are posed regularly in the literature, but still remain largely unanswered (Scarbrough, 1998).

However, in the relatively early stages of developing new theories in a much debated field, it is inevitable that attempts to resolve old questions uncover new ones. Bertels and Savage (1998), in the opening chapter of a book dedicated to expanding the theoretical and empirical base of 'Knowing in Firms' (Von Krogh et al., 1998: 7–25), observe that 'honest probing is needed now, rather than glib answers'. Whatever the weaknesses of the research base, a substantial body of studies now throws light on the part played by practical, social and emotional factors as well as by individual cognitive process in the operation of the knowledge process. The insights that we have reported in this chapter coincide (as can be seen in Part I) with an increasing attention in organisations operating in a globalising knowledge economy to the relational implications of collaborative structures, of cross-boundary linkages within and beyond the organisation, and of innovations in workplace learning stimulated by the introduction of high performance working practices.

Organisation theorists have many concerns regarding a failure in the field to recognise the organisation as a complex social institution and the consequent lack of inte-

---

Case example 7.1

The knowledge-sharing initiative at Multicorp

The product development department of a multinational food producer, Multicorp, introduced Lotus Notes groupware system in 1995 in order to get about 1,000 company users across the world to use it to inform each other in real time about what was happening on various projects, and to help make tacit knowledge explicit by explaining their informal work practices in writing. The adoption of a new methodology of knowledge sharing called 'the funnel', together with the new information system of Lotus Notes, was intended to transform the work environment from functional and individual to more horizontal, networked and team based.

Structure, culture and HR practices

However, the change was introduced in a top-down, technology-driven way and the new work system caused much confusion. Although the company was well aware of the importance of building a culture to support knowledge sharing, management had focused on training people on technical aspects but not on preparing them for the organisational implications. The researchers conducted their study of the company over a three-year period and found that during that time the organisational structure was still arranged according to functions, despite the increasing emphasis on collective, cross-functional performance. The reward system remained geared to that structure, and selection and training processes were still conducted on the basis of role-specific competencies.

Problems with tacit knowledge sharing

One reason for the failure to share knowledge, especially tacit, was because people preferred to communicate in more traditional ways. The main reason, however, seemed to be a reluctance to commit their thoughts about work in progress to the new system, which they used only to record above-the-table progress, not incomplete ideas. In part this was due to the need to write out their thoughts in accessible English, a time-consuming process and one in which the very requirement to formalise experiences and practices caused much to be lost in the telling. The researchers drew two conclusions from this:

- that knowledge creation is a rather private act that some may wish for various reasons to keep to themselves

Case example 7.1 (cont'd)

■ that sharing knowledge involves changing it:

fabulous insights have to be turned into something more prosaic to be accessible to a much wider audience. This may ultimately prove inefficient, given the additional time and effort involved. (Scarbrough, 1999: 70)

But it was clear that there were other complex forces at work also. They concerned differences in national cultures, and issues of power, departmental strength and strategic use of information.

The outcome of the various difficulties was that, during the three years when the research was going on, company users carried out formal reporting of progress on work in hand but expressed and shared little of what was happening in the informal work arena. Tacit knowledge was not surfaced or shared across workplace communities of practice, and the whole KM initiative did not achieve its objectives.

Source: Patriotta, 1999

grative approaches to many knowledge-creation initiatives (Scarbrough, 1998). Case example 7.1 illustrates one such failure. The identity of the company has been changed to preserve its anonymity, but all other information is factual.

In the Multicorp case, the dominating drive of new technology in the first three years of its introduction left other parts of the system lagging too far behind. There was a 'pre-existing organisational context, characterized by habits of working nationally, within separate, closed units, each one facing its own market' (Patriotta, 1999). The old company culture, held in place by its supporting HR policies and its communities of practice, was increasingly out of tune with the new IT system. Failure to ensure an integrative approach to the new knowledge process explained why its introduction was not a success.

The object lesson suggested by all such initiatives is that since knowledge is both product *and* process, an integrative approach to its sharing and development is essential. IT is an aid to processing and communicating information, but it facilitates only part of the knowledge process. The rest is to do with relationships between people and with their organisational context. The term 'knowledge management' is regularly used in indiscriminate fashion in organisations to refer to any knowledge-focused initiative, whether its aim is to improve information processing, to promote knowledge sharing, or to raise the level of organisationally valuable knowledge creation. The relational knowledge process cannot be 'managed', but it can be sensitively steered and facilitated. That, however, requires attention to organisational leadership, to workplace culture and to human resource policies. IT interventions on their own are unlikely to have any significant positive impact on knowledge creation.

KNOWLEDGE AS COMMODITY

Back to the machine?

Early in Chapter 2 we explained that resource-based theory (RBT) proposes that a firm's distinctive competence lies in its specialised resources, assets and skills. The knowledge that emerges from organisational learning constitutes a unique intangible asset and a core competence that can transform the competitive position of the business. RBT places particular stress on the value of tacit knowledge that is deeply embedded in the culture of the workplace (Nonaka, 1991; Hall, 1993). Because it is formed and changed by workplace relational processes its exact path of development is impossible to trace. It can be shared among organisational members without having to be made explicit, but when it does interact with new explicit knowledge or is helped to do so, both can expand, with innovation occurring as tacit knowledge becomes embodied in new products, services, strategies, processes and organisational routines (Nonaka, 1991). In companies where new knowledge is regularly developed and expressed in innovative products and processes in this way, learning processes move from the personal to the social in a 'knowledge-creating spiral' that builds on tacit and explicit knowledge (Nonaka and Takeuchi, 1995). Such a spiral can transform the workplace into a 'learning laboratory' where contribution to knowledge creation, collection and control is 'a key criterion for all activities' (Leonard-Barton, 1992: 23).

Surely such notions are to do with knowledge as relationships? Why then are we discussing them under the heading of 'knowledge as commodity?' The reason is that, perversely, RBT's very emphasis on the competitive value of 'two kinds of knowledge' can lead to a failure to grasp the interactive nature of tacit and explicit aspects of knowledge, and in consequence to a concentration on explicit knowledge as being readily observable, measurable and portable. To explain in more detail:

■ The widespread distinction now made between tacit and explicit knowledge frequently leads in practice to a preoccupation with ensuring that intangible knowledge assets are separated from the individuals in which they reside, to that they can be retained for the company's use.

The idea is that knowledge is a commodity which can be extracted (mined) from the people (repositories) in which it is buried and packaged, distributed and utilised. (Swan, 1999: 6)

■ This preoccupation with knowledge as commodity is framed by the old image of the organisation as machine. This is particularly evident in the use of terms such as 'mining', digging' and 'extracting' (Swan, ibid), and in a focus of much practitioner-oriented literature on ways of 'managing' knowledge by using information systems driven by new technology to share explicit knowledge, to combine different kinds of explicit knowledge, and to surface tacit knowledge in order to codify it (thereby losing its unique value). This kind of narrowly conceived KM approach confuses the holistic process of knowledge creation with mere information processing. It can produce an 'obsession with tools and techniques' that characterised the Multicorp case (Scarbrough et al., 1999: 24, 25).

■ The resource-based perspective has had a major influence on current notions of knowledge. However, in the view of some KM researchers, it represents an essentially theoretical approach that is flawed by its failure to draw adequately on the body of work on 'knowledge' that can be found in organisation theory. Scarbrough's outline (1998) of critical differences between the two schools of thought illustrates this. It is reproduced as Table 7.3.

■ Scarbrough finds that RB theorising is weak at 'unpacking' organisational knowledge and learning processes. It does not sufficiently take into account that

Table 7.3   *Conflicting views of organizational knowledge*

Perspective of organization theory	Perspective of the resource-based theory of the firm
Social construction of knowledge; role of crises and adaptation. Social distribution of knowledge.	Learning-by-doing; routines and skills. Path dependency.
Organizational knowledge = collective knowledge; emergent, context dependent.	Organizational knowledge = assets; aggregation of skills and knowledge.
Emphasis on tacit knowledge; shared experience of a social community.	Emphasis on functionality of knowledge; creation of innovations and new products.
Firm as a social institution, a site of power and control.	Firm as a dynamic configuration of resources.
Management as social actors, implicated in the social relations of the firm and of the wider society.	Management as decision-makers, creating intent and architecture for the development of core competencies.
Acquisition of knowledge influenced by institutional factors and the pursuit of legitimation; importance of imitation and sectoral recipes.	Acquisition of knowledge shaped by strategy and structure. Competence building is a conscious activity.

Source: Scarbrough, 1998, p. 229. Reproduced by permission of Blackwell Publishing

learning at individual, group and collective levels can bring with it skilled incompetence, rigidity and over-specialisation (see Chapter 3; also Levinthal and March, 1993; Argyris, 1996). Many of its claims relating to organisational learning are based on insights produced after the event. These do not help managers in the here-and-now 'to differentiate between those forms of learning that produce long-run competencies and those which only lead to a blind alley' (Scarbrough, 1998: 224).

■ The focus in RBT on tacit knowledge has been challenged by those who find something unsatisfactory about a concept that does not lend itself to observation or codification (Reed and DeFillippi, 1990: 100). Knowledge that is deeply embedded in the subconscious may not be fully understood even by those who possess it, so how can they share it with others? How also can the tacit and path-dependent be identified and in some way converted into meta-knowledge? (Scarbrough, 1998). How can value be placed on something that is assumed and is invisible? Seen in this light it is unsurprising that no clear links have yet been found between learning and competitive performance (Scarbrough, 1998; Eisenhardt and Santos, 2002).

Such concerns are understandable, but we have already observed that in a relatively new field there will naturally be more answers than questions. As we saw in Chapters 2 and 3, many organisations are continuing to search for ways forward in the knowledge field. The following studies in Research example 7.2 illustrate this.

Organisations such as these have to create and apply new knowledge at a rapid rate in order to fuel continuous improvement and radical innovation. Although the roots of the knowledge process, and knowledge in its tacit form, remain unclear, some of the most organisationally valuable knowledge is now seen to emerge from learning located in communities of practice.

The knowledge-development process in different organisational settings

Baumard (1999) investigated how companies such as the airline Qantas, the aluminium manufacturer Pechiney, the computer company Indigo and the financial institution Indousuez used their tacit knowledge to cope with threat in times of crisis following mergers, political turmoil and bureaucratic quagmires. Formal knowledge management systems proved to be of little use and were counterproductive in most cases. Socialising individual tacit knowledge to form a collective competence contributed far more towards the organisation's development and sustainability than information overload flowing from formal knowledge systems.

Dutrénit (2000) carried out a detailed study at the Mexican company Vitro Glass Containers into how an organisation can apply individual learning to help the entire organisation learn. Exploring the issue of how power to achieve successful technical innovation can be transformed into an organisational capability to achieve strategic innovation, she identified the importance of:

■ working on a shared view of how individual curricula and knowledge development in the organisation as a whole can support one another
■ integrating learning processes in the establishment of information systems, thereby avoiding a one-sided focus on technological innovations, such as patents, that is likely to neglect the vital learning needed in order to develop strategic capability.

Huysman and De Wit (2000) conducted a study in the Netherlands in organisations including Cap Gemini, ING Barings, KPN, Nationale Nederlanden, NS, Postbank, Schiphol, Stork, Unilever and the Ministry of Housing, Planning and the Environment. They examined structured forms of knowledge sharing within the firm and identified important considerations related to the design of knowledge-productive workplaces. Among their many findings the following are of particular relevance here:

■ The individual employee's perspective is a major factor in sharing knowledge: employees are more willing to share knowledge if such action benefits their daily activities and figures integrally in the way they work together.
■ Efforts to share knowledge must be based on a shared notion of knowledge.
■ The role of ICT tends to be overestimated, especially if there is a unilateral focus on the technical approach. In practice, personal networks are more important for sharing knowledge. ICT is probably more useful for connecting people and less relevant for gathering and disseminating knowledge.
■ Mutual concern and trust, curiosity and inspiration based on a common mission all benefit knowledge sharing.
■ A knowledge-friendly culture encourages working in teams and participating in personal and professional networks and informal gatherings.

An organisational case study

Buckman Laboratories, one of a number of KM cases collected and discussed by Scarbrough and Swan (1999, and see Appendix 2) provides the final Case example (7.2) for this chapter. We have chosen it because of the recognition given in the company to the sharing of tacit as well as explicit knowledge, and because it offers many insights into the way in which an integrative approach can stimulate and steer knowledge sharing and knowledge creation.

Case example 7.2

Transforming the knowledge process at Buckman Laboratories, 1992–98

The KM initiatives

Buckman Laboratories is a US-owned global chemical company. In 1989 Bob Buckman, the company's chief executive, pledged that knowledge would become the foundation of his company's competitive edge. The change strategy introduced in 1992 involved using new technology to capture and manage knowledge and innovative thinking. However from the start managers realised that three factors would be critical to the knowledge management (KM) programme: advanced information technology (IT), continuous culture change, and KM-focused human resource management (HRM). The technical KM initiatives were planned to emerge over time, giving flexibility to respond to new contingencies in internal and external environments.

Structural change

In 1992 the Information Systems and Telecommunications departments were consolidated to form the Knowledge Transfer Department (KTD) and the previous research and development technical information centre was renamed the Knowledge Resource Centre (KRC). The two departments are responsible for design and ongoing management of the IT network, but the monitoring and processing of the knowledge generated within the various forums subsequently set up are overseen by forum specialists and industry section leaders.

The IT system

The K'Netix knowledge creating and sharing systems used in the KM programme consist of organisational forums and codified databases. The K'Netix network was introduced in 1993. It comprises three customer-focused forums and four regional-focused forums. The systems connect knowledge bases world-wide to create a company knowledge base. This network enables electronic sharing of knowledge between the company's 1,300 associates and from them to customers in over 90 countries. This encourages group problem solving and sharing of new ideas and knowledge. 'This single knowledge network aims to encompass all of the Buckman company's knowledge and experience, empowering Buckman representatives to focus all of their company's capabilities on customer challenges' (Pan, 1999: 77).

Cultural change

Traditionally the company was a hierarchical one in which employees hoarded knowledge, with middle managers the gatekeepers. Control of scarce information was a key to power. Changing this culture was a continuing and difficult task, and leadership was crucial to its success. Bob Buckman has produced 'a managerial mindset that promotes internal co-operation and the efficient flow of information throughout the organisation worldwide' (ibid: 82). When the KM programme was introduced, he and his top HR executives contributed regularly to forums and discussion groups, demonstrating management commitment as well as monitoring proceedings. This strong leadership created the necessary role model and provided guidelines for collecting and sharing information. Gradually the culture began to change. Communities of practice evolved informally, promoting the sharing of information for specific customer problems as well as gathering knowledge for widespread corporate use. 'Their bonding is social as well as technical, and is built around informed participation' (ibid: 79). Outside these communities, sharing knowledge is very hard to enforce, and this raises the danger that they could act as barriers to organisation-wide knowledge sharing. However, the guidelines provided by leadership ensure the effective management of these communities, as does the integrated thrust of KM, cultural and HR processes.

The role of HRD

HRD has been another key in creating and sustaining an associate-driven learning culture. Until the mid-1990s training and education were delivered in traditional teacher-centred classroom fashion, but in 1996 a multilingual on-line learning centre was introduced. Its content ranges from short training and reference materials to advanced academic degrees drawn from some of the best universities in the world. Primary responsibility for managing personal and career development is now with associates, not with specialist HRD staff, and this reinforces the associate-driven KM culture.

Performance measurement and rewards

New performance measurement systems have also been introduced, not so much focused on knowledge sharing as on its results. Continuous efforts are made to identify and measure process improvement and related outcomes that company and individuals find of value. Rewards, recognition and compensation systems have also been changed in order to gear them to the realisation that people have to be given time to adjust to KM tools, to learn how to use them and to understand the long-term, as well as immediate, benefits they can bring. At Buckman Laboratories, people have had to get used to a culture of knowledge sharing and of knowledge creation, as well as to a new flatter networking structure. It has been important to reward key behaviours as well as new competencies. Monetary rewards for contribution to knowledge sharing have been offered from time to time on an individual level, but their use is only sparing and is intended as a sign of esteem by the company, not as material rewards attached to specific tasks. Careful selection has also been used along the way.

Complementing this 'reward' process there has been a 'punishment' factor, especially in the early stages when top management would write to those who did not participate in the K'Netix system, asking for their reasons and suggesting that previous ways of working were now at an end and that a new way forward was necessary to the organisation's future success.

The new managerial role

After a 'painful and strenuous' period of unlearning and relearning, managers at the company are now continuously concentrating on facilitating knowledge creation, becoming 'mentors' instead of barriers to the knowledge process:

The managerial task for the organisation is to continuously create and maintain a knowledge-enterprising culture and community whereby associates feel comfortable with knowledge and all are motivated, rewarded and entrepreneurial. Equally challenging, is the integral task of developing a knowledge-focused reward system, which can effectively replace the traditional, commission-based reward mechanism. (Pan, 1999: 81)

Knowledge productivity

By measuring the results of knowledge-sharing activities against the percentage of new products sold (always a key performance indicator at Buckman), the company has calculated that knowledge sharing has produced a 250% growth in sales in the past decade. Its global knowledge-sharing effort has helped increase the percentage of sales from products less than five years old from 14% in 1987 to 34.6% in 1996. The single key factor that has contributed to this success is a cultural change that has produced a 'shared, challenging and knowledge-entrepreneurial vision … (that) provides the focus and energy for the sharing of knowledge' (ibid: 82).

Managers have appreciated from the start that once KM is embedded in the processes in which people work it can become a process that facilitates knowledge creation and sharing through normal corporate intranets and informal communities of practice (ibid: 83). The incorporation of KM practices into company culture is intended to ensure that Buckman Laboratories achieves its mission to compete strategically on knowledge (ibid: 84).

Source: Pan, 1999

Buckman Laboratories is overcoming major geographical and cultural barriers by fostering a dedicated and distributed community of practice stretching across the world. The case demonstrates a sustained integrative approach to cultural change and to knowledge sharing and knowledge creation. In this approach HR practices focus on supporting and facilitating the knowledge process, and on rewarding its outcomes rather than its inputs. We saw in Chapter 3 the importance of such a focus in order to emphasise the need to produce knowledge that adds value for the company.

What remains unanswered in all such studies, however, are three critical questions (Rajan, 1999):

- Exactly how can tacit knowledge be encouraged and shared?
- What role can HR practices play in 'downloading' tacit knowledge? (apprenticeship and informal networks clearly have an important part to play)
- Why would anyone want to share their knowledge when, in the age of the self-employment mindset, we are all meant to be building a 'personal brand'?

Such questions have particular implications for human resource professionals, not least those working in the human resource development field (HRD). We respond to them in subsequent chapters.

ISSUES FOR HRD PRACTITIONERS

Key tasks for HRD practitioners in the KM field

The role of HRD practitioners in making KM work for organisations seems from recent research findings to be poorly defined, often leaving those practitioners unsure how to respond. The ideas fuelling KM owe little to the insights about people and learning represented by the concepts of the learning organisation that the HRD profession has done so much to develop, and the KM field is currently dominated by IT experts whose main concern is with knowledge as commodity (Roy Harrison, 1999).

Mayo (1999) observes that most accounting systems in organisations today were designed for an era in which physical and financial assets were paramount. He recommends that HRD professionals should 'take the lead in seeking useful measures for growing intellectual capital and in helping organisations to build intellectual balance sheets'. The Buckman Laboratories case offers such measures. There, the asset value of knowledge creation is assessed by identifying its outcomes in terms of continuous improvement and innovation. New measures of this kind are greatly needed, and the HRD function should be contributing to their development.

Other tasks for HRD practitioners related to the knowledge process are suggested in findings reported by Beaumont and Hunter (2002) from a wide selection of real-life case studies. They produced similar insights to those achieved by the 2002 European HRD research project (Tjepkema et al., 2002) and by the cases we have reviewed in this chapter. They stress the need for a major contribution to:

- the planning and implementation of culture change
- building internal competencies so that knowledge can be developed, transferred and retained across the organisation
- establishing communities of practice that are shaped by the common interests of participants rather than by organisational structure.

We explore these and other areas of action for HRD practitioners in the following three chapters.

At this point we have produced a second assignment in Appendix 1 that you may wish to tackle.

CONCLUSION

In this chapter our main aims have been to explain some of the major theories about knowledge in its organisational context, and to identify a variety of practical implications. The literature that we have reviewed has proved to have no unifying base, and is characterised too often by rhetoric and conceptualisation that do not lead to any substantial progress in theory building. However, no one body of theory or single notion of knowledge can ever be sufficient here. With every discovery that they make, scientists become more aware of the extraordinary complexity and workings of human cognitions and knowledge structures, while social relationships are becoming increasingly fractured in a world where the structures and cultures that formerly gave them coherence are being eroded. 'Knowledge' has no universal meaning in a world in flux.

Different notions of knowledge are lodged in different views of the world. The positivist viewpoint, from which notions of knowledge as control and commodity have emerged, sees the world as an external reality about which knowledge can be obtained through the gathering of information from within and outside the organisations. The constructivist viewpoint, from which the notion of knowledge as relational derives and to which the notion of knowledge as intelligence in part responds, sees the world as a socially constructed state. Table 7.4 outlines the impact of these two sets of views on theories of knowledge.

Changes in notions of knowledge have been stimulated through time by the failure of successive theories to provide a convincing explanation of how knowledge is formed and developed at individual, group and collective levels. There are still no conclusive answers to those questions, but research is making it increasingly clear that far more attention should be focused on how to bring workplace communities of practice together in a shared organisational purpose without, however, destroying the unique self-regulating properties that make them so attractive to individuals and so powerful in driving the knowledge process. This realisation lends further weight to the conclusions proposed in Chapter 3: that the emphasis in knowledge-creating organisations should be less on devising management systems to 'control' learning or to 'manage' knowledge, more on finding 'new ways to encourage people to think creatively and feed their thoughts back into the organisation' (Russell and Parsons, 1996: 32) and to provide the skills and support systems needed to manage the projects that arise from that creativity.

In Table 7.5 we draw together some of the most important issues raised in this chapter and set them alongside sets of key issues raised in Part I of the book. They form an agenda for the remaining chapters in Part II. We have already identified in Chapters 4 to 6 many current challenges facing the HRD function and its practitioners. Throughout Part II we shall encounter more that relate to their new tasks in knowledge-creating organisations. We evaluate these HRD challenges in our concluding chapter.

Table 7.4   *Views of the world, and their impact on notions of knowledge*

	Positivist view	Constructivist view
Basic view of the world and of the cognitive process	The world is an objective reality. The aim of the cognitive process is to create the most accurate presentations of this reality in order to enable the individual to interact effectively with it. Cognitive systems are created and recreated through a dependency of an input–output relation with the environment.	The world is not a pre-given state or an objective external reality. It is continuously brought forth through the creative act of cognition, and is continuously shaped by social interactions. Cognitive systems are created and recreated in a self-productive manner in individuals, groups and collectively.
Cognitive model	Cognitivist, rooted in traditional behavioural psychology and in open systems theory.	Autopoietic, rooted in the fields of neurobiology, physics and the social sciences.
Basic assumptions about knowledge	There is a separation between knowing and doing. Knowledge is the result of information processing, and the brain is a vehicle for human beings to attain knowledge and to solve problems.	Knowing and doing are closely interrelated processes. Knowledge is fundamentally embodied in the individual, and is developed not only in the brain but also in social interactions.
	Information is a noun, differing in quantity rather than in essence from data. Collecting accurate data and information, and using good information processing systems, will produce increasingly 'truthful' knowledge about observed phenomena. Knowledge is a type of commodity.	Information is a verb, being that part of the knowledge process whereby data are put in order. What matters is to understand the social interactions and cognitive processes that shape knowledge. Knowledge is a process as well as a product of that process. It is 'self-productive'.
Basic assumptions about learning	Learning is an individual cognitive experience. It is a process whereby the individual more accurately obtains representations of the world through 'relating incoming information to a previously acquired psychological frame of reference' (Bruner and Anglin, 1973, in Von Krogh et al., 1994: 58).	Learning is a socio-cognitive process (Ginsberg, 1994). Individuals are history-dependent and operate in a social context. Learning is situated in communities of practice, through sharing knowledge, language, conversation and narratives.

Table 7.4   *cont'd*

	Positivist view	Constructivist view
Requirements for knowledge development in the organisation	Scientifically designed systems, networks, rules, routines and procedures whereby to collect 'relevant' information and ensure its acquisition, dissemination and appropriate utilisation across the organisation.	An organisational structure and a set of informal and formal relationships that promote languaging and knowledge connectivity, and that develop shared aspects of individuals' cognitive maps.
	Job descriptions, experts, and mechanisms to regulate the flow and distribution of information from the top of the organisation to relevant organisation members.	'Self-descriptions' of the organisation that communicate its identity to all organisational members in order to signpost the kinds of knowledge that matter.
	Adequate opportunities for training, and vehicles to ensure its transfer to the job and workplace.	Use of language, myths, symbols and beliefs that develop knowledge-productive cultures. Adequate opportunities for conversations, narratives, discussion, reflection and experimentation.
Impact on learning	Produces mainly adaptive learning that fills in the gaps in current knowledge.	Produces not only adaptive but also investigative and reflexive learning that has a transformational potential for individuals and for the organisation.

Table 7.5   Issues for the strategising, organising and knowledge processes in organisations operating in a knowledge economy

Issues for the strategising process (Chapter 2)	Issues for the organising process (Chapter 3)	Issues for the knowledge process (Chapter 7)
■ It cannot be assumed that the sole strategic driver in all organisations is one of competition. In many organisations, and across different sectoral, national and international boundaries and culture there are other compelling drivers, underpinned by non-economic values. What implications does this have for strategic decision-making?	■ What kind of organisational forms can achieve an effective balance between a company's current operations and the innovatory actions needed to facilitate new capability development? And how can they be monitored and maintained?	■ How can an organisational philosophy based on mutuality of endeavour, interest and benefit be generated, and how can it then become embedded in organisational context?
■ Strategy is essentially a process, not a product. It involves the interaction of socio-political forces and of individual and collective knowledge, learning and action within and across organisations. In a fast-moving knowledge economy where no advantage obtained by one organisation can be sustained for long and where organisational boundaries are fluid and dynamic, is it not 'strategy' and 'organisation' that count, but 'strategising' and 'organising'. How can the two be integrated effectively?	■ In a knowledge-creating organisation, how should organisational performance be measured, and what kinds of incentive and reward systems are appropriate for individuals and teams?	■ What roles, actions and practices can stimulate, identify and connect strategically relevant learning at every organisational level?
	■ Since some of the most valuable knowledge emerges from workplace communities of practice, how can a productive balance be achieved between formal regulation and self-managed learning in order to maximise on that knowledge process?	■ What kind of organisational context, structure and management actions can promote and support investigative and reflective as well as adaptive learning across the organisation?
■ Human behaviour in organisations is fuelled by more than economic self-interest – and must be, if the high level of co-operative endeavour and the rapid collective learning and unlearning that is needed by organisations operating in a knowledge economy are to be achieved and sustained. How can diverse interests be identified, valued and managed effectively?	■ How should any stultifying effects of existing learning in the organisation be addressed in order to promote a culture of challenge and innovation?	■ What intra-organisational learning networks, routines and processes can stimulate the continuous development of an organisation's knowledge base?
	■ If dynamic capabilities are to emerge from all organisational levels, and also if organisations are to operate increasingly on network or cellular principles, what do such developments imply for managerial roles and skills?	■ How can tacit knowledge be shared in an organisation, and how can individuals and communities of practice be encouraged in that activity?
■ What roles and tasks are there for HRD professionals in enhancing and supporting the strategising process?	■ Is 'management' in its traditional sense becoming an irrelevant concept for knowledge-creating organisations? If it is, what might or should replace it?	■ What roles and tasks are there for HRD professionals in enhancing and supporting the knowledge process?
	■ What roles and tasks are there for HRD professionals in enhancing and supporting the organising process?	

chapter eight

The Knowledge-Productive Organisation

INTRODUCTION

In this chapter we expand on the concept of knowledge productivity to which we have referred frequently in earlier chapters. Knowledge productivity concerns the way in which individuals, teams and units across an organisation achieve knowledge-based improvements and innovations. It entails developing new knowledge in the workplace that can generate the capability for continuous improvement and also for radical innovation in operating procedures, processes, products and services.

Our purpose in this chapter is to relate the knowledge productivity concept to notions of knowledge explored in Chapter 7, and to propose a practical framework whereby to promote and sustain a knowledge-productive environment in an organisation. We call this framework the 'corporate curriculum', and in Chapter 9 we discuss research being carried out to test the construct.

As we have seen in Chapter 7, different notions of knowledge carry differing implications for knowledge creation. Viewing knowledge as control or as commodity often leads to centrally managed knowledge systems, with a strong emphasis on data collection and systems of information processing. With these perspectives, knowledge is made explicit, encoded and stored in electronic databases where it is held to represent an important asset, and serves as the basis for knowledge management. On the other hand, viewing knowledge as a web of relationships and as a capability to adapt and to transform requires an approach where knowledge is nurtured in a conducive learning environment. The emphasis is on shared knowledge development through learning situated in communities of practice.

In the context of organisations operating in an emerging knowledge economy, research offers evidence that the traditional 'knowledge as stock' (commodity) approach, focused on controlling, storing and reusing knowledge, is not likely to contribute sufficiently to the necessary regular improvement and innovation in work processes, products and services (see Tushman and Nadler, 1996). A 'flow', or processual approach to knowledge, where relationships form the focal point, offers more relevance. The development of human resources (HRD) lies at the very heart of a 'knowledge-productive' organisation, where people in the workplace embody knowledge that is critical for survival in a knowledge economy (Kessels, 1995, 1996).

In the first part of the chapter we discuss characteristics of a 'knowledge-productive' organisation and the questions it raises about traditional management roles and tasks. We then explore how such an organisation might be developed and sustained, introducing the 'corporate curriculum' framework to aid analysis of the human and organisational issues that are involved here. We identify issues that this framework raises for HRD practitioners, and the new HRD tasks that it suggests. The chapter concludes with an integrative case study.

KNOWLEDGE-PRODUCTIVE ORGANISATIONS

'Knowledge management' or 'knowledge development'?

Employees' participation in developing the knowledge of an organisation is becoming a significant theme in HRD theory. The importance of 'being smart' at all levels rather than only at the top is manifested in often desperate efforts to manage knowledge in organisations. At the same time, as we saw in Chapter 7, an increasing focus on knowledge management introduces many social tensions, raising problematic issues of ownership and utilisation of knowledge. As commentators such as Drucker (1993) and Jacobs (1996) make clear, it is knowledge development rather than knowledge management that should characterise the post-capitalist society. And in a knowledge economy it is not only specialist knowledge workers that need attention, as Case example 8.1 demonstrates.

Clearly there are issues in all such cases, whether at macro or micro level, about how to 'manage' knowledge. The danger then becomes one of a false specialisation that diverts attention from the processual nature of knowledge, converting it into simply another management function. When the importance of the production process was discovered at the dawn of the production era, we appointed production managers. When finance came to be seen as a special area of expertise, we recruited financial managers. When employees needed increasing attention, we turned to personnel managers. With the growing awareness of the importance of quality, we sought out quality managers. When we discovered the client, we created account managers. Our present focus on knowledge has given birth to knowledge managers.

Throughout, 'management' has been the key function. But might not the current interest in knowledge, its complex underlying dynamics and its economic significance, suggest an alternative possibility now? Might it not herald the end of the 'management' era? Functional management was born in a period of economic activity when there was an obsession to plan, direct, manage, measure, verify, monitor and evaluate everything considered to be important. The dominant notions of knowledge were of control and of commodity. But that was in the last century. Is it not time to question now whether we should view the concept of 'knowledge management' as the final anachronism, the watershed between two quite different eras?

In a knowledge-based economy, the capacity to develop and apply the uniquely valuable organisational process of knowledge rests equally with everyone. As we have seen in Chapter 3, in many organisations the stereotype of the authoritarian and controlling manager is now being replaced (at least in title) by the coaching, guiding, facilitating and entrepreneurial manager. We observed in Chapters 5 and 6 that similar roles are being proposed for HRD/training managers operating in a knowledge economy (Stewart and Tansley, 2002; Tjepkema et al., 2002). Such roles seem more

Case example 8.1

Agro-food complex, the Netherlands

The knowledge economy is not restricted to well-educated 'knowledge workers' in organisations that are clearly knowledge intensive. It has implications for all workers, whatever their type of workplace. For example, in the Netherlands young farmers have to deal with questions such as:

■ How can farming be economically profitable in an agricultural area with landscape value?
■ Should we raise free-range chickens, and what are the important issues here?
■ With the growing concern for food safety, can we allow free-range chickens to roam about in their excrement, or should we invest in sophisticated technology for battery cages that keep eggs separate from excrement?
■ Which combination of clover and grass should we plant to get the soil to retain nitrogen?
■ Is it wise to shift to a greater emphasis on goats' milk production?
■ But what then should we do with the inevitable large surplus of male kids that cannot be used for milk or meat production purposes?

In the Netherlands, such young entrepreneurs establish informal networks to share their experiences and to analyse new information. In his policy memorandum *Groen Onderwijs* [Green Education] the Minister of Agriculture, Nature Management and Fisheries advocated transforming traditional agriculture and livestock breeding into a knowledge-intensive agro-food complex dedicated to quality education about food, green areas, nature and landscape.

Here, a sector that we would not immediately identify as a knowledge producer is now increasingly being regarded as such. The Minister argued that important themes such as sustainability, food safety, agro biodiversity, biotechnology and integral water management should not be considered exclusively from an agricultural perspective. He believed that education about natural resources should cover the entire chain from consumers to producers, and must therefore involve relevant knowledge and expertise from adjacent disciplines, such as social sciences, medicine and ICT-related fields.

Source: Minister van Landbouw, 2000

appropriate in the context of knowledge development, but they beg the critical question: how far should someone who is essentially there to help, support, guide and collaborate still carry the title of manager?

It is not so much the title that matters here, but the focus that it produces. As we reported in our discussion of 'knowledge as commodity' in Chapter 7, Huysman and De Wit (2000) carried out a survey of 11 organisations involved in knowledge management. They found scant regard there for sharing knowledge. They criticised the use of a knowledge management concept that, in this case, disguised what was in reality a unilateral management perspective. They also criticised what emerged from their survey as a one-sided individual learning perspective that demonstrated little regard for collective organisational learning, and a one-sided information and communications technology perspective that reflected little concern for social interaction. Von Krogh et al. (2000) reached similar conclusions about the practice of knowledge management. They see it more relevant to develop knowledge using a 'steering' perspective. Malhotra (2000), who dealt extensively with such issues, concluded that a management perspective cannot be reconciled with the concept of knowledge development. He did not deny the need to find ways of managing knowledge, but he too looked to the idea of self-steering 'knowledge intrapreneurs' to achieve that.

Reflection

■ Is knowledge development – as distinct from knowledge management – given specific attention in your work environment? Do you know of any special resources that are available for knowledge development in your organisation?

■ If knowledge development is prioritised in your organisation, then who is seen to be responsible for that activity? How far do they seem to be 'managers' in the traditional sense, or to carry some other role?

Knowledge and personal 'skilfulness'

Our notion of knowledge productivity is based on two beliefs:

■ that where knowledge is a dominant concern – not just at corporate level but throughout the organisation – it follows that daily operations should be designed to support knowledge productivity (Kessels, 1996; Harrison, 2000)

■ that knowledge is both a relational process and a type of individual attribute or quality. That quality is to do with individual cognition as well as with the ability to learn in communities of practice, but it goes beyond both. It involves a personal 'skilfulness' and sensitivity that is inextricably linked with the individual concerned.

We first began to consider a concept of knowledge as a type of learnt skilfulness in our studies of successful educational programmes (Kessels, 1995; Kessels and Harrison, 1998; Kessels and Plomp, 1999). Malhotra has expressed a similar view:

> Even procedural knowledge, when translated into symbols that are later processed by another human, does not ensure that the outcome of his knowledge will rival that of the original *carrier*. Knowledge needs to be understood as the *potential for action* that doesn't only depend upon the stored information but also on the individual interacting with it. (Malhotra, 2000: 249, italics in original)

The knowledge process does not only require individuals to become involved in applying rules and procedures when dealing with standard problems. It also enables them to improve the rules, analyse new situations, devise new concepts and enhance their understanding of their own and others' learning processes. This involves the exercise of adaptive, investigative and reflexive learning, illustrated in Table 5.1, Chapter 5. It casts a new light on the distinction usually drawn between explicit and implicit knowledge (Polanyi, 1958, 1966; Nonaka and Takeuchi, 1995; Baumard, 1999; Von Krogh et al., 2000).

Explicit knowledge is not just codified, established, described, documented knowledge. It is also the expression of someone else's personal skill in codifying knowledge. When we gain access to that explicit knowledge – for example through reading a book or a Lotus Notes entry – we are also gaining access to someone else's competence in producing knowledge. But that does not make us competent too. In Chapter 7, in our discussion of 'knowledge as relationships', we explained knowledge as a self-productive process involving a continuous interaction of cognitive, emotional and relational processes for the individual. So we still have to interpret and utilise that other person's body of codified knowledge. It remains no more than information until we have processed it to form our own unique knowledge, or worked with others to do so.

We also saw in Chapter 7 that if the individuals involved in learning situated in the workplace are to become knowledgeable in ways that will benefit the organisation – in other words, if they are to become knowledge-productive – then they need help and steering of some kind. Knowledge productivity can only flourish in a conducive context. As the Case examples of Multicorp (7.1) and of Buckman Laboratories (7.2) in Chapter 7 make clear, organisational members need a shared reference point and the necessary encouragement and facilitation to develop their personal skilfulness in the knowledge process – for example by being helped to form personal networks that encourage and support the knowledge process. Information technology has a role to play here too, although mainly in a support role related to the establishment and maintenance of electronic communication networks (Hansen et al., 1999). We elaborate on this role in Chapter 10.

Huysman and De Wit (2000) draw attention to this factor of personal skilfulness when, conceptualising the sharing of knowledge as a type of organisational learning, they identified three important areas of skill:

- supporting the gathering together of individually produced knowledge of whatever form or mix of forms
- supporting knowledge exchange – a component to do with collective learning and knowledge connectivity, because it is about bringing knowledge carriers together quickly to reflect on and discuss what they have gathered
- supporting knowledge development – by creating situations where people combine their new insights to bridge gaps in existing knowledge and to produce out of it new knowledge.

Classifying knowledge

Up to this point in the book we have focused only on one way of classifying knowledge: as *explicit* and *tacit*. However, there are other classification systems that we now need to identify in order to take forward our discussion of the knowledge-productive organisation.

Gibbons et al. (1994) and Gibbons (1998) classified knowledge into that which they termed *Mode I* knowledge, exemplified by scientific knowledge structured in disciplines that regulate its elaboration, and *Mode II* knowledge, which is application-oriented and derives its significance from its specific situation or context. Mode I knowledge is the kind traditionally developed at universities and other institutions of 'learning'. In a knowledge economy there is likely to be equal concern with Mode II knowledge that is produced and shaped in an organisational context (Gibbons, 1998; Gray, 1999; Robertson, 1999). In Chapters 4 to 6 we saw how this concern, triggered usually by the introduction of new high performance practices and new technology, is leading to innovation in workplace learning processes across Europe and more widely. We saw also that it is being expressed in educational systems by a search to achieve greater collaboration between educational providers and employers in integrating Modes I and II types of knowledge in various educational programmes and curricula.

Billett (1997) made similar distinctions when he classified knowledge as *propositional*, *procedural* and *dispositional*. Propositional includes Mode I and other bodies of theoretical or codified knowledge. Procedural includes 'what we use to think and act with' (ibid) in our daily activity: in other words, Mode II knowledge. Dispositional is our learnt values, attitudes and interests that predispose us to acquire certain kinds of knowledge and to treat and use it in particular ways. Billett argues that all knowledge structures have propositional, procedural and dispositional dimensions and that in different organisational settings knowledge has different propositional, procedural and dispositional characteristics.

Such approaches to classifying knowledge demonstrate an awareness of 'the sheer complexity and diversity of factors that directly (and indirectly) shape one's learning including *what counts* in the workplace (Garrick, 1999: 226, his italics). For Garrick, 'what counts' is increasingly becoming a personal skilfulness in producing new knowledge through learning that is situated in workplace communities of practice. Therefore 'the varying characteristics of workplaces as learning environments ... become very important' (Garrick, 1999: 228). A workplace is not likely to be knowledge-productive in our meaning of that term if it is dominated by a belief in knowledge merely as a commodity consisting of objective facts or scientific theories. Individuals in such a workplace are regarded essentially as elements to control, as bins to be filled, as repositories from which knowledge is to be extracted (Swan, 1999). They are not treated as having minds capable of interpreting information in unique ways in order to produce insights and skills that can continuously improve and radically innovate in operations, products and services.

Reflection

- Consider a situation that was *either* a major learning experience for you in your organisation, *or* in which you felt frustrated in your attempts to become more knowledgeable. What type of knowledge was mainly at issue in that situation: theoretical (Mode I, propositional knowledge) or practical (Mode II, procedural and/or dispositional knowledge)?

- What kind of learning environment were you in, and how far did it help or hinder you in becoming more knowledgeable, or in developing new knowledge in others?

We have one further, crucial dimension to personal skilfulness in the knowledge process to consider, before suggesting a framework for building and sustaining a knowledge-productive learning environment in the workplace. It is the dimension of what we call *practical judgement*.

The importance of practical judgement

[NOTE: Throughout this section we draw primarily on an original account of the relationship between practical judgement and knowledge productivity by Harrison and Smith (2001: 195–213)]

Ancient Greek philosophers made distinctions between *episteme*, *techne* and *phronesis*. Our concept of knowledge productivity revolves around the relationship between these three aspects of knowledge, which we therefore expand on here.

In Aristotle's *Nicomachean Ethics* the three terms carry the following meanings:

- *episteme* represents scientific, explicit, universal knowledge
- *techne*, roughly translated, refers to the skilled competence to perform a certain task by combining the well-practised exercise of the propositional and procedural knowledge that we discussed earlier
- *phronesis* can be variously translated as practical reasoning, practical judgement or practical wisdom. It reflects personal experiences and the ability to sense and anticipate situations. It can be further explained as prudence, approximating to a practical overview of what is socially appropriate or inappropriate.

Phronesis is characterised by flexibility and attentiveness to the details of the particular, and perhaps unique, case. It therefore has distinctive emotional and ethical aspects. Questions of character, of what kind of person is performing the activity in question, are at issue here. It is not simply a matter of the competence he or she is exercising. It is about the manner of applying knowledge in the particular situation, and the human sensitivity and sense of appropriateness demonstrated. Thus for a judge, 'laws are best thought of as summaries of previous wise decisions, to be corrected where necessary by new wise decisions to meet the exigencies of unique circumstances' (Smith, 1995). The 'good judge', in other words, applies the wisdom born of experience in ways appropriate to the particular situation. This goes to the heart of the concept of 'practical judgement' and of its importance in the knowledge process.

Applying the reasoning behind *phronesis* to today's organisational context suggests a need not only for visionary leadership and facilitative management, but for 'good' leadership and management that goes about its business in a manner respectful of certain values. This has special resonance in today's business world where public confidence in corporate governance has been dramatically eroded by 'the corruption and failure of influential parts of corporate America' and by the spreading effects of that failure across the capitalist world (Marr, 2002). The reasoning has a crucial meaning for the knowledge-productive organisation where a sense of community and an inclusive approach to learning is vital.

Harrison and Smith's concept of practical judgement has four features, although they warn that no prescriptions are possible here: it is much easier to say what practical judgement *is not* than what it is. The four features are shown in Table 8.1. These features make clear the ethical nature of practical judgement, with its roots in feelings, in learning from experience, and in openness to further experience and to the continual shifts in the individual's frames of reference that this involves. The concept connects strongly with a body of strategic management literature that focuses on qualities such as trust (Dodgson, 1993; Ghoshal and Bartlett, 1994: 92; Hedlund, 1994: 84; Boisot et al., 1995), judgement (Ginsberg, 1994: 154–5), friendship and family networks (Ito and Rose, 1994; Hines and Thorpe, 1995: 679–80), and the kind of heedful interrelating to which the following writers refer:

> When we say that a collective mind 'comprehends' … we mean that heedful interrelating connects sufficient individual know-how to meet situational demands. (Weick and Roberts, 1993: 366)

McGrath and colleagues (1995: 265) use similar concepts of 'comprehension' and 'deftness' in order to explain how some groups seem to work efficiently and effectively with a 'developed collective mind'. It is this kind of skilfulness in the learning and knowledge processes that demonstrates (they claim) that the management of

Table 8.1   *Features of practical judgement*

Features of practical judgement
■ *Experience* is a necessary but not sufficient condition of practical judgement. We often need to be helped, sometimes be directly shown, how to interpret what we see in a particular situation and what to consider when formulating a response to it. If we are not helped in this way, we may import ways of understanding and coping into the workplace that prove to be barriers to learning in a community of practice where the goal is to develop collective knowledge (Levinthal and March, 1993).
■ *Character* is another feature of practical judgement. By this we mean that practical judgement is bound up with the kind of person one is. It is not so much that practical judgement *requires* certain qualities, even 'virtues', to be in place before it can develop on the basis of them, as that it partly *consists* of those qualities. These qualities have a cognitive element but they, and so practical judgement itself, have a strongly affective side. Knowledge and feelings are part of the same process.
■ *Alertness* in practical judgement is to do with how far we have a sympathetic understanding of things in their own terms, of what they mean to the agents involved. Harrison and Smith relate this to the example of the 'alert' manager who responds to the myriad complex pressures of the workplace by experiencing them accurately, distinguishing what is meant as a threat, what is a clumsy overture of co-operation, what is a response to stress, and so on.
■ *Flexibility* is closely connected with alertness. Both involve 'sensitivity or attunement', especially to others in a shared situation.

Source: Based on Harrison and Smith, 2001

learning is one of the essential determinants of long-term organisational survival: 'organisations which are fast learners are able to rapidly mobilize themselves to overcome new challenges' (ibid: 266).

Hosmer (1994: 21), discussing the agency theory approach that we outlined in Chapter 2, stresses the relevance of the Aristotelian concept of personal virtue to management's tasks in building a climate of trust in the organisation. He explains trust in managerial terms as 'confidence that the self-interests of the principal will not necessarily take total precedence over the self-interests of the agent' (ibid: 28). He argues that it is only by recognising the ethical dimensions of their decisions and actions that managers will be able to generate the trust needed to ensure shared commitment and effort across the organisation, and to build up a valued reputation in the competitive environment. They must demonstrate a concern for external as well as internal goods, the latter including the integrity of the personal well-being of employees. They must show good practical judgement in all their dealings.

The tradition in which ideas about practical judgement are rooted thus embodies values to do with citizenship and community of interest (Hosmer, 1994: 32; see also Badaracco, 1991; Dodgson, 1993; Batchelor et al., 1995). Our concept of the knowledge-productive organisation is firmly lodged in a pluralist perspective described towards the conclusion of Chapter 2. It is one in which all value systems matter, and should be treated with respect and sensitivity. We regard the exercise of such wisdom as an essential feature, not only to foster trust among stakeholders, but to ensure an inclusive approach to learning that will achieve beneficial outcomes for individuals, for the business, and for wider society.

Emotional and spiritual intelligence

Some may think that 'practical judgement' is merely another term for 'emotional intelligence' – a concept in which there is much interest currently. The two concepts are in fact quite distinct, although there are points of commonality. To explain this distinctness, it is worth at this point outlining not only the concept of emotional intelligence (EI) but also of 'spiritual intelligence' (SI) that also has relevance here.

Emotional intelligence

EI is essentially to do with the way in which emotions and cognition interact to improve thinking. EI has been explained in basic terms as:

> the understanding of emotion. The ability to perceive, to integrate, to understand and reflectively manage one's own and other people's feelings. (Jack Mayer, quoted by Pickard, 1999: 49–50)

Although EI involves the operation of social intelligence – social skills or 'knowing how to behave' – it is not to be confused with it. The emotionally adept are those who know and manage their own feelings well and who read and deal effectively with other people's feelings (Goleman, 1998). In other words, they have the capacity to think intuitively about emotion. Goleman has identified from his research five domains of EI and related sets of abilities:

- Knowing one's emotions
- Managing these emotions
- Motivating oneself
- Recognising emotions in others
- Handling relationships.

Dulewicz and Higgs (1999) have developed an EI competency framework based on these domains. It has three main components and seven dimensions:

- *The drivers* – motivation and decisiveness. These energise and drive people on to achieve their goals and tend to be inborn. They can therefore be exploited or managed through coping strategies.
- *The constrainers* – conscientiousness and integrity, and emotional resilience. These act as controls and curb excesses of drivers. They too tend to be inborn and therefore can also be exploited or managed through coping strategies.
- *The enablers* – sensitivity, influence and self-awareness. These facilitate performance and help individuals to succeed. They can be developed, using a trusted mentor/guide.

Some are scathing about EI's claims, which they find to be nothing but old wine in new bottles (Woodruffe (2001). Goleman (2001), however, argues that EI abilities have a unique significance and have been consistently undervalued compared with cognitive abilities.

Spiritual intelligence

Danah Zohar and Jacquie Drake (2000), researchers in the developing field of 'spiritual intelligence', see SI as the 'ultimate intelligence', because it represents our 'deep, intuitive sense of meaning' – our 'guide at the edge'. They observe that when the immediate environment is uncertain, people need a deep sense of inner security in order to be 'flexible, adaptable, imaginative, spontaneous, innovative, inspirational'. Access to and engagement with SI engenders a more holistic approach than traditional skills and knowledge, which are 'insufficiently robust to deal with adversity or innovation' (ibid). These claims have a particular interest when related to our observations in Chapter 7 about human behaviour in 'disorderly' environments, and the relationship between turbulence and the generation of radically new knowledge.

In Table 8.2 we outline key features of the three concepts: emotional intelligence, spiritual intelligence and practical judgement.

Table 8.2 *Emotional intelligence, spiritual intelligence and practical judgement*

Features of emotional intelligence	Features of spiritual intelligence	Features of practical judgement
(Knowing and understanding one's own emotions and being able to read, understand and deal effectively with those of others)	(A deep intuitive sense of meaning, enabling a holistic approach to adversity and innovation)	(Wisdom born of experience, expressed in a sensitive and ethical approach to applying knowledge in the particular situation)
Self-motivation – able to motivate oneself and persist in the face of frustrations	*Flexibility* – open to suggestion, surprise and change, able to cope with ambiguity	*Experience* – that shapes the individual's interpretation of unfamiliar situations and influences how he or she responds to and learns from them
Self-control – able to control impulse and delay gratification	*Self-awareness* – both reflective and self-confronting	*Character* – the personal, cognitive and affective qualities that the individual possesses and can bring to bear on situations
Self-regulation – able to regulate one's moods and keep them from swamping the ability to think	*Led by own vision*, values and sense of purpose	*Alertness* – the awareness possessed by the individual of the nature and significance of new pressures, challenges and scenarios. The degree of insight they have into the ways in which they are understood by and affect others
Sensitivity – able to empathise and to hope	*Able to learn from adversity* and turn bad experience into wisdom	*Flexibility* – sensitivity or attunement of behaviour, especially to others in a shared situation
Social skilfulness – able to recognise emotions in others and to handle relationships	*Independence and willingness* to take a stand on issues	
	Questioning – especially 'why'	
	Ability to reframe situations – new perspectives, creative alternatives	
	Spontaneity – aliveness to the moment	
	Holistic approach and welcoming of diversity	

Source: Based on Goleman, 1998; Zohar and Drake, 2000; Harrison and Smith, 2001

As Table 8.2 implies, the concept of practical judgement differs in much of its detail and in its fundamental thrust from both emotional and spiritual intelligence. Whereas EI and SI are essentially inwardly focused, concerned with how the individual uses emotional and spiritual intelligence to deal effectively with their environment in order that they can make progress within it, practical judgement is about what the individual contributes to their community in order that they can help members to move forward together. It involves a unique ethical dimension and a concern with the personal well-being of others. We return in Chapter 11 to the kinds of ethical issues that can emerge in organisations that aspire to be knowledge-productive.

Reflection

- What do you see to be the main issues that have been raised in this section about knowledge productivity? Which can you relate to your own organisational experience, and what insights can you develop from doing so?
- Why is practical judgement so essential a part of the individual's personal skilfulness in learning and knowledge processes? How do you think people can be helped to acquire this 'wisdom' in the workplace?

THE CORPORATE CURRICULUM FRAMEWORK

The concept of the corporate curriculum

The 'corporate curriculum' is a construct that refers to an organisational plan for learning (Kessels, 1996). It is not a formal educational or training curriculum. Rather, it involves transforming the daily workplace into an environment where learning and working can be effectively integrated. It facilitates the creation of a rich and diverse landscape that encourages and supports employees in the learning they need to do in order to continuously adapt and to innovate. It draws on the by no means new idea that the learning going on at and around the workplace every day is more consistently powerful in its influence on the learners and in its end products than the learning that occurs in formal courses, sessions and programmes.

Of course, there are limitations to workplaces as learning environments. Some cultures informally encourage the kinds of learning, especially dispositional, that do not support the overall purpose of the organisation. In some, there is not the necessary coaching, mentoring, counselling and expert help that may be needed to aid entry into, and integration within, a workplace community of practice (Wenger and Snyder, 2000). Some knowledge may be particularly difficult for some groups or individuals to understand, absorb, develop or utilise. The learning environment may also raise divisive cultural, philosophical, political, gender and ethical issues (Garrick: 1999: 228–9) – a dimension that we explore in Chapter 11. Some communities may use the very strength of their unique identities to hoard rather than share or build knowledge. The Multicorp case in Chapter 7 gave examples of such behaviour.

As we also saw in the Multicorp case, other negative aspects may be embedded in the management actions or performance management process of an organisation. Increased pressure to perform to demanding targets of time and cost, especially when allied to incentive payments, can lead people to cut corners and bend regulations. A hierarchy of managers who take credit for successes and blame failures on others does not promote a creative and co-operative learning culture. It teaches quite different lessons, so that employees learn to excel in mediocrity, to withdraw when the tension rises and to cover themselves in order to avoid blame. These lessons achieve an impact that cannot be reversed by a two- or three-day training course, or even by a much longer 'culture change' programme. They draw attention to the significance of that concept of practical judgement that we discussed in the previous section.

The eight pillars of learning

On the basis of the notions of knowledge and learning in a knowledge economy that we have developed in this and the previous two chapters, we conclude that the learning environment of the truly knowledge-productive organisation embodies eight inter-related learning functions, forming the 'pillars' of that organisation's corporate curriculum. They are described in Table 8.3.

Table 8.3   *The eight learning pillars of the corporate curriculum*

1. *acquiring subject matter expertise* and professional knowledge directly related to the organisation's core competencies; e.g. a bank's financial services or the care provided by a hospital.

2. *learning to identify and deal with new problems* on the basis of the acquired subject matter expertise; e.g. switching to a new tax system or introducing customer-oriented patient care.

3. *cultivating reflective skills and meta-cognitions* to find ways to locate, acquire and apply new knowledge. How do we learn from our experiences? How can we improve our ability to develop, share and utilise knowledge in the workplace, and help others to do so?

4. *acquiring communicative and social skills* that help us access the knowledge network of others, participate in communities of practice and make learning situated in the workplace more attractive and socially inclusive.

5. *acquiring skills to regulate motivation, affinities, emotions and affections* concerning working and learning. People are only smart if they want to be. You cannot be made smart against your will. It is important for knowledge-productive employees to identify personal skills that they need to develop when learning in the workplace and to have confidence and encouragement to develop them.

6. *promoting calm and stability* to enable exploration, coherence, synergy and integration, and continuous improvement of products, services and processes. Employees should receive the opportunity to master and elaborate a plan, idea or operating procedure. Of course there must be balance here. Too much calm and stability might bring about overly one-sided specialisation and an excessive internal focus, complacency or laziness.

7. *stimulating and steering creative turmoil*, which can lead to radical innovation. Creative turmoil also results from a powerful drive to resolve a tricky question. The cause is often an existential threat: a matter of winning or losing, surviving or going under, being in or out of the game. Again a warning note: not all turmoil is creative. Disturbance alone, without the drive to innovate, can be counterproductive. Turmoil may become so creative that it yields a thousand new ideas but leaves little opportunity to elaborate any of them. There is clearly a potential conflict between the learning functions of *calm and stability* and *creative turmoil*, and much thought at the practical level is needed to achieve the necessary balance between the two.

8. *developing and applying practical judgement* in order to ensure sensitivity, flexibility and attunement to the needs of the situation, and of those involved in it. Practical judgement, or wisdom, can only be developed through a continuous interplay between experience, feelings and cognitions, reflected on as they relate to a specific context. It is an individual quality, used for the benefit of the learning community and as such is one of the most difficult aspects of the corporate curriculum to describe or to achieve. Perversely, we can most easily understand it when we look at those situations in which it has clearly been absent.

Reflection ▐▬▬▬▬▬▬▬▬▬▬▬▬▬▬▬▬▬

- Consider your own work environment, or that in any organisation in which you have a special interest.
- How far does it support, or hinder, the eight pillars of learning described in Table 8.3?

Integrating 'calm' and 'turmoil'

Two pillars of the corporate curriculum stand out as in apparent opposition to one another: *promoting calm and stability*, and *stimulating and steering creative turmoil*. In Chapter 3, in our discussion of 'organising for knowledge creation', we observed the ways in which current learning can inhibit the development of new knowledge. In Chapter 7 we suggested that a degree of 'disorder' can, in certain scenarios, act as the catalyst for new knowledge to emerge. Von Krogh et al. (1994) distinguished between an organisation's need to survive (maintain its position in its current environment) and its need to advance (forge ahead in an emerging new environment). As an organisation has to contend with increasingly turbulent conditions that involve radical change in its environment, its need to advance instead of 'sticking to the knitting' also increases, and with it the need to generate quite new knowledge.

Many writers have identified the different learning processes that are at issue here (Argyris and Schon, 1978; Hedberg, 1981; Ansoff and Sullivan, 1993; Argyris, 1996). In Chapter 5 (Table 5.1) we introduced a typology produced by Guile and Young (1999), building on that of Engestrom (1995). Walz and Bertels (1995) observed that gradual improvement (involving adaptive learning) elaborates on what is already present and leads to additional refinement and specialisation. Radical innovation (involving investigative and reflexive learning) involves breaking with the past and creating new opportunities by deviating from tradition. Gradual improvement benefits from conditions of relative stability and the time to reflect on what is needed in order to improve current operations and processes. Radical innovation is more likely to flow from the creative turmoil that is one of the corporate curriculum's eight pillars of learning (Table 8.3).

A need for radical innovation can raise major organising and human resource problems. Some employees thrive on *creative turmoil* but in others it can induce high stress levels. In order to decide how best to reconcile the learning functions of *calm and stability* and *creative turmoil* in the corporate curriculum construct, there must therefore be an analysis of organisational environment and context, of the balance of needs that these suggest for adaptive and reflexive learning, and of the dispositions and competence of employees related to those learning needs.

There are critical implications here for the organising process discussed in Chapter 3, and for human resource policies to do with selection, deployment, development and rewards. There are no easy answers to the question of how to balance the need for stability with the need for 'disorder' in organisations for which regular and often radical innovation in goods, products, services and processes is a vital task. However, as the case studies and research outlined in the concluding part of Chapter 7 demonstrate, in an organisation seeking to be knowledge-productive the thrust should not be to manipulate and condition employees. That would be a return to the notions of the organisation as machine and of knowledge as control. Rather it should be to build and sustain an organisational community that values the potential offered by diversity, encouraging people in their communities of practice to apply the knowledge that they

Case example 8.2

The Corporate Curriculum of Rabobank

Rabobank, one of the largest banks in the Netherlands, has adopted the term 'Corporate Curriculum' and used it to describe 'the documents containing the principles on learning and development in Rabobank and the available learning interventions and career opportunities for specific groups of employees' (Reumkens and Snijders, 2002: 30–1).

The Rabobank Corporate Curriculum also incorporates the central values of the bank in terms of integrity, respect, professionalism and sustainability.

The need for developing a corporate curriculum is based on internal and external developments that impact on the work in the bank:

- the importance of creative capabilities and entrepreneurship of employees
- the replacement of the dominance of hierarchical modes of interaction by alliances, partnerships and network relationships
- network activities that require the capabilities of connecting, collaboration and sharing of information
- managers who adopt coaching, mentoring and facilitation approaches
- increasingly results-oriented management, performance appraisal, feedback and coaching.

The foundations of knowledge productivity and the elements of the corporate curriculum have been adopted to support these developments. Rabobank has chosen four main organising principles for their corporate curriculum:

- combining subject matter expertise and problem solving
- developing reflective and social-communicative skills
- building personal motivation
- building an effective balance between 'creative turmoil' and 'peace and stability'.

These organising principles are leading to the development of new learning services, products, activities and events to build the capacity for improvement and innovation. The learning interventions take place in classes of the Rabobank Academy as well as in the day to day work environment.

The content of the corporate curriculum comprises a clear vision on learning and development within the Rabobank, an overview of collective and individual learning interventions for about 4,000 senior staff members, diagnostic instruments, and instruments to help evaluation and transfer of learning investments.

Source: Adapted with permission from Reumkens, R. and Snijders, I. (2002) 'Het Rabobank Corporate Curriculum' [The Rabobank Corporate Curriculum]. *Opleiding en Ontwikkeling*, Vol. 15, 4: 30–3

possess to shared tasks of continuous improvement and of innovation. Case example 8.2 shows what one organisation in the Netherlands is starting to do in order to achieve this.

At this point we have provided an assignment in Appendix 1 that you might like to tackle.

ISSUES FOR HRD PRACTITIONERS

Applying the corporate curriculum construct

The corporate curriculum construct suggests a number of important principles to guide HRD professionals and others engaged in the task of creating and sustaining knowledge-productive organisations:

■ *In the knowledge-productive organisation it is essential to develop every individual's skilfulness in learning and knowledge processes.*
The knowledge that is increasingly important for an organisation comes from the exercise of individual and team competence to introduce gradual improvements and radical innovations, both in technological areas and in the ways work is organised and people participate in collaborative arrangements as well as in workplace communities of practice. Because all employees work in such communities, all directly influence the knowledge process, with either positive or negative outcomes for the organisation.

■ *Learning environments should respond positively to diversity in individuals' involvement in learning and knowledge development.*
Because knowledge emerges significantly from the exercise of personal qualities that relate to learning and knowledge processes, every individual has to develop knowledge in their own way. The individual knowledge process cannot be imparted by others, but it can be helped, encouraged and stimulated by a conducive workplace environment. That process cannot be imposed by management, nor can it be scientifically planned or evaluated. Some find the pleasure they experience from working together and being part of a community are important reasons to pursue a collective ambition. For them, the social context is one of the main attractions to getting involved in workplace learning. Others derive their zeal for learning from a specific personal interest – perhaps their drive to solve a problem, their passion for a discipline, their identification and pursuit of a personal life theme, expression of a special talent and enjoyment of an exceptional achievement. In such cases, it is the content of the particular learning situation that is the driving force.

■ *A reduction in emphasis on knowledge as a type of commodity should lead to a reduced preoccupation with designing and distributing uniform instructional content.*
Content that is irrelevant to the social context in which employees interact, or that fails to provide the opportunity for them to discuss and find solutions to substantive questions, produces negative pressures and spoils the desire to learn. Even imaginatively designed and delivered instructional material relating to the acquisition of national qualifications, or tailored to suit the organisation's vision, mission and strategy, may not achieve the active involvement of its intended audience. Concentration and the retention of learning will suffer unless the process of learning is appealing and involving for the individual learner.

■ *HRD activity should place a major focus on the effective combination of learning and working.*
Rather than a preoccupation with prescribing instructional content and a heavy reliance on planning and delivering formalised learning events, HRD practitioners should seek ways of promoting organisationally valuable learning within workplace communities of practice. They should also help and encourage various communities to come together regularly in order to strengthen horizontal linkages – sharing existing knowledge and generating new knowledge (Poell, 1998; Sprenger, 2000). New learning technology has an obvious facilitating function here.

■ *HRD practitioners should identify ways in which practical judgement can be developed and supported in the workplace.*
In the knowledge-productive workplace the exercise of practical judgement is a vital pillar of learning, manifesting itself in the personal skilfulness, sensitivity and wisdom that individuals apply to learning and knowledge processes. This

kind of wisdom is hard to define, and its roots cannot be fully known. However, by its nature it is likely to be aided by varied experience, and to be tested especially in situations that expose individuals and groups to new challenges and that encourage investigative and reflexive learning (Chapter 5, Table 5.1). The mentoring process is particularly helpful in the development in mentees of personal mastery. It is very relevant for organisations where inter-organisational collaboration is crucial, since it is a form of reflexive learning that emphasises trust, shared values and community of interest.

Practical judgement, and mentoring as a learning process, are both so intricately embedded in the socio-cognitive fabric of the particular organisation that they offer the potential to produce a uniquely 'thought-full' organisation. (Harrison and Smith, 2001)

Reflection

- How far, if at all, do HRD practices in your organisation build on people's diverse talents and interests to share and create knowledge in the workplace?
- What more might HRD practitioners do to encourage and support knowledge sharing and the creation of knowledge in that workplace?

The principles we have just outlined suggest that the tentative conclusions reached towards the end of Chapter 6 about new tasks for HRD practitioners now need to be expanded to encompass also:

- ensuring that the provision of formal training is not prioritised at the expense of the task of creating favourable conditions for knowledge-productive learning in the workplace
- producing and promoting HRD processes and initiatives to build the eight pillars of the corporate curriculum
- ensuring an inclusive learning and development system that builds on diversity in the workplace
- finding practical ways of developing a self-managing approach to knowledge sharing and to knowledge creation, utilising the support and involvement of a variety of social, occupational and professional networks to achieve this
- incorporating in training, learning and developmental processes opportunities for individuals to explore and invest in their personal domains of interest and in activity that they find personally meaningful while also having organisational relevance.

In the following three chapters we explore various issues that cast more light on these tasks. As the conclusion to this chapter, we summarise some of the work being done at Shell (Case example 8.3), one of the major companies that is promoting an inclusive development strategy to achieve collective learning, leadership capability and building commitment through respect for diversity.

AN ORGANISATIONAL CASE STUDY

Case example 8.3

The Shell Learning Initiative

The aim of the Royal Dutch/Shell Group is to meet the energy needs of society, in ways that are economically, socially and environmentally viable, now and in the future. The Group does this in a wide variety of ways. It is a supplier of fuel and lubrication products, and also explores on land and sea to find and produce oil. It has operations world-wide exploring for and producing gas and it markets gas and power internationally, to consumers and businesses alike. Its chemical products find their way into all sorts of commercial and domestic use, from mobile phones to furniture, and it has rapidly growing businesses in several of the 'new energy' sectors including hydrogen, solar, geothermal and wind energy.

Shell operates in over 135 countries, employing more than 90,000 people. All of its companies are judged on how they act, by reference to Shell's universal core values of honesty, integrity and respect for people. They strive to promote trust, openness, teamwork and professionalism.

One of the Group's major initiatives to achieve and to improve professionalism, collective learning, leadership capability and commitment is Shell Learning, launched on 1 July, 2002. After many years of a decentralised HRD policy, this constitutes a new global strategy on learning whose purpose is: 'building for tomorrow by developing the people of today'. The founding principles of Shell Learning are to:

- create an environment conducive to learning, where learning activities are accepted as a stimulating and integral part of working life
- seek to identify and action systemic issues in Shell which impact learning
- look for and utilise Group-wide synergies where possible while giving equal weight to the benefits of local solutions and delivery

- seek to bring in external learning practices as challenges to Shell thinking and be at the forefront of learning developments where that leads to competitive business advantage.

Shell Learning is a discrete unit within the global Shell People Services organisation, utilising the infrastructure and support it provides. It comprises four practices:

- *The Leadership Development Practice* is responsible for the global delivery of a range of products and services which support the assessment and development of leaders at key leadership transition levels, based on the Shell Leadership Competency Framework.
- *The Personal and Business Skills Practice* provides a portfolio of products, consultancy and event management services to assure development of personal adaptability and transferable business skills.
- *The Business Improvement Practice* contributes towards enhanced operational performance and growth of the Group by helping to drive its strategic change agenda. This is aligned with the development of people within the Group to ensure that the gains made are sustainable. BIP operates through strategic interventions, applying a portfolio of products and tools in conjunction with the businesses, and working on issues that are on the agenda of their senior leadership.
- *The Organisation Development Practice* focuses on delivering long-term solutions to align the 'whole system': strategy, work, organisation, systems, people and leadership. This unit specialises in developing relationships with senior level management to influence thinking and decision-making.

The authors and publishers thank Shell for permission to use this case

At this point we have produced a second assignment related to this chapter (see Appendix 1), which you may wish to tackle. Before you do so, you may find the following reflection helpful.

Reflection

■ How do the eight learning features of the corporate curriculum construct help to ensure a knowledge-productive workplace?

■ What issues, themes or observations in this chapter do you see to be of particular relevance to your own organisation, and why?

CONCLUSION

In this chapter we have sought to relate the knowledge productivity concept to notions of knowledge explored in Chapter 7, and have proposed a practical framework – the corporate curriculum – whereby to promote and sustain a knowledge-productive organisation. The construct rests on eight pillars or features of learning. It relates positively to the relational notion of knowledge described in Chapter 7, and negatively to the notion of knowledge as control. It is focused on building and sustaining collaborative communities of practice, and relies significantly on the exercise of practical judgement, or wisdom, to ensure respect for all value systems and to build trust that will promote knowledge productivity across the organisational community.

These requirements call into question the traditional command–control paradigm of management, and with it some widely accepted notions of knowledge management. A growing body of analysis and of empirical research suggests that knowledge-productive organisations thrive on 'emancipated' learners who participate in relatively self-controlled workplace communities of practice. In Chapters 8 and 9 we examine how that may be possible to achieve, and its implications for management and leadership in the organisation.

It has by now become clear that in addition to challenges for the HRD function that we identified in Chapter 6, there are demanding roles and tasks for HRD practitioners who are involved in promoting a corporate curriculum to stimulate knowledge productivity. We explore these in the following three chapters before reaching our conclusions on them in Chapter 12.

chapter nine

Researching Knowledge Productivity

INTRODUCTION

The purpose of this book is to explore issues affecting organisationally based human resource development (HRD) in the context of a knowledge economy. In particular we seek answers to the question: how can HRD contribute to what we term 'knowledge productivity'? In Chapter 7 we explored various notions of knowledge, and in Chapter 8 we examined in detail the concept of the knowledge-productive organisation, producing a 'corporate curriculum' framework to support it.

Because our concepts of knowledge productivity and the corporate curriculum are relatively new, it is vital to carry out research in the field in order to assess their practical utility as well as the soundness of their theoretical bases. Therefore in this chapter our purpose is to examine how to research learning processes that support the development and sharing of knowledge with the potential to produce improvement and innovation of work processes, products and services.

We start the chapter by identifying aims, research questions and taxing issues involved in research projects to do with knowledge productivity. We then outline some recent research studies that probe, and offer empirical support for, proposals for mechanisms conducive to knowledge productivity in organisations and for the corporate curriculum framework. They are inevitably exploratory, and the research questions and methodologies used differ from one study to the next, but we argue in the chapter that the outcomes that are emerging from them can be analysed convincingly using conceptual frameworks presented in this and the previous chapter. We consider the challenges that the studies present for future research of this kind, and identify the principles and tasks they suggest for HRD practitioners involved in promoting knowledge productivity in organisations. The chapter concludes with a reflection on issues meriting particular attention from researchers in the interrelated HRD, knowledge development and knowledge management fields.

The assignments related to this chapter (Appendix 1) are intended to help readers who wish to develop their research skills in the domain of HRD, and to appreciate at first hand some of the excitement involved in formulating and testing theories on knowledge productivity and the corporate curriculum.

DESIGNING RESEARCH PROJECTS ON KNOWLEDGE PRODUCTIVITY

Research aims and questions

Although academic and scientific knowledge and the outcome of R&D departments' work are traditionally held in high esteem, many challenges face researchers into learning processes that support knowledge productivity in the workplace and the role of HRD in these processes. Some of the most taxing are to do with the construction of meaningful and unambiguous concepts, the production of valid research designs, and the development of reliable research instruments.

At present the main aims of research projects on 'knowledge productivity' are to:

■ develop and test a framework that explains and clarifies the process of knowledge productivity and the variables influencing this process
■ develop and test principles and specific (learning) interventions for promoting knowledge productivity.

Key research questions in such projects are:

■ Which learning processes contribute to improvement and innovation of work processes, products and services?
■ Which variables promote or inhibit these learning processes?
■ How can these learning processes be stimulated by targeted interventions?

Knowledge productivity is to do with the way in which individuals, teams and units across an organisation achieve knowledge-based improvements and innovations (Brooks, 1997; Leonard-Barton, 1998). Researching learning processes to support the construction of the knowledge that this involves is complicated by the fact that such processes are inherently unobservable. None the less, we saw in the case of Buckman Laboratories, reported at the end of Chapter 7, that it is possible to identify the kind of impact they have on performance if the approach is related to ratio of inputs to outcomes.

The *inputs* to knowledge productivity comprise individual and team capabilities, while its *outcomes* are improvements and innovations in work processes. Specifically, those outcomes relate to:

■ effectiveness in achieving goals, objectives and conducting activities
■ efficiency of consumed resources in achieving goals, objectives and conducting activities
■ quality related to specifications and customer satisfaction
■ quality of work life in terms of employees' well-being (see also Sink et al., 1984).

It is not only learning processes that need to be studied. It is the work context in which they occur. We have explained when discussing how to integrate 'calm' and 'turmoil' in Chapter 8 that different conditions in a workplace can promote or inhibit the organisationally valuable learning in communities of practice. Knowledge productivity research therefore needs to identify and explore workplace context and the changes in rates of improvements and innovations that can be convincingly related to that context.

Reflection ████████████████████████

The production of knowledge that leads to improvement and innovation is not restricted to scientific knowledge. Consider a recent improvement or innovation in your own work environment:

■ What knowledge has been applied to produce this improvement or innovation?
■ What stimulated the development of the new knowledge and its successful application?

Variables of 'improvement' and 'innovation'

The implications for research of the views expressed thus far are that in order to establish empirical evidence for knowledge productivity it is necessary to study a subset of variables with the following elements (Kessels, 2001a; Nonaka et al., 2001):

■ active search for information
■ the development of new knowledge in the form of personal capabilities
■ gradual improvement
■ radical innovation of work processes, products and services.

The last two items raise a complex set of issues that are related to the problems of reconciling 'calm' and 'turmoil', discussed in Chapter 8.

Authors vary in their definitions of 'improvement' and 'innovation'. Often 'improvement' is treated as an incremental form of innovation, and 'innovation' as any implemented invention (Brown and Duguid, 2000: 155). We prefer to support the distinction made by Walz and Bertels (1995), reported in Chapter 8 during our discussion of ways of integrating calm and turmoil in a workplace. They define *gradual improvement* as a process elaborating on what is already present and leading to additional refinement and specialisation, and *radical innovation* as one that involves breaking with the past and creating new opportunities.

When we discussed workplace learning as competitive resource in Chapter 5, we argued that continuous improvement and radical innovation are different in kind, and so require different learning processes. In adaptive, or single loop, learning, individuals and groups act on feedback, adjusting their behaviour continuously in relation to fixed goals, norms and assumptions. Such learning enables the organisation to gradually improve in relation to attainment of required performance standards. However (as we explained in Chapter 3), it can also produce a culture that locks in present methods and so inhibits innovation. So although innovation *may* emerge from continuous improvement, it does not *invariably* do so. Reflexive, or double loop, learning on the other hand encourages radical innovation through opening up the goals, norms and deep-rooted assumptions of the organisation to questioning. Its success here, of course, depends on an organisational context where fundamental change will be accepted.

In proposing that organisations adapt most effectively to the changing environment of a knowledge economy by becoming knowledge-productive, and that knowledge productivity leads to two kinds of outcome – continuous improvement and radical innovation – we are therefore also raising the need for organisations to master a variety of different learning processes and to promote a range of different attitudes to learning and a variety of learning capabilities in the workplace.

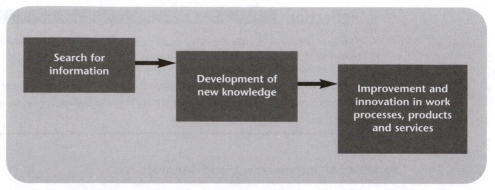

Figure 9.1   *A provisional conceptual framework for researching knowledge productivity*

An initial research framework

Figure 9.1 shows an initial conceptual framework for researching knowledge productivity. It incorporates the subsets of factors we have just discussed. As the chapter unfolds, we will expand and finalise this framework.

Reflection

We have just made a clear distinction between *gradual* improvement and *radical* innovation.

■ Try to recall examples of *each* from your own work environment, or from a work environment that you know about from reading or from others' experience.

■ When you analyse the conditions (including learning processes) that led to radical innovations and compare them with the conditions that led to gradual improvement, how did those conditions differ?

RESEARCHING KNOWLEDGE-PRODUCTIVE ORGANISATIONS

In this section we review a number of research projects conducted to probe and apply our concepts of the knowledge-productive organisation and the corporate curriculum. Given the novelty of these constructs, this means that initial research is exploratory and findings are tentative. However, as we explained at the outset of this book (Chapter 1), initial research into any new field must be exploratory, and also needs to employ a variety of methodologies. We observed in our introduction to Chapter 3 that researchers into 'organising' in an emergent knowledge economy recognise that organisational forms are still in the experimental stages. They are focusing on the innovative and the speculative in order to identify and explore the questions that these new forms raise and the skills that they highlight. The same rationale applies to researching knowledge productivity.

Researching the corporate curriculum

One of the frameworks to capture a particular set of conditions for learning in the workplace that support knowledge productivity is that of the corporate curriculum, explored in Chapter 8. A series of studies in the health and welfare sector in the Netherlands was conducted in the late 1990s to seek empirical evidence for the existence of the learning functions that constitute the corporate curriculum. They are outlined in Research example 9.1, and are detailed in full in Kessels et al. (1998) and Van Lakerveld et al. (2000).

Research example 9.1

Researching learning functions of the corporate curriculum

The studies

In the health and welfare sector, 48 institutions participated in these studies. Most of these organisations offered two departments as units of analysis, and 82 departments in all were studied. Department size varied from approximately 10 to 20 employees, and a sampling population of between three and five employees in each

department was agreed with the organisations. There were 381 respondents, of whom 271 were professional workers in the units, while 110 participants were either managers or held staff positions responsible for quality management or training.

Figure 9.2 outlines key features of the studies.

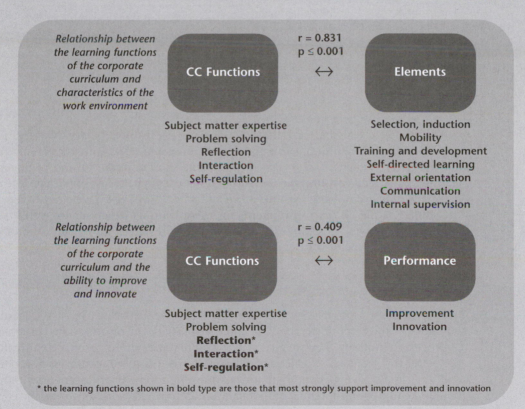

* the learning functions shown in bold type are those that most strongly support improvement and innovation

Figure 9.2 *The corporate curriculum in the health and welfare sector, the Netherlands*

Source: Van Lakerveld, Van den Berg, De Brabander and Kessels, 2000. Reproduced by permission of the authors

The findings

The main findings to emerge were that:

- the corporate curriculum's learning functions of *subject matter expertise, problem solving, reflective skills, interaction* and *self-regulation* described different sets of learning characteristics, but they related sufficiently positively to one another to justify their combination in the overarching corporate curriculum concept.
- all five learning functions related positively to improvement and innovation of work processes and services in the health and welfare sector. However, those supporting *reflection, interaction* and *self-regulation* seemed to be the most powerful in bringing about improvement and innovation.
- *Reflection* was the function most often mentioned as being adversely affected by lack of time. However, it emerged as the single

most crucial function for developing capability to improve and innovate in the day to day work environment.

Although the studies focused on learning as it occurred in the workplace, the responses showed that participants most closely associated the concept of 'learning' with formal instruction. They tended to attribute more learning outcomes to the traditional mode of participating in courses and less to workplace processes such as work-related meetings, cross-organisational co-operation, and research activities. Although most felt that their work situation could to a large extent be considered a learning environment, their instinctive definitions and beliefs about learning were most often related to classroom activities.

Source: Kessels et al., 1998; Van Lakerveld et al., 2000

The studies revealed a correlation between certain features of workplace learning and the ability of institutions to improve and innovate – that is to say, to engage in knowledge productivity. They yielded convincing substantiation for five of the eight learning functions constituting the corporate curriculum. (The supportive learning functions *calm and stability, creative turmoil* and *practical judgement* were not covered in the studies as the research instruments for these learning functions were still being developed. However, those three learning functions are part of subsequent studies, not complete at the time of writing.)

Conclusion

In these studies a positive relationship was identified between five of the learning functions of the corporate curriculum and the ability of the organisations surveyed to improve and innovate. This suggests that the more powerful the corporate curriculum, the better the organisation will be at developing the quality of its processes, products and services. By paying attention to the learning environment, an organisation should be able to improve its potential to innovate and improve its work. However, the corporate curriculum cannot be fully effective unless in the workplace there is an understanding of learning as a broad-based process, to do with informal as well as formal activity and interactions.

In the studies, *reflection* made a particularly strong contribution to improvement and innovation, but often suffered from time constraints. This suggests that the cost of creating more time for reflection could be more than offset by the benefit of employees' increased capability to adapt to the changing conditions that the organisation is facing, and respond innovatively to new challenges and to propose new ways forward.

Researching self-regulated knowledge development

Another series of studies investigated issues relating specifically to the fifth feature of the corporate curriculum framework: *self-regulation of work and learning*. The main characteristic of self-regulation as it is conceived in the framework is the taking by the employee of responsibility for permanent improvement of competencies in a job that is a primary source for learning. As the case of The Learning Company in Chapter 3 demonstrates, work processes in knowledge-intensive organisations can also act as learning processes. In such organisations the most powerful collaborative relationships are those based on mutuality of interest and reciprocal appeal. Rather than operating on the basis of power, control or contract, they do so on the basis of interest or aspiration that is relevant, motivating and meaningful for both employees and organisation.

It is central to this concept of self-regulated learning and development that management does not set the goals or determine the direction of employees' development. The main principles underpinning the concept of self-regulated knowledge development are self-direction and self-organisation, the integration of working and learning, a coaching style of leadership, collaboration, and knowledge development that has the potential to lead to improvement and innovation of products and services (see Figure 9.3).

Developmental research was conducted into an employee-driven HRD research project. It is described in outline here and is detailed in Van der Waals (2001) and in Van der Waals et al. (2002). This project consisted of three main studies. The first comprised the analysis of the design and development process of a management-driven HRD policy in ABP, the largest pension firm in the Netherlands. The second

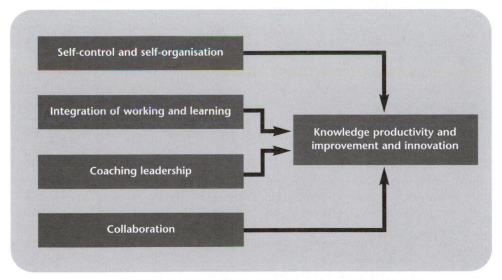

Figure 9.3   *An initial conceptual framework for self-regulated learning and development*

was a replication study with five other pension firms. The third study, described in Research example 9.2, concerned an *Insight into Client* programme that resulted in new competencies, increased co-operation, improved processes, product innovations and system innovations. The employee-driven approach to learning and development that the programme involved appeared to lead to a significant increase in customer satisfaction, employee satisfaction and productivity. Results indicated that self-regulated learning and development fitted better with organisational context than imposed employee training and development, and produced more significant improvements and innovations.

Research example 9.2

Developing self-regulated learning in a pensions firm

The study

In this study the principles of self-regulated training, learning and teamwork were systematically applied in a programme called *Insight into Clients*. The programme was developed in the Pensions and Assurance unit of MN Services, one of the five largest pension firms in the Netherlands, during 2000. It was designed in response to problems caused by increased levels of client complaints, employee dissatisfaction, lack of competence and poor collaboration and communication.

The main feature of the programme was the formation within the unit of a new client team of twelve employees, chosen as a representative sample of the unit's personnel. At the start of the programme the development of self-regulated teamwork was supported by a team activity focused on discussing existing problems, and exploring the goals of the programme *Insight into Clients*. Here, as part of the research methodology, the team was assisted throughout by two coaches. It was encouraged to experiment with new approaches to deal with the complaints of clients and to increase employee satisfaction.

The aim of the coaches was to help the team assume responsibility for work and learning processes. Although their presence throughout the period of the programme would have had an effect on its outcomes, the coaching process was an integral part of the study. The same facility was to be provided for other teams in the

unit when ultimately the programme was extended to them also.

The researchers conducted their data collection using a variety of methods and instruments in four domains: *employee satisfaction, innovation, productivity* and *customer satisfaction*.

The findings

- *Employee satisfaction.* Data were collected using a questionnaire complemented by interviews at two points in time: before the programme started and again at its conclusion. At the end of the programme the new client team was found to differ significantly in employee satisfaction from other teams in the unit. Quantitative data were compared with the output of the other teams. In additional interviews the team members expressed that they experienced more autonomy and felt greater involvement with their unit and its goals than hitherto. There was greater feedback on results, and they experienced their work as more meaningful. Co-operation was more effective and efficient, and work satisfaction higher, with increases in freedom, responsibility and variety in the work being the most frequently mentioned by team members. The members learnt from each other and expanded their professional competencies. Their motivation had increased due to their involvement in a variety of processes, and to the way in which the team organised its work processes.

Research example 9.2 (cont'd)

- *Innovation*. Data on the various improvements and innovations produced by the team were recorded in a log-book, which finally contained 106 examples. During the experiment with the new client team, other teams did not record improvements and continued working as they did before.
- *Productivity*. Data on productivity comprised the number of client questions that were dealt with by team members, and the time that elapsed between posing the question by the client and delivering the answer. According to these indices, the productivity of the new client team was 14% higher as far as the number of questions was concerned, and the elapsed time before answering was 34% shorter, compared to other teams in the unit.

- *Customer satisfaction*. Data on customer satisfaction were collected by a specialist research team, and related to client's appreciation of service level, client orientation, expertise of team members and their professional knowledge and accessibility. At the end of the programme the clients of the new client team differed significantly in their expressed customer satisfaction from the satisfaction levels demonstrated by clients of other teams in the unit. The major results related to feeling better treated as clients, perceiving an improved quality of the service, and enjoying faster and easier access to the relevant person in the unit.

Source: Van der Waals, 2001, and in Van der Waals et al., 2002

Conclusion

These results suggest the importance to knowledge development of the corporate curriculum learning functions related to *interaction* and to *self-regulation*. They are consistent with research findings into knowledge-creating organisations more widely, already discussed in our section in Chapter 3 on promoting the knowledge process. Such studies indicate that organisations that operate effectively in dynamic environments become complex adaptive systems where innovative behaviour starts when employees can regulate their learning according to the needs of that environment (Kaplan and Norton, 1996; Eisenhardt and Santos, 2002).

Researching interventions for knowledge productivity

We have consistently argued that knowledge productivity requires the organisation of the work environment so that employees are stimulated and supported to search for their own solutions, to acquire knowledge and to develop their own professional behaviour and expertise. This is the core of what is called 'constructivist design' (Lowyck, 2001), whereby employees work as a team, facilitated by a learning consultant, and pave their own route for learning. This builds collaborative learning where facilitators and learners do not use prepared learning interventions but become collaborative constructors of such interventions. Such activity forms the basis for a learning trajectory in which participants work on prototype interventions that they continuously refine and improve on the basis of feedback from users.

The study in Research example 9.3 was constructed around those principles. It is reported fully in Kwakman and Kessels (2002). It revealed that those preparing to take on HRD roles can be uncomfortable with process-oriented tasks and with the need to establish a partnership approach in their relations with clients. Many prefer the security of traditional and clear-cut training roles. This is a problematic issue that has been highlighted amongst HRD professionals quite widely, as Research example 9.4 shows.

Research example 9.3

Designing work-related learning projects: a constructivist approach

The study

To explore the feasibility of designing work-related learning projects and the roles that can be played in a constructivist approach, a series of projects was developed in partnership with 13 Dutch organisations. The projects were conducted in 2001 as part of the HRD curriculum of the University of Twente; 16 students participated and the maximum time available for any project was 40 hours. Research questions related to the design of products to support learning in the workplace, the characteristics of such products, and the role to be taken by a designer who supported a constructivist approach.

The design interventions aimed at enhancing learning in the workplace. The students carried out the assignments in 13 different organisations in various profit and not-for-profit sectors. The products they designed included competence maps, process charts, interview schedules, procedures for sharing knowledge, workshop outlines, frameworks for personal development plans, proposals for peer coaching, and advice on on-the-job instruction. The organisational participants comprised the client, members of the target group, managers, team leaders, project team, steering committee, external experts and co-workers. The active participation of the different actors varied across projects.

The findings

■ One of the most significant findings in this study was that the type of product (ready end-product, prototype, advice) that was developed by each student was determined by the type of role that the student decided to assume. The students were free to choose their roles, although all were encouraged to

focus on designing a learning environment in the workplace.
■ The four students who chose a traditional *training designer role* produced specific end-products, ready to be implemented. Those who preferred a *consultant role* participated in preparing a prototype or just offered advice. Those who chose a *facilitator role* prepared advice and prototypes as well as end-products.

Students who chose a combined role of *consultant or facilitator* operated a design process with two major characteristics:

1. The client groups had a clear input in the form of information or active participation on the design process.
2. Recurrent changes in the design process took place.

Students who took an explicit *training designer role* focusing on a ready to use end-product did not operate a design process with these two characteristics.
■ It was concluded that even students can perform adequately a role of learning consultant and facilitator who promotes collaborative learning in the workplace. Their learning here can be facilitated by working on prototypes that are subject to change and adaptation, by offering advice instead of producing end-products, and by focusing on the learning activities that take place during the design process. The students found it difficult to adopt a relational (collaborative, sharing) style, and often felt that the client expected a clear training product instead of a more process-oriented approach.

Source: Kwakman and Kessels, 2002

HRD professionals and process-oriented approaches

The findings in Research example 9.3 echo similar insights obtained during the 2002 European HRD Research Project discussed in Chapters 5 and 6. In that project an international team conducted research into HRD strategies, practices and roles across Europe (Tjepkema et al., 2002). The main aim was to investigate HRD's changing role, focusing on the challenges faced by HRD departments in so-called 'learning-oriented organisations'. Such organisations were defined as companies that strive to enhance opportunities for employee learning with the aim of evolving towards a 'learning organisation'.

These principles require HRD staff to possess skills in acting as consultants to top management, in facilitating action learning projects, in carrying out work meetings with employees and trainees, and in providing advice and assistance to line management on how to create a stimulating work environment with a healthy learning climate. The findings suggest that such skills are new to many HRD professionals, and therefore emphasise the need for a particular focus on their development in educational and training programmes for HRD specialists, and in the continuing personal and professional development of those working in the knowledge development and knowledge management fields. They are summarised in Research example 9.4.

Research example 9.4

HRD professionals' transformational tasks in knowledge-creating organisations

The study

The project comprised a total of 28 case studies in organisations in Belgium, Finland, France, Germany, Italy, the Netherlands and the United Kingdom, with each participating country offering four case studies. Each study focused on an organisation known for its initiatives aimed at transformation into a learning organisation. The research was complemented by a postal questionnaire survey in which 165 organisations participated.

At the outset of the project is was assumed that the HRD function in learning-oriented organisations is based on three main principles:

■ focus on facilitating learning instead of delivering training
■ learning as a shared responsibility of management, employees and the HRD departments
■ the integration of learning and working (Tjepkema et al., 2002a: 15).

The seven participating countries showed variations in HRD-related areas such as rights to educational leave, training taxes, fiscal deductibility of training costs, relationships between (vocational) education and HRD, and school-to-work transition practices. However, as we have seen in Chapter 6, in the learning-oriented organisations under investigation, similarities in HRD visions and practices appeared to be stronger than any trans-European differences (ibid: 17).

The findings relating to HRD, informal learning and knowledge sharing

■ The main business strategies of the companies that participated in the research focused on improving and innovating products, processes and services and on increasing client-centredness. In the companies there was a strong belief that enhanced learning leads to increased business success.

However, there was no explicit evidence to support this view, and there was scant objective evidence generally that HRD added value to the business.

- Employee development, knowledge management, knowledge sharing and creating a favourable learning culture were all major issues in the participating companies. However, the term 'knowledge management' when used by HRD professionals related mainly to sharing knowledge and making it accessible to more people in the organisation, as distinct from creating opportunities for knowledge-productive learning and development for individuals, teams and the collective whole.

- HRD strategies supported informal learning and knowledge sharing in a number of ways already noted early in Chapter 6, but the main emphasis of learning processes and initiatives was on supporting learning at the individual level. Strategies here included creating more learning opportunities, improving worker motivation for learning, supporting continuing development, and implementing a competence-based approach and personal development plans.

Source: Tjepkema et al., 2002

Conclusions

From the many conclusions reached by the researchers, the following are relevant in the context of this section (Tjepkema et al., 2002):

- In spite of a growing awareness that human assets, the ability to learn and the ability to share knowledge are at the core of the modern firm, the researchers did not find HRD to be generally well integrated into corporate strategies.
- In many organisations the HRD function was not seen as a viable mechanism for achieving competitive advantage, being regarded often as a cost to be borne in order to close certain skills gaps.
- Few HRD professionals seemed to be actively helping to build a learning culture in the organisations that were studied. Understanding and implementing the learning organisation concept often required significant changes in leadership and organisational structures and cultures, as well as involvement of HRD practitioners.
- HRD roles and strategies were too often seen and treated from the classical training perspective instead of from a learning perspective. There was an inherent tension between the desire of HRD professionals to support the business and to support individual learning. Despite a great deal of informal learning on the job and the facilitation of a work-related learning culture, many employees in the participating companies still associated learning with attending formal courses. Formal training played a leading role in these learning-oriented organisations and HRD personnel spent much time on training-related work, even though that activity was often embedded in a human resource policy to do with promoting a learning culture focused on increasing learning skills and employability.

The findings from Dutch health and welfare studies that we described earlier in this chapter suggest that when employees tend to associate learning with classroom activities, and when a culture of learning rather than of training is vital to the success of new corporate strategies, then it is also vital to develop new HRD interventions and work methods that can promote informal ways of learning and development and a sense of personal responsibility for learning. This, however, requires relevant skills in those holding HRD roles, and management support for such roles. Such skills are not always present, and such support is not always forthcoming. A significant body of research (Garavan et al., 1999; Sambrook and Stewart, 2002; Stewart and Tansley, 2002) underpins the conclusion that we suggested in Chapter 6 in our discussion of the development of managers and leaders and that we repeat here:

> Although companies rely increasingly on knowledge creation in order to gain competitive advantage and to work effectively in various collaborative arrangements, there is no significant move by trainers from their traditional roles as instructors or training providers in the workplace to new and more relevant roles of learning facilitators and strategic partners.

Reflection

Professionals and academics in the HRD field continually stress the importance of learning and development in the day to day work environment. They discourage a one-sided focus on formal training activities that are often isolated from the shop floor performance. Despite these efforts to raise awareness of the workplace as an important learning space, it appears to be extremely difficult to implement the desired approaches in a real context. The traditional role of trainer and training designer remains dominant over the more process-oriented roles of facilitator and consultant.

- What do you think are possible inhibiting factors that prevent a switch in emphasis from classroom training to workplace learning?
- What factors do you think hamper the acceptance of a facilitator and consultant role?
- What do you think causes a strict division between working and learning in an organisation?

TOWARDS A RESEARCH FRAMEWORK AND STRATEGIES

An expanded research framework

In the first section of this chapter we suggested an initial conceptual framework for researching knowledge productivity (Figure 9.1). After analysing a number of research studies into knowledge productivity and reflecting on conclusions reached in this section, we can now suggest a more comprehensive framework for research in this domain. Figure 9.4 focuses on the following elements (Keursten and Kessels, 2002):

- characteristics of the work and learning environment
- social aspects of knowledge construction
- individual motives for participating in knowledge construction
- characteristics of improvements and innovations of work processes, products and services.

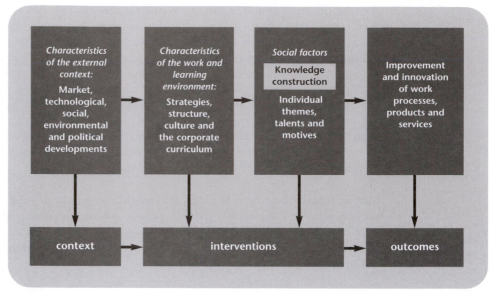

Figure 9.4   *A fuller conceptual research framework for knowledge productivity*

Strategies for researching knowledge productivity

We believe that three types of research activity are helpful in exploring the relation-ship between the characteristics of the work environment as a learning environment and the capability to bring about improvements and innovations of work processes, products and services:

1. *The reconstruction of the process of knowledge development that leads to improvements and innovations in organisations.*
    Here the researcher takes as a starting point actual improvements and innovations. Research activities focus on the reconstruction of the major events, conditions and interventions that eventually are related to the emergence of improvements and innovations. When the results of these reconstructions can be extended to a number of teams, departments or even companies, patterns of powerful combina-tions of factors that determine knowledge productivity are more likely to emerge. In these reconstruction studies the components of the conceptual framework of Figure 9.4 are investigated from the right to the left.
2. *Development research that is geared to the design and implementation of specific inter-ventions that facilitate knowledge development.*
    Here, the researcher plays an active part in the knowledge-construction process by designing interventions that strengthen the social and individual learning func-tions of the corporate curriculum. *Development* or *action-based* research is focused on gradually improving learning environments through the systematic alteration between design, evaluation, reflection and improvement. Pioneers in this field are Richey and Nelson (1996) and Van den Akker (1999). Replication of development studies offers a basis for better selection and application of specific interventions to stimulate knowledge productivity.

3. *Descriptive research that investigates the processes of improvement and innovation as they actually take place in organisations.*

Here, the researcher is an external observer who records over time events as they take place in order to track the course of improvement and innovation and identify its causes. Information has to be collected on the external environment of the firm and on its internal context with particular reference to its strategies, structure and culture, the quality of its corporate curriculum and the involvement of its individuals and teams in activities that eventually lead to improvement and innovation.

This type of research offers focused information on the conditions for collaborative learning. However, it has the same methodological problems that beset any case-based research. It is an essentially partial and speculative approach, posing particular problems of choice of organisation (or organisations, if comparative data are sought) to be studied, lack of certainty about factors that may actually influence the type and rate of improvement and innovation in that organisation (or organisations) as distinct from those that the researcher believes will do so, and ultimately lack of certainty that by the end of the period of observation, a sufficient number of improvements or innovations will have occurred to enable meaningful findings to be produced.

In our view, it is the combination of the three research strategies that is most likely to generate rich data sets on the various components of the corporate curriculum and knowledge-productivity conceptual frameworks. We have already shown in this chapter how analysis of data collected through a variety of differently designed research studies can produce valuable insights into factors that facilitate and inhibit learning processes in the work environment, and into their outcomes related to improvement and innovation. Heterogeneous rather than homogeneous research strategy seems likely to lead to an improved understanding of what interventions in particular circumstances support the capability of a team, unit or organisation to increase its knowledge productivity. Once effective interventions have been identified, they can then form the basis for describing new roles and competencies for HRD professionals and for others holding HRD responsibilities in the workplace.

Two types of research assignment – reconstructive and developmental – are provided in Appendix 1 to help readers interested in developing their skills in researching knowledge productivity in organisations.

WIDER RESEARCH ISSUES

General research uncertainties

In the new knowledge economy, competitive advantage is 'a function of an organisation's ability to continually navigate its way into realms of the unknown and concurrently develop requisite new expertise' (Venkatraman and Subramaniam, 2002: 471). As we have seen in Chapter 3, there are no certain principles to guide the organising process, no typical forms on which to base prescriptions. It is for this reason that Whittington (2002: 125) advises researchers in this field to focus their attention on pioneering firms rather than on the mass of those that reflect organisations more generally. He also urges the need to find research methodologies that will reveal what is really happening within the firm through time and its effects on firm performance.

He observes that apparently conventional structures can mask what is in reality unconventional, especially in struggling or emergent economies where 'there are strong incentives for companies to present themselves externally as multidivisionals, while inside operating very differently' (ibid).

In the literature relating to ways of organising to create and utilise knowledge for the benefit of the organisation, a surprising number of fundamental assumptions remain relatively untested. In particular, the assumption that knowledge is the most important competitive resource rests on little, if any, empirical evidence. Commenting on a wide body of research studies, Eisenhardt and Santos (2002: 159) found no significant use of actual measures of performance that can yield insights into the nature of the competitive advantage that 'knowledge' might bestow, the source of that advantage, or indeed whether that advantage exists at all.

Another assumption, implicit in many studies and writings on knowledge creation in organisations, is that all knowledge is strategically valuable. In fact, some research reveals that it is not, and also that the returns on the generation of new knowledge sometimes go to the individual, not to the firm, thereby failing to add clear value for the business. It is still unclear what constitutes organisationally valuable knowledge, when to transfer it, or whether extensive internal knowledge transfer is strategically wise or sufficiently worthwhile by other criteria, given its costs to the organisation compared with the uncertainty of its outcomes (Eisenhardt and Santos, 2002: 152) .

The studies shown in Research example 9.5 are revealing here. Findings from such research studies reflect the weaknesses inherent in any view of the firm in which knowledge is treated as primarily a commodity, rather than as also a process of knowing, where the organisation is treated as a complex activity system of knowledge emergence and application (Scarbrough, 1998; Eisenhardt and Santos, 2002). We have

---

Research example 9.5

Some findings on effective and ineffective knowledge transfer

Brown and Eisenhardt (1998) examined inter-firm co-operation in a study of 12 major computer firms. They found that more effective firms limited knowledge transfer to the most strategically valuable information, rather than all possible information. They did this by having regular meetings among business unit heads to share opportunities to collaborate, then letting those leaders choose whether or not to collaborate. The meetings created the social bonds and information necessary for collaboration to occur. The option process helped to ensure that the best opportunities were chosen.

Senior executives set the context for collaboration among businesses in the best performing firms. In less effective firms, they either ignored cross-business collaboration or forced collaboration from the top. Other research (Eisenhardt and Galunic, 2000) indicated that when knowledge was transferred effectively, business unit heads were not rewarded for collaboration, but for their own business' success (Eisenhardt and Santos, 2002: 151).

Hansen (1999) studied 120 development projects in a large electronics firm. He concluded that effective organisational design should consider the type of knowledge involved. When it is simple and easily transmitted, weak ties between members of project teams are sufficient to obtain knowledge. When knowledge is more complex, effective internal transfer requires strong ties in the form of formal mechanisms and frequent interaction.

noted in Chapter 7 that such a view underplays the importance of ensuring relatively stable communities of practice where learning can lead to the development and utilisation of strategically valuable knowledge. It also underplays the need to understand how organisational, as distinct from individual, knowledge is created, and of the part played in knowledge development by social interactions and cognitions. Eisenhardt and Santos (2002) found in their review both that the conceptualisation and measurement of knowledge is inconsistent across research studies, and that there is a need for more work on organisational context and its impact on knowledge flows. This has important implications for research strategies and questions related to exploring knowledge productivity.

Questions for research

Reflecting on the research studies outlined in this chapter and in Chapter 7, and taking into consideration the problems we have just outlined concerning research into knowledge-creating organisations, we conclude that the following issues need urgent attention from researchers in the interrelated HRD, knowledge-development and knowledge-management fields:

- Environments that encourage individuals to become expert in areas of work aligned with their personal interests and with their particular talents, ambition and motivation carry a personal appeal that stimulates curiosity and the speedy tracing of relevant information. They facilitate establishing connections with professional networks and stimulate exceptional achievement. *How, and at what kind of cost, can such personally stimulating environments be created, and what mutual support systems are needed to sustain them?*
- Specialist knowledge workers are likely to be attracted by work environments where they can enrich and expand their repertoire of competencies, have career development opportunities and enjoy stimulating working relationships with like-minded colleagues. However, an environment in which *all* employees can work on issues that interest and intrigue them, and that triggers their desire to continuously learn and apply these new learning results, should also have attractions for non-specialist knowledge workers who provide the infrastructure for their specialists colleagues. It can stimulate them to work to their full potential. *To what extent should organisations that are dependent on the rapid generation and application of knowledge invest in the development of non-knowledge workers as well as of knowledge workers (in the specialised sense of those terms)?*
- Knowledge-productive workplaces are rich learning environments in which the social context fosters collaborative efforts, but no single manager, instructor or trainer should carry exclusive responsibility for this. All organisational members need to collaborate in creating a learning environment characterised by mutual respect and recognition, integrity, and sufficient security and openness for constructive feedback and for confrontation. This requires a high standard of communication and interactive skills and the exercise of practical judgement. *How might this personal skilfulness be developed, and what role might HRD practitioners play here?*
- Formal knowledge-management systems seem to add little to an organisation seeking to develop its capability for improvement and innovation, but socialisation of experiences and development of collective competence appear to be essential. Personal networks play an especially important role in the design of

knowledge-productive workplaces. *If the traditional management model is becoming increasingly irrelevant to the domain of knowledge construction, what new model is emerging to replace it?*

■ The development of a supportive work environment and of the corporate curriculum is influenced by the organisation's strategies related to its external environment and to a range of internal factors. However, the knowledge process is highly path dependent, as we have seen from research surveyed in this chapter and in Chapter 3. *What research instruments and strategies can uncover and explore the extent and nature of that path-dependency and its effect on the organisation's capability for knowledge productivity?*

■ Much time can be taken up in the sourcing, transfer and integration within or between organisations that may ultimately prove to have no strategic value. Research also suggests that the more complex is the knowledge to be transferred, the greater is the need for formalised control systems. *In what ways can cost–benefit of the knowledge-productive workplace be assessed and measured, and what criteria can help to decide how tight or loose, formal or informal should be the ties between those involved in knowledge exchange?*

CONCLUSION

Our purpose in this chapter has been to explore ways of researching learning processes that support the development and sharing of knowledge that has potential to produce improvement and innovation of work processes, products and services. To do this we have reviewed a series of studies focused on aspects of the corporate curriculum framework introduced in Chapter 8. We have identified critical research issues and questions they raise for researchers in this field, and have concluded by producing a framework for research in the knowledge productivity domain. The three research strategies that we have linked to this research framework – reconstructive, developmental and descriptive – each have their limitations, but each also has a particular value, so we advocate using them in tandem in order to generate rich data sets.

Reflecting on many of the findings discussed in this chapter, and particularly on the demanding challenges that face researchers and practitioners in the HRD field, we have to question the extent to which those schooled in 'training' and familiar in their organisation for their 'training' role will be able to promote a learning perspective that facilitates knowledge productivity in the day to day work environment. The self-regulated learning and development project described in the case study *Insight into Clients* (Research example 9.2) was heavily based on employee initiatives on learning for improvement and innovation, and typifies a number of HRD, not training, interventions and work methods that support the development of a learning organisation.

When employees in an organisation hold perceptions of learning that are primarily associated with formal courses and classroom training, it seems clear that trainers in that organisation are not taking on genuine HRD roles. One reason for this may be that they have not the competence to do so, another that, despite having such competence, they can gain no support in the organisation for doing so. Weak integration of corporate strategies of HRD focused on knowledge productivity can explain why staff traditionally associated with formal training activity are not seen as relevant for new roles that facilitate a learning climate in the workplace. This was indicated quite strongly in findings from the 2002 European HRD Research Project (Tjepkema et al., 2002). In these situations external consultants are often brought in instead.

In such scenarios, training staff keen to enter the HRD arena should adopt a relational approach in their operations. This involves achieving external consistency – that is to say, establishing close contacts and communication with managers, supervisors and employees in order to generate shared notions of the problems to be tackled by the programmes, of the learning needs that they should serve and of how to collaborate in programme design, delivery and evaluation (Kessels and Plomp, 1997, 1999; Kessels and Harrison, 1998). Successful partnership improves the transfer of learning outcomes to the workplace and supports the embedding of formal training activities in the day to day work environment. For those HRD specialists who genuinely wish to play an active role in organisational learning processes, an important first step is to ensure external consistency for their conventional training activity, thereby gaining increased trust, support from their business partners and enhanced credibility for their initiatives (Harrison, 2002: 117–34).

chapter ten

New Technology, the Knowledge Process and HRD

INTRODUCTION

In this chapter it is our purpose to describe developments in information and communication technology (ICT) that have direct implications for the HRD function and for its practitioners. In an increasingly knowledge-based economy and in competitive environments requiring rapid organisational and skills changes, and therefore fast learning capability, it is essential to be able to apply ICT to learning processes in appropriate ways. Research studies and national surveys, however, indicate that HRD practitioners are not taking a leading role here. One of our aims is to identify some of the skills they need to acquire if they are to do so. Another is to explore aids and hindrances to the harnessing of ICT to learning and development in the workplace. Throughout the chapter we draw on research studies from across Europe.

Managers and HR practitioners need to understand how to use new information processes and systems in their own areas of work. They also need to be able to develop – or advise on the development of – an effective relationship between structure, information technology and knowledge productivity when new organisational forms are to be introduced and maintained. Research studies on the use of groupware such as Lotus Notes, of data warehousing and of collaborative technologies, some of which we reviewed in Chapter 7, all show that these high-tech approaches do not work effectively when there is inadequate understanding of the human factor. This confirms that knowledge cannot be transmitted as if it were an entity that can be passed via electronic devices from one brain to another. The notion of knowledge as a process involving the exercise of personal skilfulness in learning and knowledge development can provide a persuasive explanation for the deficient application of many so-called knowledge systems and technologies. It offers a learning perspective that has direct relevance when the work environment has to be reorganised to accommodate the introduction or expansion of new technology.

In the first section of this chapter we discuss critical aspects of the relationship between new ICT, learning and the construction of knowledge in the organisation. We then examine ways in which new technology can both aid and hinder the knowledge process, and go on to pay particular attention to uses of new collaborative technology in bringing together virtual teams to share and create knowledge. The chapter concludes by examining opportunities and challenges for HRD practitioners in relation to technology-mediated collaborative learning.

NEW TECHNOLOGY, EDUCATION AND LEARNING

Using ICT to support learning

The effective use of ICT to support learning calls for a clear vision of learning as an interactive process, and an appreciation of the need for that process to be aligned with company goals and of the importance of employee motivation to learn. It also requires the identification of perceptions in the organisation concerning how learning using ICT might best take place. A key question is: what added value might ICT bring to the learning process? The most frequent responses stress the possibility of just-in-time knowledge acquisition, greater flexibility and efficiency in learning, tailored learning, and opening up access to the most up-to-date information. However, as we hope to show in this chapter, it can make possible far more than this:

> In opening up access to the information that the learner wants, when and in the form that they want it, (electronically-based learning) can not only help them to quickly acquire targeted learning outcomes: it can also offer to them a voyage of discovery that can transform the way they see the world. It can enable them to generate knowledge and then use it in ways that they could not have predicted when they started out. E-learning can speed up the acquisition of skills; but it can also fuel the development of knowledge. This is how learning and knowledge become fused in an integrated process. (Harrison, 2002: 215)

When thinking of the power of new technology in the educational domain, one image that springs vividly to mind is that of the best professors throughout the world capturing their lectures on film, tape, CD-ROM and the Internet, thereby giving access to the latest expertise from the brightest in the field. Yet that is no new picture. In his lecture 'There should be someone who knows everything', De Swaan recollects H.G. Wells proposing in 1936, long before the Internet but shortly after the invention of the microfilm, the 'World Brain'. He envisaged a universal encyclopaedia, edited by the brightest scholars of the world, made available on microfilm (De Swaan, 2002). A similar vision emerged from the early literature of the knowledge economy and the use of technology, where Winslow and Bramer imagined the construction of an information supernetwork, connecting homes, industries, libraries and schools:

> 'Infocosm', an electronic cosmos or world teeming with information and knowledge ... ensuring that all those within the infocosm can find and use information and then supporting whatever performance needs they may have. (Winslow and Bramer, 1994: 305)

Now, such visions are becoming reality as the scenarios in Case example 10.1, picked at random from many such, illustrate.

The concept of technology opening up access to everything that is known reflects the notion of knowledge as commodity. But important though it is, the technology of book print, libraries, encyclopaedia, microfilm and of ICT does not of itself share knowledge. It can aid the process, but it cannot create it.

Case example 10.1

Harnessing new technology to training and learning processes

■ In 2000 the UK government officially launched its *University for Industry* (UfI) which, through its operating arm *learndirect*, offers on-line training packages, accessible to all, backed up by paper-based induction courses to help individuals to learn how to use the packages, and supported by on-line and face-to-face mentoring and group discussions over the Internet. The aim is that anyone, anywhere, using a computer, will be able to identify courses to meet their interests. They can enrol, pay for courses, receive learning materials and support – all electronically. Delivery methods will include interactive digital TV, video, CD-ROM and Internet. Those not yet owning a computer have only to go to a local *learndirect* centre and use one of theirs.

■ In 1999 International Computers Ltd amalgamated its six European training businesses and established a new company, KnowledgePool, to provide training services 'ranging from multisite programmes tailored for global companies to distance-learning for individuals via the Internet, intranet or CD-ROM' (Rana, 1999).

■ In March 2000 the UK Prime Minister announced that he was committing the country to a goal of universal access to the Internet by 2005, and that by 2002 all schools in Britain would be linked to the Internet. In the same month, his Minister for Education and Employment was heralding the arrival of *Universitas 21*, sponsored by the Department for Education and Employment, and linking Massachusetts Institute of Technology, Cambridge University and the UK's Institute of Enterprise in order to 'harness globalisation as a force for progressive change'. It would enable the institutions involved to 'share resourcing, facilitate staff and student mobility and use new technology to spread excellence'. The ultimate aim was to improve society: 'In a knowledge economy, expansion in high-quality higher education is critical to social justice' (Blunkett, 2000).

Reflection

■ Consider a situation you know about where ICT has added value to the learning process in an organisation or part of it. What benefits have been achieved as a result?

■ Consider now a situation where ICT has failed to add value. What seem to have been the reasons for this, and how do you think things should have been handled differently?

Do we choose technology or does technology choose us?

At first sight it may seem that we are free to decide whether to use technology and what kind of technology to use. In a learning context it is we, the actors, who appear to be in control, we who determine what aims ICT should serve, what learning strategies it should facilitate, what capabilities it should enhance. Yet in reality this is not quite the case. Our daily environment constantly if invidiously bombards us with pressures to use new technology. As a matter of course, more and more of us regularly access our emails, update our virus scan, pick up our electronic birthday cards, register for a conference on-line. Our children chat and text-message endlessly on their multiple-function mobiles, mastering complex electronic gadgets with ease. In the workplace, mysterious-sounding processes such as 'synchronous' or collaborative design carried out among dispersed teams linked electronically are now common, and the influence of ICT is shaping our entire perception of working and learning. How can we resist its force? In a digital economy, work and learning are becoming the same thing, and the use of new technology cannot now be separated from either (Tapscott, 1996).

When it comes to learning and knowledge construction, involving layered information, intensive interaction and multilateral feedback, it is wasteful to employ technology just for presenting information. The World Wide Web is 'not just a tool to provide access to existing data in more flexible, user-friendly, timely ways' (Lymer, 1996: 9–10). It is changing the way new information is generated by offering users 'a new medium through which to exchange ideas, formulate proposals and generate solutions in ways not previously possible' (ibid).

Collaborative learning in a rich learning context can probably only develop to its fullest potential when harnessed to computer and internet systems. However, the extent to which new technology's potential in this respect is realised depends in large measure on the willingness of learning designers and facilitators to exploit it to the full. That willingness is often lacking. The traditional trainer who sticks to prescribed instructional objectives and subject-matter content probably welcomed early forms of computer-assisted learning that offered programmed instruction and the quick administration of multiple choice tests. Doubtless he or she also makes good use of slide instruction steered by audiotape and of CD-ROM. Such computerised approaches reflect a didactic, trainer-oriented concept of learning. But those committed to that concept will find it much harder to adjust to on-line chatrooms and 'a-synchronous' discussion platforms (that is, platforms for discussion conducted sequentially through time) let alone incorporate them in their training courses. E-technology embodies a uniquely learner-centred philosophy.

Certainly in the UK there is no evidence of trainers or organisations leaping onto the e-based learning bandwagon, as Research example 10.1 shows.

Research example 10.1

Trainers and new technology

In 1999, research by the International Data Corporation predicted that new technology-based training would increase by more than 50% by 2002, and would become the largest delivery vehicle for corporate training. In 2002 the Chartered Institute of Personnel and Development's fourth annual training survey had a particular focus on its level of impact. The survey covered 502 respondents who were interviewed by telephone, being either training managers/directors or others who could speak on the organisation's behalf at the establishment level.

The results were disappointing. Overall, the

Research example 10.1 (cont'd)

survey presented a picture of UK establishments making extensive use of structured workplace learning but of few using new technology as a primary means of delivering that learning. Certainly since the first survey in 1999 there had been a rapid increase in the use of computer-based training, but the 2002 responses indicated that although usage was spreading rapidly, in most establishments it was not intensive. The main findings were (CIPD, 2002: 2):

■ less than a third of respondents were using e-learning for any group of employees

■ where e-learning was used, IT staff were the chief beneficiaries; it was used less often for

management and hardly at all for manual workers

■ e-learning was used most for IT and technical training, far less for soft skills training

■ most organisations using e-learning spent less than 10% of their training budgets on it

■ most training managers using e-learning thought it more effective when combined with other forms of learning and that it would have only a marginal effect on classroom training.

Source: CIPD: 2002

NEW TECHNOLOGY AND THE KNOWLEDGE PROCESS

The value-adding potential of ICT

Initial enthusiasm for new technology and subsequent failure to utilise it to the full in training and learning processes have not prevented the exploration of new applications by innovative individuals and companies. Meanwhile, as we have shown regularly throughout this book, perceptions of learning are changing – or at the least, a growing value is being placed on different perspectives of learning and knowledge processes.

Besides presenting content, ICT can help us to search for like-minded spirits, explore challenging ideas, and test fresh solutions to unusual problems. Curiosity, a passion to increase expertise, and the appeal of human interaction across many electronically facilitated networks are crucial ingredients of the knowledge infrastructure in a knowledge economy. Yet as we have just indicated, open access to the World Wide Web may seem anarchic and threatening to those holding conservative notions of learning. This is bound to change in time. After all, technology is essentially there to support, not confront. Whether or not based on electronic information systems, technology:

> simply refers to the particular way in which, in a workplace, technical systems, machinery and processes are designed to interact with human skill and knowledge in order to convert inputs into outputs. (Harrison, 2002: 211)

When any new technology is first introduced it seems revolutionary, and so creates suspicion, fear and uncertainty – but over time its usage becomes familiar, and attitudes to it change, bringing acceptance and ultimately further innovation. In the old Fordist workplace that we described in our discussion of 'the organisation as machine' in Chapter 7, the revolutionary technology was that of the mass production line and training was the critical learning vehicle that enabled individuals to acquire the routinised skills they needed. As that technology began to show its age, scientific and engineering advances in the later part of the 20th century enabled it to acquire a new sophistication. Then the advent of the first generation of computers produced another revolution, but by the turn of the century that too had lost its novelty and ICT advance was already heralding today's electronic revolution. Now, the dizzying pace of technological change on which we commented in Chapter 1 is leading to new levels of technological sophistication being regularly achieved at ever-reducing time intervals.

> In the so-called 'post Fordist' workplace, new information technology is bringing together computer-based hardware, human skills and knowledge in unique ways that are capable of changing yesterday's production line workers into today's knowledge workers. (Harrison, 2002: 211)

One of the greatest achievements of new ICT is the way in which it facilitates the process of knowing as a social construction that thrives when human minds are invited and enabled to connect. At present few HRD practitioners appear to be utilising, or even fully understanding, the full potential of ICT to stimulate the generation of knowledge as distinct from merely facilitating transmission and dissemination of information (Scarbrough et al., 1999). Yet it is inevitable that, with the widespread use of innovative ICT in work organisations, it will become ever more difficult for trainers and other HRD practitioners to maintain a stance of 'choosing' whether or not to use it in their own domain. New technology will increasingly choose them, as in the workplace it becomes a natural, fundamental part of the relational process whereby people learn and construct knowledge.

ICT and knowledge management

It is fascinating but also worrying to see how quickly the growing interest in knowledge as a business asset has been expressed in a technological approach. The frequent combination of ICT and knowledge management does not occur only in practice. In international scientific journals the majority of articles on knowledge management focus on information technology and information systems too. In their overview, Scarbrough and Swan (2001) listed 68% of articles on knowledge management as related to ICT applications. This use of ICT reflects a perception of knowledge as an objective, codified asset that can be stored, retrieved and passed on from one person to many others. However, as cases that we outlined towards the end of Chapter 7 indicated, accessing ICT systems offers much more than that: it offers the possibility of participating in a process of knowledge sharing.

In Chapter 7 we discussed the complex nature of knowledge as a relational process located in communities of practice. Hansen et al. (1999) reviewed in an ICT setting contrasting approaches of managing knowledge as a codified and objective resource, and supporting knowledge development as a personalised process. They studied consulting firms that reused codified knowledge extensively as part of their business approach, often managing it through electronic databases. They found that this stored, instrumental and case-based knowledge served as a primary resource for relatively inexperienced junior consultants whose performance, in the main, consisted of applying standardised solutions to well-defined problems. They found, on the other hand, that organisations whose prime interest was with fuzzy, ill-defined questions systematically developed much more personalised and contextualised expertise. Such organisations were concerned primarily to use information technology to support and facilitate the building of personal networks and communication processes.

The availability of advanced technologies for creating and sustaining a knowledge-based company continues to expand, and learning from the experience of others and from past situations is a favoured way of building expertise. Consider Case example 10.2.

It is intriguing to see how the continuing development of information systems leads some to conclude that such systems might one day themselves be able to learn, recall, and generalise – and how threatening others find the aim of developing such systems so that they can simulate the human brain. But we are only at the start of any such endeavour. Research shows that the human brain is still having difficulty in learning and collaborating with technology, and one of the major concerns of experts

Case example 10.2

ICT systems to support personalised learning

A case-based reasoning system

This provides a tool to support learning through cases. Essentially, it consists of a case library and a software system for retrieving and analysing similar cases and its associated information. Each case usually contains a description to capture the underlying competitive situation, the environmental condition, management priorities, experience, and values that allowed a certain strategy succeed. A software system helps indexing each case in such a way that a search yields a modest number of cases with similar features. A case-based reasoning system can thus generate details that provide a precedent for a particular decision and an explanation for past failures (Baets, 1999).

A group decision support system

This facilitates team-based learning by enabling a group of people to work interactively and simultaneously using networked hardware and software to complete the various aspects of a planning process (Baets, 1999). It represents an automated brainstorming device, supported by software that provides displays of ideas, voting, compilation, anonymous input and interaction, decision modelling, electronic mail and a bulletin board function. It brings people together and facilitates interaction by reducing communication barriers.

Mind mapping and cognitive mapping systems

These are specific tools for organising ideas, concepts or variables, and visualising their relationships. The most advanced technologies in this domain are grouped under the umbrella of Artificial Neural Networks (ANNs). The claimed potential of ANNs is that:

ANNs have the ability to learn and identify complex patterns of information and to associate these with other information. ANNs can recognise and recall information in spite of incomplete or defective input information. They can also generalize learned information to other related information. These abilities form the basis for supporting learning of the relationship among business factors/ processes. (Baets, 1999: 187)

Source: Baets, 1999

is that we may rapidly be reaching a point where technology is simply too sophisticated for the average user (Collis and Moonen, 2001).

New technology undoubtedly has vast potential in all fields of science and education, but it is difficult to imagine that even the smartest and most intelligent artificial systems will ever be able to replace the human being in the knowledge process, since when reviewing research:

> What does emerge in study after study is that … 'Knowing' is about relational and emotional as well as rational processes, social as well as psychological factors. (Harrison, 2000: 248)

In this view, ICT, no matter how sophisticated its operation, can never take more than an essentially supportive role in knowledge construction and in knowledge sharing.

ICT and knowledge sharing

The relational notion of knowledge construction, as described by authors such as Brown and Duguid (2000), is illustrated especially by Neilson's study (1997) on collaborative technologies and organisational learning. His findings indicated that information is more likely to be provided through an ICT system if employees notice that others are using it and feel a need to contribute relevant information as well. Once the system becomes an integral part of daily operating procedure, it will be used with increasing intensity.

Neilson found that the effective use of new technology requires not only specific technical skills, but also the substantial contribution of human participants. He concluded that collaborative technology is, by definition, a social device.

Huysman and De Wit's (2002) research studies indicated that groupware tools have not yet become institutionalised. One explanation seems to be that people do not use these sophisticated tools when they feel a limited need to share knowledge. The researchers concluded that the use of groupware tools will start to increase the moment that people begin to place more value on the knowledge-sharing network than on the individual acquisition of knowledge. If people are not interested in sharing, then giving them tools to share is unlikely to be enough to change their minds. As some of the case examples in Chapter 7 demonstrated, people will share ideas only when they relate to issues perceived to be of vital common concern (Dixon, 2000: 5).

Huysman and De Wit concluded that it is not enough to think just of individuals when considering how to construct and share knowledge. A broader perspective is needed – one that involves concepts of social as well as human capital:

> Human capital relates to individual learning but does not necessarily contribute to organizational learning. It is argued that the social capital provides the conditions that nurture a willingness among these intellectual humans to connect. (Huysman and De Wit, 2002: 166)

Pieper, ex vice-president of Philips, took a similar stance when discussing the 'e-mentality' in his inaugural lecture as professor in e-commerce at the University of Twente in the Netherlands. He argued that sharing knowledge requires a personal change in mentality. Only individuals able to reveal their own strengths and weaknesses will fully understand in which field they are likely to be able to add value. This revelation of personal qualities enriches the human relations network, which can only operate effectively on the basis of trust, flexibility and openness. Together, these qualities constitute the true e-mentality and those who are amply endowed with them will be the ones who derive the fullest benefit from the information society (Pieper, 2000: 50).

We have provided an assignment in Appendix 1 that you may wish to tackle at this point. Before doing so, you may find it helpful to reflect on the following questions:

Reflection

Some authors are very optimistic about the role of ICT in learning and knowledge sharing.

■ What applications do you think will become increasingly important in the future, and why?

■ In your view, what are some limitations in the use of ICT in the domain of knowledge sharing and of knowledge creation?

COLLABORATIVE TECHNOLOGY AND VIRTUAL TEAMS

Balancing ICT and face-to-face processes in virtual teams

ICT has obvious potential in helping to build and sustain virtual teams whose members are in widely dispersed locations. Such teams are a common feature of organisational life in an emerging knowledge economy, yet here too there are limits to what ICT can achieve. All successful teams are based on the creation of relationships and trust, and even though information technology has made enormous progress it is questionable whether ICT can ever of itself be enough to build such relationships. Wenger et al. (2002) suggest the following to successfully develop communities of practice that do not meet regularly face to face:

■ *Achieve stakeholder alignment.* Overcoming conflicting priorities and developing a common understanding of the potential value of co-operation takes a considerable time for distributed teams.

■ *Connect people.* Large teams may need local co-ordinators and a global facilitator who pass questions and requests to people in the network. Once contact is established, members continue the exchange of information directly via phone, email or other information technology.

■ *Whenever possible try to organise face-to-face meetings.* Face-to-face meetings seem to be very important for the success of distributed teams. The role of complex tacit forms of social communication is especially crucial, and this can only be found in such meetings (Nohria and Eccles, 1992).

Sambrook and Stewart (2002) commented in similar fashion on the conduct of research into European practices in HRD, undertaken in 1998/1999 by an international team (see Chapter 5). Reviewing problems faced in collaborative transnational comparative organisational research, they identified the greatest as being to do with reaching agreement on fundamental research concepts and terminology and on methodology, on the status of research data gathered by partners, and on claims that different researchers might support. They emphasised the need for patience, openness and mutual trust in resolving such problems, and for all research partners to meet face to face as often as possible rather than rely overmuch on email communication. They also felt strongly that key research steps should be shared by all partners, rather than being left exclusively to a project management team to execute. In their view, the function of such a team in 'virtual' collaborative endeavour must be primarily supportive.

Rice and colleagues (2000) conducted a longitudinal study to explore ways in which collaborative technology (CT) can be used to enhance knowledge sharing among dispersed teams (see Research example 10.2). It illustrates and supports the kinds of views about balancing IT with face-to-face relational processes that we have just outlined.

When discussing the use of CT to support virtual teams, one area of special interest is the way in which it can support the learning processes among professionals. Rukanova (2001) carried out an investigation into this area (see Research example 10.3). She concluded that the CT-based communication lacks richness because it cannot capture much non-verbal communication (although use of video conferencing and other imaging processes are opening up more possibilities here). She found that its value lies in facilitating collaborative work. In that capacity, it can encourage socialisation processes. However, for many professionals the technology is fairly new, and its mere availability does not automatically mean that they will use it

---

Research example 10.2

Collaborating in virtual teams

Over a 10-month field study period, the researchers observed the use of CT by an inter-organisational virtual engineering team. *The Internet Notebook* gave team members access to a project knowledge repository, enabling them to author new documents, comment on entries, sort and navigate, create a personal profile for email notification of relevant entries, use templates for frequent team activities, and so on. Team members could use the CT asynchronously or synchronously.

During the period of the study, team members collaborated with each other 61% of the time. Instead of a gradual increase in CT use, they quickly learned how to use *The Internet Notebook* and were soon applying it at a moderate level. However, there was never any consistent trend in its use, in contrast to trends that typified their use of face-to-face contact and telephone. They tended to use those modes for more ambiguous tasks to do with managing external relationships, resolving conflict, brain-

storming, and strategic direction-setting, although over time they did adjust to use of CT for some of these tasks. In particular they carried out an intense form of brainstorming via CT at a later stage in the project.

The researchers concluded that sharing knowledge when using ICT requires the development of a common language, and that team members may prefer face-to-face or phone contact when seeking to resolve fundamental differences of opinion. They found in this study that CT mainly served as an information repository and not as a gateway to the right information. It operated as a support in exchanging ideas, opinions and preferences in the team and also facilitated developing shared cognitions. But when it came to knowledge construction there seemed to be a need for a human mediating process to facilitate, motivate, and essentially reinforce group identity and purpose.

Source: Rice et al., 2000: 96

Research example 10.3

The role of collaborative technology in facilitating learning in virtual teams of professionals

Rukanova's study focused on a number of knowledge-intensive companies whose professional staff worked mainly in geographically dispersed locations. She concluded from its outcomes that communication and socialisation processes are very important for professional development, but that there is still no technology to replace that of face-to-face communication here. Even in a virtual organisation, it is essential to spend some time on such communication. Once professional colleagues get to know each other, they can disperse geographically and start using real-time collaboration and communication facilities in their CT work process.

The researcher also found that the communication process benefited particularly from the availability of buddy lists with names of friends and colleagues, thereby allowing the individual to constantly see who was on-line. Through sending an instant message, it was possible to start a communication process, whether formal or informal. In order to control the flow of instant messages, it was important to have a variety of functions such as *chat, busy, away, not available*, and so on. When team members needed to work together, this could be facilitated by real-time CT facilities.

Source: Rukanova, 2001

to its fullest potential. As the research of Rice et al. (2000) also illustrated, a certain time for learning to cope with the technology is essential, together with some compelling shared purpose.

An additional phenomenon that requires attention is the use of advanced technology for participation in synchronous activities – that is to say, in activities that are occurring simultaneously. As we have a long tradition of making wired phone calls, the use of a mobile phone does not create insurmountable problems. However, participation in a tele- or video conference requires specific skills and a disciplined approach to be effective. For many employees, these competencies are easy to talk about in theory, less easy to acquire in practice. Those only in the initial stages of using more advanced collaborative technology are likely to find the simultaneous processes of thinking, working and learning on-line quite complex, because they have not yet mastered how to combine the set of discrete capabilities that they involve.

At this point we should reconsider views expressed earlier in the chapter about the impossibility of CT ever replacing the face-to-face contact that seems indispensable for human interaction. It is possible that it is simply too early for us to judge. Perhaps it is more a matter of still having to learn how best to collaborate with members of a virtual team that we have not met face to face. Maybe there will be developments in CT that could in future help us to do this, building on such facilities as video conferencing. Once participants become accustomed to new technology they will use it more proficiently than we do now. However, there is clearly an important role for HRD practitioners in helping team members in their organisations to develop the attitudes, as well as the capabilities, needed to engage fully in virtual communities.

Reflection

- Identify and explain key competencies that you believe virtual team members need if they are to use CT effectively in their projects. Try to focus on a particular team in your own organisation.
- Then consider how these competencies might be developed, by whom, at what points in time (before, at the start of, or during the team's operations) and at what kind of time, financial and expertise cost.

Collaborative technology and sharing understanding

An important issue in using technology for supporting learning and knowledge construction, especially among dispersed team members, relates to ways in which participants develop shared understanding. To investigate this process, a series of studies (Research example 10.4) focused on the interaction between teams operating from different locations and using a variety of communication technology tools and processes. The research is detailed in Mulder and Swaak (2001) and in Mulder et al. (2002).

Research example 10.4

Interactions between geographically dispersed teams

The studies

The studies covered members of a number of virtual design teams, and gave powerful insights into types of interaction (task related, social, procedural or technology related), group learning and shared understanding, drawing on the very detailed analysis of recorded and transcribed group interactions.

From an analytical point of view the concept of reaching shared understanding was expressed as activities that included *conceptual learning*, the use of *feedback* and the expression of *motivation*. *Conceptual learning* referred to instances where team members operated on the basis of content of the information. To analyse the use of *feedback*, interactions were coded in the subcategories: *confirm, paraphrase, summarise, explain, check understanding, check action,* and *reflect*. The *reflect* code represented a feedback mode to indicate metacommunication that was not necessarily related to procedures or technology. To identify expressions of *motivation*, interactions were coded in subcategories labelled *evaluation, uncertainty,* and *impasse*.

The findings

Analysis of the results showed a predominance of task-related interactions coded as *feedback* and *conceptual learning*. These were mainly to do with accretion and tuning. Almost no social interaction could be observed, except at the end of video conferences.

One important finding was that the coded protocols yielded few expressions of *reflection*. One possible explanation is that it is inherently difficult to assess reflectivity in any empirical study. Another is that in this study little reflective activity may actually have taken place. Another is that it may be more difficult to express reflectivity in purely technology-mediated interaction – a point impossible to verify in the study, as it did not incorporate comparisons with face-to-face interactions. If it is the case that CT does not facilitate reflection easily, then the implication is that an exclusive

Research example 10.4 (cont'd)

reliance on CT hampers group learning and the reaching of shared understanding. Additional support therefore seems necessary and, if it cannot be provided by some form of ICT, then human intervention by a facilitator or learning consultant seems essential.

Source: Mulder and Swaak, 2001; Mulder et al., 2002

These findings reinforce others reviewed in this chapter in relation to social interaction. One of the conclusions reached by the researchers was that, given the importance of knowing one another if collaborative learning and shared understanding are to be achieved, team members should first meet face to face or at least exchange background personal information on a team website. Another was that as a general rule technology-related interaction could be facilitated by a virtual team receiving an introduction on optimal media use at the start of a project. Such guidelines would also be helpful for any facilitator who is starting up virtual learning teams or is intervening in technology-mediated collaborative design and problem solving.

We have provided a second assignment for this chapter, in Appendix 1. Before tackling it you may wish to reflect on the following questions:

Reflection

- If you have experience in the use of collaborative technology, has this been generally of a positive or negative kind, and what lessons have you learnt from it?
- What technological solutions do you think would help overcome the kind of shortcomings of CT discussed in this section of the chapter?
- What skills will participants need to develop if they are to engage easily in virtual collaboration?

NEW TECHNOLOGY: TASKS FOR HRD PROFESSIONALS

Enhancing the skills of HRD professionals

In the second assignment related to this chapter, the task focuses on how an HRD professional (as distinct from the many other personnel in an organisation who may carry responsibilities related to the harnessing of ICT to learning processes) might carry out a complex virtual teambuilding assignment. One striking finding of recent case-based research of 28 learning-oriented organisations across Europe where professionals with HRD roles were employed was that in only one organisation was there evidence of explicit intent or initiatives to increase the skills of HRD staff facing new challenges in their roles and tasks (Sambrook and Stewart, 2002). At this point, it is therefore relevant to include a brief section concerning the preparation of such professionals for operating effectively in the field of ICT-related learning processes and methods.

The illustrative study that we have chosen was designed specifically to enable HRD professionals to explore their role in dealing with dedicated technology for corporate learning. It is detailed in Alekseeva (2002) and outlined in Research example 10.5.

Research example 10.5

HRD professionals and the harnessing of ICT to corporate learning processes

The study

Alekseeva (2002) conducted a development study on the design of a WWW-environment for learning at Heineken University. One of the objectives was to explore the requirements for effective collaborative learning in a corporate setting using ICT.

The participants in the study comprised a group of 24 HRD professionals working in various Heineken operating companies across the world and using TeleTOP, a groupware technology designed by researchers and educationalists at the University of Twente (Collis and De Boer, 1999; http://teletop.edte.utwente.nl), in their daily operations.

Since the late 1990s TeleTOP had been extensively used and tested as a management system for formal courses in the university context, but at the time of this research study its application in a business environment was relatively new. The 24 HRD participants were invited by the staff of Heineken's corporate university to explore issues related to competency-based learning. They engaged in this virtual learning experience as part of their preparatory work for assisting at a face-to-face seminar on the same topic at Heineken headquarters, three months later. The objectives of the project were twofold:

■ to explore the use of advanced learning technology and find out what role HRD professionals should play when implementing such technology in the firm

■ to develop a learning environment for exploring the characteristics of competency-based learning, thereby offering a virtual learning experience to the HRD professionals themselves.

The findings

Some of the main findings to emerge from the study were:

■ Not all participants felt deeply motivated by the topic. In their evaluation of the project they emphasised the need for the subject of any learning experience to be appealing to the learners. Those who were not motivated collaborated only at a low level.

■ The objectives of the project were felt to be ambiguous. It was unclear to participants whether competency-based learning or collaborative learning in a WWW-based environment was the central issue. Lack of clear and concise objectives seemed to be a primary pitfall in implementing the Web-based learning support system (a point also emphasised by Collis and Moonen, 2001).

■ Care needed to be taken in selecting virtual team members. Key selection criteria should be mutual interest in the central theme, a shared language, adequate PC and Internet skills, and availability of easy and direct access to the Internet. (Such social and technological prerequisites are identified in many studies.)

■ It was felt that participation in a virtual team required a high level of self-discipline, and that the scheduled timeframe was an important factor conditioning the achievement of team goals. The physical absence of 'buddies' in a virtual environment seemed to take away some kind of 'social control' and place greater emphasis on self-control. Participants lacking intrinsic motivation found self-regulation difficult.

■ Constructive feedback from the facilitator and team members was felt essential to encourage collaboration and interaction. All communication in this study took place via written text, and the subtle nuances that are so important in learning environments had to be conveyed in English text on the computer screen. As English was not the native language of most participants, this put an extra burden on the communication process.

■ It was felt that asynchronous activities should be alternated with more direct interaction, such as on-line meetings, conference calls and chat. This could be helpful when group interactions did not occur as intended. Synchronous events, on the other hand, could fulfil the need for direct social interaction.

■ All participants made a general request to start their CT-related activity with a face-to-face meeting of the whole team. They felt that establishing personal contact between participants was particularly important for

members who did not know each other. They also felt that face-to-face contact would simplify the process of forming teams and communicating among team-mates. Where it was impossible to arrange a face-to-face session, then a video or teleconference should be organised.

Source: Alekseeva, 2002

Studies such as Alekseeva's underline how vital it is for HRD professionals and other learning facilitators to have relevant skills to motivate and support virtual team members where CT is their major communication and working mode. Similar lessons emerged from a study of the UK high-street bank Lloyds TSB's 450 learning centres in the late 1990s. Hills and Francis (1999) found some regions to be significantly better than others in achieving enthusiasm among employees for computer-based training. This was mainly because local training administrators and line managers were supportive, proactive and imaginative in their approach to learners and the learning experience. Salmon (2001: 36) offers practical help in the structuring of an on-line learning process and in explaining the skills that learning facilitators need (see www.oubs.open.ac.uk/e-moderating/fivestep.htm).

Reflection

■ Reflecting on the skills needed by HRD professionals and other learning facilitators to enable effective use of ICT by virtual teams, what principles have emerged in this section that have also been identified in research and viewpoints discussed elsewhere in this chapter?

■ From your own experience or from your wider reading, what have you found to be the main barriers and facilitators in the use of collaborative technology by virtual teams?

CONCLUSION

In this chapter our purpose has been to describe developments in information and communication technology (ICT) that have direct implications for the HRD function and for its practitioners. From the research studies and commentaries that we have discussed, two themes bear repetition here. One is the vital need for people to be motivated to learn, and the impossibility of ICT itself building that motivation:

> While technology can create or remove barriers to learning, it cannot by itself create the motivation to learn. So there is a need to plan learning and development in an integrated way. (Carnall, 1999: 54)

The other is the need to know each other before trying to learn from each other:

> Linking people up with one another is more important than capturing and disseminating knowledge. ... The possibility for personal interaction appears to be important among employees, also when knowledge sharing is supported by ICT-based knowledge systems. ... A culture that stimulates reciprocity as well as knowing who will benefit from the knowledge and for what purpose, will encourage people to add to the system. At all the organizations where we carried out research we saw this crop up again and again: personal contact wins hands down every time. (Huysman and De Wit, 2002: 178)

Some of the most important HRD implications of issues covered in this chapter concern the ways in which HRD practitioners who engage in the more formal learning settings mediated by technology will need to acquire new skills in order to make best use of new technology. The flexible harnessing of ICT to learning involves tailored learning events and processes that consume more time and effort than do most standardised training approaches. The more choices the learner has, the more demands this places on trainers and the greater the challenges facing them (Collis and Moonen, 2001).

Studies reviewed in this chapter have usually covered participants from several countries and this reflects the increasing geographical and cultural dispersal of organisational communities. With the increased use of new technology, the boundaries of HRD activity too are rapidly expanding. As well as the core skills that are indispensable for participation in a technology-mediated workspace, working with dispersed teams often requires linguistic capability and a high level of sensitivity in managing diversity. It always involves promoting meaningful social interaction within and across teams. HRD practitioners need to find ways of helping team members to establish social contact, and to exchange information about their backgrounds, motives to participate, and perceptions on individual learning objectives and on the successful completion of the project. Not all members will find such processes easy, so another task for learning facilitators is to help diverse participants in virtual teams to develop the attitudes and capabilities for engaging in virtual communities of practice.

Collaborative ICT requires new conventions not only on how to participate in such communication modes as tele- and video conferencing, but also on how to actively promote conceptual learning and encourage reflection. An enthusiasm for content is not sufficient for successful performance in a technology-mediated workplace. HRD practitioners need to develop guidelines and interventions both for operating such modes, and for communicating and interacting through them.

Because there is a clear need for expert support in becoming knowledge-productive in virtual environments, the HRD function should be able to supply local and global learning co-ordinators, learning facilitators and learning consultants who can connect dispersed team members and help them to align their interests and priorities. Generalising from that, whenever the intention is to harness ICT to learning and knowledge processes, the key role for HRD practitioners is to act as human process mediators, who facilitate and motivate, reinforcing the group's and the individual's sense of identity and purpose.

part three

HRD: Challenges in a Knowledge Economy

chapter eleven

The Ethical Dimension

INTRODUCTION

In this final part of the book our purpose is twofold: to examine some ethical implications of the theory and practice that we have discussed thus far, and to identify major themes that have emerged in order to explore both their innate significance and their particular implications for the HRD function in an emergent knowledge economy.

The changing patterns of organisations, of work and of workplaces that we have been describing raise many ethical issues. In this chapter our purpose is to explore how to identify and respond to those that can confront HRD professionals working in a knowledge economy. Such professionals have a threefold responsibility here: to the organisations for which they work, to those whose learning and knowledge they promote, and to external stakeholders. While compliance with the legal and statutory framework of the land and conformity to wider European human rights legislation is of course essential in all HRD activity, that is not the focus of our discussion. Legal and statutory frameworks vary from one country to the next. They constitute a basic area of knowledge on which it is taken for granted that all HRD practitioners will be fully informed. Our concern is with the shadowy territory of ethics, and with how HRD professionals, whose threefold responsibilities here are not always mutually reinforcing, can find a reliable pathway through it.

We saw in Chapter 5 that learning in organisations operating in a knowledge economy has been termed:

> 'the new form of labor' because it enables an organisation to achieve the expansion of knowledge that is 'one of its principal purposes (and resides) at the core of what it means to be productive'. (Zuboff, 1988: 395)

Zuboff's perspective raises a number of questions with ethical implications:

■ Does the discourse of workplace learning and knowledge creation in a globalised knowledge economy mirror a genuine break with the traditional command–control model of management, or is it based mainly on illusion?

- Which stakeholders gain the most from the development of knowledge as a key organisational asset? And who might be vulnerable in that process?
- If some of the most uniquely valuable knowledge is developed primarily through communities of practice in the workplace, then to whom does it belong – the organisation, the team, the individual? What ethical considerations arise here?

It is with such questions that we engage in this chapter. In the first section we place ethics within a business context that acts as a frame for subsequent discussion. In the second section we explore some ethical issues associated with the impact of a knowledge economy on organisations. We then examine the ethical responsibilities of HRD professionals in that economy. We conclude by introducing an ethical framework produced by Hans van Luijk (1994) that we believe has relevance for HRD professionals helping to build knowledge-productive workplaces and to implement the corporate curriculum construct that we proposed in Chapter 8.

ETHICS AND THE BUSINESS

The concept of corporate citizenship

In the wake of the 2002 Enron and WorldCom scandals, corporate governance is giving rise to many ethical concerns. Long before then, however, the charging of the former chairman of Union Carbide (now owned by Dow Chemicals) with culpable multiple homicide after the 1984 Bhopal tragedy in India had provided a high-profile example of the human cost that can follow in the wake of an organisation's failure to observe ethically responsible business practice (Glover, 2002). If the world of business is the most powerful institution in society, then it can be argued to have ethical obligations to that society. For those who hold this view, social demands and expectations come 'into the fold of conventional business management and strategy – they are something else to be managed alongside finance, marketing, production and so on' (Harvey, 1994: 4).

Not all commentators agree with the concept of corporate social responsibility. Milton Friedman regarded it as a 'fundamentally subversive doctrine' in a free society (Harvey, 1994: 3). However, the concept is growing in influence as public concern increases about the corporate governance, financial management and environmental impact of business organisations, especially those whose tentacles spread across the world. It is reinforced in many countries by government encouragement for businesses to become involved in areas such as education, inner cities, job creation and the training of the unemployed (ibid: 5). Some of the many sources that can be consulted about business ethics include (More, 2002):

- The Institute of Business Ethics, UK. info@ibe.org.uk, or website www.ibe.org.uk
- Institute for Social and Ethical Accountability: website www.accountability.org.uk
- Business for Social Responsibility – US Association: website www.ethicalcorp.com.

Ethics and corporate strategy

Barnard (1938), Simon (1945), Schendel and Hofer (1979) and Freeman and Gilbert (1988) all regarded ethics and the moral obligations of management as necessary components in the strategic planning process. However, Hosmer (1994) found that little attention had been paid subsequently in the strategic literature to this theme of integrity of common purpose among organisational stakeholders. He urged the need to return to a focus on ethics and the moral obligations of management. His context was managerial ethics as a matter not of personal virtue but of corporate strategy. In his view:

- The strategic decisions of any large-scale economic enterprise in a competitive global environment can result in both benefits and harms.
- It is the responsibility of the senior executives of the firm to distribute those benefits and allocate those harms among the stakeholders.
- Ethical principles offer the only criteria relevant for such distribution and allocation because they provide the only means of recognising and comparing the interests and rights of each of the stakeholders.
- Where this is done, this will help to develop trust in the direction of the firm.
- Stakeholders who show trust in the direction of the firm will show commitment to its future, ensuring efforts that are both co-operative and innovative and that thus lead to competitive and economic success for the firm over time.

Codes of ethics

More organisations are now drawing up ethics codes to guide behaviour at all levels. In the UK, the Institute of Business Ethics (IBE) found that in 2001 more larger companies than in 1998 were providing such a code and incorporating it into employment contracts. More, also, were showing interest in ethical and social audits, more were using their codes to give staff guidance rather than for enhancing reputation of the organisation, and more were using the Internet to deliver ethics awareness and training (Glover, 2002).

Curiously, however, the IBE found that fewer organisations than before were training their staff in business ethics, fewer were reporting on ethics in annual reports, and fewer had a process for revision of their code (ibid). This is bound to raise a question mark against intent. Unless ethical codes are supported by clear guidelines to their implementation and by positive action to ensure that implementation, they mean little. The World Bank gives an example of good practice in Case example 11.1.

Case example 11.1

The World Bank's approach to ethics

The World Bank is exempt from national law. It is therefore essential to ensure that, since employees have no recourse to national employment legislation, there is a transparently fair approach to all ethical matters and to the resolution of any conflict arising from them. For the Bank, ethics is part of a broader process, explained by a senior Bank employee as 'a holistic approach bringing together corporate governance, ethics and corporate social responsibility'.

The Bank has had an 'ethics function' since the mid-1980s, but this had not proved effective in preventing unethical behaviour within the bank, and James Wolfenson was appointed chief executive in 1995 'on a ticket to stamp out internal corruption' (*People Management*, 2002). In 1997 a

Case example 11.1 *(cont'd)*

department of institutional integrity was set up to look at fraud and corruption in bank projects. That department is now the investigating body for all misconduct both within the organisation and externally in relation to its various operations across the world. It is independent, not tied to HR, so that there is no possibility of its operation influencing career planning decisions.

The Bank's ethics policy is three-pronged:

Leadership. The ethical impetus has come from the top. Ethics is included in all manager training for senior staff, and leadership training incorporates ethical risk management.

Standards. Not only does the company have a code of conduct incorporating a handbook of organisational values, and staff rules to guide employee behaviour. The ethics office also provides an ethical decision-making tool that helps employees learn how to proceed in a dilemma, in whatever cultural environment they may be operating. The process can be studied through on-line courses with a framework of 12 questions to define the problem accurately and guide the decision-making approach. The aim is that the Bank's values and its expectations about how employees should behave, are made very clear to everyone. There are consequences when the standards of behaviour are breached.

A safe channel of communication for staff and other stakeholder. This includes a telephone hotline for whistleblowing, and the provision of confidential advice on how to handle tricky ethical issues or disputes.

Some of the Bank's lending policies are ethically controversial, but during Wolfensen's regime a start has at least been made in tackling internal corruption. The Bank accepts that there is still some way to go before that goal can be fully achieved (*People Management*, 2002).

Source: Johnson, 2002; *People Management*, 2002. See also www.worldbank.org/ethics

In the World Bank, top management is attempting to send out clear signals that ethics matter in that organisation, and to provide tools to aid problem definition and problem solving. In other organisations the messages sent out by top management can be more ambiguous. Consider Case example 11.2.

Case example 11.2

British Airways, 1980s–90s

In 1981, with British Airways in a state of virtual bankruptcy, the advent of Lord King and Colin Marshall as chairman and chief executive heralded a period of sustained and radical change. There was an organisation-wide drive by top management to communicate and embed its espoused corporate vision.

A new corporate mission to make BA 'The Harrods of the airways of the world' led to the departure of those top managers whose culture was antipathetic to that mission. There was a root and branch restructuring of the organisation and radical changes were made to its financial, technological and human resource systems (Thomas, 1985). A comprehensive HR strategy introduced new recruitment, selection, training, development and reward practices, all calculated to embed a new culture and to ensure that the organisation attracted and retained the high-calibre, customer-focused workforce that it needed in order to realise its mission. There was to be no place at BA for those who, given appropriate incentives and support, nevertheless could not –

or would not – adequately contribute to BA's new vision.

As is usual in such a reorganisation, the reality behind the corporate mission statement proved harsh for many. The new culture also masked a disturbing ethical issue. In 1993 there was an unexpected outcome to the battle that had erupted between British Airways and a small competitor, Virgin: Virgin's owner, Richard Branson, won a half-million pound court award in compensation for what was proved to be a sustained campaign of 'dirty tricks' carried out by a number of BA staff against his airline. A former BA employee testified in court that the behaviour of those staff towards Virgin had been the result of a climate and set of expectations created at the very top of the organisation. Most had felt bound to take a very aggressive line out of fear of being identified by top management as weak or lacking in commitment, with damaging job or career consequences (Blackhurst, 1993).

Such a stance by top management imposes a severe strain on the psychological contract (Chapter 2). It promotes a culture of compliance that can give rise amongst affected employees to feelings of insecurity and lack of trust, leading to diminished commitment to the organisation. In so doing, it undermines the organisation's HR strategies that aim for quite opposite outcomes. Ultimately, little may be left except an uneasy coalition temporarily held together by an interplay of power, politics, fear and self-interest.

In situations such as these, HR professionals have to be prepared to question top management's stance. As one reader of the UK journal *People Management* commented in a rather broader context:

If HR professionals want to be taken seriously, we need to be able to determine for ourselves whether the organisations in which we work are actually having a benign effect on society and to take action accordingly. (*People Management*, 2002)

To call into question the true intent of top management takes courage. It means that HR professionals must be confident that their approach is founded on sound ethical principles, and is set within a convincing ethical framework. Later in the chapter we return to this point. First, it is relevant to look at ethical issues raised by an emergent knowledge economy, and at their implications for HRD practitioners.

LEARNING AND DEVELOPMENT IN A KNOWLEDGE ECONOMY

The 'new' economy

As we have seen from the first chapter of this book onwards, a new economy has been developing in the capitalist society over the past two decades. It has been described as one in which communication technology creates and sustains global competition, innovation becomes more important than mass production, investment buys new concepts or the means to create them rather than new machines, rapid change is a constant, work is independent of location, and time to market is the critical competitive asset (Stewart and Tansley, 2002).

A central theme in the book has been that in the unique knowledge economy that is emerging from within this wider, new, fast-moving, technology-driven economy, organisations need superior speed, flexibility, adaptability and knowledge productivity. They have to:

- *think smart:* recognising new conditions as they emerge and quickly producing quite new strategies as old ones become redundant
- *learn fast:* so that they can decide which strategies to use, and rapidly develop the skills, knowledge and competencies needed to drive those strategies to success
- *adapt continuously:* regularly redeploying their human, financial and material resources and their knowledge in order to produce new strategic assets for the business
- *co-create value:* working with customers to be fully responsive to those customers' experiences and expectations (Prahalad and Ramaswamy, 2002)
- *act rapidly:* so that time to market is cut to the minimum.

We observed in Chapter 4 that the response in socio-economic policy at national and international levels to this scenario is a grand vision of 'lifelong learning for all'. The logic is persuasive at the theoretical level. For individuals, lifelong learning will enable them to cope with fundamental changes encompassing not only new organisational forms, the increasing globalisation of business, and technological innovation that is transforming work organisation, but also environmental degradation, population migrations and political landslides (Edwards, 1997: 24). For organisations, lifelong learning holds out the prospect of a skilled, flexible workforce, and for society, such a workforce will provide a vital key to wealth and sustained economic progress. Yet as we have seen in Chapters 4 and 6, the vision of lifelong learning is still a long way from being realised across Europe. The knowledge economy, too, is proving ambivalent in its impact on work organisations.

In this section we discuss three of the issues that are of particular concern in the perplexing ethical landscape of HRD in a knowledge economy. They relate to:

- the 'flexible' labour force
- new pressures in workplace learning
- coverage of training and development in the workplace.

The 'flexible' labour force

We saw in Chapter 3 that employees are commonly referred to as the major asset in knowledge-creating organisations. Work-related learning is often heralded as 'a central rallying point in this cultural shift' (Butler, 1999: 135), the vision being one of high-commitment organisations that will be populated by:

> 'new' workers who are to be highly skilled, flexible risk-takers, able to tolerate fear, uncertainty, cultural change and stress while still being able, productive and creative. (Butler, 1999: 135)

Yet although the worlds of education and work may now be closely joined, it is unclear whether this constitutes a radical break with the past, or a return to the dominance of old notions of knowledge as control and commodity that we explored in Chapter 7. In Butler's view new technologies and information industries threaten to reproduce old patterns of segregation and produce new ones in a globalised economy where the fundamental aim remains as before: increased productivity and profitability for the business. She argues that in the post-Fordist workplace it is still the case that:

> knowledge is commodified, packaged, differentially valued and costed ... as a traded good. Through workplace learning knowledge is framed as a corporate good, learners/workers as human resources/capital. (Butler, 1999: 137)

Stewart and Tansley (2002: 5), drawing on a variety of official sources, including the International Labour Organisation, the European Commission, and the World Employment Report (ILO, 2001), reflect a similar pessimism. They find that the changing nature of work in an emerging knowledge economy carries with it growth in job and income insecurity, and threatens to perpetuate existing gender inequalities in the distribution of work and jobs. Even in the 'dot.coms' that are often heralded as offering more autonomy for employees and more challenge and interest in the workplace:

> Employees generally continue to work long hours, with schedules determined by their employers, in offices rather than at home, and the old barriers to success remain. (Stewart and Tansley, 2002)

The operation of a knowledge economy threatens to intensify old labour market divisions in those countries where most new jobs are in the low-skill, low-paid sector and knowledge workers form at present only a small minority of the labour force. This is the situation in the UK, where the fastest-growing occupational groups include hairdressers, shelf-fillers, drivers and care assistants. There, data from the ESRC's *Future of Work Programme* (www.leeds.ac.uk/asrcfutureofwork) suggest that knowledge workers will form the top half of an 'hourglass economy' that will see a proportional growth in low-paid, low-skilled work. In the UK's 'flexible' labour market there are major income disparities between the better trained and educated and the less well trained. As the skilled continue to get the good jobs, the unskilled either fall out of work or adapt by taking on the low-paid work that, increasingly, is all that is left for them. In the US, a similar trend in the 1980s and early 1990s had led by the mid-1990s to 'whole segments of the population' being virtually shut out of the job market (Graham, 1994: 4). Flexibility had become a mask for high levels of poverty caused by 'the restructuring of inequality within the global drive to greater competitiveness and productivity' (Edwards, 1997: 41). It is a real possibility that in the new knowledge economy the trend will be repeated.

We have argued throughout this book that in a knowledge economy approaches to workplace learning must respect and build on diversity in order to create knowledge-productive communities of practice. If present forecasts prove valid, then in many organisations HRD professionals will struggle to achieve this while also meeting management's demand that they become 'value-adding business partners', concentrating their activity mainly on the human capital that appears to have the most asset value – knowledge workers. In the view of another respected commentator:

> For all the rhetoric of the learning economy and the breakdown of hierarchy, in reality most employees face an experience of continued subordination. (Field, 2000: 84)

Research example 11.1 offers an expansion of this view.

Is HRD in a knowledge economy to become, then, no more than a tool to achieve the kind of flexibility that profits the business but brings benefits only to an already exclusive section of the labour force? Whatever the predictions, much in practice will depend

Behind the rhetoric of the new economy

Field (2000: 84, drawing on Goudevert, 1993) narrates the case of Volkswagen, the German car manufacturer, which started in the late 1980s to experiment with teamwork, flatter hierarchies, job-sharing and shared responsibilities. From the company's viewpoint the experiment was in many ways satisfactory. Workers, however, objected to taking over traditional managerial tasks unless they were to be paid extra to do so.

He also reports Thomas and Dunkerley's 1999 study of the impact of delayering on mid-

dle managers in 50 organisations in the UK. Although higher levels of job satisfaction were experienced, so too were increased stress levels. There was also frustration at taking on greater responsibility and showing more commitment when downsizing and delayering were leading to the disappearance of opportunities to progress up a career ladder.

Source: Field, 2000

on the notion of knowledge that prevails in an organisation and on the vision and values of top management that are promoted there. If the most valuable base of knowledge is accepted as being generated 'in here' through a relational workplace process, then it is inappropriate for only one set of workers in that workplace to become the focus of HRD investment. Knowledge that resides largely in social interactions represents a widely distributed asset, and in its uniquely valuable tacit form it cannot be wrested from people. They must want and agree to put it at the service of the collective whole.

We saw in the case of Multicorp in Chapter 7 that divisive HR policies and organisational structures can result in low trust, low organisational commitment and a reluctance to share knowledge. Knowledge may then be used as a bargaining counter and knowledge management may become an exercise in power, a means of personal or group aggrandisement. Yet another case in that chapter, that of Buckman Laboratories, and the Shell case in Chapter 8 demonstrate with equal clarity how, when a genuinely co-operative and collaborative approach is taken to knowledge creation – one which the values and interests of all the parties are taken fully into account – the organisation can become a truly knowledge-productive community.

Reflection

■ In your own organisation, how far do HRD strategies and initiatives reinforce old workforce divisions, or promote new approaches to learning that help to break down such barriers?

New pressures in workplace learning

The knowledge economy, with the need it creates for collaborative and inclusive modes of learning, poses challenges for HRD specialists. As work becomes the new classroom, organisations must develop a more organic and dynamic model of HR to exploit the new ways in which people are learning in it (Rana, 2002). When learning is understood as a social process, it is difficult to disentangle from its context, since it is 'embedded in institutional cultures and structures and tied to social relationships' (ibid).

New barriers to workplace learning

The increasing interest in the workplace as a source of organisationally valuable learning is not only due to the introduction of new high performance work practices. Much is a consequence of the widespread use across Europe of national vocational training systems that use competency-based training frameworks (Solomon, 1999). Solomon observes that such systems seem at first sight to liberate learners in the workplace, since competency-focused training is intended to give learners a sense of control over their learning. It involves learner-centred approaches that emphasise group-based learning, collaboration, participation and negotiation in the learning process.

Yet by its very preoccupation with a particular set of learning processes and a particular approach to workplace learning, competency-based training can introduce new divisions in that workplace, socialising people to become certain kinds of learners, just as new high performance work practices are socialising them to be certain kinds of workers (Solomon, 1999: 123). Even systems offering accreditation of prior learning often focus on particular kinds of knowledge and experience, thus excluding others. The shift at national levels towards centralised vocational curricula is another reinforcer of 'sameness'.

Stewart and Tansley (2002) noted research reporting another significant structural and cultural barrier to workplace learning, in jobs that involve 'emotional labour' – that is to say, roles involving the need either to suppress genuine emotion or to express fake emotion (Rainbird, 2000; Sambrook, 2001; see also Mann, 1997; Taylor, 1998). They observed that those with formal responsibilities for workplace learning should 'identify how these barriers operate in their own context and [to] find ways of overcoming them that are relevant to that context' (Stewart and Tansley, 2002: 18). The likelihood of managers recognising or tackling this task seems slender as long as research continues to show that most, even in learning-oriented organisations, do not appear to have the time or inclination to add 'managing learning' to their list of responsibilities (Stewart and Tansley, 2002; Tjepkema et al., 2002).

One way of achieving new learning goals without magnifying differences between individuals or groups is through self-managed learning. It builds on, and draws benefits from, diversity by allowing participants to design their own learning agenda and curriculum to suit their specific needs, as Case example 11.3 indicates.

Case example 11.3

Birmingham City Council and race relations training

Birmingham City Council in the UK places a strong emphasis on race awareness. In the past the council ran a number of conventional training programmes, but its workforce still failed to reflect local demographics.

A consultancy firm was then appointed to tackle the problem. It introduced a self-managed learning programme at the council to support managers outside the male/white stereotype.

Under the scheme, managers are offered the chance to design their own learning programmes to meet their specific needs. The programme has resulted in a big positive shift in attitudes, and staff have started volunteering to take part in the initiative.

Source: People Management, 2002a

Such examples show that, despite the concerns of many commentators, workplace learning can be a liberating process. What is essential is that those who plan, organise or facilitate such learning have valid insights into the preferences of learners, and that they pursue learning approaches that harness diversity in imaginative ways to the pursuit of the ultimate learning goal (see IPD, 1999).

Building a knowledge-productive workplace

That final point about the ultimate goal is crucial. A survey carried out in 2002 in the UK by the Chartered Institute of Personnel and Development asked learners about learning methods that they found most and least appealing. The traditional trainer-centred method of 'being shown how to do things and then practising them' (in other words, on-the-job training) was by far the most popular, with just over half of all respondents finding it the best method. However, in an organisation seeking an enhanced capability to continuously improve and radically innovate, this is not a learning method that is likely to promote the reflective capacity and self-regulating activity that such capability involves.

What stance should the HRD professional take here? To ignore learner preferences is to risk promoting new forms of inequity amongst learners. It can put great pressure on those who do not, or cannot easily, conform to new learning norms being promoted in the workplace. They can then experience higher stress levels and demotivation, and this in turn can lead to poor performance and to the various 'punishments' or 'harms' that may follow such failure. HRD activity designed to increase conformity to norms prescribed by management needs to be handled with a positive approach to diversity. If it is not, then new learning processes may be experienced as coercion by those who are initially unwilling or unable to comply. It is in this sense that Solomon (1999: 124) sees the management of learning processes to have a 'potentially repressive power'.

The downward spiral of learning

We have just been discussing the variety of ways in which 'difference' can develop in workplaces, and the ethical implications this carries. Some of the less obvious but important differences in the context of workplace learning relate to:

■ individuals' learning style, skills and preferences
■ attitudes to change
■ ability or disposition to adapt to new cultural, emotional or performance-related norms.

The consequence of failure to recognise and tackle constructively those barriers that cause or exacerbate 'difference' in a workforce can be serious. Employees who feel that they are isolated from the majority and/or are under pressure to conform to values that they do not share are likely to become increasingly unable to play to their strengths. That is a cost not only for them but for the organisation, often intensifying workforce divides and leading to damaging loss of trust and productivity.

In such scenarios, equity becomes a real issue because we can obtain no ethically satisfactory answer to the question 'Who benefits here, and at what cost to others'? In the so-called post-Fordist workplace, the emphasis is on collaboration, trust, self-managing teams, abolition of hierarchy, self-development and visions of the 'learning organisation'. Yet despite this appearance of escape from the harsh controls of the scientifically managed Fordist workplace, many commentators argue that new forms of control have simply replaced the old. (Harrison, 2002: 147–8)

HRD professionals need to be able to recognise workplace learning processes and activity that intensify old patterns of difference between people, or create new ones. Such patterns can lead to alienation of individuals or minority groups from the very communities of practice within which valuable organisational knowledge can be created. Diversity should be reflected on and valued so that it can enhance relationships in the workplace and enrich the knowledge process. If it is treated in negative fashion, then a 'downward spiral of difference' can develop, as Figure 11.1 demonstrates.

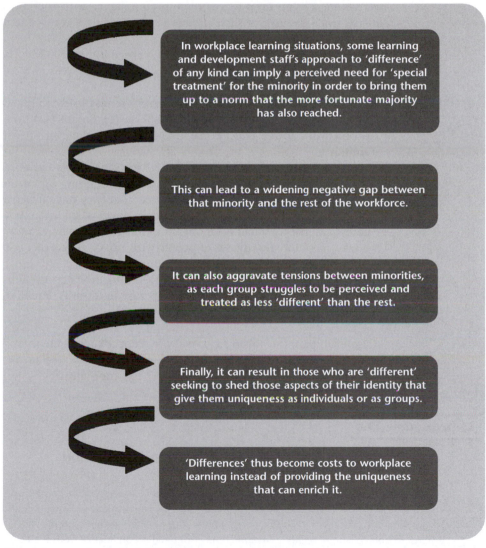

Figure 11.1   *The downward spiral of difference*

Source: Harrison, 2002, p. 149. By permission of Chartered Institute of Personnel and Development

Reflection ▰▰▰▰▰▰▰▰▰▰▰▰▰▰▰▰▰▰▰▰

- In your own workplace (or one with which you are familiar) can you see any evidence of a 'downward spiral of difference'? If so, what learning approaches might help to reverse that spiral? If not, how do you think such a spiral has been avoided?

Coverage of training and development

Lack of opportunity to show one's true potential in a learning situation is made worse by unequal access to learning processes and activities. In the UK there is a legal issue here: employers who offer traditional training programmes aimed at the stereotypical white, middle-class, able-bodied, heterosexual male, aged 25–40 risk being found institutionally racist, because that stereotype applies to only 4% of the population (*People Management*, 2002a). Even where there is compliance with the law, the ethical issue remains, since training in such situations has become a way – intended or not – to separate the haves from the have nots.

A survey of 743 people in employment, carried out in 2002 by the CIPD, found a substantial gap between those two groups:

- Employees working in smaller businesses are less likely to receive training than people in large companies or the public sector. So are part-time employees and people with lower educational qualifications, whatever the sector or size of employer.
- People with better education and in higher social classes are more likely to receive training, but are also more likely to turn down training opportunities.
- Those less qualified are more likely to feel that they have fewer training opportunities, but are also less likely to turn them down when offered. A quarter of graduates said that they had been offered training in the past 12 months but turned it down. In contrast, only 8% of people with no, or very basic, educational qualifications had not taken up offers of training.
- For all learners, and especially the less qualified, on-the-job training is the favourite method of learning yet it is not necessarily equally available for all (Cannell, 2002: 46).

Case example 11.4, taken from real life, is of a knowledge-intensive organisation where uneven coverage of training and development is acting to the disadvantage of the 'non-knowledge workers'. The case has been anonymised.

Case example 11.4

Training in a UK educational institution

The development of people in educational institutions in the UK is increasingly constrained by bureaucratic processes and by resource limitations. In one college of higher education, typical of many, lecturing staff are developed through a budget that comes primarily from the UK Department of Education and Skills, but support staff receive far less attention, being dependent on finance from the college's limited staff development budget (SDB).

In consequence, while lecturers enjoy a variety of external as well as internal training and development opportunities and processes, administrative and clerical staff are limited mainly to job-related training courses. If they wish to further their careers or expand their general knowledge through external educational programmes, they must compete for a small contribution from the SDB, and supplement that from their own purse. They must also gain permission from their line manager to attend the programmes at least in part in work time. Because of the current heavy turnover of support staff and consequent staff shortages at the college, this cannot always be given.

In this college, as in others, the specialist knowledge workers (academic staff) cannot function effectively without the support of the so-called non-knowledge workers (administrators and clerical staff). The college's frustrated learning and development manager pleads regularly with the human resource director for an expanded staff development budget, believing that it is not only equitable but also in the interest of the business to invest in a broader competency base for the support staff. She argues that:

■ It would reduce the current inequalities of access to learning and developmental opportunities that support staff perceive themselves to suffer, and that are creating a damaging divide between them and their academic colleagues.

■ It would give support staff more motivation, providing a gateway for them to greater career opportunities and thereby also no doubt reducing their currently high turnover level.

■ It could equip them with skills and knowledge that, in turn, could enable them to give a more expert support to lecturing staff.

■ It could expand their understanding of their organisation as a business concern, and develop their insights into its needs as it competes with increasing difficulty in an ever harsher market environment. This improved strategic awareness, and their recognition of the importance of their own contribution to the organisation's capability, could result in their commitment to continuously improving the services that they provide and to suggesting innovations in work processes and projects that would add value for the organisation.

At present, the L&D manager's pleas fall on deaf ears. The HR director is sympathetic, but claims that the money just isn't there – or that if it is, there are more urgent needs that must first be met. The manager, however, does not give up. She is currently researching external sources of funding and support that may be able to help her in her quest to develop knowledge workers and non-knowledge workers alike at her college into a cohesive learning and working community.

Once HRD professionals and management view the knowledge of *all* staff as equally valuable, although valuable in different ways, and once they see the issue as one of developing co-operative, not divided, communities of practice in the workplace whose shared efforts are essential if the whole organisation is to be knowledge productive, then training coverage becomes a critical issue. It has clear ethical implications, and the outcomes can either make or break that organisational community.

ETHICS AND THE HRD PROFESSIONAL

The ethical responsibilities of the HRD professional

For HRD professionals, responsibility for identifying and tackling ethical issues related to their field cannot be avoided by pleading ignorance or by turning a blind eye.

Ethics and professionalism are intertwined, since all professionals have an irreducible responsibility for what they do, for what is done in their name or with their implicit concurrence, or for what occurs within their domain:

> No professional, HR or otherwise, should venture into areas of work where they are uncertain of their own competence, if in so doing they are likely to jeopardise the duty of care they have for others. Nor should they stand silently by in situations where that duty of care is jeopardised by the incompetence of others. (Harrison, 2002: 139–40)

Not all HRD professionals recognise ethical issues when they emerge, and many are unprepared for the dilemmas that such issues can bring in their wake. Common reasons for a lack of awareness lie in HRD professional education and training programmes that do not focus on ethics as a field, in lack of HRD professionals' confidence in their abilities to deal successfully with ethical problems, or in a fear that, in openly confronting and trying to resolve what they believe to be ethical dilemmas, they will not win the support of management or of their HR colleagues. Reasons that are particularly difficult to remedy are those stemming from the individual professional's personal qualities and disposition that, because they are so deeply embedded in personality, cannot easily be rectified. This points to the importance of selection, induction and appraisal processes for HRD professionals, and of sensitive mentoring and coaching.

The role of standards

There are various codes of professional conduct that offer ethical guidelines to HRD professionals. They vary from the relatively generalised to the very detailed. Examples of the former are the UK Chartered Institute of Personnel and Development's five standards covering the learning and development (L&D) field. Each incorporates ethical considerations. The 'Generalist' standard that guides professionals operating right across the HRD field has ten performance indicators, one of which focuses on ethics. This emphasises the need for the role and tasks of the ethical practitioner to take fully into account:

■ the impact on, and implications of, diversity of people, style, and employment contracts for L&D policies and practice and organisational learning strategies
■ the information and actions needed to identify and achieve legally compliant and ethical L&D practices and processes.

It explains that HRD professionals must be fully informed about:

■ sources of information of information and guidance that help to identify and clarify ethical issues for the L&D practitioner
■ ways of creating awareness in the organisation about ethical issues involved in L&D policy and practice, and of gaining commitment to tackle them
■ sources of information and advice that clarify legal and ethical responsibilities, and help L&D practitioners to deal fairly and consistently with diversified workforces
■ how to ensure that all L&D operations and processes conform to relevant statutory, legal and ethical standards (CIPD 2001a, and on the CIPD's website, www.cipd.co.uk).

The CIPD's standards make clear what HRD professionals should be able to do, and should know about, in order to be 'ethical' in their practices, but leave it to each professional to determine what is and is not an ethical issue and to decide how best to respond to it. The US Academy of HRD, on the other hand, provides detailed guidance in its HRD Standards on Ethics and Integrity. These can be downloaded from the AHRD's website, www.ahrd.org, or can be obtained from its email address, office@ahrd.org.

The danger of detailed standards is that they impose on the practitioner a particular set of ethical values, spelt out in definitions of what is and is not 'right'. By their very comprehensiveness they tend to exclude from consideration any situation falling outside their boundaries. Contingencies that they do not cover can go unrecognised or ignored from an ethical viewpoint.

Finally, as we noted when discussing codes of business ethics earlier in this chapter, the mere presence of standards does not necessarily mean that all is well on the ground. Case example 11.5 demonstrates this. Meta standards that incorporate measures of long-term organisational effectiveness as well as of financial profitability may seem to increase the likelihood that a company will invest strategically in those HR processes – notably HRD – that will develop a high-calibre workforce for the organisation and will also act to the benefit of employees. However, when the integrity of management has been publicly found wanting, doubt is cast on all the company's strategies, including those related to HRD.

We argued in Chapter 8 that if an organisation is to be knowledge-productive, it is essential to develop a genuine learning community. This will be helped by the provision of generalised ethical guidelines relating to HRD policies and processes, backed up by appropriate diagnostic tools and aids to problem solving such as those exemplified by the World Bank's practice (Case example 11.1). However, nothing absolves HRD professionals from the responsibility to develop their own well-grounded understanding of what is 'equitable' in the particular situation, and of what actions to take. In the next section we propose a model that can aid the development of that understanding.

Case example 11.5

Xerox's adoption of meta standards

A number of leading organisations are tailoring meta standards to their own needs. Sparrow (1999) quotes Xerox, which uses a 31-measure system across six categories: leadership, human resource management, business process management, customer and market focus, information utilisation and quality tools, and results. This, he claims, is a strong base from which to build understanding about the contribution of the HR process.

Perhaps it is: but it is also of interest to note that in April 2002, Xerox was accused by the top American financial watchdog, the Securities and Exchange Commission, of a four-year scheme, master-minded by its senior management, to systematically betray its investors, using its accounting function to falsely portray the company as a business meeting its competitive challenges and increasing its earnings. The corporation did not admit its guilt, but did pay a record $10 million to settle the claims.

Reflection

■ Does your organisation have a code of ethics that is communicated to the whole workforce, and is it accompanied by tools to aid identification and diagnosis of ethical issues? If not, how are decisions made in the ethics field?

■ What do you see to be the pros and cons of detailed standards of ethical behaviour for the HRD profession?

AN ETHICS FRAMEWORK TO AID THE HRD PROFESSIONAL

Ethical approaches

There is no 'one best approach' to ethics, and problems arise when – in a particular organisation – there are no guidelines or tools to help the individuals concerned to respond to those questions. They also arise where guidelines or tools exist but do not meet the needs of a particularly knotty ethical dilemma, or where they exist but their basis in equity is dubious or non-existent. In all such cases that occur in the HRD domain, HRD professionals must be able to make ethical decisions for themselves, on convincing grounds, and to pursue them to the best of their ability. At the end of the day, whatever approach typifies the organisation's stance in relation to business ethics, and whatever codes or standards may be in place to guide HRD professionals:

> there remains a gap that only the individual can close, using as their reference point their own reasoning, core values and beliefs. Here again, though, there is a difficulty, because although [a] dictionary source defines 'ethical' as 'morally correct; honourable', we still have to ask – morally correct by whose standards? Honourable in whose eyes? Whose values do we have in mind here? (Harrison, 2002: 136)

We find a framework produced by Van Luijk (1994) to be a relevant and non-prescriptive approach for HRD practitioners. He defines ethics as being to do with practice and reflection related to norms and values that govern our relationships with others. It is not so much about what is appropriate given the requirements of law or statute, as about what should be done in order to fulfil basic moral requirements that a particular situation brings into play. Crucial ethical questions are therefore how to determine the specific interests and rights of all the parties involved in such a situation, and what principles should then guide action.

The 'model of action patterns' framework

Van Luijk observes that all human actions fall basically into three categories:

■ Self-directed (benefits come to me)
■ Other-including (we share the benefits)
■ Other-directed (benefits go to you).

Since the third category relates to an external societal rather than a business organisation context, and is concerned with actions that are purely altruistic and voluntary, we focus in this discussion on the first two categories.

Actions that are self-directed

These actions raise issues of what Van Luijk terms *recognitional ethics*. When the pursuit of actions to achieve selfish benefits produces claims from others that they have rights and issues that needs to be considered here, then the guiding ethical principle should be one of 'recognition' – that is to say, recognition that everyone has a moral duty to avoid harm being done to others, and that the rights and interests of one party can generate a duty for the other or others.

Recognitional ethics have resonance for the type of relationship between employer and employees where power is unequally distributed, and where the employer therefore has a duty of care in respect of those who work for the organisation. These ethics form the cornerstone of human rights legislation applied to the employment field, and the recognition principle is one that guides those employers who are genuinely paternalistic in their interactions with their employees.

Actions that are other-including

These actions, on the other hand, raise issues of what Van Luijk terms *transactional ethics*. Where people have common interests and either roughly equal claims or no mutual claims, yet the various parties need to collaborate in order to achieve the desired results, then there should be a search for a co-operative arrangement whereby every party contributes appropriately in order that the activity of all generates a 'surplus' that separately they could not produce.

Actions that are other-including raise the issue of *participating ethics* also. They do this when, given shared interests, it is also the case that:

- benefits desired can only be realised through participation of all the parties
- participation cannot be enforced
- no one has to participate in order to survive.

In other words, when the parties ally themselves voluntarily and commit themselves to a self-imposed and non-enforceable obligation, their relations should be guided by the exercise of a collective responsibility. They should then be governed at all times by two principles:

- *the principle of decency:* this principle holds that where a real opportunity to contribute to the common good arises and there are no insurmountable obstacles in the way, all parties should participate unless there are 'solid moral reasons' not to do so
- *the principle of emancipation:* this principle acknowledges the need for special attention to be given to the least powerful, who until now have not had the means of development – or not as much as others.

The concept of participatory ethics is appealing in the context of knowledge-productive organisations for a variety of reasons:

- It is in line with the principle that participation in knowledge creation cannot be enforced, it can only be volunteered, encouraged and facilitated.
- It resonates with the corporate curriculum pillar of 'practical judgement' (discussed in Chapter 8).

- It is in tune with the notion of the knowledge-productive organisation being one where workplace communities of practice agree freely and without coercion to move forward in partnership.
- It is relevant to the increasingly important task of organisational members to forge links with external communities of practice in order to generate knowledge that enables continuous improvement and radical innovation.
- It fits well with the shift that is taking place in the new knowledge economy from a view of value creation as a process in which the organisation's task is to cost-effectively produce goods and services, to one where its task is to be highly responsive to consumer experiences and knowledge, collaborating continuously with customers in creating added value (Prahalad and Ramaswamy, 2002).

Applying the framework

The 'model of action patterns' approach is particularly illuminating when applied to research findings on inter-organisational relationships in a knowledge economy.

If, however, the kinds of alliance discussed in Research example 11.2 are treated as being held together purely by skilful negotiating to reduce opportunistic behaviour of the participants, that threatens to reduce partnership to a calculative endeavour, where the basic stance of all the parties is assumed to be self-directed and therefore subject to continuing uncertainty and political powerplay. It would be idle to pretend that any business alliance does not involve calculative behaviour to some degree, but the extent to which such behaviour actually occurs is likely to be reduced if the fundamental nature of the relationship is agreed from the start to be one of mutual

Research example 11.2

Achieving cross-boundary knowledge creation

Elfring and Volberda (2001), in a comprehensive research review, found that accumulation of productive knowledge across the boundaries of the firm, compared to purely internal development, has become vital for organisations operating in an emerging knowledge economy where they need to regularly generate new dynamic capabilities. Such organisations increasingly rely on the knowledge of other firms to develop their competitive position, to the point where the ability of one firm to interact and share knowledge with others may be seen as an organisational competence or as a 'relational' capability (Elfring and Volberda, 2001: 255).

Research studies repeatedly demonstrate that the higher the ratio of private to common benefits, the more difficult it becomes to ensure co-operative rather than opportunistic behaviour.

Lack of commitment from one party to invest resources in projects expected to lead to common benefits may jeopardise the success of network structures that embody learning alliances.

The authors concluded that in such organisations the ability to negotiate is crucial because it can help to ensure that sufficient resources are devoted to create common instead of private benefits. That ability is also important in shaping firm boundaries, since the leading firm has to show that the committed resources will lead to benefits across the whole network (ibid: 256). The extent to which transaction costs in a leading firm network can be outweighed by benefits strongly depends on the relational capabilities of the leading firm.

Source: Elfring and Volberda, 2001

commitment rather than purely of self-interest. Once it has been accepted that ethical issues are involved in such learning alliances, there can be agreement on principles that will guide behaviour of the partners in order to secure an enduring relationship that is based on a genuine mutuality of purpose.

In the scenario described by Elfring and Volberda, the first step would be to take a view of the inter-firm partnership network as focused on 'other-including' rather than 'self-directed' actions. This would make it clear that two kinds of ethics are involved:

- *Transactional ethics*, because the firms have common interests, no mutual claims, but a need to achieve a co-operative arrangement whereby everyone makes an appropriate contribution to the partnership so that together all can generate a benefit that separately they could not produce.
- *Participating ethics*, because each party is joining the alliance voluntarily, and committing themselves to a self-imposed and non-enforceable obligation. In other words:
    - the benefits desired can only be realised through participation of all the parties
    - participation cannot be enforced
    - no one has to participate in order to survive.

Participatory ethics involve the observation by all the parties of two principles: of decency, and of emancipation. In such an alliance, therefore, by agreeing to observe these two principles in all their dealings with each other, the parties are taking on and are committed to fulfil a collective responsibility.

A further example of the utility of Van Luijk's model can be found by applying it to the case of France Telecom, the subject of the second assignment provided in Appendix 1 for Chapter 3. In that case too:

> Exchange transactions in view of mutual advantage, the recognition of asymmetrical claims between participants, and the possibility of participatory arrangements, with the accompanying varieties of transactional, recognitional and participatory ethics, are all part of the picture. (Van Luijk, 1994: 29)

Van Luijk claims that his 'model of action patterns' provides a balanced approach to ethics in business, one which, by drawing not only on philosophy but also on economics and politics, links the business world and ethical discourse. We find his flexible framework to be well suited to situations where it is important to identify what 'ethics' implies, given an internal plurality of interests, claims and business activities.

Van Luijk observes that there is more morality needed, and possible, in the market than appears at first sight to be the case. We concur with that assessment, and with the relevance of the rationale he goes on to provide (Van Luikjk, 1994: 31–2). Building on that rationale, but altering terminology to fit the context of learning and development processes in organisations operating in a knowledge economy, we conclude that there is more morality needed in the sense of a *transactional ethics*, because the regular exchange transactions and co-operative ventures that should typify learning and knowledge processes in a knowledge-productive organisation can only bear fruit when all parties adhere to moral principles of equality, honesty and reciprocity. We also conclude that there is more morality possible in the sense of a *participating ethics*, because the need for collaborative learning processes and commitment to the eight pillars of the corporate curriculum described in Chapter 8 opens ways to co-operative arrangements for common benefits that have long been blocked by the divisive nature of the old Fordist workplace and the training and development approaches associated with it.

Reflection

Consider a situation that involves training or some other form of learning and development in the workplace, and that you consider is resulting in divisive behaviour, or undue pressures on some or all of the employees involved. Then apply Van Luijk's 'model of action patterns':

a) to identify the kinds of ethical issues that the situation has raised

b) to identify the kinds of actions that would be most appropriate for the HRD professional to take in order to resolve the situation

CONCLUSION

In this chapter our purpose has been to explore how to identify and respond to ethical issues that can confront HRD professionals working in organisations in an emergent knowledge economy. In providing a framework of business ethics for our discussion, we have outlined two ways in which ethics can be treated by an organisation: as a tactic to ensure increased business benefits, or as part of a genuine attempt to act as a corporate citizen with ethical responsibilities to all organisational members and to wider society. Corporate citizenship involves ensuring an equitable distribution of benefits and of 'harms'. In terms of human resource strategies, it has a particular concern to build on diversity in ways that recognise its richness, instead of treating 'difference' as a cost to the organisation.

The knowledge economy is bringing with it many perplexing ethical issues. A body of research suggests that its operation is already perpetuating old labour market divisions and creating new barriers between the privileged knowledge workers and the non-knowledge workers. We have argued, however, that at the level of the particular organisation, much in practice depends on the notions of knowledge that prevail there, on the vision and values that are promoted by top management, and on the ways in which HRD professionals and others responsible for the planning, facilitation and evaluation of learning and development in the workplace interpret and carry out their ethical responsibilities. HRD practitioners who ignore or are insufficiently aware of those responsibilities may by their actions (or inaction) produce a downward spiral of learning in the workplace. On the other hand, those with a real concern for what is 'ethical' can help to break down old patterns of difference between learners and to prevent new barriers arising.

A central question in the chapter has been how to approach ethics. Should we take a legalistic approach where ethics becomes a set of rules to which we must conform – ethics reduced to legal compliance? Do detailed codes of practice and standards offer the best way forward for the HRD profession? In Chapter 7 we discussed the notion of knowledge as commodity. Ethics too can be treated as a commodity, and in our view the production of overly prescriptive codes or standards of ethics in the HRD field is imbued with that notion: 'ethics' becomes a packaged good for professionals to use off the shelf. We do not deny the value of codes and standards, but an excessive reliance on them as guides to thinking and action misses the crucial notion of ethics as a process, a continuing reflective dialogue between parties that can inform practical judgement. In Chapter 8 we highlighted such judgement as a central pillar of the corporate curriculum that can help to build and maintain a knowledge-productive organisation.

We therefore conclude that the help offered to HRD professional by codes of practice, tools to aid the identification and tackling of ethical issues, and standards of ethics that are built into professional educational programmes, can never stand proxy for the professional's duty to exercise his or her own wisdom in the ethical field. This is particularly vital in situations where the professional may become aware of a disturbing dissonance between what is espoused at company or at individual level and what is encountered on the ground. Unless HRD professionals develop their own understanding of business ethics and apply that understanding to their professional activity, they will find it difficult to respond appropriately and convincingly to ethical dilemmas.

In Chapter 2 in our discussion of 'the struggle for ownership' we referred to the call by Ghoshal and Bartlett (1995) for a new moral contract in HRM for all employees that would be consistent with the qualities of continuing self-development and collaborative learning needed in the new economy. We believe that Van Luijk's ethical framework (1994) is particularly relevant for HRD professionals working in organisations that must continuously improve and radically innovate. The framework makes a clear distinction between self-directed and other-including actions in the workplace. Through focusing on other-including behaviour, it suggests ethical principles that can enhance practical judgement in the workplace and help to develop and nurture a truly inclusive and knowledge-productive organisational learning community.

chapter twelve

Conclusions: Where To Now for HRD?

INTRODUCTION

In this final chapter our purpose is to summarise main themes covered in the book and identify and discuss salient issues emerging from them that relate to HRD as a field of theory, practice and professional activity.

We reiterate the concept of organisationally based HRD as a process to do with the expansion of learning capacity that can help to regenerate the organisation's knowledge base and drive its progress. Two other key concepts that underpin this final chapter are those of knowledge productivity and the corporate curriculum, and the potential they offer for enhancing the organisation's capability for improvement and innovation. It has been our argument throughout the book that in a knowledge-based economy the capability to generate and apply knowledge to continuous improvement and radical innovation in work processes, products and services is critical to organisational progress. It also raises a need for HRD practitioners to take on major new roles and tasks.

MAIN THEMES

HRD in an emerging knowledge economy

In Chapter 1 we introduced HRD as an organisational process operating in an emerging knowledge economy. There is a growing awareness at international and national policy-making levels that adding value through knowledge creation and knowledge application is becoming more important in this new economy than the availability of the traditional factors of capital, material and labour. At those levels there is a clear vision of lifelong learning that needs to be nurtured in order to build that capability. At organisational level, an appreciation of the value of the social capital that builds and sustains knowledge-productive relationships in the workplace signals major changes for business and human resource (HR) strategies and practices. Once attention is focused on workplace learning as a source of knowledge that can drive improvement and innovation, then traditional organisational forms characterised by centralisation of planning and control and the commodification of knowledge become problematic.

So too does a preoccupation with HRD activity focused primarily on training as a way of maximising employees' short-term performance only.

Tension between the need to meet immediate performance targets and to also build organisational capacity to perform effectively for the longer term is a theme that has surfaced regularly throughout the book. Another kind of tension, also introduced in Chapter 1 and discussed at various points thereafter, relates to how to ensure that the HRD investment in knowledge-based organisations both meets the needs of specialised 'knowledge workers' whose skills and motivation represent a key source of organisational advantage, and recognises the value and develops the potential of non-knowledge workers. They provide the essential infrastructure for knowledge work. They need to become part of a collective learning community if their commitment to that task is to be ensured, and if the tacit knowledge that they possess is to be surfaced, shared and used to a common advantage.

Organisational perspectives: strategising ...

In the discussion in Chapters 1 and 2 of the ways in which a new economy has been developing over the past two or three decades, it became clear that organisations' competitive advantage increasingly depends not just on the acquisition and development of superior human resources, but on the ways in which human and social capital are organised, developed and sustained through time and space. In a knowledge-based environment, such tasks call for a coupling of HR strategy to the business that is tight enough to support corporate vision and strategy across the organisation, yet loose enough to respond to differentiated needs at various organisational levels and to adapt quickly to changes in the external environment. This calls for HR practitioners (including those specialising in the HRD field) who have a thorough understanding of strategy as process, and who possess the kind of political, cultural, strategic and relational expertise not customarily acquired in a traditional HR function. Those practitioners need to be fully informed on the many pressures that are now changing the employment relationship in many organisations. They should have the skills to work with stakeholders to build, where need be, a new psychological contract based on mutuality of interest and endeavour.

In Chapter 2 we argued for this task to be framed by a pluralist perspective that treats human behaviour in organisations as driven by a multiplicity of goals and interests that are powerfully shaped by past and present context. That perspective places a high value on social capital and therefore on inclusive and equitable learning and development processes that build trust, co-operation and durable knowledge networks across and between organisations. Such processes call for HRD strategies well grounded in an understanding of the organisation's business environment, of its strategic management and of its framework of HR policies and practices. HRD practitioners must be able to build and sustain business partnerships within and beyond the organisation, and to identify and respond positively to the often conflicting demands and expectations of stakeholders in the learning and knowledge-creation processes. A key conclusion in this chapter was that if the HRD process is to be effective, it, like other HR processes, must be able to respond flexibly to the unique needs of its organisation.

... and organising

In Chapter 3 we drew attention to the dynamically interactive nature of the strategising and organising processes. In a fast-moving and globalising knowledge economy, no organisational structure retains relevance for long. Organising, not organisation, becomes a crucial activity, so that structure can change continuously to support the development of dynamic capabilities and the acquisition and use of expertise across boundaries. We argued in Chapter 3 that the organising process should be reflective, in order to fully understand what is involved in helping the firm to achieve profitability, build a committed and knowledge-productive workforce, and respond to a range of client values that increasingly include environmental responsibility, ethical business behaviour, trustworthiness and community service.

Self-organising teams, knowledge-based alliances, network and cellular structures are all innovative organisational forms that are evident in the new economy, but research consistently points to their experimental and transitory nature. An emphasis on process rather than on product in relation to both strategy and structure can only increase in a world that is no longer 'firm-centred' and that has been summarised in this way:

> You cannot create value unilaterally through the internal activities of the firm [any more] ... You have to involve customers directly and actively in helping to shape the value creation process. (Prahalad, interviewed by Arkin, 2002: 36)

Whether we look at the changes that have taken place in the retail car industry – as we did in Chapter 1 – or at those that, as Prahalad observes, have turned the doctor–patient relationship into one where the doctor no longer knows best 'but today's patients, armed with information they've picked up on the internet, will insist on being involved in determining their treatment' (ibid), the rapidity with which organisations now have to co-create with customers new knowledge that will add value is causing a 'silent but rapid morphing of industries' (ibid). For the HRD function, this again throws into relief the need to move from a preoccupation with essentially individually focused training to the continuous development of a skills base for the organisation that can create new business opportunities and adapt quickly to changing organisational forms.

HRD: country frameworks

Our review in Chapter 4 of national vocation, education and training (NVET) systems and the external policies that influence the HRD practice within organisations revealed the gap that currently exists across Europe and beyond between aspiration and reality. Examining a wide range of research, we found an increasing convergence in challenges facing VET policy in different country contexts, but significant differences at national and local levels in the ways in which these challenges are being interpreted and tackled.

Most organisations now face tensions between the need to develop skills and competencies for the future and to achieve cost efficiency and high immediate productivity. Many are introducing new high performance work practices that, driven especially by advances in new technology, are changing the nature of work and leading to innovations in workplace learning. These practices are affecting workplace communities of practice in different ways, due to variations from one country to the next in educational systems, training coverage, skill gaps, labour market trends and other factors. Macro-economic and institutional factors clearly have a strong influence on the extent to which the vision – espoused at international and national policy levels across Europe – of lifelong learning for all members of society can be implemented. Still, though, investment in HRD within organisations and its practical outcomes remain most directly shaped by organisational leadership, by management actions, by HR strategies and practice and by the expertise and business credibility of those who carry significant responsibility for the HRD process at different organisational levels.

HRD: emerging challenges and state of play

In Chapter 5 we reviewed a body of research undertaken since the mid-1990s, in order to identify the key challenges facing organisationally based HRD currently. The four that emerged consistently from that research are to do with:

- achieving strategic thrust through integration of HRD strategies with current business and HR strategies coupled with a focus on building future organisational capacity for superior speed, flexibility and knowledge creation
- facilitating culture change and building a knowledge-productive learning culture
- promoting high-quality workplace learning processes that will enhance the value of social as well as of human capital
- helping to develop managerial and leadership capability that will aid processes of strategising, organising and HRD, especially in newer organisational forms.

In Chapter 6 we explored how far these challenges are being recognised and tackled by HRD practitioners across Europe and more widely. Key research studies lead to the conclusion that, despite considerable innovation in HRD practice, there is a generalised failure to promote a learning culture in the workplace, to achieve full strategic integration for HRD and evaluation of its organisational impact, and to promote high-quality workplace learning both in informal and formal modes. Although knowledge creation is becoming a key task in many of the organisations surveyed in recent research, most HRD practitioners – like their HR colleagues more widely – do not seem to be occupying even the low ground here.

Study after study points to the impact of organisational context. Where top management's vision and values focus convincingly on knowledge productivity as an organisational capability, and where management actions, work practices and HR processes at all organisational levels support that focus and recognise the new importance of workplace learning, then a culture of learning is likely to develop and be sustained. But where context is unfavourable and/or where HR practitioners are passive, uninformed or both, culture change interventions are unlikely to take root. Our review in Chapters 5 and 6 of challenges and practice in HRD currently led us to the conclusion that even in organisations that espouse a learning orientation, the HRD function is currently failing to add sufficient value. Many of the tasks of HRD practitioners in a knowledge economy will differ greatly from those that most seem currently to perform. They are likely, too, to be more complex and strategically focused. All of this indicates a radical change agenda for the HRD profession.

Notions of knowledge

The four notions of knowledge discussed in Chapter 7 all have important practical implications for the HRD and knowledge processes in an organisational context. The notion of knowledge as primarily a relational process rather than as purely a commodity or resource underlines a need to identify ways in which workplace communities of practice can be brought together in a shared organisational purpose without, however, destroying the unique self-regulating properties that make them so attractive to individuals and so powerful in driving the knowledge process. This realisation lends further weight to earlier conclusions that the emphasis in knowledge-creating organisations should be less on devising management systems to 'control' learning or to 'manage' knowledge, and more on encouraging people to think creatively and on providing the skills and support systems that will help to disseminate and apply new knowledge in value-adding ways.

The knowledge-productive organisation

The first seven chapters in this book lead to one fundamental question for the HRD function: what are the key roles and tasks for HRD professionals in enhancing and supporting the processes of strategising, organising, workplace learning and knowledge creation? In Chapter 8 we proposed a 'corporate curriculum' to stimulate knowledge productivity in an organisation. The curriculum, with its eight 'pillars of learning' described in the chapter, suggests an answer to that question. It casts doubt on the validity in a knowledge economy of the traditional command–control paradigm of management, and of some widely accepted notions of 'knowledge management'. It rests on the belief, for which we provided a justification in the chapter, that knowledge-productive organisations thrive on 'emancipated' learners who participate in relatively self-regulated workplace communities of practice. In such organisations, HRD practitioners need to work with managers, team leaders and other internal and external partners to develop and sustain collaborative knowledge-sharing and knowledge-creating communities across the organisation. They also need to exercise a type of 'practical judgement' that is focused on equitable treatment and a respect for all value systems. This is essential if such communities are to be truly inclusive, and to operate in a culture of trust, diversity, openness, self-initiative and creativity.

Researching knowledge productivity

In Chapter 9 we reflected on many research studies that relate to knowledge productivity and the corporate curriculum, and on the demands they place on HRD researchers and practitioners. One issue that emerged with renewed urgency at this point concerned the need for practitioners schooled in 'training', and familiar in their organisation for their 'training' role, to begin to promote a different perspective: one of learning and actions that facilitate the sharing, production and application of knowledge in the day to day work environment. Research findings into HRD practice across Europe, however (summarised both in Chapter 6 and again in this chapter) provide much evidence that the dominant HRD paradigm in most organisations, even those styling themselves as 'learning oriented', is still that of 'training', not of learning in any broader sense. There are very few signs of a different perspective being held by management or being understood and promoted by HRD professionals.

In this chapter we proposed a framework for researching knowledge productivity and the corporate curriculum. We also suggested some urgent questions for those conducting future research in the field.

New technology, the knowledge process and HRD

There are major implications for the HRD function and for its practitioners in the latest developments in information, communication and collaborative technology

(ICCT) that we described in Chapter 10. These developments should expand the boundaries of HRD activity. They raise a need for HRD practitioners to possess core skills related to harnessing ICCT to learning in motivating and innovative ways, to participating in a technology-mediated workspace, and to working with geographically dispersed teams that are often also linguistically and culturally diverse.

In increasingly technologised workplaces, employees' motivation to learn new tasks, develop new work behaviours and master new work practices is vital, but new technology alone cannot build that motivation. That is a task in which HRD practitioners should be taking a lead, especially by promoting meaningful social interaction within and across teams – including virtual teams – so that people can know each other before trying to learn from each other in a technology-mediated environment. They need to find ways of enabling virtual team members to exchange information about their background, motives to participate, perceptions of individual learning objectives and of what constitutes successful completion of a project. Not everyone will find such processes easy, and another task for learning facilitators is to help diverse participants in virtual teams to develop the attitudes and capabilities for engaging in virtual communities of practice.

The ethical dimension

In Chapter 11 we explored how to identify and respond to ethical issues that can arise in organisationally based HRD practice in an emergent knowledge economy. HRD professionals have a threefold responsibility here: to the company for which they work, to the individuals whose learning and knowledge they promote, and to external stakeholders. These responsibilities are not always mutually reinforcing and raise the question of how HRD practitioners can best find their way through ethical territory.

Despite an increasing trend for businesses and the HR profession to produce codes and standards of ethical practice, not all HRD professionals recognise ethical issues when they emerge, and many are unprepared for the dilemmas that such issues can bring in their wake. Codes and standards may clarify core ethical responsibilities, but those that go beyond this are often too prescriptive, running the danger of imposing one particular set of values on the professional and also of inducing a mentality that treats as insignificant all issues and types of situations not incorporated in them. Each professional has to develop his or her own well-founded understanding of how to recognise and tackle ethical issues. In Chapter 11 we recommended a non-prescriptive diagnostic approach developed by Van Luijk (1994) as an aid to problem definition and problem solving in the territory of HRD, ethics and the knowledge-creating organisation.

For HRD professionals, the heart of the matter can perhaps be summarised as follows:

> In using learning to meet organisational ends we are intervening in a human process that goes to the heart of the individual's identity. It is vital that personnel and development practitioners understand their responsibility here. It goes beyond their organisation, being shaped by the ethical and professional values, and by the contribution they must make to society at large as well as to the organisation which employs them at a particular point in time. (Harrison, 2002: 7)

Reflecting on the themes covered in these eleven chapters, we now select salient issues that have implications for the further development of HRD in a knowledge economy, and for the education and practice of those who carry HRD responsibilities there.

WORK AND LEARNING IN A KNOWLEDGE ECONOMY

The interrelationship between work and learning

A main theme throughout this book has been the transformation of work processes that characterise a knowledge economy. Tapscott described this transformation as follows:

> When knowledge is the basis of value creation, work and learning are the same. Knowledge workers, whose 'products' often don't exist in the physical world, have a different relationship to their work and their employers, and different expectations about their professional growth. (Tapscott, 1999: ix)

As we saw in Chapters 1 and 3, historically the boundaries of work organisations have been relatively clear-cut and unchanging, and companies have controlled all business activities involved in the creation of the things they sell, the services they provide, and the processes they operate. Now, however, boundaries are fluid and control is shifting dramatically to the customer.

> Spurred by the consumer-centric culture of the Internet … the consumer's influence on value creation has never been greater. (Prahalad and Ramaswamy, 2002: 52)

In a knowledge economy as we have described it in this book, the work organisation is rapidly having to become an evolving system of knowledge production and application. It needs a highly developed capability to co-operate as well as compete, as its members at all levels work in a variety of overlapping networks and partnerships within and beyond the firm in order to create value and make progress. Recent research into training in the knowledge economy (notably Stewart and Tansley, 2002) shows that this transformation calls for HRD as an organisational process to focus on the enhancement of informal and work-based learning, and of learning skills and innovatory capacity at collective, team and individual levels.

With her pioneering book on building and sustaining the sources of innovation, Leonard-Barton (1998) was among the first to probe the relationship between successful innovators and the way they create, nurture, and grow the experience and accumulated knowledge of their organisation. Her research at Harvard led her to emphasise the need to nurture a 'love of learning' in a would-be innovative organisation:

> This love of learning is woven throughout the organization, whether the activity be problem solving across internal boundaries, creating knowledge through experimentation, importing from outside, or transferring it to other sites and nations. People who are knowingly engaged in building core technological capabilities are *curious*: they are information seekers. There is a sense of enjoyment in the work – the lightness of step that suggests that building knowledge not only makes good business sense but is *fun*. (Leonard-Barton, 1998: 261, italics in original)

This philosophy could well form the core of HRD theory in a knowledge economy. Our reasoning throughout this book has been that where work and learning are becoming inextricably intertwined in the workplace, knowledge-productive learning that can lead to continuous improvement and radical innovation is essential but cannot be forced out of people. It needs the stimulus of a genuine, engaging and inclusive collective learning partnership.

The concept of a knowledge-productive work environment not only focuses on the social aspects of a favourable learning climate, but also on the need for all individuals to explore and invest in their personal domains of interest through an interaction of work and learning that is meaningful for them as well as productive for the organisation (Kessels and Keursten, 2002). When the focus shifts from the external and internal transfer of explicit knowledge to the social construction of tacit knowledge among members of informal networks (Brown and Duguid, 1991), more emphasis has to be placed on creating favourable conditions for learning in the workplace than on organising the provision of formal training.

The issue of the transformational work environment raises additional questions for the future development of HRD:

- Does the distinction between 'knowledge workers' and 'non-knowledge workers' affect the focus of HRD?
- Should the focus of HRD be on performance or on learning?
- Where should responsibility for HRD be located?

KNOWLEDGE WORKERS AND THEIR SUPPORTING PERSONNEL

The development of 'knowledge workers'

At various points in the book a question has arisen about how best to develop 'knowledge workers' and those who provide the infrastructure for their activity. (We are using here the distinction made by Drucker (1993) between the knowledge workers who contribute to the core of economic activity in a knowledge-intensive organisation, and the service workers who facilitate that contribution.)

Looking first at knowledge workers, there is a dilemma here. We saw in Chapter 3 that such workers have considerable autonomy and are strategic players in their organisations. If they take into their own hands the necessary intellectual and social development of their careers – or, indeed, choose simply to ignore that development – what role then remains for HRD specialists? The classical role of the trainer will probably survive in domains that involve specific subject matter expertise for novices. However, research indicates that emancipated professionals such as knowledge workers tackle their need for reflection and sharing of expertise in ways that differ significantly from the directions usually taken by formal training policy (Wenger, 1998; Tapscott, 1999; Wenger and Snyder, 2000). To focus the HRD investment solely or primarily on knowledge workers may render obsolete the HRD function as traditionally conceived.

The development of 'non-knowledge workers'

And what of the so-called non-knowledge workers who will probably form the vast majority of most workforces in a knowledge economy (Field, 2000; Stewart and Tansley, 2002)? What HRD investment should they receive? Where there is a strong drive for short-termism it is likely that most resource will be spent nurturing the golden geese – that is, the high-potential specialist knowledge workers – who can bring in quick gains for the firm. This would be in line with the pattern, observed in Chapters 2, 4 and 6, that has emerged across Europe over the past 50 years, where senior management and highly educated employees have consistently received by far the most facilities and funds for training and professional development.

During that time, the HRD profession could have taken the lead in fighting to ensure for all organisational members equal rights and equality of access to opportunities for learning and development. However, it did not – or did not in any coherent and effective manner. Of course, the differing ways in which most country VET systems have operated during that time have not been helpful either. The research covered in Chapter 4 makes it clear that even now the coverage of training in most countries is unsatisfactory and that in some – notably the UK – it continues to reinforce major barriers between the 'haves and have nots' in the labour force. Patterns of provision are, however, slowly changing. Relatedly there is also a greater recognition of the importance of workplace learning, although there are reports of persistently poor standards related to its management, quality and monitoring in many organisations and of a continuing emphasis on formal learning activity. All in all, some forecast a worrying scenario unless the pace of progress increases:

> Governments that fail to acknowledge the urgency of raising national skill levels will be left with under-performing economies and hostile electorates. Better to prepare such workers for the realities of their situation, while at the same time providing them access to learning resources to improve their situation, than to face the consequences at the ballot box. (Burton-Jones, 1999: 200)

It is to be hoped that there will be radical change within the HRD profession that will produce the necessary lead in ensuring an equitable distribution of the HRD investment between knowledge workers and non-knowledge workers in the emergent knowledge economy. The task is not an impossible one if it is accepted that 'knowledge work' covers far more than work that is classified as *academic*, or *scientific* or *professional*. We argued in Chapter 1 that in today's knowledge-creating organisations knowledge work can legitimately be viewed as any that requires a certain degree of autonomy in confronting, interpreting and resolving problems and responding to customer requirements and expectations. In that sense, such work is as much located at the workplace level as it is within the offices of specialist knowledge workers. The machine operators who start investigating possible origins of failure and breakdown as soon as they receive such signals, instead of calling in the specialist maintenance crew and handing over the problems to them, are genuine knowledge workers.

So true knowledge work is not the exclusive province of those with high levels of formal education. Others at all organisational levels can participate in it also, and in a knowledge economy they should do so. Typically, a broader base of knowledge work can be achieved by reorganising the workplace, introducing new work practices, delegating authority, giving more control over work to the individual and to teams, stimulating a curiosity about the knowledge content of work, and creating a sense of excitement about the knowledge process. When learning and working are thus intertwined, non-knowledge workers should enjoy the same regime as that which applies in the case of knowledge workers: the autonomy of the learner/worker. For them to be able to do so, the HRD function's practitioners need not only to help build and sustain an inclusive learning culture in the organisation. They should also be working with management and with external agencies to facilitate the learning that many employees will need in order to acquire relevant new skills and bear new knowledge-work responsibilities.

But is this kind of transformation a realistic proposition? As we argued in Chapter 3 when discussing new organisational forms, it is important not to make excessive claims here. The traditional structures that support control and efficiency of mass production and that strive for standardised performance still have meaning because such work still exists. On the other hand, for those organisations that increasingly compete on the basis of quality improvement and innovation as well as of cost reduction, and that need to continuously co-create value with customers, there must be innovation in their approaches to the learning and development of all organisational members. For the HRD function, this supports the conclusion that:

> HRD will be increasingly concerned with facilitating the learning of individuals, teams and organizations through the design, structuring and organization of work itself. (McGoldrick et al., 2002a: 396)

However, while there is no doubt that HRD 'should be' so concerned, whether it 'will be' is open to question. Our review in this book of the current state of play both of the function and of its practitioners has revealed a sizeable gap between aspiration and reality.

WHERE TO LOCATE HRD?

The replication studies conducted by the Department of Education of the University of Twente and the Dutch Association of Trainers (NVvO) in 1993 and 2000 show that in the Netherlands the dominant profile of the HRD officer is still the traditional trainer who conducts courses in the conventional way. This profile has not changed over the last decade (Kieft and Nijhof, 2000). Tjepkema et al. (2002) reached a similar conclusion in their research into HRD practice in 'learning-oriented' organisations across Europe: although the term HRD has been adopted to cover a broad domain of work-related learning and development, its practitioners are usually regarded as 'trainers', and most are actively engaged – and expected by management to be so engaged – in little more than traditional training activity.

The theory, research and practice that have been covered in this book all support the proposition that economic performance, knowledge productivity and an organisation's learning capability at collective, team and individual levels are closely interrelated, calling for organisationally based HRD to become a type of strategic capability. A function that represents such capability is a long way from today's training function. Where, then, should responsibility for it lie? As we saw in Chapter 6, the extent to which the HRD function is currently decentralised to the line is unclear but the trend to decentralise does seem to be increasing. By and large, line managers appear to be poorly equipped and unmotivated to carry out an HRD role or to share responsibility for monitoring and evaluating its impact. They will need far more preparation and support than at present in order to ensure their commitment and competence in the HRD domain.

Developing managers' HRD skills will not be enough. Given the tendency for the pressures of a target-driven daily work routine to overshadow the value managers attach to workplace learning and development, HRD professionals will need to be able to stimulate understanding of and interest in HRD activity in all those who carry significant HRD responsibilities in the organisation. This includes encouraging every individual to take active responsibility for his or her own learning and development. The delegation of HRD responsibilities to line managers is likely to succeed only when top management and human resource (including HRD) professionals give those managers due support and encouragement, when organisational context stimulates innovation in the workplace and development of learning networks, and when managers themselves find HRD to be a credible, value-adding process.

In terms of overall responsibility for HRD, a traditional response would be to place it in the hands of a dedicated senior manager or even a board member who explicitly champions HRD in the organisation. Yet as we have tried to show in Chapters 8 and 9, in a knowledge-productive organisation the learning support that its members need is part and parcel of the day to day work environment, where learning is a substantial element of knowledge work. Learning and knowing do not constitute a specific specialist *function* and a discrete set of roles and tasks, to be planned and controlled at a senior level or to be farmed out to external specialist agencies. Rather, HRD is an organisation-wide *process* for which responsibility is shared across the organisation. Senior management, local managers, team leaders and other employees all share responsibility for the development of their capabilities, for the quality of the day to day learning environment that they construct, and for the resulting creation and combination of tacit and explicit knowledge.

The role of HRD professionals in such a scenario becomes one not of managing a specialist training or HRD function (or not exclusively) but of raising awareness of the need for all organisational members to collaborate in self-regulated learning and development, and of helping them to transform the workplace into a learning environment conducive to the sharing and creation of knowledge, and stimulating to individuals. As we saw in Chapter 6, those professionals seem to be as yet poorly equipped to carry such a role, and many are unaware that they should be preparing to do so.

PERFORMANCE VERSUS LEARNING

Another issue that has surfaced regularly throughout the book concerns the extent to which the focus of HRD should be on performance or on learning – a debate whose ramifications are spreading across the whole HRD field.

In the learning-oriented approach, HRD is about building individual and collective capacity to learn and about creating a learning culture (Watkins and Marsick, 1993). On the other hand, the 'performance' paradigm holds that the purpose of HRD is 'to advance the mission of the performance system that sponsors the HRD efforts by improving the capabilities of individuals working in the system and improving the system in which they perform their work' (Holton, 2002: 201). We have already discussed the debate in some detail in Chapters 1 and 5, and Swanson and Holton (2001) have provided a review of the underlying assumptions on which the 'learning' and 'performance' approaches rest. Here, we simply reiterate our conclusion in Chapter 5 that in a real sense the debate is misconceived because it concerns not two opposed concepts so much as two facets of a single concept: the importance of performance *and* learning in knowledge-creating organisations.

Throughout this book we have argued that an organisational capability to continuously improve and radically innovate in products, services and processes is crucial in a knowledge economy. This capability is based on the learning power of individual knowledge workers, on the social process of 'knowing', and on favourable conditions in the work environment. We have defined HRD (Chapter 1) as:

> an organisational process that comprises the skilful planning and facilitation of a variety of formal and informal learning and knowledge processes and experiences, primarily but

not exclusively in the workplace, in order that organisational progress and individual potential can be enhanced through the competence, adaptability, collaboration and knowledge-creating activity of all who work for the organisation.

This infers a central role for the HRD process in a knowledge economy where learning is no longer simply a formal prerequisite for performing a job but becomes the main characteristic of doing the job. It raises a need for a fundamental shift from conceptualising HRD as any form of learning and development that will achieve immediate performance improvement to conceptualising it as activity that will promote the long-term performance of the organisation by focusing on work-based learning and knowledge processes. In today's organisations, no matter how turbulent the environment or how innovative the organisational form, there is always a need for training and development that aid current business performance. But we contend that in a knowledge economy there is also a need to build and preserve social capital through focusing on relational learning and knowledge processes that will generate dynamic capabilities essential to future organisational performance.

Confusion within the HRD profession about its organisational purpose can only hamper the profession at a time when it needs to take on vital new roles and tasks. If HRD professionals themselves cannot agree on what they are here to do, how can they expect to convince their organisations that their activity will add real value for the business? Or motivate individuals to take the initiative in any but the most job-related learning? The performance–learning debate, while of interest at the academic level, now runs the danger of generating a false and damaging polarisation of views within the profession, and an increasingly sceptical response outside it, to HRD professionals' claims to a strategic role.

HRD ROLES AND TASKS IN A KNOWLEDGE ECONOMY

New roles and responsibilities

Having reviewed the main conclusions of previous chapters and discussed salient issues that they raise for the HRD functions and its practitioners, it now remains to suggest the kinds of roles and tasks that HRD professionals should be uniquely qualified to carry out in an emerging knowledge economy, and that therefore have implications for the education, training and continuing development of those professionals. The rationale for our strong focus on HRD as a process whose purpose is to facilitate knowledge-productive learning rather than simply to deliver training will by now be clear, as will our stance in treating learning as a responsibility to be shared between management, HRD professionals, and the individual employee. In a knowledge-productive organisation, learning and working are naturally intertwined and so responsibility for HRD should be widely, not narrowly, distributed across the organisation.

We stressed in our first section in Chapter 1 that what matters within the particular organisation is not any general definition of HRD, but a shared understanding of its role, purpose and focus *for that organisation*. When (as noted earlier in this chapter) an organisation is understood as an evolving system of knowledge production and application, then HRD practitioners have the opportunity to become strategic players. To do that, they will need mastery of expertise similar to that possessed by the human resource (HR) professionals identified in Chapter 2 who are now carrying strategic roles in globalising organisations. That expertise ranges from the ability to deal with social and cultural factors of learning situated in workplace communities of practice, to skills in coaching, counselling and mentoring individuals and teams in knowledge work. It requires strong personal networking skills, the ability to think strategically, to work in virtual contexts and to tolerate ambiguities in new business situations. It means that HRD practitioners should be working in many overlapping partnerships to create and sustain an organisational culture favourable to learning that can drive improvement and innovation. Such collaborative endeavour depends significantly on high-level political skills and on expertise in building on the rich learning opportunities offered by human diversity in the workplace.

The HRD practitioner's role in developing the organisation's social as well as human capital involves creating and nurturing social networks that can produce and share new organisationally valuable knowledge. In this sense, it is indeed about acting as 'learning architects' (University Forum, 1998) who are alert and responsive to new needs in the workplace, can raise awareness in the organisation of the importance of a culture of learning, and can follow through that awareness with action. Learning architects need a strong grasp of the organising process and of the roots and path-dependency of organisational culture and knowledge. They must be able to devise and convince others of the value of strategies that will increase motivation to create, share and apply knowledge across the organisation.

Core tasks

The territory that we have travelled in this book leads us to conclude that in organisations entering or operating in a knowledge economy there is a set of core tasks for HRD professionals to perform. We suggest that those tasks are to do with:

- identifying and investigating the implications of operating in a knowledge economy for learning and development in the particular organisation
- working in partnerships to implement business processes and developmental activity that will equip managers and team leaders at all organisational levels to fulfil their strategising, organising and knowledge-creating roles
- raising awareness across the organisation of the value of a workplace learning culture that taps into, shares and utilises explicit and tacit knowledge of organisational members, promoting continuous improvement and radical innovation in goods, services and processes
- producing well-contextualised processes and practical interventions that can help to transform the workplace into a learning environment conducive to knowledge creation, knowledge sharing and the development of new dynamic capabilities for the organisation
- working to ensure an inclusive and ethical approach to learning in the workplace. This involves building on diversity in order to access and share knowledge embedded in the grass roots of the organisational community, and contributing to a developmental performance-management process that can facilitate and value knowledge-productive learning
- stimulating and supporting self-managed learning at all organisational levels, utilising the support and involvement of a variety of social, occupational and professional networks to achieve this
- promoting HRD processes and initiatives to build the eight pillars of the corporate curriculum: acquiring subject matter expertise, learning to identify and deal with

new problems, cultivating reflective skills, acquiring communicative and social skills, developing self-regulation of motivation, affinities and emotions, promoting calm and stability, stimulating and steering creative turmoil, and developing practical judgement

- incorporating in training, learning and developmental processes opportunities for individuals to explore and invest in their personal domains of interest while also adding value through their work for the organisation
- providing expert learning support in becoming knowledge-productive in virtual environments, and helping dispersed team members to connect and align their interests and priorities. Whenever the intention is to harness collaborative and Web-based technology to learning and knowledge processes, HRD practitioners should act as facilitative and motivating human process mediators
- ensuring their own continuing professional and personal development.

The materials that we have brought together in the book indicate that the roles and tasks that we have just proposed, and the skills that they infer, are new to many HRD professionals. We urge their incorporation in educational and training programmes for HRD specialists, and in their continuing personal and professional development plans. We see this to be imperative if HRD is to be accepted in future as a process whose central organisational purpose is to do with the expansion of learning capacity that can help to regenerate the knowledge base of the enterprise and enhance both competitive and collaborative capability.

CONCLUSION

The need for sustainable economic development, and the contribution that can be made to that development by an inclusive learning society irradiated by a vision of lifelong learning for all, may be clear at macro policy level. In practice, however, there is a long road to travel. It is one where progress is frequently hampered at all levels by vested interests and authority, by short-term financial triggers and by conventional habits and dominant logics that impede critical thinking and unlearning. Material covered in our book points to an urgent need for new approaches to strategising and organising in organisations. Once the creation of knowledge and its application to the enhancement and innovation of work processes, products and services become understood as uniquely important organisational properties, then qualities of social capital, trust, respect, ethics, meaningful work, affective involvement and practical wisdom assume central significance whether in the boardroom or in the workplace.

In the new economy, many share responsibility for the learning and development that can drive organisational progress. HRD practitioners have a key role to play here, but it is not one that they can play in isolation, nor is it one that they can afford to set aside on the grounds of insufficient support from management or other powerful stakeholders. Support in a business is never given freely – it must be earned. Resorting to a culture of blame and settling for less can gain no allies for the HRD profession.

Despite unpromising findings of much current research on the state of HRD in organisations generally, we have also found, and have noted throughout the book, significant innovative knowledge-productive activity in which HRD practitioners are engaged. This, and the nature of the challenges that now confront HRD as an organisationally based process, have led us to a belief that the emergence of a knowledge economy is offering exciting opportunities as well as demanding roles to the HRD profession. We hope we have shared this belief with our readers. The challenge is to grasp these opportunities with confidence and authority. It is to work with organisational stakeholders to create a synergy between the learning, development and knowledge-creating capability of all organisational members, the thrust of strategising and organising, and the progress of the organisation as its boundaries grow ever more fluid in a turbulent world.

A quotation included in the Preface to this book provides our finishing point also:

People at all levels have accumulated knowledge about what customers want, about how best to design products and processes, about what has worked in the past and what hasn't. A company that can collect all that knowledge and share it between employees will have a huge advantage over an organisation that never discovers what its people know. (Skapinker, 2002: 1)

Appendices

Appendices

Assignments

This appendix contains the following assignments:

Chapter 2

Corporate governance in a hospital trust	*HRD task*
Strategic HRM in a multidivisional manufacturing firm	*Reflective exercise*

Chapter 3

Analysing the structure of your organisation	*Research project*
Achieving economies of expertise through knowledge networks	*Reflective exercise*

Chapter 4

Researching country frameworks for HRD	*Research project*

Chapter 5

Building a team culture	*Consultancy project*
Improving the strategy process	*HRD task*

Chapter 6

Culture change in a building society	*HRD task*
Producing an educational programme for HRD practitioners or students	*HRD task*

Chapter 7

Working in a call centre	*Consultancy project*
Tackling a failure in knowledge management	*HR task*

Chapter 8

Developing a policy on knowledge productivity   *Consultancy project*

Building knowledge productivity through
a corporate curriculum   *Reflective exercise*

Chapter 9

Conducting a reconstruction study   *Research project*

Conducting a development study   *Research project*

Chapter 10

Knowledge sharing and new technology   *Consultancy project*

Collaboration at a distance   *Reflective exercise*

CHAPTER 2 Strategising

Assignment 1

Please read through the following case and then tackle the task at the end.

CORPORATE GOVERNANCE IN A HOSPITAL TRUST

The Trust Board

You are the training manager reporting to the Human Resource (HR) and Operational Services Director on the Board of Caring Hospital Trust (the Trust controls three local hospitals and various community service units attached to them). The executive team comprises, as well as the HR director, the chief executive (CE) (see below), and the directors of Finance and Business Development, Nursing and Quality Enhancement, and Medical Services.

The executive members work well together and are generally held to be dedicated, effective health service professionals. The CE is a trained accountant with substantial managerial experience both within and outside the health service. She has done much to ensure continuously improving standards of patient care and efficiency in the Trust. She works hard with her executive team to promote a tough but fair approach to performance management, flexibility of skills, and strong, accountable management throughout the Trust.

Caring Hospital Trust: organisation and mission

Caring Hospital Trust was formed only last year from a merger between two previous Trusts. A new non-executive team has therefore had to be appointed. It consists of five non-executive directors and an experienced chairwoman. Each non-executive director devotes about 25 days a year to Trust work, in return for a small but significant salary. The chairwoman receives a substantially higher salary, but works at least three days a week at the Trust, often more.

The mission of Caring Hospital Trust is 'to achieve excellence and innovation in all we do – a local Trust to serve the needs of local people and outlying communities'. Over the next five years the Trust has three corporate goals:

■ to ensure that the Trust is the first choice of local people and is attractive to those outside the immediate area

■ to value all staff employed by the Trust, providing employment opportunities that will attract local as well as national personnel, and development and training opportunities that will meet organisational and individual needs

■ to develop clinical and community services that are recognised as being innovative, patient-oriented, and of the highest quality and standards of cost-effectiveness.

The problems

An urgent priority is to ensure that Caring Hospital Trust's strategic direction and management is in capable hands. A nearby Trust has just hit the headlines because of a series of major blunders related to patient care, staffing levels and financial management. In that Trust, two of the executive directors have been suspended and the non-executive team, including the chairman, is being held accountable for failure to identify, monitor and deal with the errors. Its members face public demands for their resignation.

The HR director has asked you to produce for the Board of Caring Hospital Trust at its next meeting a set of proposals to develop the executive and non-executive directors into an effective corporate team; and to ensure that each non-executive director acquires the essential skills and knowledge that he or she needs.

You must provide a convincing rationale for your proposals, and make clear the main practical human resource implications it might have. There must also be clarity about the kind of resources (human, physical and financial) that will be needed if your proposals are to be implemented, although at this stage no detailed figures are required.

✎ YOUR TASK

Draft your proposals for the HR director to review prior to their finalisation.

Then note for yourself what particular skills you as training manager will need in order to carry out this project for the Trust if you are invited to do so.

Assignment 2

Please read through the following case and then tackle the task at the end.

STRATEGIC HRM IN A MULTIDIVISIONAL MANUFACTURING FIRM

The firm

Russels Ltd is a well-established multidivisional manufacturing firm operating in an increasingly tough competitive environment. Over the past decade, redundancies have reduced its workforce of 2,000 to around 800, as the market has proved more and more difficult to handle. In spite of cutbacks, there has been a major investment in the company's human resource (HR) base, with a particular emphasis on recruitment and employee development. The company tends to buy in the kind of expertise it needs at different organisational levels, and then focus on learning and development interventions that will help to change the culture and structure of the organisation to one better suited to the needs of the situation – in this case, to a project-focused culture, a matrix structure, and an emphasis on continuous improvement and regular innovation in processes and products.

The HR function

Russels had a small HR specialist function that has achieved considerable credibility in the firm through its business partnerships and business-focused strategies and practices. Russels has a long track record of good employee relations, and, working with three unions, management and HR staff have achieved over the years considerable harmonisation in pay, conditions and employee contracts. However, during the recent restructuring period, the 'psychological contract' between employer and employees generally has become strained. Rebuilding commitment and enhancing flexibility are two of the main internal challenges that the company now faces in its drive to regain competitive edge.

Performance management

Performance levels are not at present a serious concern at Russels – most current business targets are being met. However, top management recognises that if the demands of an increasingly turbulent environment are to be met, these levels will have to be considerably improved. Also the project-based matrix structure is not operating with equal effectiveness across the organisation – there are pockets of poor performance – and generally the workforce needs to become more multi-skilled and more fast-adaptive to change. Finally, and of critical importance, the HR director believes that at corporate level there is a need for more innovative strategies, while conceding that at unit level there has to be a better alignment of HR strategies with corporate goals. HR initiatives work well in terms of responding to units' local needs, but in doing so have a tendency to 'drift', losing vertical fit.

You are a Human Resource consultant recently appointed to work with the firm's HR director and senior management team in devising a new HR strategy and implementation plan for Russels that will take it through what is expected to be a difficult two or three years, as it struggles to enhance its competitive capability and regain its former leading edge.

 ## YOUR TASK

Your task is not to produce the new HR strategy and plan but to prepare yourself for your part in the forthcoming strategic planning activity. Produce a memo in which you:

a. diagnose what you see to be the crucial major HR issues that must be tackled at Russels

b. draft some options for an HR strategy that could respond to those issues in feasible and relevant ways at both corporate and unit levels

c. identify who you think should be key players in implementing whatever HR strategy is finally chosen for Russels, and what – if any – development those players may need in order to ensure effective implementation.

CHAPTER 3 Organising

Assignment 1

Analysing the structure of your organisation

We suggest that you keep the following analysis by you as you read through the rest of Chapter 3, and amend or expand it from time to time.

✎ YOUR TASK

Using Drucker's and Child's guidelines on structure (Chapter 3, Introduction), produce a brief description of the structure of your own organisation (or one with which you are familiar). Then identify the main internal and/or external challenges and opportunities that *either* justify the continuation of that structure in its present form, *or* indicate a need for structural change.

Assignment 2

Please read through the following case and then tackle the task at the end.

ACHIEVING ECONOMIES OF EXPERTISE THROUGH KNOWLEDGE NETWORKS

Introduction

D'Cruz and Rugman (1994) provided an account of the way in which, in the 1990s, France Telecom developed global strategies for competitiveness in telecommunications through a co-operation-based strategy in a business network structure. The structure is geared to sharing and accessing resources with partner organisations. It provides an instructive contrast with the more traditional M-form (multidivisional) structure used by the multinational firm of Alcatel, not a direct competitor but, then and still, the largest telecom manufacturer/supplier in the world.

France Telecom and the Five Partners Model

FT is a French service provider, state-owned since 1991. It developed its Five Partners Model as 'a co-operation-based framework for organizing economic activity to create international competitiveness for globally oriented firms' (D'Cruz and Rugman, 1994: 59). FT's chosen partners to create its network are its key suppliers, customers and competitors, and the non-business infrastructure. The latter comprises non-traded service sectors, government, education, healthcare, social services and not-for-profit cultural industries. The partners yield strategic leadership role to FT as the flagship firm and undertake much of the responsibility to execute and operationalise the network's strategy.

Organising for expanded scope and expertise and for mutual benefit

The FT approach is based on the assumption that business performance can benefit from co-operative forms of organising where partners' commitment to a common purpose overrides any tendency to purely opportunistic behaviour. Each partner in the FT network has a clear role related to a shared purpose that had initially brought them together, and all gain benefits from the partnership:

The flagship firm provides strategic vision and direction related to the network's shared purpose. It carries the primary responsibility for determining the markets to be served, the products and services to be produced, and the benchmarking of network activities and processes to ensure they meet global standards.

Chosen suppliers carry much of the production responsibility, gaining in return a greater share of the value-added in the product service, and a greater than normal amount of business from the flagship firm.

Chosen customers supply input to strategies and gain in return access to those strategies and the benefits of the flagship's leadership in regard to the area of each customer's business that the flagship supplies.

Chosen competitors participate in mutually beneficial market-sharing arrangements, joint research and development projects, co-operative training ventures, and suppliers' development projects.

The non-business infrastructure that supplies much of the human and technological capital for the network gains in return funding from the flagship and can also gain physical space and human resources.

Co-operative networks to add value

The defining characteristic of a multiple partnership model is that it delivers products and services to customers through a business network rather than through a single, integrated firm. The France Telecom approach is not a way of thinking about strategy and structure that is necessarily superior to the M-form adopted by Alcatel and so many other multinationals. It is simply different, and is also a viable approach to follow in order to achieve international competitiveness. Ultimately it might prove to be superior but that, as the authors concluded at the time, 'has yet to be seen'.

In the event, France Telecom has become the principal provider of telecommunication services in Europe and one of the world leaders in its field. It is a global player, and aims to be, not the biggest, but the smartest (although during 2002 it ran into trouble when an unwise acquisition foundered). It still uses its Five Partners Model as its basic form of organising.

It will need to be smart, if experience in the telecommunications equipment industry is anything to go by. That industry is suffering from weak demand, chronic overcapacity and an uncertain future after the end of the dot.com boom and the collapse of markets post-September 11. Telecom carriers, the main customers of equipment suppliers such as Alcatel, are 'burdened with massive debts and have slashed their investment spending' (Cave, 2002). In June 2002, Alcatel announced a major profits warning and 10,000 more job losses following its downsizing of 34,000 employees worldwide since spring, 2001. In March 2003, France Telecom itself disclosed the biggest corporate loss in French history. In reality it did not signal terminal decline for the company, since the French government stepped in with a generous bridging loan. However, it provides a sombre warning that while partnership networks can achieve much, they cannot prevent the damage that can flow from suspect financial management and chaotic market conditions.

✎ YOUR TASK

The task in this assignment is to reflect on three critical issues relating to this case in order to develop your analytical and diagnostic skills:

1. The Five Partners Model represents a value-chain approach to obtaining competitive advantage. Competing in value chains, not in industries, enables a company to forge linkages with others that have advantages in other parts of the value chain. Looking at France Telecom's network of partners, in what part of the value chain does each have an advantage that France Telecom can utilise?

2. The Five Partners Model stresses collaborative behaviours that are not considered in competitive strategies. Reading the case and recalling information in Chapter 3 also, what behaviours might these be, and how might they be developed in the partnership?

3. The Five Partners Model differs significantly from the M-form structure of Alcatel. Recalling information about the M-form in Chapter 3 and perhaps from your wider reading:

   ■ What are the main ways in which the two models differ?
   ■ Why do you think that Alcatel is structured along M-form lines?

4. In an increasingly difficult competitive environment, what might be the difficulties that network forms such as that organised by France Telecom experience, and how might these be tackled?

CHAPTER 4 HRD: Country frameworks

Researching country frameworks for HRD

🖎 YOUR TASK

Making good use of the Internet as well as of written sources, carry out research that will help you to obtain an enhanced understanding of key features of *your own country's* national vocational education and training system.

Then draw up the same kind of matrix provided in Chapter 4, Table 4.1 in order to summarise those features.

Produce a report analysing the system, and commenting on its relevance for your own organisation. Your report should contain recommendations about relevant HRD initiatives that you believe could gain some external funding and other support available through the VET system.

CHAPTER 5 HRD: Emerging challenges

Assignment 1

Please read through the following case and then tackle the task at the end.

BUILDING A TEAM CULTURE

You are a human resource development consultant. A potential client has just described to you the following set of problems:

'I am one of six senior partners in a firm of employment law specialists. We are finding a number of teamwork problems as the firm is expanding and taking on bigger workloads. We feel that some training could help us, and we would appreciate your guidance here. Some of the most typical problems that I have noticed are these:

1. We have various teams in the organisation, all working independently. Each consists of between eight and ten people, and all have individual targets to achieve. Within teams, I can see that members closely guard information and are very competitive. They don't tend to help one another when there are problems, and although we have a couple of open-plan offices, it's as though there were barriers between every desk! Of course as an employment law specialist you are what you know, but there is a real reluctance to share information with others. We need to improve communications within teams, and reduce the negative impact of competitiveness while not discouraging it as a motivator.

2. Also, there is very little cross-functional communication – maybe cross-functional project groups would help here?

3. Finally, all our lawyers are technically competent, having taken their professional examinations and developed specialist expertise in a variety of legal fields. However, their interpersonal skills and self-confidence are underdeveloped when it comes to "thinking outside the box" and identifying strategic options that could take the whole firm forward. The key challenge as I see it is one of balancing technical competence with the increasing need to invest in personal and "strategic thinking" skills.'

✎ YOUR TASK

The senior partner has invited you to make a presentation in a week's time to herself and the other five senior partners, outlining your understanding of the situation indicated by the various problems she has described to you, and your proposals for tackling them. You are not the only consultant being considered for the job, and an important factor will be producing a proposal that in their view gets to the heart of the matter but will not be excessively expensive to implement – the firm has budget constraints and, given the heavy staff workloads, time and release from work are also resource factors that have to be carefully considered.

Produce your first draft of a paper for your presentation.

Assignment 2

Please read through the following case and then tackle the task at the end.

IMPROVING THE STRATEGY PROCESS

In a large government agency in the UK that is particularly exposed to an unpredictable external environment, the biggest challenge faced by the HRD function is the lack of a clearly communicated corporate strategy. The agency has recently gone through considerable change but the senior management team has been unable to agree on a strategy and vision. Without organisational vision and strategy, the HRD function is unable to prioritise its activity. While the HRD professionals can estimate what is required in developing staff for current needs, they do not know what kind of human capability and social capital they need to develop for the future. They are therefore unable to make the best use of resources by aligning them appropriately with organisational priorities. This in turn means that they are unable to make a solid case for HRD activity and produce a process for evaluating its outcomes. As a result, they only focus on immediate operational issues and on individuals' identified needs related to achievement of current targets.

The HRD professionals have discussed these problems with the senior management team. They are now working with that team on a development programme to improve the agency's strategy process and operation.

✎ YOUR TASK

Outline the kind of development programme that you think would be relevant to meet the needs described in this case study.

Provide it with a clear purpose and set of objectives, and indicate in generalised terms the kind of resources that would be needed to deliver it.

CHAPTER 6 HRD: the state of play

Assignment 1

Please read through the following case and then tackle the task at the end.

CULTURE CHANGE IN A BUILDING SOCIETY

Introduction

Today many hitherto traditional high-street businesses are developing into net-work structures that are to a large extent clusters of separate small enterprises, held together by a company brand. Dominant features are knowledge as an intangible asset, employees who are expert in their work and can operate with minimal supervision, and management achieved through performance measurements, targets and financial incentives rather than through more direct forms of control. Keywords are partnership, trust and mutual dependency. Two examples in the UK are Boots the Chemist and the Abbey National Building Society (Pickard, 2001). This case study incorporates within the fictional framework of a single organisation changes all of which have actually been introduced at those two institutions.

The context

Two years ago one of the UK's leading building societies took over a high-street bank and now offers banking services in addition to its usual services and products. The society's aim has been to maintain its reputation as a leading-edge organisation, to expand the kinds of services and products that it can offer, and to remain continuously innovative in an increasingly challenging business environment.

Organisational changes

In the past few months the organisation has begun to change its former hierarchical structure to one that more resembles that of a networked organisation held together by the former building society's familiar brand name. Management has invested heavily in new technology in order to manage all parts of its network effectively and to ensure efficient communication links.

The following features have already been introduced:

■ A new corporate mission and business strategy have been produced. These have been well publicised throughout the organisation, using a variety of methods including road shows, short training programmes and cascaded team briefings. They fit the company's new aspirations, its strong customer-focused vision, and its developing partnership-based structure.

■ Appropriate new personnel and development policies have been publicised in similar ways. Top management is committed to ensuring that at every stage of the change process there is full consultation, and that appropriate relations, reward and resourcing policies are put in place.

- The company has in the past few months opened a number of high-street 'café-banks' on a joint venturing basis with a chain of coffee shops.

- The credit card side of the company's operations and its customer relations are now managed by an international credit card organisation, also on a joint venturing basis.

Further changes on the way

Within the next three months further changes will be introduced on a pilot basis. The most important of these are:

- One third of the company's high-street branches will become pilot franchises, in which local managers can purchase a 49% stake.

- All workers in the company's call centre will be required to take on much increased personal responsibility in their work. Their role has to change from one where they simply take an enquiry and pass it on to someone with the expert knowledge to reply, to one where each call centre operator must find the answer him- or herself and call the customer back.

 YOUR TASK

Imagine that you are the HRD manager in this organisation.

1. Draft a set of proposals to take to top management whereby to start building a workplace culture for the company's call centre that will be conducive to call centre workers becoming in effect 'knowledge workers'.

2. Also produce a specific action plan detailing how to develop in local managers and call centre workers the skills and attitudes they will need in order to cope well with the changes that will be introduced on a pilot basis within the next three months.

Assignment 2

Producing an educational programme for HRD practitioners or students

YOUR TASK

Chapter 6 contains an identification and analysis of four major challenges facing HRD practitioners in their current and changing organisational environments. It has also made it clear that there are some concerns about the ability of the HRD profession to meet these challenges and to identify and respond appropriately to the tasks that they involve.

Produce an outline of an educational programme – its design, main content and learning methods – that could help the following to improve their understanding of those challenges, and to develop the skills, attitudes and confidence needed to play their due part in tackling them:

EITHER

a) a set of HRD practitioners in your own organisation

OR

b) students on a professional qualifying programme with which you are familiar that has substantial HRD content.

You do not need specialist learning design skills to tackle this task (although, of course, if you have such skills you may wish to use them). You should simply rely on your understanding of the chapter's content and your own thinking about what is likely to give most help here to either HRD practitioners or students.

CHAPTER 7 Notions of knowledge

Assignment 1

This is another assignment about call centre work, but is of a very different kind to the first assignment set for Chapter 6. Please read through the details of the case and then tackle the task at the end.

WORKING IN A CALL CENTRE

Introduction: call centre work

Many of those whom management regards as low-level labour are in fact a type of knowledge worker, and as such play a crucial part in the organisation's knowledge process. Consider, for example, the case of call centre workers. There are an estimated 203,000 call centre employees around Britain, and by 2003 it is likely that the call centre workforce will exceed that of coal mining, steel and vehicle production combined.

Almost two-fifths of these employees work at the heart of the knowledge economy, in financial services and insurance. They provide the human infrastructure for the knowledge workers who dominate those industries and are themselves a type of knowledge worker since they are in direct contact with customers and, depending on how they are managed, can have considerable autonomy in the ways in which they deal with customer queries and complaints. Their jobs are highly pressured, fast-moving and rapidly changing. They may spend 80% of their time on the phone and 'sales teams have systems which can start dialling the next number when a call is nearly over' (Brown, 2000).

The workplace context of these workers often bears more resemblance to the sweatshops of the industrial revolution than to an environment conducive to this particular kind of knowledge work. It is unsurprising that call centres so often have high rates of absenteeism and turnover. However, not all call centres use mainly casual and part-time workers, and although call centre work is highly intensive, conditions are not the same everywhere. Collective bargaining is also widespread in the industry, with organisations such as Barclays Bank and Vertex having embraced a partnership deal with their union. Staff retention rates also vary greatly, being at their lowest in the North West, Wales, the North East and London, and highest in the South East, West and Yorkshire (Hatchett, 2000).

Pressures in Australian call centres

'The way call-centre managers balance conflicting pressures, such as the need to improve service quality and reduce costs, affects employees' experience of work' (Kinnie, 2002). A study based on five call centres of a large Australian telecoms organisation drew on a survey of 480 telephone service operators. Four factors were examined: the nature of the job and work setting; social support in the organisation; personal disposition; demographic factors (Deery et al., 2002).

A key finding was high levels of emotional exhaustion in call centre workers. This exhaustion had two primary causes: difficult customers, and having to adhere closely to a predefined script. Length of service did not give employees greater competence in these areas, and they did not receive more organisational social support. Lower levels of exhaustion were associated with supportive team leaders, longer than average calls, good physical health and a positive attitude to life and work.

The researchers concluded that if more attention is not paid to employee well-being in the call centre industry, then the end result will be reduced quality and efficiency of outputs, with its consequent impact on firms' performance.

Sources: Deery et al., 2002; Kinnie, 2002

YOUR TASK

Imagine that you are an HRM consultant, asked by a firm that is shortly setting up a call centre and is currently deciding on where to locate it, for advice on how best to ensure that workers will achieve the necessary fine balance between productivity and quality of service. The chief executive (CE) believes that call centre workers will need to be given adequate recognition, support and motivation in their work so that they can cope satisfactorily with the inevitable pressures that it will involve.

Produce a paper that outlines key issues associated with call centre work. You should make good use here of the research information provided for this assignment. Conclude your paper with a set of recommendations to the CE about appropriate HRM and HRD policies and practices.

Your paper should not be a lengthy one, but it must be clear, well focused and convincing in its analysis and outline recommendations. It is not intended to be a full report, but an introductory paper that will act as a stimulus to a forthcoming detailed discussion you will be having with the CE.

Assignment 2

Please read through the following case and then tackle the task at the end.

TACKLING A FAILURE IN KNOWLEDGE MANAGEMENT

A major European bank set a goal to achieve 'global knowledge management' by developing intranet systems that would break down barriers between its different divisions. However, although the divisions invested heavily in new technology, there was a failure to consider or adequately communicate the value of their initiatives for their staff, or about the need to achieve overall integration of the various divisional intranet systems. In consequence, barriers were not reduced but were increased, because the systems introduced proved incompatible with each other, and because staff could not see what benefits they gained from the whole initiative.

Source: Based on Scarbrough, 1999

 YOUR TASK

The bank has decided to relaunch its global knowledge management initiative. This time it is determined to ensure a more integrative approach that will give it a better chance of success.

As HR Director, you have been asked to present a paper at a forthcoming initial meeting between the senior manager who is in charge of the relaunch, key IT staff who will be involved, and yourself. In your presentation you must outline the kind of HR policies and practices that you feel essential both to relaunch and to sustain the initiative. Full discussion of your ideas will take place at the meeting.

Produce your paper.

CHAPTER 8 The knowledge-productive organisation

Assignment 1

Please read through the following case and then tackle the task at the end.

DEVELOPING A POLICY ON KNOWLEDGE PRODUCTIVITY

Organisation X is operating in increasingly turbulent conditions, and has a much greater need than before for the sharing of knowledge and for fast responsiveness and innovation in a highly competitive market. You are an HRD consultant who has been asked to advise its chief executive on approaches to make the company more knowledge-productive. You have talked to many of its senior managers, and the following conversations typify the rather different perspectives that have emerged.

Manager 1

'What matters most for our company is rapid access to the best knowledge. So we need a clear vision as to where we are heading for. We need to analyse the expertise required to achieve our goals and then define the gap between what we are and where we need to be. Then, we'll have to make sure we can develop knowledge on how to bridge that gap, moving faster than our competitors. We depend on a highly skilled workforce and managers who can set goals and coach their subordinates.

The corporate vision, mission and policies must be the points of reference for the competency development, and information and communication technology should play a crucial role here. We'll need intelligent networks so that we can make best use of each others' knowledge and expertise. A superior IT-based knowledge-management system will help us to surface tacit knowledge in our employees. Then we can codify it, store it, or pass it on to others so that it can be added to or modified. If we do this and store the knowledge we produce securely, we can protect it from being copied or poached by our competitors.

As I see it, the main role for our managers in all of this is to analyse their staff's skills, organise people for the necessary learning they'll have to do, set new goals and generally inspire people. Our employees want to earn a living under reasonable conditions. As long as they are motivated by their managers and get a fair salary, they'll give their time, energy and loyalty in return.'

Manager 2

'What this company needs most is to develop its capability to quickly adapt and innovate. We can't just rely on our research and development experts here – we need to tap into the knowledge all our employees have about how to deal with everyday questions. So let's have a critical review of business routines that don't serve a useful purpose any more. Let's find out better ways of co-creating value with our customers. Let's get everyone in the organisation to go on the alert for new information and develop their antennas for picking up interesting developments and practices wherever and whenever they happen.

Our people want to earn a living under reasonable conditions. They know that their careers depend on their own skills and talents and how they develop them. They all value working somewhere where they find trust, mutual respect and good workplace relationships. They're each driven in a different way but they are all what I'd call "passionate experts". However, they are very well aware of their talents and of their high market value. They'll only stay with us as long as we offer a work environment that they also find is an inspiring learning environment.'

Source: Based on Kessels and Van der Werff, 2002: 23–5

YOUR TASK

- Identify and analyse the notions of knowledge and learning that emerge from these two conversations.

- Then, as the HRD consultant, write a briefing paper for the company's chief executive, to prepare her for a meeting you will both shortly be having. In it you should outline your analysis of the issues that you believe to have been raised by the two conversations, and produce recommendations to help the company move towards being a knowledge-productive organisation.

Assignment 2

Please read through the following summary of key concepts in Chapter 8 and then tackle the task at the end.

BUILDING KNOWLEDGE PRODUCTIVITY
THROUGH A CORPORATE CURRICULUM

Key concepts

■ Knowledge productivity represents the ability of a team, unit or organisation to signal relevant information on the basis of which to develop new capabilities and to apply these to gradual improvement and radical innovation in operating procedures, products and services.

■ The corporate curriculum is a construct that refers to an organisational plan for learning. That plan facilitates the creation of a rich and diverse environment that encourages and supports employees in the learning they need for continuous improvement and innovation.

■ A well-developed corporate curriculum therefore facilitates the process of knowledge productivity.

■ The corporate curriculum's 'pillars' of promoting calm and stability and stimulating creative turmoil must be skilfully balanced. There is a tension between the need to promote the calm and stability that help to achieve adaptation and improvement, and the creative turmoil from which radical innovation can flow.

■ Another pillar, that of practical judgement, has an ethical nature. Its roots lie in feelings, in learning from experience, in respecting all value systems, in responding positively to diversity in the workplace, and in openness to further experience and to the continual shifts in the individual's frames of reference that this involves.

✎ YOUR TASK

You have been asked to prepare a report on how your organisation (or one with which you are familiar) could increase its knowledge productivity and you are thinking through what you should include.

Draft a memo for yourself to help this reflective process, using the key concepts of Chapter 8 as guiding principles and taking it for granted that your report will need to contain answers to three fundamental questions:

■ What kind of improvements and innovations are we striving for?

■ What kind of capabilities do we need to further develop?

■ What pillars of our corporate curriculum need further reinforcement?

CHAPTER 9 Researching knowledge productivity

Assignment 1

Conducting a reconstruction study

Designing and conducting a reconstruction study provides an insight into a situation that has taken place in the past in a specific department or unit, through carrying out desk review and interviewing key actors. At the same time it puts the observer at a distance from the situation studied.

Please carry out the following task to develop your skills in reconstructive research.

🖎 YOUR TASK

1. Choose a client or principle who is interested in the investigation of a recent improvement or innovation of a work process, product or service.

2. Obtain from them detailed information about the nature of that improvement or innovation, and record that information.

3. Select relevant components from the general framework shown in Figure 9.4, and design your instruments for data collection (list of topics, questions, interview schedule and so on).

4. Identify the actors who were involved in the process leading to the improvement or innovation.

5. Tailor your data collection instruments to those actors and to the kind of role they played in the process of knowledge construction.

6. Carry out your data collection in order to discover what actually happened in the chosen unit that produced the recent improvement or innovation identified in step 2.

7. When you have done this, ask the respondents to validate the data.

8. Analyse the data and display your main findings in a matrix.

9. Identify how many aspects from organisational context, workplace environment, learning functions, knowledge-construction process and specific interventions appear to relate to the improvement or innovation you have studied.

10. Produce convincing conclusions for your findings.

11. Produce informed recommendations for interventions to increase the likely number of future improvements and innovations.

Assignment 2

Conducting a development study

Designing and conducting a development study provides an insight into interventions that support the process of knowledge construction that leads to improvements or innovation of work processes, products or services. It does so by actively involving the researcher in the learning process, thereby resulting in him or her losing the 'safe' position of observer at a distance that is offered by a reconstruction study.

Please carry out the following task to develop your skills in developmental research.

✎ YOUR TASK

1. Choose a client or principle who is interested in the enhancement of work-related learning that may lead to improvement or innovation.

2. Select components from the general framework shown in Figure 9.4 that could play an important role in developing effective interventions to produce improvement and innovation in a unit.

3. Meet with the members of the unit. Start building a working relationship with them, sharing perceptions on the assignment you are about to conduct.

4. Develop interventions and prepare advice that will help those who have agreed to take part in your study to share experiences, collect new information, and reflect on their learning activities.

5. Identify factors that typically facilitate or inhibit the learning process and the construction of knowledge in the workplace. Design instruments for data collection relating to these factors (list of topics, questions, interview schedule and so on).

6. Tailor your data collection instruments to the participants in your study and to the role they appear to have in the process of knowledge construction in the unit.

7. Carry out your data collection once the interventions have run for a sufficient length of time.

8. When it is concluded, ask the respondents to validate the data.

9. Analyse the data and display your main finding in a matrix.

10. Identify how many characteristic aspects from organisational context, work environment, learning functions, the knowledge-construction process and the specific interventions you have carried out seem to relate to outcomes in terms of improvement or innovation.

11. Produce convincing conclusions for your findings.

12. Review with respondents the interventions that you developed in step 4. Your aim is to decide how best to strengthen the relationship between specific interventions, collaborative learning processes and eventual improvements and innovations.

13. Produce informed suggestions for interventions likely to increase the number of future improvements and innovations.

CHAPTER 10 New technology

Assignment 1

Please read through the following case and then tackle the task at the end.

KNOWLEDGE SHARING AND NEW TECHNOLOGY

The company

Company X is a consulting firm offering services in environmental engineering. It develops systems for purifying and recuperation of water and waste. It is expert in 'clean' production. It has invested much money and effort in developing a knowledge-management system to support the conduct of large-scale projects and to facilitate learning from each other's experiences. The systems contain project-management tools, formats for preparing proposals, timelines, cost overviews, and descriptions of a variety of roles including project manager, analyst, designer, facility manager and administrative support staff. Staff must use standardised formats for new projects and to store project proposals and evaluation reports in the system.

The knowledge-management system

The chief knowledge officer who maintains the knowledge-management system has just uncovered a number of problems, of which the most significant are the following:

■ The number of entries made in the system is dramatically decreasing.

■ Currently almost none of the consultants prepare evaluation reports to be added to the system.

■ Proposals for new projects that can be retrieved from the system have not been formatted according to the prescribed templates.

■ Consultants complain about the time-consuming procedures involved in putting everything onto the computer, and feel hampered by the formal procedures that in their view do not fit the need for tailor-made projects.

✎ YOUR TASK

Imagine that you have been invited to explore the background of the poorly functioning knowledge-management system in Company X:

■ After studying the various types of research strategy described in Chapter 9, what elements do you think would be helpful as a framework for analysis of this case – and why?

■ If you were asked to develop an alternative approach for improving professional knowledge sharing in Company X, what would you recommend?

■ What role could technology play to support the sharing of knowledge?

Assignment 2

Please read through the following case and then tackle the task at the end.

COLLABORATION AT A DISTANCE

Introduction

You are one of the national HRD officers of an airline company with ground staff in most European countries, and in the US, Africa and Asia. Due to new and stricter safety regulations, the treatment of customers as clients has deteriorated. You have been invited by senior management to create a new project in which ground staff are invited to develop new ideas about how to increase the level of customer service.

From previous projects, management has learnt that it is useless for headquarters to impose new and uniform procedures for client-centredness. The cultural diversity in this globally operating service industry is vast and requires local attention and initiatives as well. On the other hand, a high level of quality across the whole company needs to be assured, since passengers travel to all manner of destinations and must be treated with consistency wherever they go.

Project specification

Staff from most of the countries in which the company is active will participate in your new project. Senior management wants to experiment with the idea of 'a dispersed learning team'. In many ways it is a novel approach for the company.

The management wants the project to have the following key features:

■ It should enable the participants to jointly develop new knowledge on how to increase the level of customer service.

■ It should lead to a general, global framework for customer service, but one that is flexible enough to take account of local diversity.

■ It must incorporate a high level of collaborative information and communication technology (ICT), since due to the long distances between the participants' workplaces, it will be impossible to organise regular meetings for them. The company is willing to heavily support the project in this way.

■ This will be a pilot project to generate new knowledge about how to organise collaboration between dispersed teams.

✎ YOUR TASK

Produce a set of briefing notes for yourself, containing your thoughts on how best to deal with the following issues:

■ As an HRD professional, how should you prepare yourself for this assignment?

■ What ICT tools and processes might you use to support the team as they carry out the project?

■ Specifically, having taken into account the results of various research projects and experiments on distance collaboration that you know about (if only from Chapter 10), how will you enhance co-operation and learning in your team?

■ How should you start the project?

■ How should you select the project team participants?

This is not essentially a design task. Its aim is to stimulate your thinking on how generally to handle your assignment and on a variety of approaches to virtual collaboration – both ICT-aided and face to face – that you could employ.

Case Companies

Case name	Sector	Type of organisation	KM initiative	Outcome
Expert Consulting	consultancy	small scientific consultancy creating customised products and services	organisation-wide knowledge sharing and creation	relatively successful – cross-disciplinary knowledge sharing
Ebank	financial services	very large global bank	KM via development of global internet tool	many problems – disintegrated intranet development
JBA	software	medium-sized international software developer	KM for integrated software development project	largely successful – project completed on schedule
NET project	public sector university	small multi-disciplinary, multi-institutional research team	knowledge sharing and creation across team members	many problems – disintegration among team members
Brightco	manufacturing and service	medium-sized, multinational, material-handling equipment manufacturer and service provider	KM for introduction of IT sales/service support across all sites	largely successful – project on schedule
CommCo	telecommunications	very large global telecom company	creation of 'virtual university' for becoming a learning organisation	many problems – project eventually cancelled
Multicorp	manufacturing and supply	very large global manufacturer, supplier of consumer goods (dental care division)	KM for product development via 'innovation funnel' tool	many problems – tool not used as intended
Buckman Labs	manufacturing and supply	large global chemical company	global knowledge sharing via IT (K'Netix) and human resources management	very successful – integrated knowledge architecture

Source: Reported in Scarbrough and Swann, 1999, p. ix. Reproduced by permission of Chartered Institute of Personnel and Development

References

Ackroyd, S., Burrell, G., Hughes, M. and Whitaker, A. (1988) 'The Japanisation of British industry?' *Industrial Relations Journal*. Vol. 19, 1: 11–23.

Ahlstrand, B. and Purcell, J. (1988) 'Employee relations strategy in the multi-divisional company'. *Personnel Review*. Vol. 17, 3: 3–11.

Alekseeva, M. (2002) *Design of a WWW-environment for collaborative learning at Heineken University* (HRD Masters Thesis). Moscow/Enschede: University of Twente.

Alheit, P. (1999) 'On a contradictory way to the 'Learning Society': a critical approach'. *Studies in the Education of Adults*. Vol. 31, 1: 66–82.

Allard-Poesi, F.A. (1996) 'The emergence process of a collective representation in a decision-making group: a case study'. *Paper presented at European Institute for Advanced Studies in Management, 4th International Workshop on Managerial and Organisational Cognition: Management in the thought-full enterprise*. Stockholm: Stockholm School of Economics and Linkoping University, 29–30 August.

American Society for Training and Development. (1999) *Work Force Investment Act of 1988 Fact Sheet*. www.astd.org/virtual_community/public_policy.

Amit, R. and Schoemaker, J.H. (1993) 'Strategic assets and organizational rent'. *Strategic Management Journal*. Vol. 14, 1: 33–46.

Ansoff, H.I. and Sullivan, P.A. (1993) 'Optimizing profitability in turbulent environments: a formula for strategic success'. *Long Range Planning*. Vol. 26, 5: 11–23.

Argyris, C. (1996) 'Skilled incompetence'. In K. Starkey (ed.) *How Organizations Learn*. London: International Thomson Business Press, pp. 82–91.

Argyris, C. and Schon, D.A. (1978) *Organizational Learning: A Theory of Action Perspective*. Reading, MA: Addison Wesley.

Argyris, C. and Schon, D.A. (1996) *Organizational Learning II: Theory, Method and Practice*. New York: Addison Wesley.

Arkin, A. (2002) 'Rewrite the rules'. *People Management*. Vol. 8, 20: 36–7.

Ashton, D., Sung, J., Raddon, A. and Powell, M. (2001) 'National frameworks for workplace learning'. In *Chartered Institute of Personnel and Development Workplace Learning in Europe* [summary of the European Workplace Learning Seminar, London, 2 April 2001]. London: CIPD, pp. 35–60. Available to download from: www.cipd.co.uk.

Badaracco, J.L. (1991) *Knowledge Link: How Firms Compete Through Strategic Alliances*. Boston, MA: Harvard Business School Press.

Baets, W.R.J. (1999) *Organizational Learning and Knowledge Technologies in a Dynamic Environment*. Dordrecht: Kluwer Academic Publishers.

Barnard, C.I. (1938) *The Functions of the Executive*. Cambridge, MA: Harvard University Press.

Barney, J. (1991) 'Firm resources and sustained competitive advantage'. *Journal of Management*. Vol. 17: 99–120.

Bartlett, C.A. and Ghoshal, S. (1993) 'Beyond the M-form: toward a managerial theory of the firm'. *Strategic Management Journal*, Winter Special Issue. Vol. 14: 23–46.

Bassanini, A. and Scarpetta, S. (2001) 'Does human capital matter for growth in OECD Countries? Evidence from pooled mean-group estimates' *OECD Economics Department Working Paper No. 283*. OECD: Paris.

Batchelor, J., Donnelly, R. and Morris, D. (1995) 'Learning networks within supply chains'. *Working paper, Coventry Business School*. Coventry: Coventry University, Priory Street, Coventry, CVI 5FB.

Bates, D.L. and Dillard, Jr., J.E. (1993) 'Generating strategic thinking through multi-level teams'. *Long Range Planning*. Vol. 26, 5: 103–10.

Baum, J.A.C., Calabrese, T. and Silverman, B.S. (2000) 'Don't go it alone: alliance network composition and startups' performance in Canadian biotechnology'. *Strategic Management Journal*. Vol. 21, 3: 267–81.

Baumard, P. (1999) *Tacit Knowledge in Organisations*. London: Sage.

Beardwell, I. and Holden, L. (eds) (1995) *Human Resource Management – A Contemporary Perspective*. London: Pitman.

Beaumont, P. and Hunter, L. (2002) *Managing Knowledge Workers: The HRM Dimension. Research Report*. London: Chartered Institute of Personnel and Development.

Becker, B. and Gerhart, B. (1996) 'The impact of human resource practices on organizational performance: progress and prospects'. *Academy of Management Journal*. Vol. 39: 779–801.

Becker, G. (1975) *Human Capital: A Theoretical and Empirical Analysis with Special Reference to Education*, 2nd edn. New York: Columbia University Press.

Becker, G.S. (1993) *Human Capital: A Theoretical and Empirical Analysis with Special Reference to Education*, 3rd edn. Chicago: University of Chicago Press.

Beer, M. (1980) *Organization Change and Development*. Santa Monica, CA: Goodyear.

Bertels, T. and Savage, C.M. (1998) 'Tough questions on knowledge management'. In G. von Krogh., J. Roos and D. Kleine (eds) *Knowing in Firms: Understanding, Managing and Measuring Knowledge*. London: Sage, pp. 7–25.

Bettis, R.A. and Hitt, M.A. (1995) 'The new competitive landscape'. *Strategic Management Journal*, Summer Special Issue Vol. 16: 7–19.

Bettis, R.A. and Prahalad, C.K. (1995) 'The dominant logic: retrospective and extension'. *Strategic Management Journal*. Vol. 16: 5–14.

Billet, S. (1997) 'Dispositions, vocational knowledge and development: sources and consequences'. *Australian and New Zealand Journal of Vocational Education Research*. Vol. 5, 1: 1–26.

Blackhurst, C. (1993) 'Branson to demand "millions" from BA'. *Independent on Sunday, Business Section*. 24 January: 1.

Blunkett, D. (2000) 'Digital dimensions'. *Guardian Higher Education Supplement*, 15 February: 1h.

Bohn, R.E. (1994) 'Measuring and managing technological knowledge'. *Sloan Management Review*. Vol. 36, 1: 61–73.

Boisot, M., Griffiths, D. and Moles, V. (1995) 'The dilemma of competence: differentiation versus integration in the pursuit of learning'. *Paper prepared for the Third International Workshop on Competence-based competition*. Ghent: November 16–18.

Bolman, L.G. and Deal, T.E. (1991) *Reframing Organizations: Artistry, Choice and Leadership*. San Francisco, CA: Jossey-Bass.

Bood, R.P. (1996) 'Wandering in a cognitive field'. *Paper presented at European Institute for Advanced Studies in Management, 4th International Workshop on Managerial and Organisational Cognition: Management in the thought-full enterprise*. Stockholm: Stockholm School of Economics and Linkoping University, 29–30 August.

Boud, D. and Garrick, J. (1999) 'Understandings of workplace learning'. In D. Boud and J. Garrick (eds) *Understanding Learning at Work*. London, Routledge, pp. 1–11.

Bournois, F., Chauchat, J.-H. and Roussillon, S. (1994) 'Training and management development in Europe'. In C. Brewster and A. Hegewisch (eds) *Policy and Practice in European Human Resource Management: The Price Waterhouse Cranfield Survey*. London: Routledge, pp. 122–38.

Bowen, D.E., Gilliland, S.W. and Folger, R. (1999) 'HRM and service fairness: how being fair with employees spills over to customers'. *Organizational Dynamics*. Winter: 7–23.

Bowman, E.H., Singh, H. and Thomas, H. (2002) 'The domain of strategic management: history and evolution'. In A. Pettigrew, H. Thomas and R. Whittington (eds) *Handbook of Strategy and Management*. London: Sage, pp. 31–51.

Brewster, C. (1999) 'Strategic human resource management: the value of different paradigms'. In R.S. Schuler and S.E. Jackson (eds) *Strategic Human Resource Management*. Oxford: Blackwell, pp. 356–72.

Brewster, C. and Hegewisch, A. (eds) (1994) *Policy and Practice in European Human Resource Management: The Price Waterhouse Cranfield Survey*. London: Routledge

Brewster, C., Harris, H. and Sparrow, P. (2002) *Globalising HR: Executive Briefing*. London: Chartered Institute of Personnel and Development.

Brewster, C., Hegewisch, A., Mayne, L. and Tregaskis, O. (1994) 'Appendix 1: Methodology'. In C. Brewster and A. Hegewisch (eds) *Policy and Practice in European Human Resource Management: The Price Waterhouse Cranfield Survey*. London: Routledge, pp. 230–45.

Brickley, J.A. and Van Drunen, L. (1990) 'Internal corporate restructuring: an empirical analysis'. *Journal of Accounting and Economics*. Vol. 12: 251–80.

Briggs, P. (1991) 'Organisational commitment: the key to Japanese success?' In C. Brewster and S. Tyson (eds) *International Comparisons in Human Resource Management*. London: Pitman, pp. 33–43.

Brooks, A.K. (1997) 'Power and the production of knowledge: collective team learning in organizations'. In D. Russ-Eft, H. Preskill and C. Sleezer (eds) *Human Resource Development Review: Research and Implications*. Thousands Oaks, CA: Sage, pp. 179–205.

Brown, D. (2002) 'Top down and bottom up'. *People Management*. Vol. 8, 17: 18.

Brown, J.S. and Duguid, P. (1991) 'Organisational learning and communities-of-practice: towards a unified view of working, learning and innovation'. *Organization Science*. Vol. 2, 1: 40–57.

Brown, J.S. and Duguid, P. (2000) *The Social Life of Information*. Boston: Harvard Business School Press.

Brown, P. (2000) 'Trained to cope with anything'. *Times,* 22 February: 45.

Brown, S.L. and Eisenhardt, K. (1998) 'The art of continuous change: linking complexity theory and timepaced evolution in relentlessly shifting organizations'. *Administrative Science Quarterly*. Vol. 42: 1–34.

Bruner, J. and Anglin, J.M. (1973) *Beyond the Information Given*. New York: W.W. Norton and Co.

Buchanan, P., Claydon, T. and Doyle, M. (1999) 'Organizational development and change: the legacy of the 1990s'. *Human Resource Management Journal*. Vol. 9, 2: 20–37.

Buckingham, M. (2001) 'What a waste'. *People Management*. Vol. 7, 20: 36–40.

Burgoyne, J. (1999) *Develop Yourself, Your Career and Your Organisation*. London: Lemos and Crane.

Burton-Jones, A. (1999) *Knowledge Capitalism. Business, Work, and Learning in the New Economy*. Oxford: Oxford University Press.

Butler, E. (1999) 'Technologising equity: the politics and practices of work-related learning'. In D. Boud and J. Garrick (eds) *Understanding Learning at Work*. London: Routledge, pp. 132–50.

Campbell, M. (2002) 'Bridge of death sends warning to Schröder'. *Sunday Times*, 8 September, 1: 26.

Cannell, M. (2002) 'Class Struggle'. *People Management*. Vol. 8, 5: 46–7.

Cappelli, P. (1995) 'Rethinking Employment'. *British Journal of Industrial Relations*. Vol. 33, 4: 563–602.

Carnall, C. (1999) 'Positive e-valuation'. *People Management*. Vol. 5, 17: 54–7.

Carroll, R. (1987) 'Organizational approaches to strategy: an introduction and overview'. *California Management Review*. Vol. 30, 1: 8–9.

Carter, P. and Jackson, N. (1990) 'The emergence of postmodern management?' *Management Education and Development*. Vol. 21, Part 3: 219–28.

Castells, M. (1998) *End of Millennium*. Malden, MA: Blackwell.

Caulkin, S. (2001) *Raising UK Productivity: Why People Management Matters*. London: Chartered Institute of Personnel and Development.

Cave, A. (2002) 'Alcatel rings the alarm as even more jobs go'. *Daily Telegraph*, 27 June: 31.

CEDEFOP (The European Centre for the Development of Vocational Education) (1996) *The Role of the Company in Generating Skills – The Learning Effects of Work Organisation, The Netherlands Country Study*. Luxembourg: CEDEFOP.

CEDEFOP (The European Centre for the Development of Vocational Education) (1997) *Identification, validation et accreditation de l'apprentissage antérieur et informel*. France: CEDEFOP.

Centraal Planbureau (2002) *De peilers onder de kenniseconomie. Opties voor institutionele vernieuwing.* [The pillars of the knowledge economy. Options for institutional renewal] The Hague: CPB.

Chakravarthy, B.S. and White, R. (2002) 'Strategy process: forming, implementing and changing strategies'. In A. Pettigrew, H. Thomas and R. Whittington (eds) *Handbook of Strategy and Management.* London: Sage, pp. 182–205.

Chandler, A.D. (1962) *Strategy and Structure: Chapters in the History of the American Industrial Enterprise.* Cambridge, MA: MIT Press.

Chartered Institute of Personnel and Development (2001) *Workplace Learning in Europe* [summary of the European Workplace Learning Seminar, London, 2 April 2001]. London: CIPD. Available to download from: www.cipd.co.uk.

Chartered Institute of Personnel and Development (2001a) *CIPD Professional Standards.* London: CIPD. Available to download from: www.cipd.co.uk.

Chartered Institute of Personnel and Development (2002) *Training and Development 2002 Survey Report.* London: CIPD. Available to download from: www.cipd.co.uk.

Child, J. (1977) *Organization: a Guide to Problems and Practice.* London: Harper & Row.

Child, J. (1988) 'On organizations in their sectors'. *Organization Studies.* Vol. 9, 1: 1–32.

Ciborra, C.U. (1996) 'The platform organization: recombining strategies, structures and surprises'. *Organization Science.* Vol. 7, 2: 103–18.

Codol, J.P. (1984) 'On the system of representations in an artificial social situation'. In R.M. Farr and S. Moscovici (eds) *Social Representations.* Cambridge: Cambridge University Press, pp. 239–53.

Cohen, W.M. and Levinthal, D.A. (1990) 'Absorptive capacity: a new perspective on learning and innovation'. *Administrative Science Quarterly*, Vol. 35, 1: 128–52.

Collins, N. (2002) 'How globalisation slayed the dragon of inflation'. *Daily Telegraph*, 22 July: 17.

Collis, B. and Moonen, J. (2001) *Flexible Learning in a Digital World.* London: Kogan Page.

Collis, B.A., and De Boer, W. (1999) 'The TeleTOP Decision Support Tool (DST)'. In J. van den Akker, R.M. Branch, K. Gustafson, N. Nieveen and Tj. Plomp (eds) *Design approaches and tools in education and training.* Dordrecht: Kluwer Academic Publishers, pp. 235–48.

Commission of the European Communities (1993) *The Outlook for Higher Education in the European Community: Responses to the Memorandum.* Luxembourg: Office for Official Publications of the European Communities.

Coopey, J. (1995) 'The learning organization, power, politics and ideology'. *Management Learning.* Vol. 26, 2: 193–213.

Coulson-Thomas, C. (2001) 'Fashion victim'. *People Management.* Vol. 7, 17: 51.

Cray, D., Haines, Jr. G.H. and Mallory G.R. (1994) 'Programmed strategic decision making: the view from Mintzberg's window'. *British Journal of Management.* Vol. 5: 191–204.

Crouch, C., Finegold, D. and Sako, M. (1999) *Are Skills the Answer?* Oxford: Oxford University Press.

Cunningham, I. and Hyman, J. (1999) 'Devolving human resource responsibilities to the line: beginning of the end or a new beginning for personnel?' *Personnel Review.* Vol. 28, 1/2: 9–27.

Cyert, R.M. and March, J.G. (1963) *A Behavioural Theory of the Firm.* Englewood Cliffs, NJ: Prentice Hall.

Daft, R.L. and Weick, K.E. (1984) 'Toward a model of organizations as interpretation systems'. *Academy of Management Review.* Vol. 9, 2: 284–95.

Darling, J., Darling, P. and Elliott, J. (1999) *The Changing Role of the Trainer.* London: Institute of Personnel and Development.

Davidow, W.H. and Malone, M.S. (1992) *The Virtual Corporation.* New York: HarperCollins.

D'Cruz, J.R. and Rugman, A.M. (1994) 'The Five Partners Model: France Telecom, Alcatel, and the Global Telecommunications Industry'. *European Management Journal.* Vol. 12, 1: 59–66.

De Swaan, A. (2002) 'Iemand moet toch alles weten'. [There should be someone who knows everything] *Vrij Nederland.* Vol. 63, 27: 49–51.

Deery, S., Iverson, R. and Walsh, J. (2002) 'Work relationships in telephone call centres: understanding emotional exhaustion and employee withdrawal'. *Journal of Management Studies.* Vol. 39, 4: 471–96.

Dehnbostel, P. and Molzberger, G. (2001) 'Combination of formal learning and learning by experiences in industrial enterprises'. In J.N. Streumer (ed.) *Proc. 2nd Conference on HRD Research and Practice Across Europe: Perspectives on learning at the workspace.* University of Twente Enschede, The Netherlands, 26–27 January: pp. 77–88.

Department for Education and Employment (1998) 'The Learning Age'. Green Paper. London: HMSO.

DiMaggio, P.J. and Powell, W.W. (eds) (1991) *The New Institutionalism in Organizational Analysis*. Chicago: University of Chicago Press.

Dixon, N. (2000) *Common Knowledge: How Companies Thrive by Sharing What They Know*. Boston: Harvard Business School Press.

Dodgson, M. (1993) 'Learning, trust, and technological collaboration'. *Human Relations*. Vol. 46, 1: 77–95.

Dore, R. (1987) *Taking Japan Seriously: A Confucian Perspective on Leading Economic Issues*. London: The Athlone Press.

Dougherty, D. (1999) 'Organizing for innovation'. In S.R. Clegg, C. Hardy and W.R. Nord (eds) *Managing Organizations: Current Issues*. London: Sage, pp. 174–89.

Drost, E.A., Frayne, C.A., Lowe, K.B. and Geringer, J.M. (2002) 'Benchmarking training and development practices: a multi-country comparative analysis'. *Human Resource Management*. Vol. 41, 1: 67–86.

Drucker, P. (1974) 'New templates for today's organizations'. *Harvard Business Review*. Vol. 52, 1: 45.

Drucker, P. (1993) *Post-capitalist Society*. Oxford: Butterworth Heinemann.

Drucker, P. (2001) 'A century of social transformation. Emergence of knowledge society'. In *The Essential Drucker*. New York: Harper Business, pp. 299–320.

Dulewicz, V. and Higgs, M. (1999) *Making Sense of Emotional Intelligence*. ASE (Tel. (UK): 01753 850333).

Dutrénit, G. (2000) *Learning and Knowledge Management in the Firm: From Knowledge Accumulation to Strategic Capabilities*. Cheltenham: Edward Elgar.

Dybowski, G. (1998) 'New technologies and work organization – impact on vocational education and training'. In CEDEFOP, *Vocational Education and Training – the European Research Field: Background Report*. Thessaloniki: CEDEFOP: Vol. 1.

Edwards, R. (1997) *Changing Places? Flexibility, Lifelong Learning and a Learning Society*. London: Routledge.

Eisenhardt, K.M. and Brown, S. (1999) 'Patching: restitching business portfolios in dynamic markets'. *Harvard Business Review*. May–June: 72–80.

Eisenhardt, K.M. and Galunic, D.C. (2000) 'Coevolving: at last, a way to make synergies work'. *Harvard Business Review*. January/February: 91–101.

Eisenhardt, K.M. and Santos, F.M. (2002) 'Knowledge-based view: a new theory of strategy?' In A. Pettigrew, H. Thomas and R. Whittington (eds) *Handbook of Strategy and Management*. London: Sage, pp. 139–64.

Elfring, T. and Volberda, H.W. (2001) 'Schools of thought in strategic management: fragmentation, integration or synthesis'. In H.W. Volberda and T. Elfring (eds) *Rethinking Strategy*. London: Sage, pp. 1–25.

Elfring, T. and Volberda, H.W. (2001a) 'Multiple futures of strategy synthesis: shifting boundaries, dynamic capabilities and strategy configurations'. In H.W. Volberda and T. Elfring (eds) *Rethinking Strategy*. London: Sage, pp. 245–85.

Emery, F.E. and Trist, E.L. (1960) 'Socio-technical systems'. In C.W. Churchman and M. Verhulst (eds) *Management Science, Models and Techniques*, Vol. 2. London: Pergamon, pp. 83–97.

Engestrom, Y. (1995) *Training and Change*. Geneva: International Labour Office.

European Commission (1996) 'Teaching and Learning. Towards the Learning Society'. *Le Magazine*, Issue 5: 3–5.

Evans, K., Hodkinson, P., Keep, E., Maguire, M., Raffe, D., Rainbird, H., Senker, P. and Unwin, L. (1997) *Issues in People Management No. 18: Working To Learn – a Work-based Route to Learning for Young People*. London: Institute of Personnel and Development.

Fayol, H. (1949) *General and Industrial Administration*. London: Pitman.

Field, J. (2000) *Lifelong Learning and the New Educational Order*. Stoke-on-Trent: Trentham Books.

Filella, J. (1991) 'Is there a Latin model in the management of human resources?' *Personnel Review*. Vol. 20, 6: 14–23.

Floyd, S.W. and Wooldridge, B. (1992) 'Middle management involvement in strategy and its association with strategic type: a research note'. *Strategic Management Journal*. Vol. 13, 2: 153–67.

Floyd, S.W. and Wooldridge, B. (1994) 'Dinosaurs or dynamos? Recognizing middle management's strategic role'. *Academy of Management Executive*. Vol. 8, 4: 47–57.

Follet, M.P. (1941) *Dynamic Administration*. London: Longman.

Fombrun, C., Tichy, N.M. and Devanna, M.A. (eds) (1984) *Strategic Human Resource Management*. New York: Wiley.

Freeman, R. and Gilbert, D. (1988) *Corporate Strategy and the Search for Ethics*. Englewood Cliffs, NJ: Prentice Hall.

Further Education Unit (1992) *Vocational Education and Training in Europe: A Four-country Study in Four Employment Sectors*. London: FEU.

Galbraith, J.R. and Nathanson, D. (1978) *Strategy Implementation*. St. Paul, MN: West Publishing.

Garavan, T., Heraty, N. and Barnicle, B. (1999) 'Human resource development literature: current issues, priorities and dilemmas'. *Journal of European Industrial Training*. Vol. 23, 4/5: 169–79.

Garrick, J.R. (1999) 'The dominant discourses of learning at work'. In D. Boud and J. Garrick (eds) *Understanding Learning at Work*. London: Routledge, pp. 216–29.

Garvey, B. and Williamson, B. (2002) *Beyond Knowledge Management: Dialogue, Creativity and the Corporate Curriculum*. London: Financial Times and Prentice Hall.

Ghoshal, S. and Bartlett, C.A. (1994) 'Linking organizational context and managerial action: the dimension of quality of management'. *Strategic Management Journal*, Special Summer Issue. Vol. 15: 91–112.

Ghoshal, S. and Bartlett, C.A. (1995) 'The new moral contract: guaranteeing employability'. *20th Anniversary Euroforum Conference: Strategic Leadership Programme*. London Business School, 15–16 September.

Gibbons, M. (1998) 'Higher Education Relevance in the 21st Century'. *Association of Commonwealth Universities: draft paper*. London: ACU.

Gibbons, M., Limoges, C., Nowotny, H., Schwartzman, S., Scott, P. and Trow, M. (1994) *The New Production of Knowledge*. London: Sage.

Giddens, A. (1994) 'Living in a post-traditional society'. In U. Beck, A. Giddens and S. Lash (eds) *Reflexive Modernization. Politics, Tradition and Aesthetics in the Modern Social Order*. Cambridge: Polity Press – Blackwell, pp. 56–109.

Ginsberg, A. (1994) 'Minding the competition: from mapping to mastery'. *Strategic Management Journal*, Winter Special Issue. Vol. 15: 153–74.

Gioai, D.A. and Poole, P.P. (1984) 'Scripts in organizational behaviour'. *Academy of Management Review*. Vol. 9, 3: 449–59.

Gleave, S. and Oliver, N. (1990) 'Human resource management in Japanese manufacturing companies in the UK: 5 case studies'. *Journal of General Management*. Vol. 16, 1: 54–68.

Glover, C. (2002) 'A common good'. *People Management*. Vol. 8, 20: 38–9.

Goleman, D. (1998) *Working with Emotional Intelligence*. London: Bloomsbury.

Goleman, D. (2001) 'Nothing new under the sun'. *People Management*. Vol. 7, 3: 51.

Gonczi, A. (1999) 'Competency-based learning: a dubious past – an assured future?' In D. Boud and J. Garrick (eds) *Understanding Learning at Work*. London: Routledge, pp. 180–95.

Goold, M. and Campbell, A. (1987) *Strategies and Styles*. Oxford: Blackwell.

Goudevert, D. (1993) 'Welche Zukunft hat die Arbeit?' [What is the future of labour?] *Die Welt*, 22 April: 12.

Gouldner, A.W. (1965) *Wildcat Strike*. New York: Harper.

Graham, G. (1994) 'Lack of training shuts out poor'. *Financial Times*, 14 March: 4.

Grant, R.M. (1991) *Contemporary Strategy Analysis: Concepts, Techniques, Applications*. Oxford: Blackwell.

Gray, H. (1999) 'Re-scoping the university'. In H. Gray (ed.) *Universities and the Creation of Wealth*. Buckingham: The Society for Research into Higher Education and Open University Press, pp. 3–17.

Grieves, J. and Redman, T. (1999) 'Living in the shadow of OD: HRD and the search for identity'. *Human Resource Development International*. Vol. 2, 2: 81–102.

Groupe Esc Toulouse (2002) 'Call for Papers' – *Fourth Conference on HRD Research and Practice across Europe 2003: Lifelong Learning for a Knowledge Based Society*. France: Toulouse Business School (Groupe ESC Toulouse), the University Forum for HRD (incorporating EURESFORM) and the Academy of HRD.

Grunewald, U. and Moraal, D. (downloaded 2000) 'Approaches and obstacles to the evaluation of investment in continuing vocational training' – *Discussion and case studies from six member states of the European Union*. Webpage: www.trainingvillage.gr/download/publication/panorama/5078/index_en.html.

Guardian (2002) 'Things can only get better – or can they?' *Guardian*, 10 September: 7 (see also www.guardian.co.uk/september11/oneyearon).

Guest, D.E. (1987) 'Human resource management and industrial relations'. *Journal of Management Studies*. Vol. 24: 503–21.

Guest, D.E. (1990) 'Human resource management and the American dream'. *Journal of Management Studies*. Vol. 27, 4: 377–97.

Guest, D.E. (1997) 'Human resource management: A review and research agenda'. *The International Journal of Human Resource Management*. Vol. 8, 3: 263–76.

Guest, D. and Baron, A. (2000) 'Piece by piece'. *People Management*. Vol. 6, 15: 26–30.

Guest, D. and Hoque, K. (1994) 'The good, the bad and the ugly: employment relations in new non-union workplaces'. *Human Resource Management Journal*. Vol. 5, 1: 1–15.

Guest, D. and King, Z. (2001) 'Personnel's paradox'. *People Management*. Vol. 7, 19: 24–9.

Guile, D. and Young, M. (1999) 'The question of learning and learning organisations'. *Working Paper. London: Lifelong Learning Group, Institute of Education, University of London*. 55, Gordon Square, WCIH ONT.

Gurdon, G. (1994) 'Toyota U-turn to end "jobs for life"'. *Daily Telegraph*, 22 January: B7.

Hall, R. (1993) 'A framework linking intangible resources and capabilities to sustainable competitive advantage'. *Strategic Management Journal*. 14: 607–18.

Hamel, G. (1991) 'Competition for competence and inter-partner learning within international strategic alliances'. *Strategic Management Journal*. Vol. 12: 83–103.

Hamel, G. and Prahalad, C.K. (1993) 'Strategy as stretch and leverage'. *Harvard Business Review*. Vol. 71, 2: 75–84.

Handy, C. (1995) *The Age of Unreason*. London: Arrow Business Books.

Hansen, M.T. (1999) 'The search–transfer problem: the role of weak ties in sharing knowledge across organizational subunits'. *Administrative Science Quarterly*. Vol. 44,1: 82–111.

Hansen, M.T., Nohria, N. and Tierney, T. (1999) 'What's your strategy for managing knowledge?' *Harvard Business Review*. March–April: 106–16.

Harrell-Cook, G. and Ferris, G.R. (1997) 'Competing pressures for human resource investment'. *Human Resource Management Review*. Vol. 7, 3: 317–40.

Harris, S.G. (1994) 'Organizational culture and individual sensemaking: a schema based perspective'. *Organization Science*. Vol. 5, 3: 309–21.

Harrison, R. (1999) 'Need to know'. *People Management*. Vol. 5, 3: 31.

Harrison, R. (2000) 'Learning, knowledge productivity and strategic progress'. *International Journal of Training and Development*. Vol. 4, 4: 244–58.

Harrison, R. (2002) *Learning and Development*, 3rd edn. London: Chartered Institute of Personnel and Development.

Harrison, R. and Miller, S. (1999) 'The contribution of clinical directors to the strategic capability of the organisation'. *British Journal of Management*. Vol. 10, 1: 23–39.

Harrison, R. and Smith, R. (2001) 'Practical judgement: its implications for knowledge development and strategic capability'. In B. Hellgren and J. Lowstedt (eds) *Management in the Thought-full Enterprise. A Socio-cognitive Approach to the Organization of Human Resources*. Bergen: Fagbokforlaget, pp. 195–213.

Harrison, Roy (1996) 'Action learning: route or barrier to the learning organization?' *Employee Counselling Today, The Journal of Workplace Learning*. Vol. 8, 6: 27–38.

Hart, S. and Banbury, C. (1994) 'How strategy-making processes can make a difference'. *Strategic Management Journal*. Vol. 15, 4: 251–69.

Harvey, B. (1994) 'Introduction'. In B. Harvey (ed.) *Business Ethics: A European Approach*. London: Prentice Hall, pp. 1–11.

Hatchett, A. (2000) 'Ringing true'. *People Management*. Vol. 6, 2: 40–1.

Hayes, C., Anderson, A. and Fonda, N. (1984) 'International competition and the role of competence'. *Personnel Management*. Vol. 16, 9: 36–8.

Hedberg, B.L.T. (1981) 'How organizations learn and unlearn'. In P.C. Nystrom and W.H. Starbuck (eds) *Handbook of Organizational Design, 1*. New York: Oxford University Press, pp. 15–23.

Hedlund, G. (1994) 'A model of knowledge management and the N-Form corporation'. *Strategic Management Journal*, Special Summer Issue. Vol. 15: 73–90.

Hendry, C. (1994) 'The Single European Market and the HRM response'. In P.A. Kirkbride (ed.) *Human Resource Management in Europe: Perspectives for the 1990s*. London: Routledge, pp. 93–113.

Hendry, C. (1995) *Human Resource Management: A Strategic Approach to Employment*. London: Butterworth Heinemann.

Hills, H. and Francis, P. (1999) 'Interaction learning'. *People Management*. Vol. 5, 14: 48–9.

Hines, T. and Thorpe, R. (1995) 'New approaches to understanding small firm networks – the key to performance, managerial learning and development'. In *Proceedings of the 18th ISBA National Conference*. Paisley: November, pp. 669–86. a.hines@mmu.ac.uk and r.thorpe@mmu.ac.uk.

Hodgkinson, G.P. (1996) 'The cognitive analysis of competitive structures: a review and critique'. *Working Paper (June)*. Leeds: School of Business and Economic Studies, University of Leeds.

Hodgkinson, G.P. and Johnson, G. (1994) 'Exploring the mental models of competitive strategists: the case for a processual approach'. *Journal of Management Studies*. Vol. 31, 4: 525–51.

Holton III, E.F. (2002) 'Theoretical assumptions underlying the performance paradigm of human resource development'. *Human Resource Development International,* Vol. V, 2: 199–215.

Homan, G. and Shaw, S. (2000) 'Reframing the role of higher education in the process of lifelong learning – a UK perspective'. *Paper presented at the Conference on Convergence and Divergence in the European HRD Agenda: Comparing and Contrasting Research and Practice*. Kingston, Kingston University, 15 January.

Hosmer, L.T. (1994) 'Strategic planning as if ethics mattered'. *Strategic Management Journal*, Summer Special Issue. Vol. 15, 17–34.

Huemer, L., von Krogh, G. and Roos, J. (1998) 'Knowledge and the concept of trust'. In G. von Krogh, J. Roos and D. Kleine (eds) *Knowing in Firms: Understanding, Managing and Measuring Knowledge*. London: Sage, pp. 123–45.

Huff, A.S. (1982) 'Industry influences on strategy reformulation'. *Strategic Management Journal*. Vol. 3: 119–31.

Hurst, D.K., Rush, J.C. and White, R.E. (1996) 'Top management teams and organizational renewal'. In K. Starkey (ed.) *How Organizations Learn*. London: International Thomson Business Press, pp. 381–409.

Hurwitz, J., Lines, S., Montgomery, B. and Schmidt, J. (2002) 'The linkage between management practices, intangibles performance, and stock returns'. *Journal of Intellectual Capital*. Vol. 3, 1: 51–61.

Huselid, M.A. (1995) 'The impact of human resource management practices on turnover, productivity and corporate financial performance'. *Academy of Management Journal*. Vol. 38: 635–70.

Huysman, M. and De Wit, D. (2000) *Kennis delen in de praktijk*. [Knowledge sharing in practice] Assen: Van Gorcum/Stichting Management Studies.

Huysman, M. and De Wit, D. (2002) *Knowledge Sharing in Practice*. Dordrecht: Kluwer Academic Publishers.

Incomes Data Services (1993) *European Management Guides: Training and Development*. London: Institute of Personnel Management.

Inkpen, A. and Choudhury, N. (1995) 'The seeing of strategy where it is not: towards a theory of strategy absence'. *Strategic Management Journal*. Vol. 16: 313–23.

Institute for Prospective Technological Studies (2000) *The IPTS Futures Project Conference Proceedings*, Brussels.

Institute of Personnel and Development (1999) *Managing Diversity: Evidence from Case Studies*. London: Institute of Personnel and Development.

International Labour Organization (2001) *World Employment Report 200: Life at Work in the Information Economy*. Geneva: ILO.

International Survey Research (2002) *UK plc: Leader or Follower?* London: ISR and www.isrsurveys.com.

Ito, K. and Rose, E. (1994) 'The genealogical structure of Japanese firms: parent–subsidiary relation-ships'. *Strategic Management Journal*, Summer Special Issue. Vol. 15: 35–51.

Jackson, S.E. and Schuler, R.S. (1995) 'Understanding human resource management in the context of organizations and their environments'. *Annual Review of Psychology*. Vol. 46: 237–64.

Jacobs, D. (1996) *Het Kennisoffensief. Slim concurreren in de kenniseconomie*. [Knowledge offensive. Smart competition in a knowledge economy]. Alphen aan den Rijn: Samsom.

Jaques, E. (1952) *The Changing Culture of the Factory*. London: Tavistock.

Jenkins, A. (1992) 'France: Two decades of innovation in training'. In *Proceedings of the Third Confer-ence on International Personnel and Human Resource Management*. Ashridge College with Universi-ties of Illinois and Bond. 2–4 July.

Jensen, M.C. and Meckling, W.H. (1976) 'Theory of the firm: managerial behaviour, agency costs and ownership structure'. *Journal of Financial Economics*. Vol. 3: 305–60.

Johnson, R. (2002) 'Trust funding'. *People Management*. Vol. 8, 19: 36–9.

Jones, G. (1984) 'Task visibility, free riding and shirking: explaining the effect of structure and tech-nology on employee behaviours'. *Academy of Management Review*. Vol. 9: 684–95.

Kamoche, K. (1996) 'Strategic human resource management within a resource-capability view of the firm'. *Journal of Management Studies*. Vol. 33, 2: 213–33.

Kaplan, R.S. and Norton, D.R. (1996) 'Using the balanced scorecard as a strategic management system'. *Harvard Business Review*. Vol. 74, 1: 75–87.

Katz, D. and Kahn, R.L. (1966) *The Social Psychology of Organizations*. London: Wiley, pp. 14–29.

Keep, E. (2001) 'The skills system in 2015'. In D. Wilson, E. Lank, A. Westwood, E. Keep, C. Leadbeater and M. Sloman (eds) *The Future of Learning for Work: Executive Briefing*. London: Chartered Institute of Personnel and Development, pp. 24–31.

Kessels, J.W.M. (1995) 'Opleidingen in arbeidsorganisaties: Het ambivalen-te perspectief van de kennisproduktiviteit' [Training in organisations: The ambivalent perspective of knowledge produc-tivity] *Comenius*. Vol. 15, 2: 179–93.

Kessels, J.W.M. (1996) 'Knowledge productivity and the corporate curriculum'. In J.F. Schreinemakers (ed.) *Knowledge Management, Organization, Competence and Methodology*. Würzburg: Ergon Verlag, pp. 168–74.

Kessels, J.W.M. (2001) 'Learning in organizations: A corporate curriculum for the knowledge economy'. *Futures*. Vol. 33: 479–506.

Kessels, J.W.M. (2001a) *Verleiden tot kennisproductiviteit* (Inaugural lecture) [Tempting for knowledge productivity]. Enschede: University of Twente, 8 February.

Kessels, J.W.M. and Harrison, R. (1998) 'External consistency: the key to success in management devel-opment programmes?' *Management Learning*. Vol. 29, 1: 39–68.

Kessels, J. and Keursten, P. (2002) 'Creating a knowledge productive work environment'. *LLinE, Lifelong Learning in Europe*. Vol. 7, 2: 104–12.

Kessels, J.W.M. and Plomp, Tj. (1997) 'The importance of relational aspects in the systems approach'. In C.R. Dills and A.J. Romiszowski (eds) *Instructional Development Paradigms*. Englewood Cliffs, NJ: Educational Technology Publications, pp. 93–126.

Kessels, J.W.M. and Plomp, Tj. (1999) 'A systematic and relational approach to obtaining curriculum consistency in corporate education'. *Journal of Curriculum Studies*. Vol. 31, 6: 679–709.

Kessels, J.W.M. and Van der Werff, P. (2002) 'What is beyond knowledge productivity?' In T. van Aken and T.M. van Engers (eds) *Beyond Knowledge Productivity*. Utrecht: Lemma Publishers, pp. 19–27.

Kessels, J., Leeuw, H. and Van Wijngaarden, P. (2002) 'A competency-based approach to cooperative education in the university curriculum'. *Paper presented at the Iére Conférence internationale du Ceraltes (Centre d'Etudes et de Recherche pour ALTernance dans L'Enseignement Superieur [Study and Research Centre for Cooperative Higher Education]): L'Alternance dans l'enseignement superieur: dispositifs et enjeux pédagogiques [In cooperative education school-based training and work experience alternate]. Group ESIEE*, 5 Novembre. Paris, pp. 93–9.

Kessels, J.W.M., Van Lakerveld, J. and Van den Berg, J. (1998) 'Knowledge productivity and the corpo-rate curriculum'. *Paper presented to AERA 1998 Annual Educational Research Conference*. San Diego, CA: 13–17 April.

Keursten, P. and Kessels, J.W.M. (2002) 'Knowledge productivity in organizations: towards a framework for research and practice'. Paper presented to European Consortium for the Learning Organisation Conference: Delivering Learning in the Workplace. Amsterdam: 16–18 May.

Kieft, M. and Nijhof, W.J. (2000) *HRD-Profielen 2000. Een onderzoek naar rollen, outputs en competencies van bedrijfopleiders* [HRD-profiles 2000. Investigation of the roles, output and competencies of trainers]. Enschede: Twente University Press.

Kinnie, N. (2002) 'How the pressures of call centres can lead to emotional exhaustion'. *People Management*. Vol. 8, 16: 45.

Kirjavainen, P. (2001) 'Strategic learning in a knowledge-intensive organisation'. In H.W. Volberda and T. Elfring (eds) *Rethinking Strategy*. London: Sage, pp. 172–90.

Knowles, M. (1970) *The Modern Practice of Adult Education: from Pedagogy to Andragogy*. Chicago: Follett Publishing Company.

Koenig, C. and Van Wijk, G. (2001) 'Managing beyond boundaries: the dynamics of trust in alliances'. In H.W. Volberda and T. Elfring (eds) *Rethinking Strategy*. London: Sage, pp. 116–27.

Kogut, B. and Zander, U. (1992) 'Knowledge of the firm, combinative capabilities, and the replication of technology'. *Organization Science*, Vol. 3, 3: 383–97.

Kogut, B. and Zander, U. (1996) 'What do firms do? Coordination, identity, and learning'. *Organization Science*. Vol. 7: 502–17.

Koike, K. (1988) *Industrial Relations in Modern Japan*. London: Macmillan – now Palgrave Macmillan.

Kolb, D.A. (1984) *Experiential Learning: Experience as the Source of Learning and Development*. Englewood Cliffs, NJ: Prentice Hall.

Kwakman, K. and Kessels, J.W.M. (2002) 'Ontwerpen van leren op de werkplek'. [Designs for learning in the workplace]. Paper presented to ORD 2002 29th Annual Educational Research Conference. Antwerp: 29–31 May.

Larsen, H.H. (1994) 'Key issues in training and development'. In C. Brewster and A. Hegewisch (eds) *Policy and Practice in European Human Resource Management: The Price Waterhouse Cranfield Survey*. London: Routledge, pp. 107–21.

Lave, J. and Wenger, E. (1991) *Situated Learning: Legitimate Peripheral Participation*. Cambridge: Cambridge University Press.

Leadbeater, C. (2000) *Living on Thin Air: The New Economy*. London: Viking.

Legge, K. (1989) 'Human resource management: a critical analysis'. In J. Storey (ed.) *New Perspectives on Human Resource Management*. London: Routledge, pp. 19–40.

Legge, K. (1995) *Human Resource Management: Rhetorics and Realities*. London: Macmillan – now Palgrave Macmillan.

Lengnick-Hall, C.A. and Lengnick-Hall, M.L. (1988) 'Strategic human resources management: a review of the literature and a proposed typology'. *Academy of Management Review*. Vol. 13, 3: 454–70.

Leonard-Barton, D. (1992) 'The factory as a learning laboratory'. *Sloan Management Review*. Fall: 23–38.

Leonard-Barton, D. (1998) *Wellsprings of Knowledge: Building and Sustaining the Sources of Innovation*. Boston: Harvard Business School Press.

Levinthal, D.A. and March, J.G. (1993) 'The myopia of learning'. *Strategic Management Journal*, Special Issue. Vol. 14: 95–112.

Levy, D. (1994) 'Chaos theory and strategy: theory, application, and managerial implications'. *Strategic Management Journal*, Special Summer Issue. Vol 15: 167–78.

Lindblom, C.E. (1959) 'The science of muddling through'. *Public Administration Review*. Vol. 19, 2: 79–88.

Lorenz, C.L. (1994) 'Cross-border victory, national casualty'. *Financial Times*, 6 May.

Lowyck, J. (2001) 'Ontwerpen van leertrajecten' [Designing learning trajectories]. In J.W.M. Kessels and R.F. Poell (eds) *Human Resource Development: Organiseren van het leren* [Organising learning] Alphen aan den Rijn: Samsom, pp. 165–80.

Luhmann, N. (1986) 'The autopoiesis of social systems'. In F. Geyer and J. van der Zouwen (eds) *Sociocybernetic Paradoxes*. Beverly Hills, CA: Sage, pp. 172–92.

Lundvall, B.A. (2000) 'Understanding the role of education in the learning economy: the contribution of economics'. In *OECD Knowledge Management in the Learning Society*. Paris: OECD, pp. 11–35.

Lymer, A. (1996) 'Educational impacts of the World Wide Web'. *Account*. Vol. 8, 1: 9–10.

Mabey, C. and Salaman, G. (1995) *Strategic Human Resource Management*. Oxford: Blackwell.

Malhotra, Y. (2000) 'Role of organizational controls in knowledge management: is knowledge management really an "oxymoron"?' In Y. Malhotra (ed.) *Knowledge Management and Virtual Organizations*. Hershey: Idea Group Publishing, pp. 245–57.

Malloch, H. (1990) 'Strategic management and the decision to subcontract'. In P. Blyton and J. Morris (eds) *Flexibility in the 1990s*. Berlin: Walter de Gruyter, Ch. 10.

Malloch, H. (1992) 'Human resource strategy in Hutton Borough Council'. In D. Winstanley and J. Woodall (eds) *Case Studies in Personnel*. London: Institute of Personnel Management, pp. 245–51.

Malloch, H. (1992a) 'Human resource strategy in Hutton Borough Council'. In D. Winstanley and J. Woodall (eds) *Case Studies in Personnel: Tutors' Manual*. London: Institute of Personnel Management, pp. 133–5.

Mann, S. (1997) 'Emotional labour in organizations'. *Leadership and Organizational Development Journal*. Vol. 18, 1: 4–12.

Marr, A. (2002) 'Politicians pay the price of ignoring corporate crookery'. *Daily Telegraph*, 3 July: 22.

Marsick, V.J. (1994) 'Trends in managerial reinvention: creating a learning map'. *Management Learning*. Vol. 25, 1: 11–33.

Maturana, H. and Varela, F. (1980) *Autopoesis and Cognition: The Realization of Living*. London: Reidl.

Mayo, A. (1999) 'Called to account'. *People Managment*. Vol. 5, 7: 33.

Mayo, A. (2001) *The Human Value of the Enterprise: Valuing People as Assets – Measuring, Managing, Monitoring*. London: Nicholas Brealey Publishing.

Mayo, E. (1933) *The Human Problems of an Industrial Civilisation*. New York, Macmillan.

McGoldrick, J., Stewart, J. and Watson, S. (eds) (2002) *Understanding Human Resource Development: A Research-based Approach*. London: Routledge.

McGoldrick, J., Stewart, J and Watson, S. (2002a) 'Postscript: The future of HRD research', in J. McGoldrick, J. Stewart and S. Watson (eds) *Understanding Human Resource Development. A Research-based Approach*. London: Routledge, pp. 395–98.

McGrath, R.G., MacMillan, I.C. and Venkataraman, S. (1995) 'Defining and developing competence: a strategic process paradigm'. *Strategic Management Journal*. Vol. 16, 4: 251–75.

Méhaut, P. (1989) *Production et usage de la formation par et dans l'entreprise. Tome 4*. [Production and use of training by and in the enterprise. Vol. 4]. Paris: CEREQ.

Miles, R.E. and Snow, C.C. (1986) 'Organizations: new concepts for new forms'. *California Management Review*. Vol. 28, 3: 62–73.

Miles, R. and Snow, C. (1995) 'The new network firm: a spherical structure built on a human investment philosophy'. *Organizational Dynamics*. Vol. 23, 4: 5–18.

Miles, R.E., Snow, C.C., Mathews, J.A., Miles, G. and Coleman, Jr. H.J. (1997) 'Organizing in the knowledge age: anticipating the cellular form'. *Academy of Management Executives*. Vol. 11, 4: 7–20.

Miller, D. (1993) 'The architecture of simplicity'. *Academy of Management Review*. Vol. 18, 1: 116–38.

Miller, P. (1987) 'Strategic industrial relations and human resource management – distinction, definition and recognition'. *Journal of Management Studies*. Vol. 24: 347–61.

Miller, P. (1991) 'A strategic look at management development'. *Personnel Management*. Vol. 23, 8: 45–7.

Miller, S., Hickson, D.J. and Wilson, D.C. (1999) 'Decision-making in organizations'. In S.R. Clegg, C. Hardy and W.R. Nord (eds) *Managing Organizations: Current Issues*. London: Sage, pp. 43–62.

Minister van Landbouw, Natuurbeheer en Visserij (2000) *Beleidsbrief groen onderwijs*. [Green education] Den Haag: Ministerie van Landbouw, Natuurbeheer en Visserij. Directie wetenschap en Kennisoverdracht. Trcdwk/2000/3418.

Mintzberg, H. (1983) *Structure in Fives: Designing Effective Organizations*. Englewood Cliffs, NJ: Prentice Hall.

Mintzberg, H. (1994) 'Rounding out the manager's job'. *Sloan Management Review*. Vol. 36, 1: 11–26.

Mintzberg, H. (1994a) 'The fall and rise of strategic planning'. *Harvard Business Review*. January–February: 107–14.

Mintzberg, H. and Waters, J. (1985) 'Of strategies, deliberate and emergent'. *Strategic Management Journal*. Vol. 6: 257–72.

Mohrman, S.A. and Lawler III, E.E. (1999) 'The new human resources management: creating the strategic business partnership'. In R.S. Schuler and S.E. Jackson (eds) *Strategic Human Resource Management*. Oxford: Blackwell, pp. 433–47.

More, E. (2002) 'How to set up a CSR programme'. *People Management*. Vol. 8, 20: 50–1.

Morgan, G. (1997) *Images of Organization*, 2nd edn. London: Sage.

Morris, J. (1991) 'Action learning: the long haul'. In J. Prior (ed.) *Handbook of Training and Development*. Aldershot: Gower, pp. 611–28.

Mulder, I. and Swaak, J. (2001) 'A study on globally dispersed teamwork: coding technology-mediated interaction processes.' In T. Taillieu (ed.) *Collaborative Strategies and Multi-organisational Partnerships*. Leuven: Garant, pp. 235–43.

Mulder, I. Swaak, J. and Kessels J. (2002) 'Assessing group learning and shared understanding in technology mediated interaction'. *Educational Technology and Society*. Vol. 5, 1: 35–47.

Mulder, M. and Tjepkema, S. (1999) 'International Briefing No. 1: Training and Development in the Netherlands'. *International Journal of Training and Development*. Vol 3, 1: 63–73.

Mumford, A., Robinson, G. and Stradling, D. (1987) *Developing Directors: The Learning Processes*. Sheffield: Manpower Services Commission.

Nakamoto, M. (1995) 'Signs of ebbing strength at home'. *Financial Times*, 1 March: 21.

Neilson, R.E. (1997) *Collaborative Technologies and Organizational Learning*. Hershey: Idea Group Publishing.

Nelson, R.R. and Winter, S.G. (1982) *An Evolutionary Theory of Economic Change*. Cambridge, MA: Harvard University Press.

Newsweek (1991) 'The best schools in the world'. 2 December: 38–50.

Nohria, N. and Eccles, R.C. (1992) 'Face-to-face: making network organizations work.' In N. Nohria, and R.C. Eccles (eds) *Networks and Organizations: Structure, Form and Action*. Boston: Harvard Business School Press, pp. 288–308.

Nonaka, I. (1991) 'The knowledge-creating company'. *Harvard Business Review*. November–December: Vol 69: 96–104.

Nonaka, I. (1994) 'A dynamic theory of organizational knowledge creation'. *Organization Science*. Vol. 5, 1: 14–37.

Nonaka, I. (1996) 'The knowledge-creating company'. In K. Starkey (ed.) *How Organizations Learn*. London: International Thomson Business Press, pp. 18–31.

Nonaka, I. and Takeuchi, H. (1995) *The Knowledge-creating Company*. Oxford: Oxford University Press.

Nonaka, I., Toyama, R. and Byosière, P. (2001) 'A theory of organizational knowledge creation: understanding the dynamic process of creating knowledge'. In M. Dierkens, A.B. Antal, J. Child and I. Nonaka (eds) *Handbook of Organizational Learning and Knowledge*. New York: Oxford University Press, pp. 491–517.

OC&W (1998) Nationaal Actieprogramma Een Leven lang Leren. [Dutch National Action Plan on Lifelong Learning] Letter from the Minister of Education, Culture and Science to the Members of the Parliament, 27 January.

Organization for Economic Co-operation and Development (2001) T*he Well-being of Nations. The Role of Human and Social Capital*. Paris: OECD.

Organization for Economic Co-operation and Development. (2001a) *The New Economy: Beyond the Hype*. The OECD Growth Project. Paris: OECD.

Orr, J.E. (1990) 'Sharing knowledge, celebrating identity: community memory in a service culture'. In D.S. Middleton and D. Edwards (eds) *Collective Remembering*. Newbury Park, SA: Sage, pp. 169–98.

Pan, S.L. (1999) 'Knowledge management at Buckman Laboratories'. In H. Scarbrough and J. Swan (eds) *Case Studies in Knowledge Management*. London: Institute of Personnel and Development, pp. 76–84.

Parker, S.K., Mullarkey, S. and Jackson, P.R. (1994) 'Dimensions of performance effectiveness in high-involvement work organisations'. *Human Resource Management Journal*. Vol. 4, 3: 1–21.

Patriotta, G. (1999) 'Multicorp: knowledge management in product development'. In H. Scarbrough and J. Swan (eds) *Case Studies in Knowledge Management*. London: Institute of Personnel and Development, pp. 68–75.

Patterson, M.G., West, M.A., Lawthom, R. and Nickell, S. (1997) *Impact of People Management Practices on Business Performance*. London: Institute of Personnel and Development.

Pedler, M., Burgoyne, J. and Boydell, T. (1991) *The Learning Company: A Strategy for Sustainable Development*. Maidenhead: McGraw-Hill.

Pennings, J.M. (2001) 'Configurations and the firm in current strategic management'. In H.W. Volberda and T. Elfring (eds) *Rethinking Strategy*. London: Sage, pp. 240–244.

Penrose, E.T. (1959) *The Theory of the Growth of the Firm*. Oxford: Blackwell.

People Management (2002) 'World Bank fails to "set an example on corruption"'. Letters page. Vol. 8, 21: 26.

People Management (2002a) 'Trainers face race risk'. News Section. Vol. 8, 9: 11.

Perrow, C. (1967) 'A framework for the comparative analysis of organizations'. *American Sociological Review*. Vol. 32, 2: 194–208.

Pettigrew, A. (1973) *The Politics of Organizational Decision Making*. London: Tavistock.

Pettigrew, A.M. (1985) *The Awakening Giant: Continuity and Change in ICI*. Oxford: Blackwell.

Pettigrew, A.M. (1987) 'Context and action in transformation of the firm'. *Journal of Management Studies*. Vol. 24, 6: 649–70.

Pettigrew, A., Thomas, H. and Whittington, R. (eds) (2002) *Handbook of Strategy and Management*. London: Sage.

Pettigrew, A., Thomas, H. and Whittington, R. (2002a) 'Strategic management: the strengths and limitations of a field'. In A. Pettigrew., H. Thomas and R. Whittington (eds) *Handbook of Strategy and Management*. London: Sage, pp. 3–30.

Pickard, J. (1999) 'Sense and sensitivity'. *People Management*. Vol. 5, 21: 48–56.

Pickard, J. (2001) 'How Abbey are they?' *People Management*. Vol. 7, 25: 27.

Pieper, R. (2000) *e-WERELD. De ingrediënten van de netwerkmaatschappij*.[e-World. Ingredients of the network society] Amsterdam: Koppelith and Co. www.roelpieper.com.

Poell, R.F. (1998) 'Organizing work-related learning projects. A network approach'. PhD dissertation. Nijmegen: Katholieke Universiteit Nijmegen.

Polanyi, M. (1958) *Personal Knowledge*. Chicago, IL: University of Chicago Press.

Polanyi, M. (1966) *The Tacit Dimension*. New York: Anchor Day Books.

Porac, J., Thomas, H. and Fuller, C.B. (1989) 'Competitive groups as cognitive communities: the case of the Scottish knitwear manufacturers'. *Journal of Management Studies*. Vol. 26, 4: 397–416.

Porter, M., Takeuchi, H. and Sakakibara, M. (2000) *Can Japan Compete?* Basingstoke: Macmillan – now Palgrave Macmillan.

Prahalad, C.K. and Bettis, R.A. (1986) 'The dominant logic: A new linkage between diversity and performance'. *Strategic Management Journal*. Vol. 7, 6: 485–501.

Prahalad, C.K. and Ramaswamy, V. (2002) 'The co-creation connection'. *Strategy and Business*. Issue 27, 2nd quarter: 50–61.

Pugh, D.S. (ed.) (1971) *Organization Theory: Selected Readings*. Harmondsworth: Penguin.

Purcell, J. (1995) 'Corporate strategy and its link with human resource management strategy'. In J. Storey (ed.) *Human Resource Management: A Critical Text*. London: Routledge, pp. 63–86.

Purcell, J., Kinnie, N., Hutchinson, S. and Rayton, B. (2000) 'Inside the box'. *People Management*. Vol. 6, 21: 30–8.

Putnam, R. (2000) *Bowling Alone: The Collapse and Revivial of American Community*. New York: Simon & Schuster.

Quinn, J.B. (1980) *Strategies for Change – Logical Incrementalism*. Homewood, IL: Irwin.

Quinn, J.B. (1992) *Intelligent Enterprise: A Knowledge and Service Based Paradigm for Industry*. New York: Free Press.

Rainbird, H. (2000) *The Learning Society and the Knowlege Economy: The Contribution of Workplace Learning to a Learning Society*. Coventry: National Advisory Council for Education and Training Targets lecture series.

Rajan, A. (1999) 'Informed judgement: case studies in knowledge management'. *People Management*. Vol. 5, 14: 55–6.

Rana, E. (1999) 'Failure to embrace online learning will hit firms hard'. *People Management*. Vol. 5, 16: 19.

Rana, E. (2002) 'A class above the rest'. *People Management*. Vol. 8, 9: 15.

Raper, P., Ashton, D., Felstead, A. and Storey, K. (1997) 'Toward the learning organisation? Explaining current trends in training practice in the UK'. *International Journal of Training and Development*. Vol. 1, 1: 9–21.

Ray, T. (2002) 'Managing Japanese organizational knowledge creation: the difference'. In S. Little, P. Quintas and T. Ray (eds) *Managing Knowledge: an Essential Reader*. London: Sage, pp. 102–38.

Reed, R. and DeFillippi, R. (1990) 'Causal ambiguity, barriers to imitation, and sustainable competitive advantage'. *Academy of Management Review*. Vol. 15, 11: 88–102.

Reitsperger, W.D. (1986) 'Japanese management – coping with British industrial relations'. *Journal of Management Studies*. Vol. 23, 1: 72–87.

Reumkens, R. and Snijders, I. (2002) Het Rabobank Corporate Curriculum [The Corporate Curriculum of Rabobank] *Opleiding & Ontwikkeling. Tijdschrift voor Human Resource Development*, Vol. 15, 4: 30–3.

Revans, R.W. (1969) 'The Enterprise as a Learning System'. In M. Pedler (ed.) *The Origins and Growth of Action Learning*, Chartwell-Bratt, 1982. Reprinted in M. Pedler (ed.) *Action Learning in Practice*, 2nd edn. 1991. Aldershot: Gower.

Rice, R., Majchrazak, A., King, N., Ba, S. and Malhotra, A. (2000) 'Computer mediated interorganizational knowledge sharing: insights from a virtual team innovating using a collaborative tool'. In Y. Malhotra (ed.) *Knowledge Management and Virtual Organizations*. Hershey: Idea Group Publishing, pp. 84–100.

Richey, R.C. and Nelson, W.A. (1996) 'Developmental research'. In D. Jonassen (ed.) *Handbook of Research for Educational Communications and Technology*. London: Macmillan – now Palgrave Macmillan, pp. 1213–45.

Roberts, K.H. and Grabowski, M. (1999) 'Organizations, technology and structuring'. In S.R. Clegg, C. Hardy and W.R. Nord (eds) *Managing Organizations: Current Issues*. London, Sage, pp. 159–73.

Roberts, Z. (2002) 'Unions "to lead in training"'. *People Management*. Vol. 8, 17: 7.

Robertson, D. (1999) 'Knowledge societies, intellectual capital and economic growth'. In H. Gray (ed.) *Universities and the Creation of Wealth*. Buckingham: The Society for Research into Higher Education & Open University Press, pp. 18–35.

Rosenberg, M.J., Coscarelli, W.C. and Hutchison C.S. (1992) 'The origins and evolution of the field'. In H.D. Stolovitch and E.J. Keeps (eds) *Handbook of Human Performance Technology*. San Francisco: Jossey-Bass, pp. 14–31.

Rukanova, B. (2001) *Personal Development in Virtual Organisations (HRD Masters Thesis)*. Enschede: University of Twente.

Russell, C. and Parsons, E. (1996) 'Putting theory to the test at the OU'. *People Management*. Vol. 2, 1: 30–2.

Salmon, G. (2001) 'Far from remote'. *People Management*. Vol. 7, 19: 34–6.

Sambrook, S. (2001) 'Developing a model of factors influencing work-related learning: findings from two research projects'. Paper presented to ECER 2001 European Conference on Educational Research. Lille, France: Charles de Gaulle University, 5–8 September.

Sambrook, S. and Stewart, J. (2002) 'Reflections and discussion'. In S. Tjepkema, J. Stewart, S. Sambrook, M. Mulder, H. ter Horst and J. Scheerens (eds) *HRD and Learning Organisations in Europe*. London: Routledge, pp. 178–87.

Sanchez, R. (1995) 'Strategic flexibility in product competition'. *Strategic Management Journal*. Vol. 16: 135–59.

Sawyers, D. (1986) 'The experience of German and Japanese subsidiaries in Britain'. *Journal of General Management*. Vol. 12, 1: 5–21.

Scarbrough, H. (1998) 'Path(ological) dependency? Core competencies from an organizational perspective'. *British Journal of Management*. Vol. 9, 3: 219–32.

Scarbrough, H. (1999) 'System error'. *People Management*. Vol. 5, 7: 68–74.

Scarbrough, H. and Swan, J. (eds) (1999) *Case Studies in Knowledge Management*. London: Institute of Personnel and Development.

Scarbrough, H. and Swan, J. (2001) 'Explaining the diffusion of knowledge management: the role of fashion'. *British Journal of Management*. Vol. 12, 1: 3–12.

Scarbrough, H., Swan, J. and Preston, J. (1999) *Knowledge Management: A Literature Review*. London: Institute of Personnel and Development.

Schein, E.H. (1985) *Organizational Culture and Leadership*. San Francisco: Jossey-Bass.

Schendel, D. and Hofer, C. (1979) *Strategic Management: A New View of Business Policy and Planning*. Boston, MA: Little, Brown.

Schmidt, J.A. (2002) 'Measuring, managing the intangible: taking stock of human and organizational capital'. *CRN News*. Vol. 7, 3: 1, 25, 31.

Schmidt, J.A. and Lines, S. (2002) 'A measure of success'. *People Management*. Vol. 8, 9: 34.

Schoonhoven, C.B. and Jelinek, M. (1990) 'Dynamic tension in innovative high technology firms: managing rapid technological change through organizational structure'. In M. von Glinow and S. Mohrman (eds) *Managing Complexity in High Technology Firms*. Oxford: Oxford University Press, pp. 90–115.

Schuler, R.S. and Jackson, S.E. (eds) (1999) *Strategic Human Resource Management*. Oxford: Blackwell.

Schultz, T.W. (1961) 'Investment in human capital'. *American Economic Review*. Vol. 51, 1: 1–17.

Scott, W.R. (1995) *Institutions and Organizations*. Thousand Oaks, CA: Sage.

Selznick, P. (1957) *Leadership in Administration*. New York: Harper & Row.

Senge, P.M. (1990) *The Fifth Discipline: The Art and Practice of the Learning Organization*. New York: Doubleday.

Seth, A. and Thomas, H. (1994) 'Theories of the firm: implications for strategy research'. *Journal of Management Studies*. Vol. 31, 2: 165–91.

Silverman, D. (1970) *The Theory of Organisations: a Sociological Framework*. London: Heinemann.

Simon, H.A. (1945) *Administrative Behavior: A Study of Decision-making Processes in Administrative Organization*. New York: Free Press.

Simon, H.A. (1955) 'A behavioural model of rational choice'. *Quarterly Journal of Economics*. Vol. 69: 99–18.

Simon, H.A. (1956) 'Rational choice and the structure of the environment'. *Psychological Review*. 63: 129–38.

Sink, D.S., Tuttle, T.C. and DeVries, S.J. (1984). 'Productivity measurement and evaluation: what is available?' *National Productivity Review*. Vol. 3, 3: 265–87.

Sisson, K. and Storey, J. (1988) 'Developing effective managers: a review of the issues and an agenda for research'. *Personnel Review*. Vol. 17, 4: 3–8.

Skapinker, M. (2002) *Knowledge Management: The Change Agenda*. London: Chartered Institute of Personnel and Development.

Sloman, M. (2002) 'Ground Force'. *People Management*. Vol. 8, 13: 42–6.

Smith, R. (1995) 'The rationality of practice'. *Curriculum Studies*. Vol. 3, 2: 209–15.

Solomon, N. (1999) 'Culture and difference in workplace learning'. In D. Boud and J. Garrick (eds) *Understanding Learning at Work*. London: Routledge, pp. 119–31.

Sparrow, P. and Hiltrop, J.-M. (1994) *European Human Resource Management in Transition*. Hemel Hempstead: Prentice Hall.

Sparrow, P. R. (1999) 'Is human resource management in crisis?' In R.S. Schuler and S.E. Jackson (eds) *Strategic Human Resource Management*. Oxford: Blackwell, pp. 416–32.

Spender, J.-C. (1994) 'Knowing, managing and learning: a dynamic managerial epistemology'. *Management Learning*. Vol. 25, 3: 387–412.

Spender, J.-C. (1996) 'Making knowledge the basis of a dynamic theory of the firm'. *Strategic Management Journal,* Winter Special Issue Vol. 17: 45–62.

Sprenger, C.C. (2000) Leerpraktijken. Een studie naar de wijze waarop leren vorm kan krijgen in op leren gerichte organisaties. [Learning practices. A study of learning practices in learning organisations]. PhD dissertation. Rotterdam: Erasmus Universiteit.

Stacey, R.D. (1995) 'The science of complexity: an alternative perspective for strategic change processes'. *Strategic Management Journal*. Vol. 16, 6: 477–95.

Starkey, K. and McKinlay, A. (1993) *Strategy and the Human Resource: Ford and the Search for Competitive Advantage*. Oxford: Blackwell.

Starkey, K. and McKinlay, A. (1996) 'Product development in Ford of Europe: undoing the past/learning

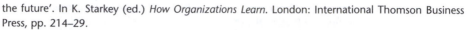

the future'. In K. Starkey (ed.) *How Organizations Learn*. London: International Thomson Business Press, pp. 214–29.

Steedman, H. (1990) 'Speaking practically, the French have it'. *Independent*, 5 September.

Stelzer, I. (2002) 'All change as consumers call the tune'. *Sunday Times Business section*, 21 July: 3.4.

Stern, E. and Sommerlad, E. (1999) *Workplace Learning, Culture and Performance*. London: Institute of Personnel and Development.

Sternberg, R.J. (1994) 'PRSVL: an integrative framework for understanding mind in context'. In R.J. Sternberg and R.K. Wagner (eds) *Mind in Context: Interactionist Perspectives on Human Intelligence*. Cambridge: Cambridge University Press: pp. 218–32.

Stevens, J. (2001) 'Summary report of seminar proceedings'. In Chartered Institute of Personnel and Development *Workplace Learning in Europe* [summary of the European Workplace Learning Seminar, London, 2 April 2001]. London: CIPD, pp. 7–12.

Stevens, J. and Ashton, D. (1999) 'Underperformance appraisal'. *People Management*. Vol. 5, 14: 31–2.

Stewart, J. (1999) *Employee Development Practice*. London: Financial Times Pitman Publishing.

Stewart, J. and McGoldrick, J. (eds) (1996) *Human Resource Development: Perspectives, Strategies and Practice*. London: Financial Times Pitman Publishing.

Stewart, J. and Tansley, C. (2002) *Training in the Knowledge Economy. Research Report*. London: Chartered Institute of Personnel and Development.

Stiles, J. (2001) 'Strategic Alliances'. In H.W. Volberda and T. Elfring (eds) *Rethinking Strategy*. London: Sage, pp. 128–39.

Stjernberg, T. and Werr, A. (2001) 'Consulting thought-fully'. In B. Hellgren and J. Lowstedt (eds) *Management in the Thought-full Enterprise: European Ideas on Organizing*. Bergen: Fagbokforlaget, pp. 259–80.

Stolovitch, H.D. and Keeps, E.J. (1992) 'What is human performance technology? Human performance interventions of an instructional nature'. In H.D. Stolovitch and E.J. Keeps (eds) *Handbook of Human Performance Technology*. San Francisco: Jossey-Bass, pp. 3–13.

Storey, J. (1991) 'Do the Japanese make better managers?' *Personnel Management*. Vol. 23, 8: 24–8.

Storey, J. (1992) *Developments in the Management of Human Resources*. Oxford: Blackwell.

Storey, J. (1995) *Human Resource Management: A Critical Text*. London: Routledge.

Swan, J. (1999) 'Introduction'. In H. Scarbrough and J. Swan (eds) *Case Studies in Knowledge Management*. London: Institute of Personnel and Development, pp. 1–12.

Swanson, R.A. (1995) 'Human resource development: performance is the key.' *Human Resource Development Quarterly*. Vol. 7, 3: 203–7.

Swanson, R.A. and Holton III, E.F. (2001) *Foundations of Human Resource Development*. San Francisco: Berrett-Koehler.

Swart, J., Kinnie, N. and Purcell, J. (2003) *People and Performance in Knowledge-intensive Firms. Research Report*. London: Chartered Institute of Personnel and Development.

Swidler, A. (1986) 'Culture in action: symbols and strategies'. *American Sociological Review*. Vol 5: 273–86.

Tapscott, D. (1996) *The Digital Economy: Promise and Peril in the Age of Networked Intelligence*. New York: McGraw-Hill.

Tapscott, D. (1999) 'Introduction'. In D. Tapscott (ed.) *Creating Value in the Network Economy*. Boston: Harvard Business School Publishing, pp. vii–xxvi.

Taylor, H. (1991) 'The systematic training model: corn circles in search of a spaceship?' *Management Education and Development*. Vol. 22, part 4: 258–78.

Taylor, R. (2002) *Britain's World of Work – Myths and Realities*. Gloucestershire: Economic and Social Research Council Publications. Also on www.esrc.ac.uk.

Taylor, S. (1998) 'Emotional labour and the new workplace'. In P. Thompson and C. Warhurst (eds) *Workplaces of the Future*. Basingstoke: Macmillan – now Palgrave Macmillan.

Teather, D. and Elliott, L. (2002) 'Deep wounds keep sombre Wall Street under a cloud'. *Guardian*, 10 September: 6.

Teece, D., Pisano, G. and Schuen, A. (1997) 'Dynamic capabilities and strategic management'. *Strategic Management Journal*. Vol. 18, 7: 509–22.

Ter Horst, H. and Tjepkema, S. (2002) 'Cases from The Netherlands'. In S. Tjepkema, J. Stewart, S. Sambrook, M. Mulder, H. ter Horst and J. Scheerens (eds) *HRD and Learning Organisations in Europe*. London: Routledge, pp. 114–32.

Terry, M. and Purcell, J. (1997) 'Return to slender'. *People Management*. Vol. 3, 21: 46–7.

Thomas, M. (1985) 'In search of culture: holy grail or gravy train'. *Personnel Management*. Vol. 17, 9: 24–7.

Thomas, R. and Dunkerley, D. (1999) 'Careering downwards? Middle managers' experience in the downsized organisation'. *British Journal of Management*. Vol. 10, 2: 157–69.

Tjepkema, S. (2002) 'Conclusions from case studies and survey'. In S. Tjepkema, J. Stewart, S. Sambrook, M. Mulder, H. ter Horst and J. Scheerens (eds) *HRD and Learning Organisations in Europe*. London: Routledge, pp. 156–77.

Tjepkema, S., Stewart, J., Sambrook, S. Mulder, M., Ter Horst, H. and Scheerens, J. (eds) (2002) *HRD and Learning Organisations in Europe*. London: Routledge.

Tjepkema, S., Ter Horst, H. and Mulder, M. (2002a) 'Learning organisations and HRD'. In S. Tjepkema, J. Stewart, S. Sambrook, M. Mulder, H. ter Horst and J. Scheerens (eds) *HRD and Learning Organisations in Europe*. London: Routledge, pp. 6–19.

Tjepkema, S. and Wognum, A.A.M. (1996) 'From Trainer to Consultant? Roles and Tasks of HRD Professionals in Learning Oriented Organisations'. *Paper presented at ECLO Conference: 'Growth through Learning'*. Copenhagen.

Tosey, P. (1993) 'Interfering with the interference: a systemic approach to change in organisations'. *Management Education and Development*. Vol. 24, part 3: 187–204.

Trist, E. and Bamforth, K. (1951) 'Some social and psychological consequences of the longwall method of coal-getting'. *Human Relations*. Vol. 4: 3–38.

Truss, C. and Gratton, L. (1994) 'Strategic human resource management: a conceptual approach'. *International Journal of Human Resource Management*. Vol. 5, 3: 663–86.

Tushman, M. and Nadler, D. (1996) 'Organizing for innovation'. In K. Starkey (ed.) *How Organizations Learn*. London: International Thomson Business Press, pp. 135–55.

Ulrich, D. (1998) 'A new mandate for human resources'. *Harvard Business Review*. January–February: 124–35.

University Forum for HRD (1998) *Unpublished Report from the Standing Committee for professionally focused university postgraduate programmes in HRD to AGM*. 1 May. Oxford: The Executive Secretary, UFHRD, 58, Picklers Hill, Abingdon, OX14 2BB.

Urwick, L. (1944) *The Elements of Administration*. London: Harper & Row.

Van den Akker, J. (1999) 'Principles and methods of development research'. In J. van den Akker, R.M. Branch, K. Gustafson, N. Nieveen and Tj. Plomp. (eds) *Design Approaches and Tools in Education and Training*. Dordrecht: Kluwer Academic Publishers, pp. 1–14.

Van der Klink, M. and Mulder, M. (1995) 'Human resource development and staff flow policy in Europe'. In A-W. Harzing and J. van Ruysseveldt (eds) *International Human Resource Management*. London: Sage, pp. 157–78.

Van der Waals, J. (2001) *Van managergestuurd naar mederwerkergestuurd opleiden en leren*. [*From manager-driven to employee-driven HRD*]. PhD dissertation. Enschede: University of Twente.

Van der Waals, J., Kessels J.W.M. and Euwema, M. (2002) 'Towards employee-driven HRD.' In *Proceedings of the 3rd Conference on Human Resource Development Research and Practice across Europe: Creativity and Innovation in Learning* (CD-ROM). Edinburgh: 25–26 January.

Van Lakerveld, J., Van den Berg, J., De Brabander, C. and Kessels, J. (2000) 'The corporate curriculum: a working–learning environment'. In *Proceedings of the Annual Academy of Human Resource Development Conference: Expanding the Horizons of Human Resource Development* (CD-ROM). Raleigh-Durham NC.

Van Luijk, H. (1994) 'Business Ethics: the Field and its Importance'. In B. Harvey (ed.) *Business Ethics: A European Approach*. London: Prentice Hall, pp. 12–31.

Venkatraman, N. and Subramaniam, M. (2002) 'Theorizing the future of strategy: questions for shaping strategy research in the knowledge economy'. In A. Pettigrew, H. Thomas and R. Whittington (eds) *Handbook of Strategy and Management*. London: Sage, pp. 461–74.

Von Foerster, H. (1984) 'Principles of self-organization in socio-managerial context'. In H. Ulrich and G.J.B. Probst (eds) *Self-organization and Management of Social Systems*. Berlin: Springer-Verlag, pp. 2–24.

Von Krogh, G. and Roos, J. (1995) 'A perspective on knowledge, competence and strategy'. *Personnel Review*. Vol. 24, 3: 56–76.

Von Krogh, G., Ichijo, K. and Nonaka, I. (2000) *Enabling Knowledge Creation*. Oxford: University Press.

Von Krogh, G., Roos, J. and Kleine, D. (eds) (1998) *Knowing in Firms: Understanding, Managing and Measuring Knowledge*. London: Sage.

Von Krogh, G., Roos, J. and Slocum, K. (1994) 'An essay on corporate epistemology'. *Strategic Management Journal*, Summer Special Issue. Vol. 15: 53–71.

Vygotsky, L.S. (1978) *Mind in Society: The Development of Higher Psychological Processes*. Cambridge, MA: Harvard University Press.

Walsh, J.P., Henderson, C.M. and Deighton, J. (1988) 'Negotiated belief structures and decision performance: an empirical investigation'. *Organizational Behaviour and Human Decision Processes*. Vol. 42: 194–216.

Walton, J. (1999) 'The emerging concept of human resource development', *Strategic Human Resource Development*. London: Financial Times Pitman Publications, pp. 51–80.

Walz, H. and Bertels, T. (1995) *Das intelligente Unternemen. Schneller: Lernen als der Wertbewerb*. [The Intelligent Enterprise: Learning Faster than the Competitor] Landsberg: Moderne Industrie Verlag.

Waples, J. (1999) 'Revolting investors'. *Sunday Times Business Focus*, 31 January: 3.5.

Warmerdam, J. and Tillaart, H. (1998) *Sectoral Approaches to Training Synthesis Report on Trends and Issues in Five European Countries*. Luxembourg: CEDEFOP.

Watkins, K. (1989) 'Business and industry'. In S. Merriam and P. Cunningham (eds) *Handbook of Adult and Continuing Education*. San Francisco: Jossey-Bass, pp. 422–30.

Watkins, K.E. and Marsick, V.J. (1993) 'Building the learning organisation: a new role for human resource developers'. *Studies in Continuing Education*. Vol. 14, 2: 115–29.

Watson, J.B. (1924) *Psychology from the Standpoint of a Behaviourist*. London: Lippincott.

Weber, M. (1947) *The Theory of Social and Economic Organization*. London: Oxford University Press.

Weick, K.E. and Roberts, K.H. (1993) 'Collective mind in organization: heedful interrelating on flight decks'. *Administrative Science Quarterly*. Vol. 8: 357–81.

Wenger, E. (1998) *Communities of Practice. Learning, Meaning, and Identity*. Cambridge: Cambridge University Press.

Wenger, E., McDermott, R. and Snyder, W.M. (2002) *Cultivating Communities of Practice*. Boston: Harvard Business School Press.

Wenger, E.C. and Snyder, W.M. (2000) 'Communities of practice: the organizational frontier'. *Harvard Business Review*, January–February: 139–45.

Wernerfelt, B. (1984) 'A resource-based view of the firm'. *Strategic Management Journal*. Vol. 5, 2: 171–80.

Westwood, A. (2001) 'Drawing a line – who is going to train our workforce?' In D. Wilson, E. Lank, A. Westwood, E. Keep, C. Leadbeater and M. Sloman (eds) *The Future of Learning for Work: Executive Briefing*. London: Chartered Institute of Personnel and Development, pp. 17–22.

Wheelwright, S.C. and Clark, K.B. (1992) *Revolutionizing Product Development*. New York: Free Press.

Whitehead, M. (1999) 'Firms ignore staff needs in key areas of the economy'. *People Management*. Vol. 5, 3: 16.

Whitley, R. (1999) *Divergent Capitalisms*. Oxford: Oxford University Press.

Whittington, R. (2002) 'Corporate structure: from policy to practice'. In A. Pettigrew, H. Thomas and R. Whittington (eds) *Handbook of Strategy and Management*. London: Sage, pp. 113–38.

Whittington, R. and Mayer, M. (2002) *Organising for Success in the Twenty-first Century: A Starting Point for Change. Research Report*. London: Chartered Institute of Personnel and Development.

Whittington, R., Pettigrew, A. and Thomas, H. (2002) 'Conclusion: doing more in strategy research'. In A. Pettigrew, H. Thomas and R. Whittington (eds) *Handbook of Strategy and Management*. London: Sage, pp. 475–88.

Williamson, O.E. (1985) *The Economic Institutions of Capitalism: Firms, Market and Relational Contracting*. New York: Free Press.

Winslow, C.D. and Bramer, W.L. (1994) *Future Work. Putting Knowledge to Work in the Knowledge Economy*. New York: Free Press Macmillan.

Wissema, J.G., Brand, A.F. and Van der Pol, H.W. (1981) 'The incorporation of management development in strategic management'. *Strategic Management Journal.* Vol. 2: 361–77.

Woodruffe, C. (2001) 'Promotional Intelligence'. *People Management.* Vol. 7, 1: 26–9.

Wouters, M. (1992) *Adult Education in the 1990s: Needs, Perspectives and Policy Recommendations on Adult Education in Europe*. Leuven: Catholic University of Leuven.

Wright, P.M. and McMahan, G.C. (1992) 'Theoretical perspectives for strategic human resource management'. *Journal of Management*, Vol. 18, 2: 295–320.

Zohar, D. and Drake, J. (2000) 'On the whole'. *People Management.* Vol. 6, 8: 55.

Zuboff, S. (1988) *In the Age of the Smart Machine*. New York: Basic Books.

Author Index

A

Ackroyd, S., 75–6
Ahlstrand, B., 24
Alekseeva, M., 194–6
Alheit, P., 15
Allard-Poesi, F.A., 132
Amit, R., 21
Anglin, J.M., 142
Ansoff, H.I., 98, 157
Argyris, C., 44, 95, 98, 136, 157
Aristotle, 150
Arkin, A., 224
Ashton, D., 25, 65–6, 68, 70–5, 79

B

Badaracco, J.L., 152
Baets, W.R.J., 188
Bamforth, K., 126
Banbury, C., 46, 97
Barnard, C.I., 35, 37, 202
Barney, J., 21
Baron, A., 24
Bartlett, C.A., 6, 34, 39, 51–2, 55–9, 121, 151
Bassanini, A., 12
Batchelor, J., 152
Bates, D.L., 98
Baum, J.A.C., 43
Baumard, P., 137, 148
Beardwell, I., 85

Beaumont, P., 140
Becker, B., 24, 34, 87
Becker, G.S., 12
Beer, M., 126
Bertels, T., 133, 157, 165
Bettis, R.A., 6, 8, 32, 44, 102
Billet, S., 150
Blackhurst, C., 205
Blunkett, D., 184
Bohn, R.E., 43–4
Boisot, M., 151
Bolman, L.G., 101
Bood, R.P., 132
Boud, D., 62
Bournois, F., 71, 115
Bowen, D.E., 26
Bowman, E.H., 6, 29
Bramer, W.L., 183
Branson, R. , 205
Brewster, C., xvii, 4, 7, 22–3, 35, 37, 59, 84, 93
Brickley, J.A., 42
Briggs, P., 76
Brooks, A.K., 164
Brown, D., 88
Brown, J.S., 15, 44, 129, 165, 189, 229
Brown, P., 255
Brown, S.L., 55, 178
Bruner, J., 142
Buchanan, P., 55
Buckingham, M., 92–3
Burgoyne, J., 95

Burton-Jones, A., 230
Butler, E., 206–7

C

Campbell, A., 98
Campbell, M., 67
Cannell, M., 212
Cappelli, P., 26, 29
Carnall, C., 196
Carroll, R., 127
Carter, P., 37
Castells, M., 11
Caulkin, S., 24–5
Cave, A., 247
Chakravarthy, B.S., 99
Chandler, A.D., 40
Child, J., 30, 39
Choudhury, N., 83–4, 99
Ciborra, C.U., 41
Clark, K.B., 50
Codol, J.P., 125
Cohen, W.M., 43
Collins, N., 7
Collis, B.A., 189, 195, 197
Coopey, J., 95
Coulson-Thomas, C., 116–17
Cray, D., 127
Crouch, C., 68
Cunningham, I., 115
Cyert, R.M., 43, 125–6

D

Daft, R.L., 129
Darling, J., 89
Davidow, W.H., 41
D'Cruz, J.R., 246
De Boer, W., 195
De Brabander, C., xviii
De Swaan, A., 183
De Wit, D., 137, 147, 149, 189, 197
Deal, T.E., 101
Deery, S., 255
DeFillippi, R., 136
Dehnbostel, P., 69
Dillard, J.E. Jr., 98
DiMaggio, P.J., 132
Dixon, N., 189
Dodgson, M., 151, 152
Dore, R., 75
Dougherty, D., 51, 92
Drake, J., 154
Drost, E.A., 118
Drucker, P., 11, 17, 39, 63, 146, 229
Duguid, P., 15, 44, 129, 165, 189, 229
Dulewicz, V., 153
Dutrénit, G., 137
Dybowski, G., 69

E

Eccles, R.C., 190
Edwards, R., 62, 63, 78, 206–7
Eisenhardt, K.M., 8, 9, 12, 43, 46, 50, 54–5, 136, 171, 178–9
Elfring, T., 33, 41, 43–4, 50–1, 218
Elliott, L., 82
Emery, F.E., 126
Engestrom, Y., 96, 157
Evans, K., 73

F

Ferris, G.R., 27, 30
Field, J., 11, 15, 63, 207–8, 229
Filella, J., 115
Floyd, S.W., 98
Follett, M.P., 123
Fombrun, C., 36

Francis, P., 196
Freeman, R., 202

G

Galbraith, J.R., 36
Galunic, D.C., 178
Garavan, T., 175
Garrick, J.R., 62, 150, 155
Garvey, B., 5
Gerhart, B., 24, 34
Ghoshal, S., 6, 34, 39, 51–2, 55–9, 121, 151
Gibbons, M., 149
Giddens, A., 11
Gilbert, D., 202
Ginsberg, A., 142, 151
Gioai, D.A., 125
Gleave, S., 77
Glover, C., 202–3
Goleman, D., 153–4
Gonczi, A., 113
Goold, M., 98
Gouldner, A.W., 93
Grabowski, M., 40–1
Graham, G., 207
Grant, R.M., 21
Gratton, L., 34
Gray, H., 149
Grieves, J., 84
Grunewald, U., 68
Guest, D.E., 24–5, 36
Guile, D., xvii, 96–7, 157
Gurdon, G., 76

H

Hall, R., 135
Hamel, G., 53
Handy, C., 41
Hansen, M.T., 149, 178, 187
Harrell-Cook, G., 27, 30
Harris, H., xvii, 23
Harris, S.G., 125
Harrison, Rosemary, xvii, 63, 72–3, 95, 101, 112–13, 148, 150, 154, 160, 181, 183, 186–7, 189, 211, 214, 216, 227
Harrison, Roy, 140
Hart, S., 46, 97
Harvey, B., 202
Hatchett, A., 255
Hayes, C., 74, 77
Hedberg, B.L.T., 157

Hedlund, G., xvii, 43, 46, 151
Hegewisch, A., 84
Hendry, C., 72, 92–3
Higgs, M., 153
Hills, H., 196
Hiltrop, J.M., xvii, 24, 32, 61, 71, 89–93, 99, 104–5, 114, 118
Hines, T., 151
Hitt, M.A., 6, 8, 32
Hodgkinson, G.P., 125, 132
Hofer, C., 202
Holden, L., 85
Holton III, E.F., 5, 17, 232
Homan, G., 12
Hoque, K., 36
Hosmer, L.T., 152, 202
Huemer, L., 130
Huff, A.S., 30, 132
Hunter, L., 140
Hurst, D.K., 46
Hurwitz, J., 88
Huysman, M., 137, 147, 149, 189, 197
Hyman, J., 115

I

Inkpen, A., 83–4, 99
Ito, K., 151

J

Jackson, N., 37
Jackson, S.E., 4, 20–1
Jacobs, D., 146
Jaques, E., 123
Jelinek, M., 55
Jenkins, A., 69–71
Jensen, M.C., 31
Johnson, G., 125
Johnson, R., 204
Jones, G., 31

K

Kahn, R.L., 126
Kamoche, K., 21, 28, 31
Kaplan, R.S., 171
Katz, D., 126
Keep, E., 73
Keeps, E.J., 17

Kessels, J.W.M., xviii, 5, 64, 145, 148, 155, 165, 167–8, 171–2, 175, 181, 229, 259, 275
Keursten, P., 175, 229
Kieft, M., 231
King, Z., 24–5
Kinnie, N., 255
Kirjavainen, P., 28, 47, 52
Knowles, M., 129
Koenig, C., 53
Kogut, B., 43
Koike, K., 76
Kolb, D.A., 129
Kwakman, K., 171–2

L

Larsen, H.H., 107–10, 115
Lave, J., 10, 129
Lawler III, E.E., 20, 22, 27
Leadbeater, C., 109
Legge, K., 24, 36
Lengnick-Hall, C.A., 21
Lengnick-Hall, M.L., 21
Leonard-Barton, D., 135, 164, 228
Levinthal, D.A., 43, 99, 136, 152
Levy, D., 101, 126–7
Lindblom, C.E., 33
Lines, S., 88
Lorenz, C.L., 42
Lowyck, J., 171
Luhmann, N., 130
Lundvall, B.A., 11
Lymer, A., 185

M

Mabey, C., 36, 85
Malhotra, Y., 147–8
Malloch, H., 32–3
Malone, M.S., 41
Mann, S., 209
March, J.G., 43, 99, 125–6, 136, 152
Marr, A., 151
Marsick, V.J., 98, 232
Maturana, H., 130
Mayer, M., 54–5, 58, 60, 99–100
Mayo, A., 88, 140
Mayo, E., 124
McGoldrick, J., 5, 85, 231

McGrath, R.G., 151
McKinlay, A., 45–6, 127
McMahan, G.C., 22
Meckling, W.H., 31
Méhaut, P., 70
Miles, R.E., 41, 43, 50
Miller, D., 44, 88
Miller, P., 24, 76
Miller, S., 101, 125–6
Mintzberg, H., 33, 45, 98, 101
Mohrman, S.A., 20, 22, 27
Molzberger, G., 69
Moonen, J., 189, 195, 197
Moraal, D., 68
More, E., 202
Morgan, G., 122
Morris, J., 95
Mulder, I., 193–4
Mulder, M., 63, 67, 78
Mumford, A., 101

N

Nadler, D., 52–3, 145
Nakamoto, M., 75
Nathanson, D., 36
Neilson, R.E., 189
Nelson, R.R., 43, 50
Nelson, W.A., 176
Nijhof, W.J., 231
Nohria, N., 190
Nonaka, I., 5, 50, 75, 91, 129, 135, 148, 165
Norton, D.R., 171

O

Oliver, N., 77
Orr, J.E., 129–30

P

Pan, S.L., 138–9
Parker, S.K., 92
Parsons, E., 141
Patriotta, G., 134
Patterson, M.G., 93
Pedler, M., 95
Pennings, J.M., 42
Penrose, E.T., 21
People Management, 203–5, 209, 212
Perrow, C., 126
Pettigrew, A.M., 4, 32–4, 41

Pickard, J., 153, 252
Pieper, R., 190
Plomp, Tj, 148, 181
Poell, R., 159
Polanyi, M., 148
Poole, P.P., 125
Porac, J., 125
Porter, M., 64
Powell, W.W., 132
Prahalad, C.K., 7, 8, 33, 44, 51, 102, 206, 218, 228
Pugh, D.S., 123
Purcell, J., 24, 85, 93–4
Putman, R., 88

Q

Quinn, J.B., 33, 43

R

Rainbird, H., 209
Rajan, A., 140
Ramaswamy, V., 7, 8, 33, 206, 218, 228
Rana, E., 184, 208
Raper, P., 110–11
Ray, T., 27, 65, 75–7, 81
Redman, T., 84
Reed, R., 136
Reitsperger, W.D., 76
Reumkens, R., xvii, 158
Revans, R.W., 95
Rice, R., 191
Richey, R.C., 176
Roberts, K.H., 40–1, 151
Roberts, Z., 72
Robertson, D., 149
Roos, J., 129, 131
Rose, E., 151
Rosenberg, M.J., 17
Rugman, A.M., 246
Rukanova, B., 191–2
Russell, C., 141

S

Salaman, G., 36, 85
Salmon, G., 196
Sambrook, S., 85, 95, 108, 110, 175, 190, 194, 209
Sanchez, R., 8
Santos, F.M., 8–9, 12, 43, 46, 50, 54, 136, 171, 178–9
Savage, C.M., 133

Sawyers, D., 75, 77
Scarbrough, H., xviii, 132, 134–5, 137, 178, 187, 257, 266
Scarpetta, S., 12
Schein, E.H., 91
Schendel, D., 202
Schmidt, J.A., 88
Schoemaker, J.H., 21
Schon, D.A., 95, 98, 157
Schoonhoven, C.B., 55
Schuler, R.S., 4, 20–1
Schultz, T.W., 87
Scott, W.R., 132
Selznick, P., 21
Seth, A., 30
Shaw, S., 12
Shepherdson, I., 76
Silverman, D., 33, 126
Simon, H.A., 125–6, 202
Sink, D.S., 164
Sisson, K., 97
Skapinker, M., xiv, 236
Sloman, M., 90
Smith, R., 150–1, 154, 160
Snijders, I., xvii, 158
Snow, C.C., 41, 43, 50
Snyder, W.M., 10, 155, 229
Solomon, N., 11, 209–10
Sommerlad, E., 72, 113, 118
Sparrow, P.R., xvii, xviii, 8, 23, 24, 26–8, 30, 32, 61, 71, 89–93, 99, 104–5, 114, 118, 215
Spender, J.C., 16, 30, 129
Sprenger, C.C., 159
Stacey, R.D., 127
Starkey, K., 45–6, 127
Steedman, H., 66
Stelzer, I., 7
Stern, E., 72, 113, 118
Sternberg, R.J., 10
Stevens, J., 25, 96, 114
Stewart, J., 4, 85, 86, 90, 95, 108–10, 116–8, 146, 175, 190, 194, 205, 207, 209, 228–9
Stiles, J., 53
Stjernberg, T., 132
Stolovitch, H.D., 17
Storey, J., 34, 76, 85, 97
Subramaniam, M., 8, 39, 42–3, 53–4, 59, 177
Sullivan, P.A., 98, 157
Swaak, J., 193–4

Swan, J., 135, 137, 150, 187, 266
Swanson, R.A., 5, 17, 86, 232
Swart, J., 49
Swidler, A., 92

T

Takeuchi, H., 75, 135, 148
Tansley, C., 4, 85, 90, 109, 116–18, 146, 175, 205, 207, 209, 228–9
Tapscott, D., 185, 228–9
Taylor, F., 123
Taylor, H., 101
Taylor, S., 209
Teather, D., 82
Teece, D., 43, 50
Ter Horst, H., 106
Terry, M., 93, 94
Thomas, H., 30
Thomas, M., 204
Thomas, R., 208
Thorpe, R., 151
Tillaart, H., 67
Tjepkema, S., 4–5, 67, 83–4, 95, 105–8, 110, 115, 117–18, 140, 146, 173–4, 180, 209, 231
Tosey, P., 101
Trist, E., 126
Truss, C., 34
Tushman, M., 52–3, 145

U

Ulrich, D., 60
Urwick, L., 123

V

Van den Akker, J., 176
Van den Berg, J., xviii
Van der Klink, M., 63, 78
Van der Waals, J., 169, 171
Van der Werff, P., 259
Van Drunen, L., 42
Van Lakerveld, J., xviii, 167–8
Van Luijk, H., 202, 216, 219, 227
Van Wijk, G., 53
Varela, F., 130
Venkatraman, N., 8, 39, 42–3, 53–4, 59, 177

Volberda, H.W., 33, 41, 43–4, 50–1, 218
Von Foerster, H., 130
Von Krogh, G., 101, 125, 129–31, 133, 142, 147–8, 157
Vygotsky, L.S., 10, 129

W

Walsh, J.P., 125
Walton, J., 85
Walz, H., 157, 165
Waples, J., 29
Warmerdam, J., 67
Waters, J., 33
Watkins, J.B., 87
Watkins, K.E., 232
Watson, J.B., 123
Weber, M., 123
Weick, K.E., 129, 151
Wells, H.G., 183
Wenger, E.C., 10, 129, 155, 190, 229
Wernerfelt, B., 21
Werr, A., 132
Westwood, A., 72–3
Wheelwright, S.C., 50
White, R., 99
Whitehead, M., 72
Whitley, R., 40
Whittington, R., 40–3, 54–5, 58, 60, 99–100, 177
Williamson, B., 5
Williamson, O.E., 30
Winslow, C.D., 183
Winter, S.G., 43, 50
Wissema, J.G., 97
Woodruffe, C., 153
Woolridge, B., 98
Wouters, M., 63
Wright, P.M., 22

Y

Young, M., xvii, 96–7, 157

Z

Zander, U., 43
Zohar, D., 154
Zuboff, S., 96, 201

Subject Index

bold page numbers
indicate principal
references

A

ABB *see* Asea Brown
    Boveri
Abbey National
    Building Society,
    252
ABP (NL), 169
absorptive capacity, 43,
    46, 127–8
abstract thinking, 98
academic values, 64
Academy of Human
    Resource
    Development
    (AHRD), 86, 90, 215
accreditation of prior
    learning and
    workplace learning,
    64, 66, 209
Acer, 41
action learning, 95,
    101
adaptability, 87, 89,
    118
adaptive capability, 126
adaptive learning,
    96–7, 101, 143–4,
    148, 157, 165,

adaptive systems, 171
administration theory,
    123
adult education, 16, 66
Adult Education
    Centres in
    Germany, 68
adult learning, 84
Adult Learning
    Inspectorate (Ali)
    (UK), 112
agency costs, 31, 53–4
agency theory, 30, 34,
    152
agro-food complex, 147
AHRD *see* Academy of
    Human Resource
    Development,
Alcatel, 247
alertness, 154
alignment, 24
alliances, 40
ambiguity, 98
ambition, 179
Americas, 57
appraisal, 20, 76, 214
apprenticeship, 61, 65,
    70, 72, 101, 140
Artificial Neural
    Networks (ANNs),
    188
Asea Brown Boveri
    ABB, 55–9, 98, 100
Asia, 32, 57
assessment centres, 14

ASTD American Society
    for Training and
    Development, 74
a-synchronous
    discussion
    platforms, 185
AT&T, 74
Australia, 255
authoritarian manager,
    146
authority, 230, 235
authority (in
    bureaucracy), 123
authority,
    decentralised, 51
authority, line of *see
    also* Chandler
    (1962), 40
autonomy, 52, 230
autopoiesis, 130, 142

B

Baccalauréat
    Professionnelle, 70
Baccalauréat
    Technologique, 70
Barclays Bank, 255
Belgium, 65, 83, 84,
    173
benchmarking, 105,
    132
best practice activity,
    132
Bhopal India, 202
biotechnology, 64

Birmingham City Council (UK), 209
blended learning *see also* e-learning, 107
blue- and white-collar workers, 76
Boots, 252
bottom-up processes, 41
boundary spanning, 52, 102
bounded rationality, 125
brainpower, 25
brainstorm, 51, 188, 191
British Airways, 204–5
British Telecom, 72
Buckman Laboratories, 137–40, 149, 164, 208, 266
buddies in virtual teams, 192, 195
bulletin board, 188
bundling of HR practices, 36, 41
bureaucracy *see also* Weber (1947), 123
business development, 23
Business for Social Responsibility (US), 202
business policy, 4
business skills, 161
business strategy, 24, 31, 101
business units, 40
business-focused HRD, 107

C

call centre *assignment*, 253, 255
calm and stability *compare* creative turmoil, 157, 164, 168, 235
Cambridge University, 184
camp sessions, 51
Canon, 50–1
Cap Gemini, 137
capabilities, 21
capability development (Brewster, Harris and Sparrow, 2002), 23, 50, 59,
capability development (Elfring and Volberda, 2000a), 51–2
capitalism, 75
capitalist society *see also* post-capitalist society (Drucker, 1993), 205

career development, 115–16
case-based reasoning, 188
Catholic Church, 123
CD-ROM, 183–5
CEDEFOP, 61, 66, 71, 111
cellular organisation *see also* Acer and ABB, 41, 53, 57
central management model, 115
centres of excellence, 23
Certificate of Training Practice, CIPD, 112
certification of skills (Singapore), 79
chaebol (Korea), 40
chambers of commerce, 68, 80
chaos theory *see also* science of complexity, 126, 128
Chartered Institute of Personnel and Development *see* CIPD,
chat, 185, 192, 196
China, 40, 76
CIPD, Chartered Institute of Personnel and Development, 22, 49, 61, 69, 73–4, 79, 85, 111–12, 114, 1117–1117–18, 185–6, 210–12, 214–15
Classical School *see also* structure, 40
classroom-based instruction, 75
client expectations, 30
client-centredness, 173
coaching, 15, 52, 85, 101–2, 105, 116, 155, 158, 169–70, 214, 234
codes of (professional) conduct *see also* standards, 204, 214
codification, 136
codified knowledge *see also* explicit knowledge, 187
coercion, 210
cognitions, collective, 33
cognitive map, 125, 143, 188
cognitive model; basic assumptions about knowledge and learning, 142
cognitive psychology, 125, 130, 132, 142
collaboration, 28, 59, 169, 209, 210
collaborative arrangement, 74

collaborative design, 185
collaborative engineering, 6
collaborative ICT, 197
collaborative learning, 183, 185, 194–5, 219, 221
collaborative organizational cultures, 99
collaborative relationships, 25, 169
collaborative technology, 182, 189, **190–2**, 235
collaborative work, 191
collective agreement, 66–7, 70–1
collective ambitions, 159
collective labour agreement, 14
collective learning, 34, 132, 160–1
COLO (NL), 66
command–control paradigm, 162, 201, 226
commitment, 25–6, 36, 89
commonality of purpose, 47, 59
communication workers, 74
communication,
    lateral, 51
    line of *see also* Chandler (1962), 40
    non-verbal, 191
communities of practice, 10, 44, 49, 54, 88, 96, 129, 131, 132, 136, 140, 142, 144–5, 148, 155, 159, 162, 164, 179, 187, 190, 197, 202, 213, 218, 227
community involvement and service, 59
community of interest, 160
company as family *see also* China and Japan, 40, 65, 76
compensation policies and systems, 20, 55, 139
competence, 89
    building, 136
    development, 85
    managers, 115
    managers *definition* Ter Horst and Tjepkema (2002), 106
    collective, 179
competencies, 8, 24
    practical, 64
    relational, 42

competency frameworks and schemes, 81, 92, 94, 161
competency-based approach to VET, 65
competency-based curriculum, 64
competency-based learning, 195, 209
competency-based standards, 62
competition, 63
competitive advantage, 21, 38, 174, 178
competitive capability, 20, 109
competitive drive, 32
competitive performance, 136
competitive perspective, 53
competitive pressures, 105
compliance, 30
computer software, 64
computer-assisted learning *see also* e-learning, 185
computer-based training *see also* e-learning, 196
conceptual learning, 193
configuration theory, 41
conflict, 36–7
constructivism, 129, 141–2, 171, 172
consultant, 172–3
consumer-centric culture, 7
contextualist paradigm *see also* universalist paradigm, 37, 59
continuing education, 14, 62
continuing vocational training (CVT), 70
contract workers, 27
contracting-out, 29
control, 87, 169, 180
co-operation, 13, 16, 36
co-operative enterprise, 48
co-operative perspective, 53
core business processes, 22
core competence, 135
core competencies of HR-specialists, 23
corporate citizenship, 202, 220
corporate curriculum, 5, 145, 157–8, 162–3, 166–8, 177, 202, 217, 219, 221–2, 226, 234

corporate curriculum *assignment*, 260
corporate curriculum *definition*, **155**
corporate goals, 35, 101
corporate governance, 58, 151, 202–3
corporate governance *assignment*, 241
corporate learning, 194
corporate management, 30
corporate mission statement, 205
corporate responsibility, 202
corporate university, 195
corporate values, 30
corporate venturing, 53
cost cutting and reduction, 45, 59
Council for Professional and Technical Education, (Singapore), 78
counselling, 102, 155, 234
CPB (Dutch National Planning Office), 15
craft-level qualifications, 72
Cranfield HRM survey (1994), 84, 108–9
creative capabilities, 158
creative turmoil *compare* calm and stability, 156–8, 168, 235
creativity, 87, 226
critical thinking, 235
cross-cultural awareness, 105
cultural capacities, 93
cultural diversity, 23
culture, 98
    change, 55, 92, 103–4, 111, 138, 140, 156, 225, 252
    definition, **91**
    processes, 42
    typologies *see also* Schein (1985), 91
culture, national, 105, 134
curiosity, 179, 186, 230
curriculum, national, 64
customer
    collaboration, 218
    equity, 87
    expectations, 30
    satisfaction, 164, 170–1
customers, connected, 7
customisation, 96
cybernetics theory, 125

D

data, 131,142
data as distinct from information and knowledge, 130
data warehousing, 182
data workers, 15, 17
decency, 217, 219
decision-making, 39, 125, 188
defensive routines (Argyris, 1996), 44
Dell Computers, 41
'Delors' law, 69
Denmark, 65–6, 115
Department for Education and Employment (UK), 63, 212
deployment, 76, 116
deskilling, 62
development, 20, 58
developmental process, collective, 99
dialogue, 51
digital economy, 185
disengagement, 25
Disney Corporation, 92
dispersed learning team *assignment*, 264
dispersed teams *see also* distributed teams *and* virtual teams, 191,193, 235
distributed teams *see also* virtual teams, 190
diversity, 52, 59,160, 197, 207, 209–10, 234
diversity *assignment*, 264
dot.coms, 207
double-loop learning *compare* single-loop learning, 91, 103, 165
Dow Chemicals, 202
downsizing, 57
drop out, 14
dual educational system *see also* VET, 63–4, 67–8, 80, 82
Dutch Association of Trainers (NVvO), 231
dynamic capabilities, 8, 11, 52, 54, 59, 60, 87, 100, 144, 218, 224, 234
dynamic network *see also* Dell Computers, 41

E

Eastern Europe, 32
e-based learning *see* e-learning,
EC *see* European community,
e-commerce, 189
Economic Development Board in Singapore, 78
economic growth, 62
economic motive, 59
economic rationality, 125
economic self-interest, 35
economies of expertise, 8, 53, 58,
economies of expertise *assignment*, 246
economy, digital, 185
economy, globalised, 206
economy, hourglass, 207
economy, knowledge, xiv, 3, 6, 18, 222
economy, learning (Field, 2000; Lundvall, 2000), 11, 207
economy, transformational knowledge (Drucker, 1993), 11
economy, new, 205, 208
education, formal, 16
education frameworks, 61
education policy, 14
educational leave, 173
educational system, 63
educational underclass, 64
e-learning, 73, 114, 116, 183, 186
electronic mail, 188
electronic shamrock organisation *see also* F International, 41
electronically based learning *see also* e-learning *and* technology-based education, 73
email, 190–1
emancipation, 162, 217, 219, 226, 229
e-mentality (Pieper, 2000), 189
emotional intelligence, 153–5
emotional labour, 209
emotional process, 189
employability, 27, 79
employability consultants, 14

employee,
  development, 85, 174
  involvement, 25
  motivation, 36
  relations, 20
  satisfaction, 170
  training and development *see also* ETD, 89–90
employee-driven approach, 170
employer/union partnership in training (USA), 74
employment, 4, 20, 26, 32, 38, 86
employment, lifetime, 27, 76
Enron, 202
entrepreneur, 52, 158
entrepreneurial manager, 146
entrepreneurial process, 56
entrepreneurial unit, 56
environmental responsibility, 59
episteme (scientific knowledge), 150–1
equality, 219
equity, 210
Ericsson, 106
ESRC, 26, 207
ETD employee training and development, 89–90
e-technology *see also* e-learning, 185
ethics *see also* Van Luijk (1994), 11, 28, 37, 59, 155, **201**, 202–5, 213–16, 219, 220, 227, 234–5
ethics *see also* Institute for Business Ethics (IBE) (UK), 202–3
ethics *see also* Nicomachean Ethics (Aristotle), 150
EURESFORM, 90
Europe, 5, 32, 45, 55, 57, 62, 65, 78, 82, 84, 86, 90, 105, 107–8, 112–14, 190, 206, 209, 224, 226, 229, 231, 247
European Centre for the Development of Vocational Training *see* CEDEFOP
European Commission *see also* EC, 61–3, 207
European Community (EC), 12, 15

World Initiative on Lifelong Learning, 12
European HRD Research Project 2000 *see also* Tjepkema (2002), 83–5, 105, 107–10, 115–16, 118, 140, 173, 180
European human rights legislation, 201
European Market, 12, 42
European qualifications structure, 13
European Social Chapter, 29
evaluating training, 61
executive reward strategies, 29
executives, senior, 178
experiential learning, **101**
expertise, 59
experts, 125
external consistency, 181

F

F International, 41
face-to-face meeting, 190–2, 194, 196
facilitator, 172, 194, 196–7
family networks (China), 40
Federal Institute of Vocational Training and Education BIBB (Germany), 69
feedback, 179, 193, 195
FEU Further Education Unit, 63, 78
Finland, 83, 109, 173
flexibility, 36, 154, 190, 207
Ford, 45, 127
Fordist workplace, 187, 211, 220
Formation Professionnelle Continué, 70
France, 14, 62, 65–6, **69**–71, 78, 80, 82–3, 108, 114–15, 173
France Telecom, 219, 246
front-line teams, 100
Future of Work Programme *see also* ESRC, 207

G

Gallup, 92
gap analysis, 87
gatekeepers, 52

gender inequalities, 207
General Electric, 40, 51
General Motors, 33
German Model VET, 67
Germany, 14, 62, 64–5, **67–9**, 71, 78, 80, 82–3, 115, 173, 208
global factory *see also* Asea Brown Bovari ABB, 57
globalisation, 7, 22
Green Paper, *The Learning Age*, 63
greenfield sites, 37
Groupe Esc Toulouse, 85
groupware tools, 189
Guardian, 76, 82

H

Harrods, 204
Harvard University, 88, 228
Harvard's mutuality model, 36
Heineken University, 195
heterarchy, 50
High Frequency Economics, 76
high-commitment model, 36
high-velocity environments, 54
historical path *see also* path dependency, 54
Hitachi, 77
Honda, 50–1, 84
HR (human resources), 20
  paradigms, 20
  philosophies, 20
  planning, 20, 76, 109
  policies, 20, 94, 157
  practices, 20
  professionals, 58
  strategy, 4, 31, 34
HR, globalising, 22
HRD, 86
  as a subset of HRM, 90
  as an organisational process, 9
  centralisation and decentralisation, 108
  definition, 4, 89
  definition Stewart and McGoldrick (1996), 85
  educational programme *assignment*, 254
  function, xvi, 17, 83, 104, 174

practitioners, xvi, 86, 88, 115–16
process, 85, 86
professionals, 17, 85, 107
professionals as strategic players, 11
roles, 108, 116, 139, **233**
skills, **117**
specialists, 85
strategic integration of HRD, 104, 106, 118
strategies, 104, 108
tasks, **234**
terminology and meanings, **84**
HRD, an integrative approach to, 107, 134, 140
HRD–HRM relationship, 90
HRM (human resource management), 20, 94
HRM, e-enablement of, 23
human agency, 124
human capital *compare* social capital, 12, 16–17, 19, 21, 27, 29, 37–8, 63, 87–8, 97, 103–4, 113, 189, 207, 225
human cognitions, 141
human exchange, 30
human interaction, 186
human relations, 126
human resource base, 21
human resource development *see* HRD,
human resource management *see* HRM,
human resource *see* HR,
human rights legislation, 217
Hutton Borough Council, 32

I

ICCT *see also* ICT, 227
ICI (UK), 41, 58
ICT, 137, 184, 186, 188, 194–5, 197
ICT *assignment*, 263–4
ICT literacy, 13
identity, 197, 211
identity, group, 191
IiP *see* Investors in People,
Ill-defined problems *compare* well-defined problems, 188

ILO *see* International Labour Organisation,
implicit learning, 148
improvement, 25, 157, 165, 167–8, 176
improvement, continuous, 22, 222
independent judgement, 16
India, 202
Indigo, 137
individual cognition, 33, 148
individual development, 59
individual learning accounts, 13
Indousuez, 137
induction, 92, 186, 214
industrial relations, 69
industrial revolution, 4, 49
industry councils US, 73
Industry Week, 59
inertia, 44, 53
'Infocosm' (Winslow and Bramer, 1994), 183
information, 142
information access, WWW, 7
information and communication technology *see also* ICT, 10, 14, 149, **182**
information as distinct from data and knowledge, 131
information processing, 125, 135, 145
Information Society (Giddens, 1994), 11
information systems, 6
ING Barings, 137
innovation, 3, 22, 25, 34, 59, 137, 157, 165, 167, 168, 170–1, 176, 222
innovative capacity, 46
innovative drive, 55
innovators, 228
in-service training, 68
Institute for Business Ethics (IBE) (UK), 202–3
Institute for Social and Ethical Accountability, 202
Institute of Enterprise (UK), 184
Institute of Personnel and Development *see also* IPD and CIPD, 89
Institute of Physical and Chemical Research (Japan), 77

instruction, formal, 168
instructional content, 159
instructional objectives, 185
integrity, 59, 152–3, 158, 161, 179, 203–4, 215
Intel, 53
intellectual capital, 8, 116, 140
intellectual property, 87
intelligence, spiritual, 153–5
interaction, 167–8, 171
interfirm co-operation, 178
International Brotherhood of Electrical Workers (US), 74
International Computers Ltd, 184
International Data Corporation, 185
International Labour Organisation (ILO), 207
International Monetary Fund, 63
international transactions (Brewster, Harris and Sparrow, 2002), 23
Internet Notebook, The, 191
Internet *see also* WWW, 7, 114, 183, 186, 203, 228
Internet skills, 195
inter-organisational relationships, 218
intranets, 186
intra-organisational learning, 144
intrinsic motivation, 195
intuition, 98
Investors in People IiP, 71–2, 74
IPD *see also* CIPD, 210
ISR, 76
IT networks, 105
IT systems, 134, 138
Italy, 65, 71, 78, 83–4, 115, 173

J

Japan, 5, 27, 32, 55, 62, 64–6, **75**–7, 81–2, 105, 114–15
job descriptions, 143
job design, 25, 122
job enrichment, 75
job performance, 108
job rotation, 77
joint ventures, 27, 40

K

keiretsu (Japan), 40, 75
KLM, 43
KM *see* knowledge management,
knowing, 9, 129–30, 142, 178, 189, 232
knowing in firms *see also* Von Krogh (1998), 133
knowledge, xv, **121**
    as a process, 18, 182, 225
    as a resource, 9, 18
    as commodity, 18, **134**–5, 159, 178, 183, 206–7, 220, 225
    as control, **122**, 157, 206
    as intelligence, **124**, 127
    as relationships, **129**, 132, 149
    as social construction, 136
    as stock *see also* knowledge as commodity, 145
    cognitivist view, 125
    connectivity, 131, 143, 149
    construction, 176, 191
    creativity, 94
    development, 57, 87, 146, 176
    digging, 135
    extracting, 135
    flow, 8, 46
    integration, 46, 54, 55
    'intrapreneurs' *see also* Malhotra (2000), 148
    management *assignment*, 257, 263
    management and ICT, **187**
    management *compare* knowledge development, 146
    management, KM, 4, 22, 25, 46, 84, 90, 107, 121, 134–5, 137–40, 145–7, 162, 174, 208
    mining, 135
    networks *assignment*, 246
    partnerships, 59
    productivity, xv, 5, 139, **145**, 148, 162–3, 169, 176–7, 180, 206, 222, 226

productivity *assignment*, 258, 260
productivity *definition*, **145**
sharing, 133–4, 137, 149, 234
sharing *assignment*, 263
sourcing, 46
structures, 141
systems, 182
transfer, 46, 178
work, 16, 230
workers, 15, 27, 47, 49, 114, 147, 179, 187, 207, 220, 223, 228–9
KnowledgePool, 184
knowledge, collective, 132
knowledge, disposition, 150
knowledge, explicit *compare* tacit knowledge, 44, 129, 135, 148, 151, 229, 234
knowledge, implicit *see* tacit knowledge *compare* explicit knowledge,
knowledge, measurement of, 179
knowledge, Mode I and II (Gibbons et al., 1994), 149
knowledge, procedural, 148, 150–1
knowledge, propositional, 150–1
knowledge, relational, 134
knowledge, reservoir of, 54
knowledge, tacit *compare* explicit knowledge, 5, 17, 19, 44, 47, 81, 129, 133–7, 140, 144, 208, 223–4, 229
knowledge-based businesses, 57
knowledge-based economy, 222
knowledge-construction, 87
knowledge-creating activity, 89
knowledge-creating enterprises, 50
knowledge-creation, 18, 25, 58–9, 117–18, 133, 234
knowledge-creation capability, 75
knowledge-intensive employment, 15

knowledge-intensive firms (KIFs), 28, 47
knowledge-productive learning, 117, 174
knowledge-productive organisation, 226
knowledge-productive relationships, 38
knowledge-productive teams, 111
KPN, 137

L

labour costs, 20
labour force, flexible, 206
labour market, 62–3, 70, 75
labour, division of, 122–3
Lander (Germany), 67–8
'languaging', 131, 143
Latin management model, 115
leadership, 204
leadership capability, 84, 97, 103–4, 114, 160–1, 225
leadership, directional, 59
leanness, 94
learner-centred approaches, 209
Learning Age, Green Paper, 63
learning and development standards (CIPD), 112
Learning and Skills Councils, (UK) (LSCs), 72, 81
learning architects, 88, 90, 117, 234
learning capability, 128, 231
learning centres, 73
learning climate, 13, 107, 229
learning community, 38, 88, 221
Learning Company, 48, 59, 169
learning consultant, 171–2, 194, 197
learning culture, 18, 25, 84, 91, 100, 103–4, 109–11, 118, 155, 174, 225
learning economy (Field, 2000; Lundvall, 2000), 11, 207
learning environments, 17, 159
learning facilitators, 117
learning functions, 167

learning groups, 105
learning islands (Germany), 68–9
learning laboratory, 135
learning networks, 25
learning organisation LO, **94**–5, 140, 173–4, 180, 211
learning partnership, 107, 228
learning society, 235
Learning Society (European Commission, 1996), 11
learning systems, 96
learning to learn, 111, 128
learning typology *see also* Engestrom (1995) *and* Guile and Young (1999), 96
learning
    continuous, 18–19
    formal, 69–70, 230
    informal, 69, 97, 101, 174
    investigative, 96, 143–4, 148, 157
    lifetime, 79
    relational, 233
    self-regulated, 169–70, 180, 232
    team-based, 188
learning-by-doing, 136
learning-oriented organisations, 83, 105–6, 108
levy/grant system, 71
lifelong learning, 5, 14, 110, 206, 222, 235
lifelong learning policy *see also* European Community World Initiative Lifelong Learning, 12, 62
lifelong vocational training, 70
Lloyds TSB, 196
Lotus Notes, 133, 182
Lucent Technologies, 74
Luxembourg, 65

M

machine bureaucracy (Mintzberg, 1983), 45
machine operators, 230
management, 49, 60, 144
    development, 85

education, 105
roles, 8, 109
styles, 24
succession, 115
team, 98
training and development (MTD), 97, 101
management, facilitative, 59
management, people, 49, 115, 203–5, 209, 212
management, senior, 161, 229
    chief executive, 29, 98
management, strategic, 20–1, 102
managerial capability, **97**, 103–4, 114
managers, line, 109, 196, 231
managers, middle, 56, 100, 138
market competition, 33
market need, 21
market partners, 14
Marks & Spencer, 92
mass production, 59, 231
Massachusetts Institute of Technology, 184
matrix organisation, 56
Mazda, 45
McDonald's, 43
mental maps, 126
mentoring, 52, 101, 105, 116, 139, 155, 158, 160, 184, 214, 234
Mercedes Benz AG, 69
mergers, 105
meta standards, 215
meta-cognitions, 156
meta-knowledge, 136
metaphors, 122, 124
M-form or multidivisional structure *compare* N-form structure, 41, 47, 55–6, 247
Microsoft, 53
mind mapping, 188
Minister of Agriculture, Nature Management and Fisheries (NL), 147
Ministry of Housing, Planning and Environment (The Netherlands), 137

Ministry of International Trade and Industry (Japan), 75
Ministry of International Trade and Industry (Singapore), 78
minority groups, 27
mission, 51
MN Services, 170
mobilisation of workers, 70
monitoring, 87
moral contract, 28, 221
moral principles, 219
moral requirements, 216
morality, 33, 219
motivation, 193
MTD see management, training and development,
Multicorp, 134–5, 149, 155, 208, 266
multicultural corporation, 57
multiple choice test, 185
multi-skilled workforces, 6
multiskilling, 25, 62
multi-task work, 77
mutual co-operation, 34
mutual interest, 195
mutuality model, 36

N

narratives, 142–3
National Centre for Competitiveness (UK), 116
National Health Service, 33
National Learning and Skills Council (NLSC), 72–3, 112
National Skills Recognition System (Singapore), 79
National Vocational Education and Training system see also NVET, 61
Nationale Nederlanden, 137
Netherlands, 14, 62, 65–7, 72, 78, 80, 82–3, 108, 111, 115, 147, 167, 169, 173
network principles, 53
network relationships, 54, 158
Network Society (Castells, 1998), 11
networking, WWW, 8
networking skills, 234

networks, 13, 105, 234
New Deal welfare to work programme (UK), 71
Newsweek, 64
N-form structure compare M-form structure, 47, 54
Nicomachean Ethics (Aristotle), 150
Nikkei index, 75
Nippon Telegraph and Telephone (NTT), 77
non-knowledge workers compare knowledge workers, 16, 27, 179, 212–13, 220, 223, 229
Nordic management model, 115
Norton-Kaplan Balanced scorecard, 30
Norway, 114–15
NS Dutch Railways, 137
NVET, 71–3, 76–9, 82, 209, 224
NVET assignment, 249
NVET funding, 65
NVET systems, 67, 80

O

OECD, 12–13, 15–16, 61–3
Office of Management and Budget (US), 88
off-the-job programmes, 101
OJT 2000 Plan Singapore, 78
OJT 21 Singapore, 79
Olivetti, 41
'One-Stop Centers' (US), 74
on-line learning, 192
on-line meetings, 195
on-the-job experience, 101
on-the-job training, 212
open learning centres, 106
open systems theory, 126
organisation
    as a network of relationships, 43, 53
    as a portfolio of dynamic capabilities, 43, 50
    as a repository of knowledge, 43
    as a reservoir of knowledge, 43
    as a brain, 124
    as a culture, 129
    as a machine, 135, 157
    as an organism, 126

Organization for Economic Co-operation and Development see OECD
organisation, team-based, 6
organisation, virtual, 192
organisational behaviour, 47
organisational capability, 9, 21, 23, 96, 115
organisational competence, 218
organisational context, 93, 111
organisational culture, 47
organisational design, 8, 39, 178
organisational identity, 51
organisational inertia, 98
organisational knowledge, 132, 136, 179
organisational learning, 4, 84, 95, 106, 136, 149, 189
organisational performance, 25, 144
organisational policies and practices, survey, 84
organisational resources, 21
organisational routines, 55
organisational rules, 55
organisational structure, 59, 99
organisational viability, 29
organisationally based HRD, 5
organising, 34, 39, 46, 55, 60, 99, 103, 117, 128, 144, 166, 223–5
organising capabilities, 100
organising principles, 56
organising skills, 99–100
ownership, 28, 221

P

paid training leave (CIF France), 70
participating ethics see also Van Luijk (1994), 217, 219
partnership, 27, 40, 42, 172, 218
patents, 137
path-dependency, 59, 180
peace and stability see also calm and stability, 158
Pechiney, 137

pension funds, 29
People Developer Standard
    in Singapore, 79
performance, 59, 87, 167,
    223
    appraisal, 158
    control, 8
    improvement, 5, 18–19,
        85–6, 113, 233
    indicators, 214
    management, 25
    measurement, 139
    metrics, 55
    paradigm see also
        performance–learning
        debate, 232
    plans, 88
    standards, 56, 165
    targets, 123
performance, company, 36
performance, job, 108
performance–learning
    debate, 17, **86**, 233
performance-oriented units,
    55
personal
    brand, 140
    capabilities, 165
    development, 15
    development paths, 16
    development plans, 106,
        174
    interaction, 197
    networks, 137, 179, 188
    skilfulness, 148–50, 179,
        182
Philips, 189
phronesis (practical
    reasoning), 150–1
platform organisation see
    also Olivetti, 41
pluralist perspective of
    organisations, 20, 37–8,
    223
political skills, 234
politics, 33, 205
Portugal, 108, 114
positivist view, 127, 141–2
post-16 education, 72
Postbank (NL), 137
post-capitalist society
    (Drucker, 1993), 146
post-Fordist workplace, 11
power, 33, 134, 169, 205,
    210
power-play, 126

practical judgement, 150–1,
    154–6, 159, 162, 168,
    179, 217, 221, 226, 235
practical reasoning see
    phronesis, 151
practical wisdom, 16, **151–2**,
    162, 235
Price Waterhouse-Cranfield,
    84
principal see also agency
    theory, 30
problem-centred learning,
    116
problem-solving, 25, 77, 158,
    167–8
process-oriented approach,
    171–2
Procter & Gamble, 100
product life cycle, 53
productivity, 170–1
Productivity and Standards
    Board in Singapore, 78
professional, xvi
    development, 106, 117,
        229, 235
    growth, 228
    networks, 179
    rules, 30
    standards, 113
professionalism, 158, 161
profitability, 59
programme design, 181
programmed instruction,
    185
project management, 115,
    191
psychological contract, 26,
    93, 118, 205, 223
psychometric testing, 124

Q

Qantas, 137
qualifications, 63, 65
quality, 36, 164
    circles, 75, 77
    deployment processes, 6
    improvement, 59
    standards, 30

R

Rabobank Academy, 158
rational economic man
    (Simon, 1995), 125
rationalisation of costs, 22

RBT see resource-based
    theory,
RBV see resource-based view
    of the firm,
recession, 75
reciprocal appeal, 169
reciprocity, 219
recognition of prior learning,
    62
recognitional ethics see also
    Van Luijk (1994), 217
recruitment, 20, 24, 58, 76,
    92, 116
redeployment of people, 25
reflection, 16, 167, 193
reflection-in-action, 67, 111
reflective learning, 144
reflective skills, 156, 158,
    168, 235
reflexive learning, 96–7, 101,
    128, 143, 148, 157, 160,
    165
relational approach, 123,
    181
relational capability, 218
relational process, 189
relational style, 172
research
    action-based, 176
    case-based, 177
    collaborative, 190
    descriptive, 177, 180
    design, 164
    development study, 169,
        176, 180
    development study
        assignment, 262
    framework, 175
    instruments, 164, 180
    methodology, 190
    reconstruction study, 180
    reconstruction study
        assignment, 261
    replication study, 176
resource configuration, 50
resource-based view of the
    firm (RBV), 21, 32–3
resourced-based theory
    (RBT), 134–5
respect, 59, 158, 160–1, 179,
    235
responsiveness, 94
reward, 58, 76, 116, 122, 124
Riboud Report, 70
RIKEN (Japan), 77
risk-sharing, 31
role model, 101–2

Royal Dutch/Shell Group *see* Shell
Royal Mail (UK), 110

S

Saturn Corporation, 33
scarcity value, 21
Schiphol (NL), 137
school-to-work transition, 13
scientific knowledge *see* episteme,
scientific management, 40, 122–3, 127
secondments, 105
Sector Skills Councils (UK), 72
sectoral organisations, 67
Securities and Exchange Commission (US), 215
selection, 20, 76, 122, 167, 214
self-awareness, 153–4
self-control, 154, 195
self-co-ordination, 51
'self-descriptions' (Von Krogh, 1994), 131, 143
self-development, 28, 211, 221
self-directed learning *see* self-managed learning,
self-directed working *see* self-management,
self-direction, 15, 169
self-employment, 140
self-managed learning, 59, 117, 144, 167, 209, 234
self-management, 25, 41, 48–50, 67, 69, 75, 111, 169, 186, 210
self-motivation, 154
self-organisation *see* self-management,
self-productive , 142, 149
self-productive knowledge *see also* autopoiesis, 130–1
self-regulation, 106, 154, 167–9, 171, 195, 210, 235
Semco, 34
seniority pay, 27
service workers *see also* non-knowledge workers, 15, 17, 229
service-oriented economies, 42

shared values, 160
shared ideology, 51
shared language, 195
shared ownership, 48
shared understanding, 193–4
shareholder value, 22, 29
Sharp, 44
Shell, 92, 160–1, 208
SHRM *see* strategic human resource management HRM
Siemens, 114
simultaneous engineering, 45
Singapore, 62, 65, **78**, 114
single-loop learning *compare* double-loop learning, 165
situated learning, 129
skilfulness, 159
skilled competence *see* techne,
skilled incompetence (Agyris, 1996), 44, 88, 92, 98, 127, 136
skills aquisition, 25
skills development, 25
skills
    business, 161
    creative, 64
    interactive, 179
    Internet, 195
    key, 69
    life-, 94
    networking, 234
    organising, 99–100
    political, 234
    reflective, 156, 158, 168, 235
    social (communicative), 156, 158, 235
    soft, 114
SMEs, small and medium-sized enterprises, 67
social audits, 203
social capital *compare* human capital, 16–17, 19, 21, 27, 37–8, 76, 87–8, 97, 103–4, 113, 189, 222–3, 225, 233, 235, 251
social class, 212
social cohesion, 62
social community, 136
social construction, 17, 187
social context, 159, 179
social control, 195
social dialogue, 69
social exclusion, 12
social intelligence, 153

social interaction, 142, 193, 196, 197, 227
social mobility, 69
social network, 102, 234
social partners, 65, 70
social pressures, 105
social relationships, 130, 141, 208
social rules, 30
social science, 132
social skilfulness, 154
social system, 126
socialisation, 42, 179, 191, 192, 209
socio-cognitive process, 142
socio-technical theory, **126**
Spain, 115
sponsors, 52
stakeholders, 190, 202
standardisation, 52, 87
standards, 30, **113**, 204, 214, 220–1
standards, CIPD, 113
standards, occupational and vocational, 13, 65, 85, 112–13
State Workforce Investment Board (US), 73, 80
Statoil (Norway), 114
stockholder influence, 29
Stork (NL), 137
strategic alliances, 27
strategic awareness, 87
strategic capability, 102, 137, 231
strategic decision-making, 144
strategic human resource development, 85
strategic human resource management (SHRM) *assignment*, 22, 24–5, 34–6, 38, 243
strategic integration of HRD, 104, 106, 118
strategic partnerships, 22
strategic roles, 98
strategic thinking, 45
strategic thrust, 84, **89**, 91, 103, **104**, 225
strategising, 8, **20**, 34, 46, 60, 97, 99, 103, 117, 128, 144, 223, 235
strategy, 46, 101
    assignment, 251
    as a process, 33, 38
    as a product, 33

strategy, stretch model *see also* Hamel and Prahalad (1993), 34, 51
strategy, intended, 46
structural continuities, 42
structural reconfiguration, 8, 33
structure, 39–40
structure *definition*, 42
subject matter expertise and content, 156, 158, 167–8, 185, 229, 234
Sun Microsystems, 41
supervision, 167
supply chains, 40
Sweden, 65, 115
Switzerland, 115
synchronous design, 185
systematic training cycle, 113, 124

T

talents, 176, 179
task group structures, 111
task rotation, 111
team culture *assignment*, 250
team-based learning, 188
team-based organisations, 6
teambuilding, 25
teamworking, 69, 96, 115
techne (skilled competence), 150–1
technical qualifications, 72
technology, 186
technology, collaborative, 182, 189, **190–2**, 235
technology, new *assignment*, 263
technology, web-based, 235
technology-based education, 73
technology-mediated interaction, 193
technology-mediated workspace, 197
TeleTOP, 195
Texas Instruments, 44
theoretical qualifications, 64
thrust *see* strategic thrust
tolerance of risk, 98
top management, 205, 220, 231
total quality management, 30, 75, 186
Toyota, 50, 51, 76

TQM *see* total quality management
trainers, 231
training, 16, 20, 122, 180, 223, 226
    budgets, 111
    centre, 67
    designer role, 172
    evaluation, 61
    standards, 124
    tax, 69, 71, 173
training, continuous, 70
training, cross-functional, 45, 104
training, formal, 70, 174
training, funding of, 65, 112
training, youth, 65
transaction costs, 30–1, 53–4
transactional ethics *see also* Van Luijk (1994), 217, 219
transferability of qualifications, 13
transformational knowledge economy *see also* Drucker (1993), 6, 11
transnationalism, 105
trust, 13, 16, 28, 34, 59, 63, 76, 88, 95, 137, 152, 160–1, 181, 190–1, 203, 205, 208, 210, 226, 235
Turkey, 108

U

UK *see* United Kingdom
UNESCO, 12
Unilever, 137
Union Carbide, 202
unions, 27, 37, 68, 70, 72–4, 81
unitary approach *see also* universalist model, 36
unitary view of organisations, 20
United Kingdom (UK), 14, 27, 29, 30, 32, 34, 41, 49, 62, 64–5, 71–4, 76, 78, 81–3, 85, 89, 94, 108, 111, 113–16, 173, 185, 196, 207–8, 210, 212, 230
United States of America (USA), 5, 15, 30, 40, 55, 57, 62–3, 65, 73, 78, 80, 82, 86–8, 90, 105, 114, 207

universal knowledge, 151
universalist model, 36
universalist paradigm *compare* contextualist paradigm, 35, 59
Universitas 21 (UK), 184
University Forum for Human Resource Development (UFHR), 88, 90, 234
University of Bath (UK), 49
University for Industry Ufl (UK), 73, 184
University of Twente (NL), 172, 189, 195, 231
unlearning, 101, 139
US *see* United States of America

V

value chain, 57
value systems, 37
Vertex, 255
VET vocational education and training, 9,14, 62, 71, 73, 113, 230
video conference, 191–2, 196
Virgin, 92, 205
virtual communities, 192, 227
virtual corporation *see also* Sun Microsystems, 41
virtual environments, 235
virtual organisation, 192
virtual team, **190–2**, 194, 197
virtual team *assignment*, 264
Vitro Glass Containers, 137
vocational education and training *see also* VET and NVET, 9, 12, 61, 63–4, 97, 105
vocational qualifications, national (UK), 114
vocational standards, 13, 65
Volkswagen (VW), 69, 208

W

web-based technology, 235
well-defined problems *compare* ill-defined problems, 188
whistleblowing, 204
Work and Employment Research Centre (WERC), 49

work-based learning, 228, 233
work-based training, 112
workers
  blue-collar and white-collar, 76
  communication, 74
  contract, 27
  data, 15, 17
  goods-producing, 15
  knowledge, 15, 27, 47, 49, 114, 147, 179, 187, 207, 220, 223, 228–9
  management, 15
  non-knowledge, 16, 27, 179, 212–13, 220, 223, 229
  service *see also* non-knowledge workers, 15, 17, 229
  temporary, 27

Workforce Investment Act (WIA) (US), 73–4
work-integrated learning *see also* in-service training, 68
workplace assessment, 62
workplace cultures, 24
workplace education, 112
Workplace Learning in Europe *see also* CIPD, 66, 73–4, 79, 111, 114
workplace learning *see also* work-related learning, 14, 19, 67, 71, 78, 84, **95**, 104, 109, **112**, 114, 208–10, 222, 225
work-related learning, 16, 172, 206
World Bank, 63, 203, 204, 215
World Brain *see also* Wells, H.G. (1936), 183

World Employment Report (ILO, 2001), 207
World Wide Web, (WWW) 4, 7, 185–6, 195
Worldcom, 202

X
Xerox, 215

Y
youth training, 65

Z
zaibatsu (Japan), 75
zero defect groups, 77